From the 1919 Revolution to the 2011 Arab Spring

Focused on three Egyptian revolutions—in 1919, 1952, and 2011—this edited book argues that each of these revolutions is a milestone which represents a meaningful turning point in modern Egyptian history.

Revolutions are typically characterized by a fundamental change in political and social infrastructures as well as the establishment of new values and norms. However, it should be noted that this may not be entirely applicable when examining the context of the three Egyptian revolutions: the 1919 revolution failed to liberate Egypt from British colonial hegemony; the 1952 revolution failed to rework the country's social and economic systems and unify the Arab world; and the "Arab Spring" revolution of 2011 culminated in a chaotic economic and social catastrophe, thus failing to solve the young generation's crisis. Nevertheless, by revisiting and redefining these revolutions through diverse theoretical frameworks, the book proposes that each of them played a significant role in shaping Egypt's political, social, and cultural identity.

This book is specifically of interest for students, historians, and social scientists with a keen interest in Egyptian history and the Middle East, offering fresh perspectives and insights into these transformative moments in Egypt's history.

Uzi Rabi is the Director of the Moshe Dayan Center for Middle Eastern and African Studies, Head of the Department of Middle Eastern and African History, and a senior researcher at the Center for Iranian Studies, all at Tel Aviv University. His research focuses on the modern history and evolution of states and societies in the Middle East, Iranian–Arab relations, oil and politics in the Middle East, and Sunni–Shiʿi dynamics.

Mira Tzoreff is a Senior Lecturer at the Department of Middle East and African History and a Senior Researcher at the Moshe Dayan Center—both at Tel Aviv University. Her areas of research are the socio-cultural history of modern Egypt, women and gender in Arab and Islamic societies, and youth in the Middle East and North Africa.

Routledge Studies in Middle Eastern Politics

117 **Perspectives on International Conflict Resolution**
Theological Debates on the Israel–Palestinian Peace Process
Shameer Modongal

118 **Conflict and Peace in Western Sahara**
The Role of the UN's Peacekeeping Mission (MINURSO)
Edited by János Besenyő, Joseph Huddleston and Yahia H. Zoubir

119 **Western Democracy and the AKP**
A Dialogical Analysis of Turkey's Democratic Crisis
Mehmet Celil Çelebi

120 **Islamic Identity and Development after the Ottomans**
The Arab Middle East
Ozay Mehmet

121 **Polarization and Consensus-Building in Israel**
The Center Cannot Hold
Edited by Elie Friedman, Michal Neubauer-Shani and Paul Scham

122 **Turkey's Relations With Israel**
The First Sixty Two Years, 1948-2010
Ekavi Athanassopoulou

123 **From the 1919 Revolution to the 2011 Arab Spring**
A History of Three Egyptian *Thawras* Reconsidered
Edited by Uzi Rabi and Mira Tzoreff

For a full list of titles in the series:
https://www.routledge.com/Routledge-Studies-in-Middle-Eastern-Politics/book-series/SE0823

FROM THE 1919 REVOLUTION TO THE 2011 ARAB SPRING

A History of Three Egyptian *Thawras* Reconsidered

Edited by Uzi Rabi and Mira Tzoreff

TEL AVIV UNIVERSITY
MDC
The Moshe Dayan Center for Middle Eastern and African Studies

Routledge
Taylor & Francis Group
LONDON AND NEW YORK

First published 2024
by Routledge
4 Park Square, Milton Park, Abingdon, Oxon OX14 4RN

and by Routledge
605 Third Avenue, New York, NY 10158

Routledge is an imprint of the Taylor & Francis Group, an informa business

British Library Cataloguing-in-Publication Data
A catalogue record for this book is available from the British Library

Library of Congress Cataloging-in-Publication Data

Names: Rabi, Uzi, editor. | Tzoreff, Mira, editor.
Title: From the 1919 Revolution to the 2011 Arab Spring : a history of three Egyptian Thawras reconsidered / edited by Uzi Rabi and Mira Tzoreff.
Description: London : New York : Routledge, 2024. | Series: Routledge studies in Middle Eastern politics ; 123 | Includes bibliographical references and index. |
Identifiers: LCCN 2023037870 (print) | LCCN 2023037871 (ebook) | ISBN 9781032398273 (hardback) | ISBN 9781032398280 (paperback) | ISBN 9781003351580 (ebook)
Subjects: LCSH: Egypt--Civilization--20th century. |
Egypt--Civilization--21st century. | Arab Spring, 2010- |
Egypt--History--Revolution, 1952. | Egypt--History--Insurrection, 1919 |
Egypt--Politics and government--1919-1952. | Egypt--Social condtions--20th century. | Egypt--Social condtions--21st century.
Classification: LCC DT107.826 F76 2024 (print) | LCC DT107.826 (ebook) |
DDC 962.05--dc23
LC record available at https://lccn.loc.gov/2023037870
LC ebook record available at https://lccn.loc.gov/2023037871

ISBN: 978-1-032-39827-3 (hbk)
ISBN: 978-1-032-39828-0 (pbk)
ISBN: 978-1-003-35158-0 (ebk)

DOI: 10.4324/9781003351580

Typeset in Palatino
by The Moshe Dayan Center for Middle Eastern and African Studies, Tel Aviv Univeristy, Israel

Publisher's Note
This book has been prepared from camera-ready copy provided by the editors. Every effort has been made to contact copyright-holders. Please advise the publisher of any errors or omissions, and these will be corrected in subsequent editions.

Contents

Figures vii
Table viii
Contributors ix
Note on Transliteration from Arabic xii

Preface 1

REVOLUTIONS IN EGYPT—A THEORETICAL FRAMEWORK

1 **The Conceptualization of the 1919, 1952, and 2011 Uprisings: *Thawra* or Revolution?** 7
Shimon Shamir

2 **The Burden of History** 25
Shlomo Avineri

EGYPTIAN REVOLUTIONS FROM WITHIN: POLITICS, SOCIETY, ECONOMY, AND REGIONAL ROLE

3 **Who Has Governed Egypt—Ruler, Regime, or State? Egypt's Unrevolutionary 1971 Revolution** 33
Nathan J. Brown

4 **Historic Pathways in Two Revolutions: 1919 and 2011** 45
James Whidden

5 **Vertical Versus Horizontal: Egypt's State–Religion Discourse Before and After the 2011 Uprising** 67
Limor Lavie

6 **The Lonely Minority? Assessing the Modern Story of Egypt's Copts and their "Return to Tradition"** 87
Heather J. Sharkey

7 **Egypt: The Inevitable Consequences of Inconsistent Socio-Economic Policies** 111
Onn Winckler

8 **From Leader to Partner: Egypt's Declining Role in the Arab System (1952–2020)** 137
Elie Podeh

HOW SHOULD A REVOLUTION BE REMEMBERED? HEGEMONIC COLLECTIVE MEMORY VERSUS COUNTER-COLLECTIVE MEMORIES

9 State Efforts to Establish Museums for the 1952 Revolution in Egypt 161
Joyce van de Bildt-de Jong

10 The Jubilee Celebrations of Egypt's 1952 Revolution and the Construction of Collective Memory 177
Alon Tam

11 Language, Humor, and Revolution in Contemporary Egypt 203
Gabriel M. Rosenbaum

12 Young Egyptians Conquer the Public Sphere of Taḥrīr Square, Reshaping Egyptian Collective Memory and Identity through Graffiti 241
Mira Tzoreff

Index 269

Figures

1.1	A Two-Stage Revolution Model.	13
7.1	Egypt's real GDP growth rate, 1961–2019 (%).	112
7.2	Egypt's inflation rate (consumer prices), 1961–2018 (%).	112
7.3	Egypt's population, 1897–2050 (de facto population, thousands).	115
7.4	Egypt's natural increase rate, 1907–2019.	115
7.5	CBR of Egypt, Iran, Turkey, Brazil, Mexico, and South Korea, 1960–2018.	117
7.6	Egypt's military expenditures, 1960–2019 (% of GDP).	119
11.1	*Rab'a,* a sign made with the fingers.	208
11.2	The *milyonīyya* manifesto, Friday, May 27, 2011.	209
11.3	The dentist.	211
11.4	Mubarak wants to replace the people.	212
11.5	*Irḥal* (Leave!).	215
11.6	Just leave! My hand hurts!	215
11.7	Leave! My shoulder hurts!	215
11.8	Leave! I miss my wife…	216
11.9	The *ṣa'īdi* with his *irḥal* board.	216
11.10	*irḥal* in mirror writing.	217
11.11	Leave (in hieroglyphics).	217
11.12	Leave (in Hebrew).	217
11.13	Go! I am freezing!	218
11.14	*Hatimshi* and *ingiz* (Go and hurry up!)	218
11.15	Even for one day…	219
11.16	Come back again, President.	219
11.17	I would like to have been Egyptian.	220
11.18	Take from us… 'Alā''s father.	221
11.19	Poison, podium, and Facebook.	222
11.20	Al-Sisi demands small change.	226
11.21	Sorry, I can't give you money.	227
11.22	[Sa'd Zaghlūl:] There is no change.	228
11.23	*Inzil* in al-Sisi's election campaign (a).	229
11.24	*Inzil* in al-Sisi's election campaign (b).	229
11.25	Three Egyptian presidents.	230

Table

Contributors

Shlomo Avineri is Professor of Political Science at the Hebrew University of Jerusalem and member of the Israel Academy of Sciences and Humanities. He served as Director-General of Israel's Ministry of Foreign Affairs in the first cabinet of Prime Minister Yitzhak Rabin. Avineri is the recipient of the Israel Prize, the country's highest civilian decoration. His books on Hegel, Marx, and Zionist thought have been translated into many languages. His most recent book is *Herzl: Theodor Herzl and the Foundation of the Jewish State.*

Joyce van de Bildt-de Jong received her PhD in History from Tel Aviv University. Her dissertation examined the contested memory of the 1952 revolution in Egypt during the periods of Anwar al-Sadat and Hosni Mubarak. Her research interests include contemporary Egyptian history, collective memory, and identity politics. She has published several journal articles and book chapters, dealing with questions of memory and nostalgia in Egypt. She has worked with the Historical Society of Jews from Egypt, researching the effect of Egypt's wars with Israel on the Egyptian Jewish community.

Nathan J. Brown has a PhD in politics and Near Eastern Studies from Princeton University. His dissertation received the Malcolm Kerr award from the Middle East Studies Association in 1987. He is Professor of Political Science and International Affairs at George Washington University, and has served as a Guggenheim Scholar, a fellow at the Woodrow Wilson Center, and a Carnegie Fellow. Brown's most recent book is *Arguing Islam after the Revival of Arab Politics*. His areas of expertise are government and politics of the Middle East, democratization and constitutionalism and the rule of law in the Arab world.

Limor Lavie received her PhD from the Hebrew University of Jerusalem. She is a Lecturer in the Department of Arabic at Bar Ilan University. Her areas of research include the political history of contemporary Egypt, state–religion relations in the Middle East, the Muslim Brotherhood, the Arab uprisings, and state–media relations in the Arab world. Her book, *The Battle over a Civil State: Egypt's Road to June 30, 2013*, was published in 2018. Her most recent article is "Lessening Anti-Jewish Hate Speech in Service of the Egyptian Regime: State Media under Mubarak, Re-Examined," published in *Die Welt des Islams*.

Elie Podeh (PhD Tel Aviv University, 1991) holds the Bamberger and Fuld Chair in the History of the Muslim Peoples at the Department of Islamic and Middle East Studies, and is a senior research fellow at the Harry S. Truman Institute for the Advancement of Peace—both at the Hebrew University of Jerusalem. Since 2016, he has served as the President of the Middle East and Islamic Studies Association of Israel (MEISAI). His research interests are modern Egypt, inter-Arab relations, the Arab–Israeli conflict, education, and culture in the Middle East and Israeli foreign policy.

Uzi Rabi (PhD Tel Aviv University, 2000) is the Director of the Moshe Dayan Center for Middle Eastern and African Studies, Head of the Department of Middle Eastern and African History, and a senior researcher at the Center for Iranian Studies, all at Tel Aviv University. His research focuses on the modern history and evolution of states and societies in the Middle East, Iranian–Arab relations, oil and politics in the Middle East, and Sunni–Shiʿi dynamics. His book *The Return of the Past: State, Identity, and Society in the Post-Arab Spring Middle East* (Lexington Books, November 2019), is a translation of his best seller in Hebrew *Back to the Future—The Middle East in the Shadow of the Arab Spring* (Resling, 2016).

Gabriel M. Rosenbaum received his PhD from Tel Aviv University in 1995. He is professor emeritus at the Department of Arabic Language and Literature at the Hebrew University of Jerusalem. He is also the director of the Israeli Academic Center in Cairo since 2006, and a visiting fellow at Wolfson College, Cambridge (UK). His research and publications focus on the language, literature, drama, and popular culture of modern Egypt, as well as modern spoken Egyptian Judeo-Arabic. He also writes prose fiction and poetry (in Hebrew), and recently published a novel titled "The First Supper."

Shimon Shamir (PhD Princeton, 1961) is Professor Emeritus of the history of the Middle East at Tel Aviv University. He was the founding director of the Shiloah (now Dayan) Center for Middle Eastern Studies in Tel Aviv and of the Israeli Academic Center in Cairo. Shimon Shamir served as Israel's ambassador to Egypt and as first ambassador to Jordan. His research focuses on the modern history of Egypt, Jordan, and the Palestinians, on intellectuals and ideology in the Arab world, and on the Arab–Israeli conflict.

Heather J. Sharkey is Professor in the Department of Near Eastern Languages and Civilizations at the University of Pennsylvania. She holds degrees from Yale (Anthropology, BA), the University of Durham (Middle Eastern Studies, MPhil), and Princeton (History,

PhD). Her most recent books are *A History of Muslims, Christians, and Jews in the Middle East* (2017), and a volume co-edited with Jeffrey Edward Green, *The Changing Terrain of Religious Freedom* (2021).

Alon Tam is a social historian of modern Egypt and of its Jewish community. He has written, among others, about the social and political history of Cairo's coffeehouses, about Cairo's Jews and their place in its urban history, and the Blackface in Egyptian theater. Tam received his PhD from the Department of Near Eastern Languages and Civilizations at the University of Pennsylvania, where he also held a postdoctoral fellowship. He held postdoctoral fellowships also at Columbia University, and the University of California in Los Angeles.

Mira Tzoreff is a Senior Lecturer at the Department of Middle East and African History and a Senior Researcher at the Moshe Dayan Center—both at Tel Aviv University. Her areas of research are the socio-cultural history of modern Egypt, women and gender in Arab and Islamic societies and youth in the Middle East and North Africa. Mira Tzoreff is the editor of a special issue of *The Near East* titled "Women and Gender in Middle Eastern Spheres" (2018), and author of "The Quiet Revolution: Saudi Women Heading a Revolution from Within" (*The New East*, 2018) and of "Humoresque and Satire in 'Ali Salem's Writing as a Means for Social and Political Criticism" (*Middle Eastern Studies*, 2021).

James Whidden is Professor of History at Acadia University, Canada. His PhD dissertation was written in 1998 at the School of Oriental and African Studies, University of London, where he produced a biographical dictionary in 1926. His research primarily deals with colonialism and politics in Egypt; book-length works include *Egypt: British Colony, Imperial Capital* (2017) and *Monarchy and Modernity in Egypt: Politics, Islam and Neo-Colonialism Between the War* (2013).

Onn Winckler (PhD University of Haifa, 1994) is Professor in the Department of Middle Eastern and Islamic Studies at the University of Haifa. He is the author of *Demographic Developments and Population Policies in Ba'thist Syria* (1999); *Arab Political Demography: Population Growth, Labor Migration and Natalist Policies* (2005, 2009, 2017); and *Behind the Numbers: Israel Political Demography* (2015, Hebrew). He is also the co-editor with Elie Pdeh of *Rethinking Nasserism* (2004); The Third Wave: Protest and Revolution in the Middle East (2017, Hebrew); and *Between Stability and Revolution: A Decade to the Arab Spring* (2021, Hebrew).

Note on Transliteration from Arabic

The transliteration of Arabic words in this book generally follows the system of the International Journal of Middle East Studies, with slight changes made to facilitate reading.

Very common names such as Gamal, Hosni, Mohammad, and the like are freely transcribed according to the forms in general usage. Names of Egyptian and Arab personalities who usually spell their names in English or French forms were left in those forms.

In some names and terms, the Egyptian pronunciation of the letter (ج) as "G" was preferred to the Modern Standard Arabic transliteration as "J." Words transcribed from the Egyptian vernacular (mainly in Gabriel M. Rosenbaum's chapter) are the only exception to this translation system. While the transliteration of the vernacular, too, adheres to the general rules of the same system, some modifications were required to represent the different pronunciation of the vernacular.

Preface

While the "Arab Spring" upheavals of 2011 bred hopes for political reform and a better future, they resulted in several failed states and overarching frustration. Even Egypt, which managed to weather the revolutionary storm and restore stability, suffers from an underlying sense of shattered dreams. This sense of failure in 2011 mirrored past attempts at reform, from the unsuccessful 1919 revolution to end British colonial hegemony, to the broken and unfulfilled promises of the 1952 revolution to rework the country's social system and unify the Arab world. In spite of these three ultimately unsuccessful efforts to achieve their defined objectives, each milestone does in fact represent a meaningful turning point in modern Egyptian history. These three catalysts, upheavals, or more commonly referred to as revolutions, helped propel Egypt into the twenty-first century. The present volume is a by-product of a three-day workshop which took place at Tel Aviv University in January 2018. It deals with these three revolutions, re-examined by American and Israeli scholars who specialize in modern and contemporary Egypt, to reassess their significance in Egyptian history. We were privileged to have the well-known Egyptian sociologist Sa'd al-Din Ibrahim as a key-note speaker. In his comments, Ibrahim argued that the Egyptian youth are not an exception, as young people around the globe, regardless of their location, want to express themselves, raise their voices, and protest against tyranny and injustice. Indeed, the slogan of the movement against Mubarak was *Kifayah*! ("Enough!") wielded by civil society—young women and men who felt they were at the end of their rope. Bureaucrats or military personnel were not among the protesters. Under the threat of his son Gamal inheriting the Egyptian presidency, from 13–15 million young people signed petitions demanding Mubarak to reform the Egyptian political system. While his back against the wall, the president rejected their demand claiming that Egypt was not Tunisia. Indeed, as Ibrahim claimed, Tunisia was the Cinderella of the Arab Spring revolutions that was not replicated elsewhere, but did serve as an inspiration for the Egyptian youth in a non-violent manner.

Therefore, Ibrahim argues, the connection between three historical events—the ʻUrabi Revolt (1879–1882), the 1919 revolution, and the 2011 Arab Spring—in Egypt's history must be reconsidered. The first, the ʻUrabi Revolt began as an uprising initiated by army officers, which snowballed into a popular upheaval against the British occupation of Egypt. Next is the 1919 revolution, which broke out after the British colonial authorities refused to allow leaders from the Egyptian national movement (including Saʻd Zaghlūl and ʻAli Fahmy) to promote Egyptian independence at the Paris Peace Conference in the spirit of the American President Woodrow Wilson's call for self-determination. Defying the Egyptian national leadership, the British High Commissioner remarked, "Who do you actually represent? You represent nobody but yourself, certainly not the Egyptian nation!" triggering some 6 million out of 30 million Egyptians to sign a petition nominating Zaghlūl as their representative. This powerful moment demonstrating the potency of civil society was embedded in the collective memory of the young Egyptians who founded the *Kifayah* movement and filled Taḥrīr Square in 2011. The days of this revolution were seen as a festival, reminiscent of the Roman Forum in its practices. Demanding the ousting of President Mubarak, the youth were met by violence, and hundreds of dead and injured demonstrators at the hands of the regime.

The chapters are grouped in three parts. The volume opens with two chapters providing a theoretical framework aiming at understanding revolutions in Egypt. The first is a chapter by Shimon Shamir probing the fluctuating connotations of the term "revolution" and its Arabic counterpart *thawra* in their common use across the Arab world, assessing their validity in each 1919, 1952, and 2011. Next, Shlomo Avineri suggests a broad and global historical context for Egypt's revolutionary experiences.

The second part of this volume takes an internal look at Egypt's revolutions, investigating politics, society, economy, and regional issues. It opens with Nathan Brown's chapter which shows how in the course of the Nasserite Revolution "ruler, regime, and the state in Egypt became difficult to disentangle" from the country's foreign policy. James Whidden follows with a comparison of the consequences of the 1919 and 2011 revolutions, concluding that they both "betray an enduring pattern of authoritarian restoration" on the domestic front. Limor Lavie discusses the state–religion discourse, showing its expansion after the 2011 upheaval to a "wide, segmentally organized and multi layered," relative to the past. While Lavie's chapter focuses on the place of Islam in the state, Heather Sharkey's deals with developments facing the

Coptic community. She suggests that these developments "moved in step with Egyptian history and remained integral to it" only until the 1960s, marking "important departures that changed Coptic connection to Egypt." Onn Winckler follows, examining Egypt's deteriorating socio-economic conditions following the Nasserite period, which in his analysis, was caused mostly by the deficient implementation of necessary economic policies. Finally, Elie Podeh analyzes Egypt's declining regional position from Nasser's revolution to the rise of ʿAbd al-Fattah al-Sisi following the ousting of Mubarak, based on the typology of leadership roles.

The third and final part of this collection looks at the hegemonic collective memory versus the counter-collective memories of these revolutions. Joyce van de Bildt-de Jong describes the attempts made by the Mubarak regime to establish a museum of the 1952 revolution and the difficulties the project faced, as well as the unsuccessful attempts to revive the project after the 2011 uprising. Alon Tam focuses also on the collective memories of the July Revolution, dealing with the 2002 celebrations of its Golden Jubilee. He identifies a variety of ways through which the Nasserite period is remembered according to the changing agenda of the regime. Gabriel Rosenbaum presents through an extensive study of Egyptian linguistic quandaries the culture of humor that found expression in the revolution of 2011 and its aftermath. Mira Tzoreff's chapter concludes this volume, focusing on the various ways young Egyptian protestors employed in establishing both their "right to the city" and their right to reconstruct the Egyptian collective memory of the Arab Spring revolution as well as the layers of the Egyptian collective identity through graffiti.

Uzi Rabi and Mira Tzoreff

REVOLUTIONS IN EGYPT—
A THEORETICAL FRAMEWORK

The Conceptualization of the 1919, 1952, and 2011 Uprisings: *Thawra* or Revolution?

Shimon Shamir

The Merits of *Thawras*

The enthusiasm generated by the remarkable success of the Taḥrīr demonstrators to overthrow a powerful ruler, and subsequently the spreading disillusionments as Islamists and generals filled the vacuum created by the rebels—inspiring a lively discussion among Egyptians on the place of revolutions in their political life. In newspaper columns, in the social media, and also in several books, discussants went back to previous chapters in Egypt's modern history—mostly to the events of 1919 and 1952—seeking to find meaning in the successive upheavals that have swept over the country in the last hundred years and hopefully derive reassurance from these past experiences. "The contestation over the significance of these events," wrote Dina Shehata, "continues to define the national debate in Egypt."[1]

Opinions expressed in this retrospection represent a broad range of approaches but broadly speaking it emerges that nationalistic premises and beliefs dominate this discussion. Many assert that the Egyptian people are the prime movers of their history and that in face of oppression they always rise up claiming their rights and defying their oppressors. In this conception, the three insurgencies—of March 1919, July 1952, and January 2011—were all manifestations of the ingrained spirit of the Egyptian people and thus all were essentially equivalent. Congruently, it is also maintained that the three events represented continuity, comprising stages in a linear development. Above all, the three are seen as laudable revolutions.

Thus, in a recent book dealing with collective memories of the Egyptians from the *thawra* of 1919 to that of 2013, Dr. ʿAwāṭef ʿAbd al-Raḥmān writes that all these *thawra*s "arose from identical circumstances and issued from the same idea, namely, that the people have the final word and the people have supreme sovereignty."[2]

A better-known thinker, Muhammad Hassanein Heikal, elaborated on this concept. In an article written shortly after the eruption of the Arab Spring in Egypt and published later in his book *Miṣr ʾilā ʾayn?* (Whither Egypt?), he articulated it in the following way:

> *Thawrat al-shabāb* [of 2011] completed the *thawra* of 1919 in which the people, led by the big landowners' class, rose up seeking to realize the evacuation of the British forces by means of negotiations, and demanding the proclamation of a constitution, be it even granted by the King.
>
> [...] It also completed the *thawra* of 1952, which was executed by members of a vanguard from the Egyptian military. They were embraced and supported by the people who shared with them the great deeds they accomplished for Egypt in the regional and global spheres. Yet, for whatever reasons, they did not manage to realize democracy for the entire people.
>
> Then finally arrived the youth of 2011. Their action not only continued but also surpassed the preceding experiences, because this time [...] they did not follow the leadership of the big landowners, who had preferred to negotiate, nor did they follow the *thawra* of the military vanguard, which though supported by the masses was unable, due to its circumstances, to advance on their chosen road beyond three-quarters of its length. This time, in 2011, the people rose up in its entirety, including all the generations, all the social classes, and all the religious communities [...] millions after millions. Thus, for the first time in Egypt's modern history, we witnessed a total turnout, a complete *thawra* by and for the entire people.[3]

Heikal's reading of these events does not claim that the previous *thawra*s were flawless: he grants that 1919 was led by a non-revolutionary upper class, and 1952 was launched by a military clique which was not adequately democratic. Yet all these *thawra*s (actually starting from the 1882 *thawra* of Orabi) represent for him a chain of basically similar events progressing gradually from one stage to another and culminating in the *thawra* of 2011. In this interpretation, *thawrat al-shabāb* is endowed with historical logic—it is the fruition of the struggles of previous generations. The term *thawra* is thus employed by Heikal, as by most Egyptian historians and writers, as a coherent and meaningful concept, a useful tool for interpreting Egypt's modern history.

The Multiple Meanings of *Thawra*s

But does "*thawra*" effectively serve this purpose? Does labeling all three events by the same term make them really connected? Can it provide a coherent, well-defined concept for interpreting their meaning?

In fact, as all readers of Arab historiography know, the term *"thawra"* is excessively broad, being applied to a wide range of different types of political actions. In modern Arab history, whenever a junta of ambitious military officers seized power from the ruling government, it conveniently appropriated for its coup the appellation *"thawra."* Moreover, the term was used also to denote power struggles within the junta: thus, when Hafez al-Asad removed his fellow Baathists from government positions he declared the act to be a *thawra taṣḥīḥīyya* (corrective *thawra*), just as Sadat's purge of his fellow Nasserites entrenched in the "centers of power" was termed *thawrat al-taṣḥīḥ* (the *thawra* of correction). When Iraqi tribes resisted the impositions of centralization on their traditional privileges by the British–Iraqi authorities, their strife went by the name *thawrat al-ʻishrīn*. When, in World War I, Bedouin irregulars fought against the Turks beside the British troops, their struggle was heralded as *al-thawra al-ʻarabīyya al-kubrā*. And recently, as numerous violent conflicts erupted among local forces in the countries of the Arab Spring, many labeled their struggles as *thawra*. The term thus covers a variety of political actions: *coups d'état*, anti-government riots, mutinies, regular and irregular warfare, purge of rivals, terrorist campaigns, civil wars, and, yes, also revolutions. In some cases, political schemes with questionable legitimacy and followings adopted the designation *thawra* to obscure and glorify their true character. Hence, to say that a certain political event was a *thawra* simply does not mean much.

The various types of *thawra*s had a normative connotation. They all presumed to represent a struggle of "good" against "evil" and to be somehow associated with "the people." *Thawra*s were depicted as heroic, liberating, standing on the right side of history, and leading to a better future. Furthermore, the term sometimes simply served as an approving adjective. In the political vocabulary of the Nasserite regime, for example, the adjective *"thawrī"* would just mark something as positive, correct, or useful.

The Historical Ambiguities of *Thawra*

The usefulness of the term *"thawra"* for methodical analysis is questionable not only because of its multiple meanings and inherent value judgment, but also because its etymology is quite problematic. When the term *"thawra"* first appeared in a political context, it referred usually to the French Revolution and subsequently to other revolutions in the West. The connotations were clearly negative. Within nineteenth-century Muslim mainstream, *thawra*s were seen as upheavals disrupting "the good order of things." The stability of the political system was regarded as serving the common good, hence attempts to upset it were denounced as detrimental. *Thawra*s were associated with *fitna,* namely, sedition and internal strife. References to *thawra* in this derogatory sense can be found in Arabic writings of the time, such as Boutros Bustani's encyclopedia *Dā'irat al-Ma'āref* (1882):

> A *thawra,* in political language, is what the Arabs call *fitna.* It means a drastic change and a severe unrest. [...] A *thawra* leads to conspiracies and then to disturbances. Eventually, [...] the foundations of government are shaken, much blood is shed, and complete turmoil prevails.[4]

The rejection of *thawra*s has roots in the Islamic tradition. Orthodox Islam, which has developed as an all-inclusive system regulating all spheres of life including the political, regarded the stability of the political community as a basic requirement of religious praxis, reasoning that *'ibāda* (worship) cannot be performed without the existence of an organized community. It followed that the authority of the leaders, whose function is to maintain the stability of the system, must be obeyed. The frequently quoted verse of the Quran that lays down this principle is the directive يَا أَيُّهَا الَّذِينَ آمَنُوا أَطِيعُوا اللَّهَ وَأَطِيعُوا الرَّسُولَ وَأُولِي الْأَمْرِ مِنْكُمْ ("You who believe, obey God and the Messenger, and those of you who are in authority"—*al-nisā'* 59).

The question to what extent there may exist circumstances in which, in spite of this precept, it would be legitimate to rise against a Muslim ruler and depose him is an issue which has been widely debated among Islamic jurists. Some argue that since the *imām,* namely, the ruler, has clearly pronounced duties—notably sustaining the sharī'a and dispensing justice (*'adāla*)—his legitimacy is contingent on fulfilling these obligations, and therefore neglecting them would expose him to possible removal. This view is rejected by the mainstream in Islamic orthodoxy. For example, Abu Ḥāmed al-Ghazāli, quoting the *ḥadīth* that says, "Religion and political power are twins," asserts that the good system of religion can be maintained only by an *imām* who is obeyed. Overthrowing even a tyrannical sultan is inexcusable: it would only result in disorder and confusion. Even those few jurists who condone the possibility of uprising do not speak of a full-fledged rebellion, nor of anything close to a Western concept of revolution. What they condone is simply the enforced replacement of one ruler by another.[5]

No wonder that the immediate reactions to the French Revolution were a mixture of shock and condemnation. The Muslim observers not only denounced the revolution but actually projected the Islamic logic of prohibiting *thawra*s on this non-Muslim polity. Just as in Islam an uprising against the political authority was regarded as an assault on religion, so the revolt against the French monarchy was seen as naturally linked to the attacks on the institutions of their religion. Religion and polity were perceived as inherently connected in Europe just as they were in Islam. Thus, a memorandum on the French Revolution, sent by Reis ül-Kütab to the Ottoman *divan*, stated that "in the conflagration of [political] sedition and wickedness that broke out a few years ago in France [...] none took offence at the closing of churches, the killing and expulsion of monks, and the abolition of religion."[6]

The shift from the negative view of *thawra* as a form of *fitna* to the contemporary, essentially positive image of *thawra*s resulted from changing historical realities. After the establishment of European control over most Arab lands, the implications of *thawra* were reversed. No longer threatening the stability of Islamic entities, *thawra*s now turned against the non-Muslim foreign rulers and gained legitimacy. In this situation, they drew vitality from their association with the rapidly spreading ideologies of nationalism and patriotism. Subsequently, with the withdrawal of the European powers from the region and the emergence of various types of Arab nation-states, *thawra*s lost their common focus and split up into the great diversity described above, sometimes still retaining their mobilizing capabilities. All of which leads to the conclusion that the concept of "*thawra*," with all its volatility and ambiguities, can hardly offer an effective paradigm for the study of issues in the political history of contemporary Egypt.

How Revolutionary Were the Three *Thawra*s?

The term "revolution"—existing with slight variations in most Western languages—seems to be representing a more precise meaning and a commonly understood concept. Even in scholarly writings, in such disciplines as history and social sciences, the term is often used as though it has a universally recognized unique meaning. In fact, however, "revolution" is a multiple-meaning term whose intention depends on the context. The term can denote any deep and wide-reaching change in social, economic, political, or cultural life—such as the "industrial revolution," the "sexual revolution," or the "digital revolution." In popular usage, the term can be applied to any kind of drastic change. Narrowed to politics, it would be applied without distinction to various types of clashes with powerful authorities, including mutinies, mass demonstrations, coups at the top, underground subversions, and guerrilla raids. And, of course, *thawra*s in writings on the Arab world would generally be translated as "revolution."

Accordingly, the attempt ventured here to probe, in historical and socio-political terms, the question how "revolutionary" were the events of 1919, 1952, and 2011, must start with stating an appropriate definition of revolution. The scholarly literature on the subject deals with many types of revolutions yet the most fundamental among them is the one that fits the historic revolutions that took place in modern times in France, Russia, and China, and more recently in countries like Cuba and Iran. The term "revolution" in these cases signifies above all a comprehensive transformation. Basically, it comprises two stages: first, the overthrow and substitution of the ruling power (often with some participation of the masses); and second, the restructuring of the political and socio-economic systems.

The exact wording of definitions depicting this model may vary from one theoretician to another. Naturally, they all articulate their thoughts in the framework of their preferred general theory or ideology—be it structuralism or Marxism or other—but the two-stage model is always upheld. A widely quoted, long-standing definition is that of De Tocqueville who, inspired by the French Revolution, was among the first in modern times to probe the nature of revolutions. His definition, as cited by Tanter and Midlarsky, was the following: "An overthrow of the legally constituted elite, which initiates a period of intense social, political and economic change."[7] An example of essentially similar definitions in later scholarly literature could be that of the sociologist Jeff Goodwin, who stated that "revolutions entail not only mass mobilization and regime change, but also more or less rapid and fundamental social, economic, and/or cultural change during or soon after the struggle for state power."[8]

According to this conception, uprisings that fail to seize power from the ruling government, or those which do take over the government but basically leave the existing system intact, will not be considered revolutions. They may be termed revolts, but not revolutions. Antonio Gramsci scorned uprisings that failed to implement the second stage, labeling them "revolutions without a revolution."[9] Likewise, the implementation of the second stage without going through the first would be regarded as reform rather than revolution.

The existence of stages in this model underscores the fact that revolution is essentially a process. A two-stage revolution evolves in a linear course, progressing from the pre-revolutionary situation to the final results. Several criteria positioned along this process assess its accomplishments and its fulfillment as a genuine revolution. The following schematic chart, worked out from the vast theoretical literature on revolutions, lists these criteria with brief illustrations of their components. The nature of the 1919, 1952, and 2011 events in Egypt will be considered subsequently in the prism of this model and chart.

Phase 1: Seizing Power

"Revolutionary Situation"

Hardships and oppression, growing frustration and resentment, readiness to act, weakening of the ruling elite, of the system, of legitimacy

▼

Participation

Masses, classes, sectors, associations, army

▼

Organization

Leadership, movement, political parties, coalitions

▼

Ideology

Creed, vision, program of action, organs, exponents

▼

Intensity

Rage, "moment of enthusiasm," violence, energy

▼

Action

Strategy, arenas, operations, duration

▼

Ruler's Reaction

Capabilities, resolve, delegitimization of insurgents, actions

▼

External Players

Sympathetic support, hostile intervention

Phase 2: Restructuring

Depth

1. Replacement of rules; 2. Regime change; 3. Socio–economic transformation

▼

Pace

1. Immediate decrees; 2. Gradual transformation; 3. Subsequent developments

▼

Source

1. From below; 2. From above

▼

Sustainability

1. Counter-revolution; 2. "Themidorian reaction"; 3. Decline; 4. Stabilization

Figure 1.1: A Two-Stage Revolution Model.

Phase 1: Seizing Power

"Revolutionary Situation"

Conditions in Egypt in 1919 were clearly worse than those that would prevail on the eve of the 1952 and 2011 *thawras*. The exploitation of Egypt's resources by the British for the requirements of the war exacted a heavy toll on the people: 1.5 million Egyptians were in forced labor corps; there were extensive requisitions, food dearth and other economic hardships. In 1919 Egyptians lived under the Protectorate, known in Arabic by the humiliating name *ḥimāya*. They suffered from various forms of degradation: the exigencies of the martial law, harassment by British troops, and arrests and expulsions culminating in the banishment of popular leaders. Consequently, there emerged a widespread readiness to take action, partly even violent, against the British authorities.

The conditions in 2011 were also bad enough—striking industrial workers, unemployment particularly among educated youth, rising cost of living, corruption in the politico–economic system and widening gaps between rich and poor. Politically, the public suffered from police-state measures, harassment of the opposition, and manipulation of the elections. To crown it all, the president's son appeared as the designated successor, an act that was attributed to the regime's *"Gumlūkīyya"* ("republican–monarchist") style, and generated great public resentment. All these predicaments did not amount to the level of the misery in 1919, but they were enough to breed readiness, among parts of Egyptian society, for mass demonstrations calling for the fall of the leadership and regime in power.

Ironically, the *thawra* of July 1952, the most successful of the three, was also the one that least obviously emanated from a "revolutionary situation." True, poverty within the rapidly increasing population was severe, the political system lost credibility due to corruption and rivalries at the top, and public order was occasionally disrupted by such disturbances as the Black Saturday riots. Yet all these adversities were not channeled into significant readiness within the public at large to rise up against the governing system.

Participation

The social composition of the groups that carried the main burden of the uprising varied from one *thawra* to another. The 1919 *thawra* was the most inclusive: fellahs sabotaged railways and communication lines and killed British personnel in the countryside, while government employees, merchants, high school and 'Azhari students, transportation workers, professionals, and clergy participated in demonstrations and strikes in the cities.

The coup of July 1952 was executed by a group of middle-rank army officers, mostly from the middle class or the lower middle class, without the participation of masses of any kind. The 18-day demonstrations that ousted Mubarak in January 2011 were spurred by urban educated youth and had considerable mass participation, including industrial workers.

Organization

The level of organization in the three *thawra*s represented three basic types: loose, strong, and nonexistent. In 1919, the demonstrators, belonging to various associations in the cities, were loosely coordinated by activists of Zaghlūl's Wafd and by improvised local committees, whereas the insurgents in the countryside had no organization at all. The coup of 1952 was conducted by the tight network of the Free Officers. The 2011 demonstrators in Taḥrīr were coordinated mostly through social networking—a virtual bond that could not serve as a substitute to real organization. Directives through mobile phones were unable to effectively direct political actions or transform the initial success into the establishment of a new reality.

Whereas the *thawra* of 1919 was inspired by the widely acclaimed figure of Sa'd Zaghlūl, and that of 1952 was competently directed by the charismatic leadership of Abd al-Nasser—the 2011 demonstrators in Taḥrīr were actually leaderless.

Ideology

The three *thawra*s had much in common in terms of doctrines and programs needed for guiding political action. None of the three, at the time of their uprising, possessed an articulated ideology. The goals they proclaimed were very broad and concentrated on the immediate and the negative: the removal of those in power. Thus, the initial demand in 1919 was *galā'*—ousting the British Protectorate; in 1952, it was *taṭhīr*—purging the political elite and the military high command; and in 2011, *irḥal*—overthrowing the president. The question of what exactly should be the following step remained at that stage unanswered.

Full-fledged doctrines and programs were not prepared in advance not only because of the abruptness of the three *thawra*s, but also because of the diversity of orientations among their participants: the partnership between the magnate landowners and the popular classes in 1911 was inevitably limited and temporary; the 12 leading Free Officers of 1952 were almost evenly divided between Left, Right, and Muslim Brotherhood; and the Taḥrīr activists, as the discussions among them revealed, were split between "minimalists," "reformers," and "radicals." At most, they were united by some very broad values: by the nascent concept of Egyptian nationalism in 1919, by some populist notions of patriotism and reformism in 1952, and by unspecific beliefs in democracy and distributive justness in 2011. Accordingly, they rallied around very general slogans, such as *al-istiqlāl al-tamm* in 1911, *al-taḥarrur wal-islāḥ* in 1952, and *'eish, ḥurrīyya wa-'adāla igtimā'īyya* in 2011.

Intensity

The participants of all three *thawra*s were driven by deep feelings of humiliation and anger. In 1919, they were enraged by the high-handed and ruthless conduct of the British, augmented by the killing of hundreds of Egyptians as the *thawra* evolved. In 1952, the Free Officers were infuriated by the corruption of politicians and the palace who were regarded, among others, as responsible for the mortifying defeat in Palestine and the persistent presence of the British in Egypt. And in 2011, the demonstrators were angered both politically, by the brutality of the security machineries and the manipulations of the regime, and socially, by the degrading gap between the tycoons around Mubarak (including his exploitative sons) and the poorer classes.

In spite of the similarities in the motivations of the perpetrators of the three *thawra*s, their actions had different levels of intensity. The high intensity of the 1919 *thawra* was manifested in the massive demonstrations that brought together people from all social classes, asserting with great enthusiasm their newly crystalized Egyptianess. July 1952 was different. The military conspirators, unsure about the scale of support they could expect from other political forces, acted with great restraint, focusing cautiously on limited targets; the intensity of their movement evolved only later. The intensity of the 2011 Taḥrīr demonstrations recalled those of 1919, even though there were differences between the two rallies: unlike the participants of the 1919 *thawra*, the 2011 protesters did not represent such a broad alliance of social classes nor were they linked to a national leadership. Yet the fact that the Islamists, albeit reluctantly, joined their demonstration, and military leaders executed their principal demand—the removal of the president—reflected their intensity.

Considering the intense anger that drove the insurgents, the level of violence exercised in the three *thawra*s was remarkably low. In 1919, demonstrators in the cities were instructed, in proclamations issued by personalities around Zaghlūl's Wafd, that the struggle should be conducted *bi-turuq silmīyya* (peaceful means). The disturbances in the countryside were more violent but even there less than 40 Britishers lost their lives. The July 23 seizure of power was a remarkably bloodless putsch, especially compared to other *coups d'état* in the region (notwithstanding the ten Kafr al-Dawar workers who were executed three weeks later). Demonstrators in Taḥrīr Square, like those of 1919, often declared their commitment to peaceful protest.

Regardless of what each *thawra* managed or failed to accomplish in concrete political terms, all three can be credited for endowing the people with a spirit of dignity and pride. The very fact that Egyptians had the courage to take action against their powerful oppressors generated a mood of elation. In 1919, Egyptians experienced what Tawfīq al-Ḥakīm expressed by the words *'awdat al-rūḥ* (the return of the spirit), even hailing the event as "the rebirth of Egypt." Nasser's speeches, proclaiming the restoration of *al-'izza w'al-karāma* (glory and honor), were jubilantly cheered by the crowds. And the demonstrators in Taḥrīr, acclaimed as those who dared to "break the barriers of fear," shared with the public their newly acquired sense of pride by the graffiti they painted around the square—one of them calling upon every Egyptian: *irfa' ra'sak foq—inta maṣri* (Raise your head high—you are Egyptian). This feeling of restored dignity is considered by many as the most notable achievement of the three *thawras* and the strongest connection between them.

Action

There were remarkable similarities between the modi operandi of the insurgents in March–April 1919 and those employed in January–February 2011. In both cases the principal political activities consisted of massive demonstrations. The protesters' objective was: to take over central parts of the urban space (mostly through marches in 1919 and sit-ins in 2011); to proclaim their demands by chanting slogans and waving banners; to mobilize people for expanding the circle of protests; to display energy and determination; and to oppose forcefully the measures taken by the authorities for crushing their campaign—in 1919 by the British, and in 2011 by the State's security forces including the bizarre "camel riders."

The July 1952 takeover was entirely different. In typical *coup d'état* manner, the officers, employing their troops (some of whom were not even aware of the purpose of their action), seized key government and communication installations and proclaimed a *thawra*. Only in the following years did they manage to mobilize popular support and eliminate, one by one, the institutions of the previous political system. Of the three *thawras*, this was the only one that managed to topple and replace the existing regime.

In all three *thawra*s the capital city of Cairo was the key arena of operations. Unlike many revolts and revolutions elsewhere, which attempted to seize control by gathering forces in the periphery and storming the capital from the outside, the Egyptian *thawra*s challenged the rulers from the inside, especially from the streets of Cairo. They knew that in Egypt controlling the capital makes it possible to dominate the whole country.

Rulers Reaction

The identities of the powers challenged by the three *thawra*s varied: in 1919, the British rule was targeted; in 1952, the Free Officers aimed at the Egyptian elite in the first place and the British presence in the second; and in 2011, the protesters focused on the Egyptian president and by implication on the whole system that backed him up.

The reactions of the targeted powers also differed from one case to another. In 1919, the challengers faced the resolve of the British rulers, still holding on to imperialist convictions, hardened by the exigencies of the recent world war, and determined to crush the resistance. Initially, the British authorities felt no need for constraint: more than 800 Egyptians were killed, villages were burned down, and harsh sentences were passed by military courts. Only in the subsequent stages did the British tone down their policy.

A different constellation existed in 1952. The reaction of the Egyptian government was debilitated by discords among the politicians, by the shortcomings of the internal security system, and by the belief that sooner or later the officers and their troops would return to their barracks. Consequently, the officers seized power almost effortlessly. The British on their part, uncertain about the nature of the coup and at this stage less imbued with Imperialist resolve, did not move from their Suez Canal bases to interfere in the situation, as feared by the officers.

The reaction of the regime to the Taḥrīr rallies during the crucial 18 days until Mubarak's resignation was tougher. In 2011, the president fought to defend his authority more aggressively than the king had done in 1952. The means he possessed in this struggle were considerable. He had at his disposal an extensive and experienced security apparatus, comprising, in various categories, almost a million personnel. In addition, he could trust elements of the "deep state" (eventually termed *al-fulūl*) to stand for continuity and stability. Accordingly, Mubarak did not desist from using brutal force against the demonstrators, killing 300 of them in the first week. Yet, when the demonstrations kept spreading, and above all when the army abandoned him, Mubarak's resolve dwindled and he gave up.

External Players

The fate of the three *thawras* was determined exclusively by internal players, that is, if the British forces of the Protectorate could be regarded as internal. Yet, external public opinion did play some role. The Wilsonian political climate that was spreading after World War I, supporting self-determination for dominated peoples, encouraged Egyptians to claim their freedom. It should also be seen in the background to Zaghlūl's determination to present his demands at the Peace Conference in Paris, a political step which having been thwarted by the British ignited the 1919 *thawra*.

Public opinion in the democratic world never looked favorably on coups by military juntas. Yet the takeover by the Free Officers in 1952 was met with mixed feelings. Public opinion in the West, for quite some time, had been observing with uneasiness the excesses of the Egyptian elite around Farouk's palace and the old-style imperialistic schemes of the British in Egypt and the whole region. Since the officers rose against both, they gained for their coup considerable approval. Disenchantment with the problematic situation of Egypt in mid-century could be linked also to the CIA's decision to conspire with Nasser and his fellow officers. The collaboration between the two did not last for too long, but it gave the Nasserites significant backing at the crucial stages of their coup.

Positive involvement of external public opinion was noteworthy in 2011. The young demonstrators in Taḥrīr Square, many of them educated and English-speakers, attracted broad sympathy. They were frequently shown on television screens throughout the world, being interviewed by well-wishing, albeit not always well-informed, reporters. Spectators gained the impression that they were watching an actual revolution moving to replace an incumbent oppressive rule by an enlightened democratic system. Commentators and other observers placed this uprising in the context of the global democratization trend that had previously embraced Eastern Europe, Latin America, and other parts of the world. As it was explicated, now came the turn of the countries of the "Arab Spring," led by Egypt, to join this democratization trend. This worldwide attention and approval evidently encouraged the demonstrators and it may have contributed also to Mubarak's despair and renunciation.

Phase 2: Restructuring

Depth, Source, Pace, and Sustainability

An analysis of the three *thawras*' accordance with the criteria of the second phase should start with the *thawra* of 1952. It was the only one that developed a full-fledged restructuring of the system, and was implemented entirely by those who initiated the uprising.

The *thawra* of July 1952 started with an *inqilāb*-type seizure of control and within two years it advanced into a total replacement of the political regime. The Nasserites abolished the monarchy, the old parliament, and the constitution, and all the political parties (including the movement of the Muslim Brotherhood). Instead, they established a system of "guided democracy": all powers were concentrated in the hands of the Revolutionary Council, a one-party system was formed, and a republic was proclaimed leading to the creation of a new constitution and institutions. Further on, in 1961–1962, the Nasserites completed a socio–economic transformation into a new system ambitiously titled Arab Socialism. It consisted of governmental control of the economy, nationalization of industry and private companies, expanding agrarian reform, and proclamation of a "Revolution of Workers and Fellahs." All these innovations were interwoven into a Nasserist ideology centered on Arabism and anti-imperialism (*Depth*).

Accordingly, this *thawra* differed from revolutions which proceed directly from overthrowing the incumbent political power to demolishing the prevailing socio–economic system: it took the Nasserites a whole decade to finalize a comprehensive conversion of the system (*Pace*). Revolutionary changes were conceived by the leaders at the top and enacted through various types of decrees, matching the model known as "Revolution from Above."[10] Once the Nasserite system took shape, it was implemented consistently for another decade, albeit with declining achievements and credibility. In the end, Nasserism did not survive the death of Nasser. Sadat, his successor, launched a de-Nasserization campaign which eliminated, one by one, all the elements of the inherited system (*Sustainability*).

The *thawra* of 1919 was not the kind of uprising that brings down a government and seizes the power to take its place. Hence, the question to be asked is not to what extent the system was restructured by new rulers in power—there were in fact no new rulers—but what were the system-changing results that emanated, directly or indirectly, from the fact that the 1919 uprising had taken place (*Depth, Pace*).

The abolition of the Protectorate and evacuation of the British, the main demands of the demonstrators, were scarcely achieved. Three years after the 1919 *thawra* the British did finally abolish the Protectorate and grant Egypt some kind of formal independence, but the basic power situation has hardly changed. The British remained in Egypt for over a third of a century and, as their humiliating intervention in the governance of Egypt in 1942 demonstrated, in spite of the limitations on their presence that were agreed with Egyptians, they kept the ability to impose their will on the Egyptian polity.

In Egypt's national politics, the consequences of the *thawra* were more substantial. Out of the 1919 demonstrations, there emerged a genuine nationalist movement, framed by the Wafd Party, enjoying extensive popular support and headed by a widely acclaimed leader—Sa'd Zaghlūl, acclaimed as *"za'īm al-'umma"* (the leader of the nation). The promulgation of the 1923 Constitution, which guaranteed individual rights and freedom of expression and assembly, can also be attributed largely to the *thawra*. Yet periods of Wafdist governance started long after the *thawra* and remained sporadic. The seven prime ministers who held office after 1919 were not of the Wafd; they mostly opposed it. Zaghlūl reached the premiership only in 1924, led more reformist that revolutionary policies, and was replaced in less than a year by what was described as a "counter-revolution." Egypt's political life after 1919 can be characterized as a continuous and fluctuating bickering between four forces: the palace, the British, the Wafd, and the conservative parties—a reality that was a far cry from the vision of the 1919 *thawra*.

A socio–economic transformation was not among the goals of the 1919 uprising. "The leadership of the *thawra*," wrote its leading Egyptian historian, "entirely neglected the economic aspect."[11] The dominance of the landed magnates in Egyptian life persisted after 1919 and in fact even increased. Yet, the *thawra* was influential in the socio–economic field as well. It nurtured a realization, especially within business circles, that political independence could not be expected without developing an independent economy liberated from the preeminence of the foreigners. Inspired by the patriotic spirit of 1919, Egyptian businessmen established Banque Misr and, subsequently, other exclusively Egyptian institutions.

The uprising of 2011 accomplished the removal of the ruler at the helm but did not go beyond that. Hopes of the demonstrators to change the whole political order and create a sound democracy, as expressed in their slogans *('isqāt al-niẓām)* and discussed within their aspirant circles, did not materialize. They certainly did not expect that the void they created would be filled by a government of Muslim Brothers. Nor did they expect the subsequent return of military officers to power, instituting a system which does not essentially differ essentially from that of the deposed ruler. The creation of a novel, comprehensive socio–economic system was not even contemplated (*Depth, Sustainability*). Whether the 2011 uprising is likely to yield meaningful results in the long run, is too early to tell.

Conclusion

Although the 1919, 1952, and 2011 *thawra*s had several common features, highlighted and sometimes overstated in Egyptian historiography, they were dissimilar events. They took place in different political circumstances, employed different methods in their struggle, had different objectives, and led to different results. The existence of congruous continuity between the three was denied by the perpetrators themselves: exponents of Nasserism condemned the 1919 *thawra* as a failed uprising hijacked by the big landowners, while Taḥrīr demonstrators denounced the long-standing rule by military officers which was initiated by the 1952 coup. At most, they sometime linked their uprising to that of 1919, pointing out that, among other similarities, women and Copts played important roles in both.

In the general literature on the three Egyptian events their appellation as *"thawra"* is usually and legitimately translated as "revolution." The two terms, heavily loaded with multiple meanings, are quite close to each other. Whether they can also be rendered as "revolutions" in the strict sense of the term as defined in historical and social studies (see above), is a different question. The examination of this issue conducted in this chapter leads to the conclusion that the three approximated this model to different degrees but none corresponded to it totally.

- The *thawra* of 1952 was essentially a *coup d'état* which only at a later stage became a revolution.
- The *thawra* of 1919 did not seize power or restructure the system, but some of its long-term consequences had revolutionary traits.
- The *thawra* of 2011 overthrew the incumbent ruler but failed to bring about meaningful changes and cannot not be considered a revolution.

In spite of their limitations, the significance of the *thawra*s in Egypt's life should not be underrated. These dramatic events—to which the *thawra* against the French in 1798 and *thawrat Orabi* in 1882 should be added—characterized the image of Modern Egypt. Their presence in the collective memory of the Egyptians, as a mixture of facts and myths, nourished their self-image. *Thawra*s played a key role in Egypt's cotemporary nation-building process. They represent turning points in the country's modern history. With each of the three events, new forces came into play. Egypt after each *thawra* was not the same as Egypt before it.

Notes

1. Dina Shehata, "1919 vs 1952," *Al-Ahram Weekly*, April 8, 2019.
2. 'Awatef Sarrāj al-Dīn, *Ayyām fi dhākirat al-Miṣrīyyīn: min thawrat 1919 'ilā thawrat 30 yūniyū 2013* (Cairo: Markaz al-Ahrām lil-Nashr, 2016), 9.
3. Muhammad Hassanein Heikal, *Miṣr 'ilā 'ayn? Mā ba'da Mubārak wa-zamānihi* (Cairo: Dar al-Shuruk, 2012).
4. Buṭrus al-Bustāni, *Dā'irat al-Ma'āref* (Beirut: 1882), vi, 337–338, quoted in Ami Ayalon, "Thawra," *EI*[2] X, 444.
5. Erwin Rosenthal, *Political Thought in Medieval Islam* (Cambridge: Cambridge University Press, 1962), 38–43.
6. Ahmed Cevdet, *Tarih-i Cevdet* (Istanbul: 1301–1309 AH), vol. vi, 311f. Quoted in Bernard Lewis, *The Emergence of Modern Turkey* (London: Oxford University Press, 1961), 65–66.
7. Raymond Tanter and Manus Midlarsky, "A Theory of Revolution," *J. of Conflict Resolution* XI/3 (1967), 264–280.
8. Jeff Goodwin, *No Other Way Out: States and Revolutionary Movements, 1945–1991* (Cambridge: Cambridge University Press, 2001), 8.
9. Antonio Gramsci, *Scritti Politici 1* (Rome: Editori Riuniti, 1967), quoted in Billie J. Brownlee and Maziyar Ghiabi, "Passive, Silent and Revolutionary: The 'Arab Spring' Revisited," *Middle East Critique* 25, no. 3 (2016), 299–316.
10. Ellen Kay Trinberger, *Revolution from Above: Military Bureaucrats and Development in Japan, Turkey, Egypt and Peru* (New Brunswick: Transaction Books, 1978).
11. 'Abd al-Raḥmān al-Rāfe'i, *Thawrat 1919*, 4th ed. (Cairo: Dār al-Ma'āref, 1987), 582.

Selected Bibliography

Brownlee, Billie J., and Maziyar Ghiabi, "Passive, Silent and Revolutionary: The 'Arab Spring' Revisited," *Middle East Critique* 25/3 (2016), 299–316.

Goodwin, Jeff, *No Other Way Out: States and Revolutionary Movements, 1945–1991* (Cambridge: Cambridge University Press, 2001).

Sarrāj, Awatef al-Dīn, *Ayyām fi dhākirat al-Miṣrīyyīn: min thawrat 1919 'ilā thawrat 30 yūniyū 2013* (Cairo: Markaz al-Ahrām lil-Nashr, 2016).

Tanter, Raymond, and Manus Midlarsky, "A Theory of Revolution", *Journal of Conflict Resolution* 11, no. 3 (1967), 264–280.

Trinberger, Ellen Kay, *Revolution from Above: Military Bureaucrats and Development in Japan, Turkey, Egypt and Peru* (New Brunswick: Transaction Books, 1978).

The Burden of History

Shlomo Avineri

During the 1882 attempt under Ahmed Orabi to resist British control of Egypt, a European observer writing from London made the following skeptical assessment: "We know little about Orabi, but I am prepared to wager ten to one that he is an ordinary pasha who does not want to let the financiers collect the taxes because in good Oriental fashion he prefers to put the taxes in his own pocket. It is again the story of peasant countries from Ireland to Russia and from Asia Minor to Egypt... It seems to me you are defending the so-called National Party too much."

This harsh judgment, tinged with what we would call today typical Victorian orientalism, appears in a letter from Friedrich Engels to the German Social Democratic leader and theoretician Eduard Bernstein, dated August 9, 1882. Bernstein, like many European progressive thinkers, saw in the Orabi insurrection the beginning of a wider anti-colonial movement. The more skeptical Engels, on the other hand, added a wise caveat: "I think we can well be on the side of the oppressed fellahin without sharing their illusions (a peasant people has to be cheated for centuries before it becomes aware of it from experience) and be against the English brutalities without at the same time siding with their military adversaries of the moment."

In retrospect, Engels' doubts, for all their eurocentric prejudices, did point out the crucial need to consider the concrete historical context in any analysis of political and social development, and not to impose general theories of history grounded in the European experience on societies that have to come to terms with—and overcome—very different legacies. This was what both he and Marx had learned from the failures of the 1848 European revolutions and their aftermath, and such insights can be helpful too when addressing the past century of Egyptian history. It is clear that the latter must be viewed primarily within the context of overall Middle East developments. Nevertheless, given what happened in central Eastern Europe following the collapse of Communism and the dissolution of the Soviet Union, and the subsequent comparisons between those phenomena and the Arab Spring, it also seems necessary to investigate recent Egyptian history against the background of post-1989 developments in Europe. Though parallels between them are obvious, the differences are perhaps even more striking, making a convincing argument that the success of revolutions in Egypt hinges on a complex set of circumstances not aligned with European precedents.

We can begin with one of the most significant lessons of post-Communism. When the Communist regimes collapsed, these countries all shared a similar political and economic structure: they were one-party states, with the state party enjoying not only a monopoly of political power, but also control of a nationalized economy and the spheres of culture and education. Despite these commonalities, however, after 1989, these societies developed in different ways—from Russian quasi-czarist neo-authoritarianism to the political multi-party pluralism of Visegrád countries. These differences cannot be explained by quantifiable data such as GNP per capita, degrees of industrialization or urbanization, or similar dimensions.

It turns out that the one set of data which would best predict any country's development toward democracy and a market economy was its historical legacy. For those countries that possessed a tradition of civil society, some forms of representative institutions, a multi-party system, and a legacy of municipal and academic autonomy of one sort or another—like the Visegrád countries, despite the clear differences among them—the transition to democracy was relatively easy. In other countries like Russia, where such traditions were weak or non-existent, the path to democracy was much more difficult and was eventually blocked. Despite recent populist authoritarian tendencies in countries like Hungary and Poland, their political structures today still differ significantly from contemporary Russia's authoritarianism or Ukraine's inability to develop a coherent political system. And even the current nationalist tendencies in Hungary and Poland hark back to pre-1939 legacies that survived communist ideology and suppression. In other words, historical legacies and burdens cannot be discounted, and they appear to be more powerful than general concepts of universalism and democracy. Far from experiencing an End of History, the resilience of history sometimes brings about some kind of Return to History.

Historical legacies are of course difficult if not impossible to quantify; but to deny their impact would mean to end up in a blind alley which has led astray many believers in an almost messianic hope for a smooth, one-way road to democracy throughout Eastern Europe. The reality turned out to be much more complex than such simplistic determinism.

A similar deterministic worldview seems to have accompanied what was optimistically called the Arab Spring, which projected the demonstrations that challenged and toppled military dictatorships in some Arab countries as the harbinger of a general wave toward democracy across the Arab world. While the final verdict is not yet out, it is clear that no such historical determinism is at work.

Studying the comparative historical dimension immediately points out the singularity of Egypt. The very existence of countries like Iraq, Syria, Libya, and Sudan—whose status as distinct political entities is an outcome of Western imperialistic powers having divided among themselves the spoils of the declining Ottoman Empire—was seriously challenged by the turmoil of mass demonstrations (and in the case of Iraq, the US-led military invasion). Some of them may never recover. Yet Egypt, for all its recent tribulations, stands out as a coherent polity, deeply anchored in the consciousness of its population. This strong identity as a nation and polity helps to overcome whatever tensions exist between the Muslim majority and the Coptic community, which cannot be said of the relations between communities in Iraq and Syria. Egypt is one of the oldest states in the world, not a patchwork of disparate provinces stitched together by Western imperialists, and this distinguishes it from most of its neighbors in the region.

But this strength is accompanied by a Pharaonic, hierarchical, and pyramidal state structure. It protects Egypt from the kind of dismemberment and disintegration experienced by modern concoctions like Libya, Syria, or Sudan; yet it also means that its state structure and its coherence have built-in elements of a powerful authoritarian tradition that runs through Egyptian history from Pharaonic and Hellenistic times to the Mameluk period. While many Arab countries in the Middle East were set up as Western-style nation-states and ended, in one way or another, as failed states, Egypt's existence as a distinct polity has never been questioned. Even Nasser's attempts to integrate it into a wider pan-Arab commonwealth were far from universally accepted, and in the end proved futile: Egypt remained exclusively Egypt.

This political tradition also survived in the era of imperialism. Egypt never became a colonial territory and maintained its identity, even if in an attenuated form, under British hegemony. Yet it also meant that Egypt's path to modernity was linked with the deepening and strengthening of this Pharaonic tradition.

It was linked, similarly, with the army. It was no accident that Muhammad ʻAli's attempts at modernization were focused on the military, which became a symbol of Egypt's entry into the modern world and of its identity. This could not be said of the Syrian or Iraqi armies, which eventually became the power base of Baʻathist factions anchored in sectarian minority groups. More than in any Arab country, Egypt's army is identified with its nation, and since 1973 also with its pride. During the turmoil that led to Mubarak's downfall, the army enhanced its legitimacy by claiming that "the people and the army are hand in hand." This was not an empty boast: beyond its wide economic and other social roles, the army truly saw itself—and was seen—as the embodiment of the Egyptian nation.

A similar phenomenon, though in a different register, came to define the role of the Muslim Brotherhood. The fact that the Brotherhood was founded in Egypt, from within its social and political culture, and was identified in one way or another with the country's struggle against the British occupation, gave it legitimacy in a local, patriotic, and national context that it lacked in other countries which imported its ideology from Egypt. Paradoxically, the politics of the military officers in power helped to enhance the Brotherhood's salience and significance in Egyptian society.

While the Brotherhood was banned as a political party and its leaders were persecuted, jailed, and in some cases executed, its social outreach grew. Many social programs—in education, welfare, anti-alcoholism, anti-prostitution, and other fields—which the government bureaucracy, typically engaged in regime protection, often neglected, were successfully carried out by civil society groups linked one way or another with the Ikhwan. Moreover, many of the high-visibility professional associations, which hold great power in Egypt's corporate structure, were slowly taken over by people and groups linked to the Brotherhood: the associations of doctors, engineers, writers, journalists, lawyers, and others eventually came to be headed by Brotherhood supporters. So while the Brotherhood was banned politically, it became the most powerful factor in civil society and, next to the army, the most powerful entity in the country.

All this set the stage for the first free elections after the fall of Mubarak. The "TV effect" of CNN or Al Jazeera—media images of thronged demonstrators at Taḥrīr Square—suggested to international viewers that these were masses of young, Western-clad people with Facebook and Twitter accounts, many of them English-speakers. The illusion created was that this represented Egypt, while in fact Egypt comprised at the time almost 90 million people, mostly traditional and conservative in their ways and beliefs, who do not have Facebook accounts and do not speak English. Though the Taḥrīr demonstrators got their 10 percent of the vote, when the masses of citizens got the chance to vote in a free election for the first time, the preponderant majority voted for the Islamists, the people they knew, who helped their neighborhoods and their children, and stood by them in their times of need. The Islamists received a majority not because most Egyptians are Islamist fundamentalists, but because voting for young guys and girls in T-shirts does not sit well with their traditional norms. They voted for familiarity—people they knew and the basically traditional ideas with which they were comfortable.

This changed, of course, when the Brotherhood-led government started to impose its views on a population which was traditional but not extremist; it also turned some of the anti-Mubarak demonstrators into reluctant supporters of the military. That many in the Coptic community would perceive themselves more secure with an authoritarian military leader, who could at least protect them, rather than an Islamist government is obvious; it was a hard choice, but its logic cannot be denied. At the end of the day, when the army and the Brotherhood were the two strongest forces in the country, both enjoying a profound sense of legitimacy within the country's historical narratives, the outlook for a liberal, rule-based, secular, and egalitarian democracy was not bright.

It should never be forgotten that the transition to democracy in the West was painful and prolonged. France went through a series of revolutions and counter-revolutions; the USA failed to abolish slavery by constitutional means and went through a terrible civil war whose consequences still haunt the country; and Germany, Italy, and Spain, to name just a few European nations, had to overcome fascism through sometimes tough external intervention. To imagine that traditional Middle Eastern societies can move easily and quickly from different forms of authoritarianism to consolidated democracy is a variety of Western intellectual imperialism, which may be well intentioned but overlooks historical realities.

A further lesson, gleaned both from Eastern Europe and the Arab Spring, is that massive, popular demonstrations can bring down oppressive regimes, but they are not sufficient in themselves to establish and maintain a consolidated democracy. That calls for historic, institutional, and cognitive building blocks, anchored in tactical behavior and memory. Abstract slogans and theories do not suffice.

Paradoxically, in the case of Egypt, its strong state tradition can actually raise the hope that the current authoritarian regime might slowly move toward a phased liberalization without endangering the essential unity and cohesion of the country, something that cannot be said of brittle polities like Syria or Iraq, let alone Sudan or Libya. If this should happen, Egypt—the oldest, continuously existing country in the Arab world—may yet become a model for the whole region. It will require a lot of patience and probably a long time, but the option is there, precisely because of the dialectical possibilities manifest in Egypt's history.

EGYPTIAN REVOLUTIONS FROM WITHIN: POLITICS, SOCIETY, ECONOMY, AND REGIONAL ROLES

Who Has Governed Egypt—Ruler, Regime, or State? Egypt's Unrevolutionary 1971 Revolution

Nathan J. Brown

Over the century beginning in 1919, Egyptians experienced five events that were officially deemed "revolutions": in 1919, 1952, 1971, 2011, and 2013. Standard definitions of the term—involving a combination of radical political change and popular mobilization, and sometimes a redistribution of property rights—do not fit any of them (though the 1919 and 2011 events may come close). But all except one had at least one of those characteristics. All events claimed the title—or Egypt's rulers bestowed the title on them—not so much as an act of scholarly classification but in order to anchor them in an aura of profound popular legitimacy, placing them beyond political contestation, and enabling those who spoke in their names to claim a popular mantle.

The exceptional event among these—or rather the single event on the list of "revolutions" that seems utterly unexceptional—is the "Corrective Revolution" of May 15, 1971. It consisted largely of a purge by President Anwar al-Sadat (who had acceded to the presidency the previous September) of some of his rivals. Memory of this event gradually faded during the subsequent presidency of Hosni Mubarak, and by the time it was abolished as a public holiday it had been long forgotten.

But in some ways the events of 1971 mark an important turning point in Egyptian political history. Up to that point, the distinctions among ruler, regime, and state had been in progressive decline. Since that time, they have recovered. However, the use of those terms has not always reflected the shift, obscuring some fundamental changes in Egyptian governance. The changes have been evolutionary rather than revolutionary in nature, but that does not diminish their significance.

Indeed, it is common to refer to governance in Egypt by a single proper name: Nasser's Egypt, Sadat's Egypt, Mubarak's Egypt, and so on. Sometimes the ruler gives his name to a regime, for example, "the

Nasser regime." Sometimes an even more extensive (and often explicit) association is made between ruler and state: it is not uncommon for scholars to explain the behavior and nature of key state structures—the military, the judiciary, the religious establishment—in terms of the motivations of the rulers.[1] The "Nasserist state" is a common phrase, and the political liberalization of the 1970s is often explained purely in terms of Sadat's motives, as are similar waves of liberalization that waxed, before waning, under Mubarak.

Such wording seems odd. The Egyptian state has many institutions, some of which have deep historical roots; to reduce the entire apparatus to a single individual risks missing much of the country's politics in the country. To refer to a regime by a single name suggests that there is no distinction between ruler and regime, and that there was not merely a change in the occupant of the presidency but also a change of regime when Hosni Mubarak succeeded Anwar al-Sadat.

Such vocabulary is based not simply on journalistic shorthand but on an implicit political argument regarding the centrality of the presidency as an institution, and the president as an individual, to the Egyptian state. In this chapter, I seek not only to make this implicit argument explicit, but also to assess its usefulness. I will argue, in contrast to prevailing implicit usage, that the role of the presidency as an institution and the president as a person has varied considerably over time. I take three moments in Egyptian politics over the past half century—the height of the Nasserist experiment in 1960s; the middle of the Mubarak presidency in the 1990s; and the Sisi presidency after 2014—to show how the president/regime/state elision varies in its accuracy and usefulness for analyzing and understanding Egyptian politics.

And in the process, I show the true turning point that 1971 represents—one that was quite profound, even if it has dropped from the pantheon of Egypt's "revolutions."

The Egyptian State, 'Abd al-Nasser, and the Nasserist Regime

During the 1960s, at the height of the Nasserist period, ruler, regime, and state had become particularly difficult to disentangle. This did not mean that every inspector of scales in provincial market places acted at the personal whim of the president, but it did mean that the regime was personalized and that a series of structures and procedures had been devised, often incrementally and in a jerry-rigged fashion, to diminish the autonomy of state institutions and make them accountable to the regime and the ruler.

At the center of this ruler/regime/state fusion stood the presidency and the president himself. The presidency was a new institution in Egypt, created only upon the abolition of the monarchy in 1953. The creation of that office was accompanied in the previous and following years by other steps restructuring the state and the political sphere: the abolition of the monarchy, the disbanding of political parties, the formation of the Liberation Rally, the assault on *Majlis al-Dawla* (a set of administrative courts and legal advisory structures), the suspension of the parliament, the taming of the labor unions, the suppression of the Muslim Brotherhood, and the construction of exceptional courts—that had the cumulative effect of eliminating much competition and pluralism within the state apparatus and in Egyptian politics more generally. As Gamal 'Abd al-Nasser assumed the presidency in 1954, he began to establish a personal dominance over the regime that would have been difficult to anticipate. By the late 1950s, ruler and regime had become fused.

More slowly but just as certainly, a set of set of structures was built (or deeply modified) that not only institutionalized the centrality of the presidency but also subordinated most of the state apparatus to regime and ruler. Two obvious structures that accomplished this task were the military and security services. The military, formerly an apolitical institution, furnished the regime with key personnel and was subordinated to it. Mid-ranking officers in the Free Officers' Movement came to populate leadership roles throughout the state apparatus and even in the military itself. The security services policed dissent with a ruthlessness previously unknown in Egyptian political life and provided the intelligence necessary to maintain what became a police state.

But a third critical structure, perhaps underappreciated at the time and since, was the Arab Socialist Union (ASU). The ASU was established initially to occupy political space and propagate ideology, but it had a far-reaching effect on the state structure. The ideology it propagated was vague but unmistakably statist. But more important was the way it brought various structures in the Egyptian political order to heel. It controlled access to the parliament, turning Egypt's legislature into a rubber stamp. It owned the country's newspapers, thus controlling the media. The ASU brought the country's professional associations and unions under its wing. And it was headed by the president.

To be sure, there were a few structures that escaped its grasp—such as the judiciary. But even there, the late 1960s saw serious discussion about folding the judiciary into the ASU. While that step was never taken, a series of other decisions taken in 1969 (known collectively as "the massacre of the judiciary") effectively subordinated one of the last autonomous bodies in the Egyptian state.

Regime, State, and Ruler during the Mubarak Presidency: The Fruit of the 1971 Corrective Revolution

But if ruler, regime, and state were fused in the 1960s, and "Nasser's regime" or even "Nasser's Egypt" turn out to be accurate phrases, Egypt's political system evolved in different directions in the 1970s. Some of the roots of this lay in long-term structural factors connected to the overreach (chiefly in the foreign policy and economic realms) that began a trip up (or tie down) the Nasserist state even in the late 1960s. Others lay more in short-term tactical decisions as Anwar al-Sadat assumed control of the presidency.

And it is in this regard that the 1971 Corrective Revolution is a key turning point. Finding key state bodies in control of potential rivals, challenging his dominance of both the regime and the state, Sadat first purged those rivals and introduced some institutional changes to make it unlikely that their power bases could be used in the future.

Those power bases—the security services and the ASU—were treated as centers of power that needed to be contained or counterbalanced. The military, which had been turned into 'Abd al-Ḥakīm 'Āmer's fiefdom until he was purged in 1967, was not deemed one of the centers of power. But it was treated similarly as a possible power base for rivals.

Such bodies were placed under the control of allies. Older institutions that had been sidelined or subdued by the ASU or the military and security services were given a bit more autonomy. This was most notably the case with the ordinary judiciary (where the victims of the "massacre of the judiciary" were reinstated); *Majlis al-Dawla* (which took on a particularly prominent role[2]); and the parliament (where ideologically distinct platforms were allowed that evolved into independent political parties). Some of the socialist policies were gradually reversed, allowing a significant private sector to re-emerge. Former dissidents were released; some were allowed to write for the press; and even the Muslim Brotherhood was allowed to resume some of its activities (apparently in hope that it would focus on social activity rather than politics).[3] Opposition student groups were treated with disdain, but rather than revive the harsh repression of the Nasser years, rival Islamic groups were allowed to contest the role of the left. The Corrective Revolution did not merely change personnel and lead to a strategy of balancing political forces, it made institutional changes as well. The military was gradually ushered out of the political sphere, the ASU was gradually disestablished, and some (sharply limited and varying but still real) measure of pluralism returned to Egyptian party and political life.

These steps were all allowed by the regime and the ruler, but apparently for tactical reasons. They led over time to a significant set of structural changes, however, that cannot be understood simply as a product of ruler intentions or regime tactics. Indeed, by the 1980s, these trends had evolved to create a different kind of system. Key Egyptian state institutions—the judiciary, the religious establishment, the media, the military, and the internal security apparatus—achieved a greater level of autonomy. To be sure, three aspects of this autonomy kept the situation manageable for overall presidential domination.

First, these sectors were all divided internally. The judiciary, for instance, comprised distinct branches for administrative law, constitutional law, and regular civil, criminal, commercial, and personal status matters; the religious establishment was divided among al-'Azhar, Dār al-'Iftā', and the Ministry of 'Awqāf.

Second, their autonomy often led them to maneuver jealously against each other. For instance, the judiciary sometimes issued decisions to rein in the security services, which in turn developed new tools and tricks to avoid the judiciary.

Third, and perhaps most important, each institution was generally headed by a reliable, pro-regime figure. The president retained significant authority in this regard sometimes directly (such as appointing the prosecutor-general), sometimes indirectly (with presidiential loyalists in the *Majlis al-Shūrā*, for instance, approving strongly pro-regime figures to head elements of the national press).

By the 1990s, the overall result of these developments was a political system in which ruler, regime, and state were linked but no longer fused. The president, by then Hosni Mubarak, presided over the state but hardly micro-managed it. Even the regime—if by that we mean the cohort of leading figures dominating the political system—contained some who represented not merely themselves but also broader constituencies. Leading figures in the business community built links with the National Democratic Party; leading judges curried favor with their colleagues by securing material benefits; editors of the national press evinced loyalty to the system as a way of obtaining subsidies for their enterprises and padded payrolls for their supporters.

Meanwhile, the state apparatus itself became progressively Balkanized. Egyptian cabinets evolved to include ministers who primarily represented their own sectors. The minister of justice was always a senior judge; the minister of foreign affairs was a senior diplomat; the minister of defense was the top officer in the armed forces; and so on. The heads of each sector were to remain loyal to the ruler and to the regime, but the sector as a whole was often free to manage most of its internal affairs. The military became a fiefdom (or set of fiefdoms), kept away from most political issues but free to defend the country's borders, build residential quarters for officers, run economic enterprises, and purchase armaments. The religious sector was given control of mosques, some schools, and the complex of institutions subsumed under al-'Azhar, which was able to police its own members to some extent but was not to concern itself with political affairs.

The autonomy accorded each sector, while far from complete, allowed various parts of the Egyptian state to develop in an insular fashion. Some became virtually self-perpetuating in nature (as senior judges filled judicial ranks with descendants of judicial families; the police academy also turning to familiar families to induct new members; and so on. And they were able to some extent to develop not merely their corporate identity and secure material benefits on a corporate basis, but also to articulate a sense of corporate mission. Judges stood for the rule of law; religious officials stood for Islam; the military stood for external security, and so on. Each sector came to see itself as the most essential part of the Egyptian state: there could be no state without law, judges intoned; 'Azharīs would present themselves as helping Egyptians hew to the divinely sanctioned path; generals asserted that without their protection of the state there would be no state to protect and provide for ordinary citizens.

And some began to resent the extent of presidential interference, especially in senior appointments. This contest exploded most publicly in a confrontation between dissident judges and the regime in the 2000s. Similar, less dramatic tussles played out in other sectors as well.

It was the presidency that held this Balkanized state together. Until it came apart.

The Wide State Reassembles Itself after 2013

There are many ways to understand the tumultuous events of 2011. Egypt's ruler was forced to depart, and the ensuing contest for his seat took more than three years to resolve. The regime was reshaped in some fundamental ways. But most significantly, in 2011, the Egyptian state stopped working as a unit.

This was most apparent in February of that year. Egypt's first coup since 1952 came about legalistically when the Supreme Council of the Armed Forces (SCAF) issued its "Communiqué Number One," a document that said virtually nothing. But it was signed by Field Marshall Muhammad Hussein Tantawi—and yet the SCAF was headed by statute by the president of the republic. Over the next three years, the SCAF continued to act not merely as a state within the state but also as a state above the state.

Other state bodies also demonstrated their autonomy and sometimes pressed for more. Al-'Azhar secured a law rendering its leadership self-perpetuating, accountable only to itself. The country's Supreme Constitutional Court did the same. By the time that Egypt's first freely elected president took office in 2012, he stepped into a position that had been stripped of many of the tools his predecessor had used to coordinate and direct state bodies. And those state bodies were hardly enthusiastic about hewing to the entreaties of a figure from outside the state apparatus—Muhammad Morsi, an engineering professor from Zaqaziq whose publicly engaged career had been spent in the Muslim Brotherhood.

By 2013, when Morsi was overthrown, and 2014 (when 'Abd al-Fattah al-Sisi, Tantawi's successor as SCAF leader, was elected president), the Egyptian state apparatus had begun to act as if it were a collection of autonomous entities that could come together for a concerted purpose (such as the overthrow of Morsi and the crackdown on the Brotherhood.

Sisi initially stepped into the same office that Morsi had occupied. Though he had the active support rather than the hostility of large parts of the state apparatus, he lacked the tools that previous presidents had wielded. Various state bodies—the intelligence services, al-'Azhar, the judiciary, and the military—had dominated the process of drafting the constitution: they played a strong role in the 2012 constitution, written under the supervision of the Brotherhood, and a commanding one in the 2014 constitution. Most were headed by figures who did not owe their position to the new president.

Consequently, much of what passed for politics in Egypt in the ensuring years was in fact the friction among state institutions. The regime, now consisting of the president and the leaders of security-minded bodies, successfully quashed most forms of organized political life in 2014 and 2015. But there are still state bodies and institutions that do not have to answer mechanically to the nation's nominal leaders. The president, for example, can make demands of al-'Azhar, which he has done quite publicly, going so far as to tell the Sheikh of al-'Azhar on one infamous occasion, "You're wearing me out." Nevertheless, the institutions can deflect, delay, and ignore. The courts have been known to issue verdicts that caused headaches for the regime.

And the ruler and regime are slowly mending the situation—through legislation (amending the judicial law), emergency measures (with a renewal of the state of emergency in a constitutionally dubious manner), and pressure. A set of constitutional amendments cemented some of these changes in 2019, increasing the president's control over the judiciary, for instance. Not all tools are legalistic. Recalcitrant state officials are hounded or purged, and their rivals encouraged to undermine them. There is no political party to fulfill the previous role of the ASU (a loose "Future of the Homeland" party was assembled to take part in the 2020 parliamentary elections, allowing the regime to organize its parliamentary majority a bit more easily without creating the kind of center of power that the ASU became). The fiefdoms that grew up from the 1970s until 2011 are now identified as a problem by the country's rulers and there are quiet moves to bring one under closer control.

The result is that the Balkanized state of the Mubarak era is being replaced by one in which the military and security services clearly guide the state apparatus. Though political parties are allowed by law, they are not permitted to be active in practice except as electoral alliances that support various loyalist forces. Independent voices—in *Majlis al-Dawla*, the press (both private and state-owned), the state auditing bureau, and the religious establishment—are purged or vilified. Security services and the military provide guidance to such entities, feeding the press with stories and delineating acceptable positions. Major economic initiatives are pursued with the military's guiding hand and participation.

In these ways, the Egyptian state has been reconstituting itself since its panic in 2011, but it has been doing so in ways that do not resemble the past. The three periods of ruler/regime/state relations discussed in this chapter are distinguished by the extent to which the distinctions among these terms can be made.

In Egypt's 1952 revolution, a group of army officers overthrew the old regime and constituted a new one. But the military as an institution, while influential, did not rule. And those officers placed their allies in command of state institutions, forming an informal network. The 2013 revolution was led by a coalition of state institutions: the military, al-'Azhar (a reluctant participant), the security services, and the judiciary. It was the chief justice of the Supreme Constitutional Court who served as interim president in the aftermath of the 2013 coup; after a new constitution was written, it was the military chief of staff who became president in 2014, only after obtaining the formal blessing of the Supreme Council of the Armed Forces for his candidacy. Unlike 'Abd al-Nasser and Anwar Sadat, Egypt's current president, Sisi, spent his entire career in the military (with no record of youthful political activity). He thus seems to be a product of the military bubble that the 1971 Corrective Revolution helped create and has surrounded himself largely with military personnel.

While the authority of the president as an individual is returning, the presidency as an institution is now ruling the Egyptian state in conjunction with the military and security establishment, whose leadership has been reshaped to ensure its loyalty. There exists no real political apparatus like the ASU to coordinate or lead. The sinews of authority seem to be populated mainly by men in various uniforms.

On April 28, 2018, in an address commemorating the return of the Sinai Peninsula to Egypt in 1982, President Sisi spoke of his admiration for Sadat's vision (one that, he hinted, was not understood at the time) and the late president's ability to restore the strength army. Narrating his understanding of recent Egyptian political history from the perspective of the military as an institution, he ended by stating: "The question of the coherence and cohesion of the state is the responsibility of all, especially intellectuals and media."[4] This remark likely puzzled many, but for a figure like Sisi, its meaning was clear: Egypt depends on the military as the major pillar of the state; the presidency is a lonely office; and all Egyptians and all state bodies are required to follow the leadership of those two institutions.

Notes

1. See, for instance, Tamir Moustafa, *The Struggle for Constitutional Power: Law, Politics, and Economic Development in Egypt* (Cambridge: Cambridge University Press, 2007), in which he explains the emergence of a strong constitutional court largely as a function of regime and ruler intentions. To be fair to Moustafa, my own earlier work, *The Rule of Law in the Arab World: Courts in Egypt and the Gulf* (Cambridge: Cambridge University Press, 1997), explained the emergence of the Egyptian judicial system partly in terms of regime intentions.
2. James H. Rosberg, "Roads to the Rule of Law: The Emergence of an Independent Judiciary in Contemporary Egypt." (PhD diss., Massachusetts Institute of Technology, 1995).
3. This was the Brotherhood leadership's understanding of the regime's implicit offer. ʿAbd al-Munʿim Abu al-Futūḥ. Personal interview by author, Cairo, 2008.
4. "Six Messages from Sisi to the People at the Educational Seminar of the Armed Forces," *Veto*, April 28, 2018, accessed October 30, 2020, http://www.vetogate.com/3159785.

Selected Bibliography

Brown, Nathan J. *The Rule of Law in the Arab World: Courts in Egypt and the Gulf* (Cambridge: Cambridge University Press, 1997).

Moustafa, Tamir. *The Struggle for Constitutional Power: Law, Politics, and Economic Development in Egypt* (Cambridge: Cambridge University Press, 2007).

Rosberg, James H. "Roads to the Rule of Law: The Emergence of an Independent Judiciary in Contemporary Egypt" (PhD diss., Massachusetts Institute of Technology, 1995).

Historic Pathways in Two Revolutions: 1919 and 2011

James Whidden

From one perspective, the Egyptian leader ʿAbd al-Fattah al-Sisi was Egypt's savior, bringing about a second revolution that heroically spared Egypt from further Islamist disorder.[1] This familiar viewpoint obscures the fact that military governance has been part of the problem in recent Egyptian history.[2] Before the revolution of 2011, the Egyptian military was an essential part of the "regime" or "deep state" alongside the president, the security services, and their clientele in the vast civilian bureaucracy—private and state-owned businesses.[3] On the eve of the revolution, this state was malfunctioning and virtually delegitimized; its military monopolized national wealth and controlled most of the nation's profitable industries while the majority of its people lacked basic social services and human rights.[4] In a country where half the population lived near the poverty line and 20 percent below it, the revolution was largely a protest of all those excluded from the military's entitlements. "Bread and Social Justice" was, not surprisingly, the slogan of the revolution.

At first, the revolution found its support among labor unions, youth groups, and primarily middle-class political activists.[5] Some members of the Muslim Brotherhood also joined the revolutionary protests, particularly younger members who had broken with the conservative leadership of an organization that worked closely with the government of Hosni Mubarak. "Revolutionaries" of all types observed that after Mubarak was forced to resign in February 2011, there were signs of an arrangement between the military leadership (The Supreme Council of the Armed Forces, SCAF) and the Muslim Brotherhood.[6] They both could find common ground in their misgivings about the revolutionaries (the April 6 Movement and other radical groups comprising youth and union activists). However, a year after the Brotherhood took office in 2012, the revolutionaries themselves turned to the military as the guardian of revolutionary hopes. In a move that mirrored Nasser's in 1954, the new regime outlawed the Brotherhood in December 2013, framed a constitution that empowered the military, police, and judiciary in January 2014, and finally, in April 2014, outlawed the very group that had led the revolution, the April 6 Movement. All this transpired during a general repression of the opposition: by 2016, there were an estimated forty to sixty thousand political prisoners in Egypt.[7]

Revolutionary youth claimed from early on that the military manipulated events, posing as defenders of the people to camouflage their restoration of the "remnants" of the old regime.[8] Some independent journalists have supported this interpretation, arguing that the military intended all along to steer the revolution in a direction that would enhance military power.[9] Toward this end, the military let the revolutionaries decimate its civilian rivals in the "deep state," while alienating the revolutionaries from the Islamists, Christians from Muslims, and conservatives from liberal reformers. Others have pointed to the weaknesses of the revolutionary movement, a coalition of diverse, competing ideological units that could not find consensus and, in many cases, abjured the political arena altogether for utopian dreams, whether leftist or Islamist.[10] Even the front-line revolutionaries, youth and labor, failed to cooperate.[11] And the revolutionary crowd—the "street," the "people," or however one defines the inchoate forces that filled public squares—proved fickle, storming the police and military barricades through 2011 and then throwing their support behind the military in 2013.

Why the revolution took such turns will remain a difficult question to answer definitively until hard evidence comes to light. Yet history offers comparative examples of earlier revolutions, supported by archival materials. Some studies point to the similarity between Egypt's 2011 and 1952 revolutions.[12] However, comparisons with the 1919 revolution reveal an enduring pattern of authoritarian restoration. To corroborate the comparison of the 1919 and 2011 revolutions, some of the terms popularly used to describe 2011 are herein applied to 1919. For instance, the archival material shows that the institutional integrity of the "deep state" survived the revolutionary outburst of 1919, which enabled the regime's "remnants" to marshal counter-revolutionary resources; the opening for the old regime came after the national leadership fragmented into competing divisions, as radical revolutionaries vied first with liberal-constitutionalists and later with the conservative monarchists; finally, the events of 1924 proved that counter-revolution, or a "second revolution," had social support, resulting in the toppling of a popularly elected party, the Wafd or Delegation, in 1924, not unlike the fall of the Brotherhood from office in 2013.[13]

Similarities between the two revolutions suggest that in each case events followed what has been referred to as historic pathways. Raymond Hinnebusch has offered a theory of "authority-building," derived from Ibn Khaldun and Max Weber, that combines the bureaucratic state with charismatic leadership.[14] A comparison of 1919 and 2011 supports that theory, particularly regarding the effective alliance of populist movements with remnants of the old regime, which, in the first revolutionary "stage" seemed to consolidate revolutionary gains, but in the second phase provided a pathway for the old regime's restoration.[15] This chapter will demonstrate, first, the strategy of regime survival by alliance with a populist movement, the Wafd (comparable to SCAF allying with the Muslim Brothers); second, the divisions within the revolutionary, popular movement; and third, the manipulation of populist forces in a counter-revolution. In the fourth section, a brief history of the 2011 revolution will summarize the similarities of regime restoration across a century.

Old Regime Remnants

From 1919, the old regime survived by seeking cover behind the revolutionary Wafd and directing the ire of radical nationalists toward the "liberal" or moderate nationalists. Though not a conventional interpretation of events, there was nevertheless a strategic alliance that allowed the monarchy to provide support for the Wafd by leveraging the electoral constituencies in 1923. In exchange, the Wafd refrained from direct attacks against the king, thereby enabling the monarchy to rebuild its popularity and legitimacy. This deal fell apart only in 1924 after the Wafd Party formed a government.

Normally, the monarchy has been regarded as a vehicle of British colonial influence. To some degree, the British did use the monarchy to reverse the Wafd's fortunes; however, the monarchists also managed to maneuver independently. From the beginning of massive demonstrations in early 1919, British agents in Cairo supported the career ministers, notably Hussein Rushdi and ʿAdli Yakan, envisioning them as the source of a moderate party that would counter the Wafd's revolutionary radicals. The popularity of the Wafd made this seem unlikely until a wave of violence in 1921 was credited to the Wafd. An intervention of imperialists, led by Winston Churchill, called for the protection of Alexandria's foreign communities, and British diplomatic agents at the High Commission in Cairo began lobbying the British government to make concessions to moderates to check the Wafd's uncompromising, revolutionary nationalists.[16] That policy was accepted by the British cabinet following another wave of popular demonstrations in December 1921. An Egyptian cabinet of "liberals," that is, neither monarchists nor revolutionaries, was formed in February 1922 upon the unilateral declaration of Egyptian independence, which was designed to give the liberals legitimacy. A party known as the "Liberal Constitutionals" (*aḥrār dustūriyyūn*) was established with former or "dissentient" members of the Wafd, led by old regime statesmen of ministerial rank like ʻAdli Yakan and ʻAbd al-Khāleq Tharwat, but also including liberal intellectuals such as Muhammad Hussein Haykal and ʻAbd al-ʻAzīz Fahmī. The British chose to support this group of mostly career bureaucrats by making concessions to nationalist demands. As a result, with the 1922 declaration, the British underwrote the creation of the Liberal-Constitutional Party on the assumption that, together with career bureaucrats, the Liberal-Constitutionals would be able to control the constitutional and electoral processes that followed the 1922 declaration and thus temper the revolutionary enthusiasm of the Wafd.

Though the Wafd remained popular and easily mobilized constituencies, its radicalism alienated elements of elite political society and its clienteles, hence there was a base of support for the Liberal-Constitutionals. The monarch, Ahmad Fu'ād, appeared to be neutral in these contests. However, British state papers show that he advised British agents against conceding to Liberal-Constitutional demands for elections and a ministry responsible to a parliament.[17] Moreover, to undermine the democratic experiment and restore royal autocracy, the monarchy began campaigning in 1922 against the Liberal-Constitutionals, not the Wafd, for instance, by purchasing political journals that attacked them.[18] Meanwhile, the Wafd directed its own campaign at the Liberal-Constitutionals, not the king. This covert alliance between the king and the Wafd was cemented in May 1923 when Hasan Nash'at, previously a member of the Wafd, began acting as liaison between Sa'd Zaghlūl, leader of the Wafd Party, and the king. The king's strategy involved, first, destroying the Liberal-Constitutionals, and second, separating a "conservative" faction from the Wafd Party.[19]

To destroy the Liberal-Constitutionals, the king's supporters pressured the Ministry of Interior's department that was responsible for drawing up electoral districts.[20] Zaki Bey Ibrāshī, a client of the king, and Mahmud Fahmi Nuqrāshī, a confident of Zaghlūl, together drew up the constituencies to benefit the Wafd's candidates.[21] Members of the Wafd controlled a department set up in 1923 to organize the agricultural cooperatives, which were then transformed into vehicles to corral voters. Similarly, from February 1922, the Liberal-Constitutional government used its powers of state patronage to pack the administration with its clients, who in turn leaned on constituents in electoral campaigns. However, the alliance of the Wafd Party and monarchists checked this strategy by controlling a wider selection of candidates and thus the elections did not follow the pattern envisaged by the Liberal-Constitutional government and their British advisers.[22] In other words, the monarchy was able to trade its influence over the "deep state" for the Wafd's popular support to undermine the Liberal-Constitutionals. Was a similar deal worked out between the military and the Muslim Brotherhood to weaken the revolutionary youth from 2011 to 2013?

After defeating the Liberal-Constitutionals in the elections of 1923, the government formed by the Wafd Party in 1924 was led by the highly charismatic Sa'd Zaghlūl. Perhaps because of the Wafd's covert alliance with the monarchists, the Zaghlūl ministry also included statespersons representative of previous governments that had collaborated with the British and the ruling family. This alienated the more revolutionary members of the Wafd. Though there was not yet a monarchist party, the king was able to insert his agents into the Wafd government and parliament, who then attempted to split the Wafd Party between radicals and conservatives.[23] To do so, the monarchists won over individuals who had supported the Wafd at its inception, like Hasan Nash'at and 'Ali Maher, as well as prominent Liberal-Constitutionals who were disappointed by their party's performance in 1923, like Ismā'īl Ṣidqī. Meanwhile, the radical revolutionaries unwittingly played their part in fragmenting the Wafd Party by encouraging the demands of feminists and labor activists, thereby alienating conservative opinion. In short, the political ideologies generated by the revolution proved difficult to control, even by a gifted leader like Zaghlūl (a less charismatic figure, Muhammad Mustafa al-Barādi'ī, faced similar challenges from 2011 to 2013).

Ideological Divisions

The division of the revolutionaries into moderate and radical camps was a feature of the second stage of the revolution, opening the path to counter-revolution. The first schism in the Wafd came after Zaghlūl failed to negotiate a treaty with Lord Curzon in 1920, beginning with the defection of prominent members of the Wafd, like Ismā'īl Ṣidqī. These moderates then supported the decision of 'Adli Yakan, one of the ministers in the wartime government of Hussein Rushdi, to enter talks with the British government in 1921. The origin of the Liberal-Constitutional Party was in this split. After Yakan abandoned his leadership aspirations in the teeth of Wafd opposition, 'Abd al-Khāleq Tharwat officially formed the party following the British unilateral declaration of Egyptian independence in February 1922.

With the defeat of the Liberal-Constitutionals in the elections of 1923, only the Wafd Party stood in the way of monarchist ambitions. The contest between the Wafd and the monarchy revolved around the constitutional issue of whether the monarch or the elected representatives held ultimate authority. That question had remained unresolved during the deliberations of the constitutional commission in 1922. The former prime minister, Hussein Rushdi, chaired the commission and, alongside other old regime elements, ensured that the revolutionary nationalists of the Wafd were not represented. A few pliable former Wafdists were appointed to the commission alongside Liberal-Constitutionals. The constitution that was drafted enshrined the king's powers of patronage, securing the "traditional" rights of the hereditary Islamic prince. Observers noted that these powers marked the beginning of a monarchist party.[24] The constitution was ambivalent about whether the ministers were to act according to the will of the parliament, the "people," or the will of the monarch. This was the first issue Zaghlūl addressed when a Wafd-dominated ministry was created in January 1924, declaring that the elections had legitimized the parliament as the sole representative of the nation. He said that a constitutional system should be founded on the principle of the natural right (*haqquha al-tabī'ī*) of the nation to sovereignty, not on the inclination of a hereditary monarch. Previously, he said, the state had regarded the people as a hunter regards its prey, rather than a leader its army, but the present government had the trust (*thiqa*) of the nation.[25]

With these words, the Wafd leadership seemed to suggest that it rejected the compromises worked out by the liberals and monarchists in 1922 and 1923, including deference to the monarch's authority. The other point emphasized in this speech was the unity of government and people, and it was reiterated when parliament was convened in March 1924. In typically republican, revolutionary language, Zaghlūl described the king as one "foreign" to the nation, whereas, "We the ministry are not foreign to you, we are part of you."[26] The implication: the political authority held by the monarchical remnants of the old regime would be replaced by a new government, representative of the nation.

However, Zaghlūl had difficulty finding consensus even within his own party. The parliament of 1924 was disorderly, a result of the inability of the Wafd's leadership to control various factions within it. Parliamentary factions emerged representing constituencies with vested interests and supporting a variety of policies. Armed with petitions from their constituents, parliamentarians seized control of state resources (diverting water resources, for example), which were turned like weapons against their opponents from previous governments.

Liberal-Constitutionals resigned from the administration, others were purged and re-entered private life. A prominent Liberal-Constitutional, Muhammad Mahmud, was undermined by state officials appointed to his home constituency in Asyut. The estates of Liberal-Constitutionals in other provinces were also attacked by groups carrying revolutionary banners calling for the redistribution of land to the lower classes. There were industrial disturbances in Alexandria and Cairo.[27] On Bastille Day, Zaghlūl made a speech praising the part of the lower classes in the national struggle.[28] Furthermore, the complexion of the government changed in October 1924 with the appointment of more revolutionary members of the Wafd to ministerial positions, like Ahmad Maher. At the ministry of religious endowments (*awqāf*), Nash'at had been stirring up religious opinion against the Wafd government.[29] In reaction, the Wafd attempted to block the king's constitutional powers to make religious appointments on the constitutional principle that these appointments were subject to the oversight of the elected representatives.

All of these events had an impact on conservative opinion, particularly among the influential bureaucratic class, an entitled and wealthy group, and rural notables, who were dependent on the delivery of state services, notably irrigation.[30] The wealthiest landholders appear to have made the decision to strike at the Wafd while they still had some measure of control over their local constituencies, as testified by Muhammad Badrāwī 'Āshūr, the largest landowner in lower Egypt.[31] Loyalty to the ruling family as guardian of the integrity of the Egyptian state was another factor. Zaghlūl's rhetoric, a veiled republicanism, was regarded by some as a direct threat to the monarchy.[32] A speech he gave at San Stephano Casino in Alexandria on October 24, 1924, contained merely perfunctory recognition of the king. Acknowledging that national aspirations had yet to be fully realized, he said, "My life is short, but the nation lives on. The fathers must teach its principles and dogmas to their sons."[33] The Arabic version, *"In kānat hayāti qaṣīra fa-inna hayāt al-umma ṭawīla,"*[34] is a paraphrase of the republican French formula: "I am mortal, but the nation is eternal."[35] With such statements, Zaghlūl gave the monarchists the ideological ammunition they needed to stage a counter-revolution. In unison, British intelligence reports called such speeches revolutionary incitement after the assassination of Sir Lee Stack on November 19, 1924, which they interpreted as an act of nationalist extremism, not monarchist calculation.[36] In fact, evidence suggests that it was actually a monarchist plot: according to police investigations, the assassins were close to monarchist agents.[37] Violence is typically a tactic used by counter-revolutionaries to sway public opinion during a transitional stage of a revolution.[38]

It was political violence that created the opportunity for the restoration of the old regime in 1924.[39] It bred uncertainty and fear among the bureaucrats and landholders, as well as the resident foreign colonies. After the assassination, a significant sector of Egyptian parliamentarians abandoned the Wafd, and even some Liberal-Constitutionals turned to the monarchy.[40] The British "Oriental secretary" admitted that Stack's assassination created the opening for a British intervention,[41] but the restoration was led by monarchists. In a letter in *al-Akhbār* in December 1924, Prince ʻOmar Ṭūsūn claimed that Zaghlūl had sacrificed the interests of the country for personal ends, and that factional disputes were contrary to a "true love of country."[42] Expressing disillusion with the liberal experiment, Ṭūsūn enjoined the leaders of the parties to "forget past offenses and sink their personalities in the sole personality of the beloved nation."[43] Echoes of this language would be heard in Sisi's pronouncements after the brutal summer of 2013.

Popular Forces

British intelligence reports claimed that the Wafd Party's "nepotism" and "terrorism" in 1924 alienated many, who then turned to a reconstituted old regime.[44] Figures like Ṣidqī, Nash'at, ʻAli Maher, and Mahmud Abu Naṣr helped reorganize the bureaucracy, ran the royalist organization, and articulated a new conservative ideology. To achieve the last, the monarchists purchased the Wafd's French-language journal, *La Liberté*, and established new Arabic-language journals, *al-Ittiḥād* (The Union) and *al-Shaʻb al-Maṣrī* (The Egyptian People).

The organizers of the royalist counter-revolution were not people tied by aristocratic pedigree to the royal family, but lawyers and professionals like Maher and Nash'at, who had supported the Wafd previously. The monarchist organization was able to win support from the Wafd general membership and the executive committee.[45] They were adept in the Wafd's type of political mobilization but imagined a political system secured by heredity, hierarchal social relations, and deference to authority. These monarchists organized a "counter-organization" in late 1924; it took the name Union Party, *ḥizb al-ittiḥād*, evoking a national coalition as the Wafd had done in 1919.[46] The evidence in the Egyptian National Archives shows that each of these parties relied on the social power of the "middle stratum" of Egyptian society: rural notables (*aʻyān*), urban notables, and professionals, including merchants (*tājer*), property owners (*dhū* or *ṣāḥeb al-amlāk*), lawyers (*muḥāmi*), journalists (*ṣiḥāfī*), doctors (*ṭabīb*), and engineers (*muhandis*). This "class" was a key factor in mobilizing larger constituencies that extended into the lower strata.[47] Equally important for this purpose were the bureaucrats, high and low: among the ranks of party members could be found ministers of state, inspectors, judges, mayors, police, clerks, and district inspectors (*wazīr, mufattish, ḥākem, 'umda, ghafīr, kāteb, naẓīr al-qism*). There were also significant numbers of religious scholars (*'ulamā'*), including the posts of sheikh, *qādi*, imam, *sayyid*, and muezzin (*mu'adhdhin*). Among the constituencies of Cairo and Alexandria, the most common professional category in Ittiḥād membership lists was "lawyer," whether in *ahliyya* (civil) or *sharī'a* (religious) courts, but whenever specified it was most often stated as *sharī'a* lawyer (*muḥāmi shar'ī*).[48]

The monarchists appealed largely to conservative, middle-class notables, bureaucrats, and professionals, as well as a significant number of people with a religious orientation. Not yet Islamist per se, the monarchy nevertheless laid the foundations for the organization of Islamist groups. Those with religious educations had suffered marginalization in the state hierarchy, dominated as it was by graduates of the professional schools, the *effendiyya*. This too is apparent in the membership lists. Honorary titles among the Ittiḥād and Wafd members included *pāshā, bey*, hajj, sheikh, *ustādh* (teacher), and *effendi*. In a list of party candidates for the elections of 1925, the Wafd had the most candidates, 194, among whom were 9 *pashas*, 62 *beys*, 94 *effendis*, and 27 sheikhs. In the same collection of candidates were one 122 Ittiḥādists, who posed the greatest electoral challenge to the Wafd. The Ittiḥād list included 6 *pāshās*, 41 *beys*, 22 *effendis*, and 26 sheikhs. The obvious difference between these parties was the larger percentage of sheikhs (religious notables) in the ranks of the Ittiḥād, reflecting that party's appeal to graduates of al-'Azhar. Its percentage of *effendis* was lower than the Wafd's. It is clear that the Ittiḥād Party enlisted the support of the rich and powerful as well as marginal members of the modern state system, particularly Islamic scholars, who were seeking a way to re-establish their role in government. This accounts for the higher place given to religious ideology by the Ittiḥād Party and the enthusiastic crowds that supported the king through late 1924 and 1925. At the same time, it should be noted that each party's base of support was similar: the middle stratum of society, an influential and substantial group capable of mobilizing popular forces.

During the 1925 electoral campaign, a correspondent of *The Times* described an Ittiḥād rally in Kafr al-Shaykh attended by about 1,500 "stout country folk." The rally, he wrote, was "nothing like the delirious enthusiasm which used invariably to mark the least Zaghlūlist [Wafd] gathering." Apparently most Ittiḥādists supporters were moved by the idea that a royalist government "would pay better and really last." However, while the "folk" of Kafr al-Shaykh came out to the streets to voice their support for the king, the neighboring town remained totally quiet, suggesting a politically divided society. The monarchists represented order, a party which the conservative middle class could regard as a guarantor of their historic role as patricians of their local communities. Ḥilmī 'Īsā Pasha, the campaign orator in Kafr al-Shaykh, announced that the Ittiḥād Party had the benefit of the king's guidance. Also attending was a religious notable, Sayyid Muhammad al-Biblāwī, who headed a Sufi brotherhood (*naqīb al-ashrāf*). For him, Ittiḥād's most important appeal was for national unity and the abolition of party feuds, a political virtue which he said could be found beneath the royal banner.[49] The monarchists were able to recruit support in the populace on that basis. *Al-Siyāsa*, a Liberal-Constitutional journal, admitted as much when it said that much of the monarchists' support came from conservative property holders who "deceived the simple minds of those who still live simply as laborers, promising them the best or defending them from evil."[50]

Something of the appeal of the monarchist counter-revolution can be found in a letter addressed to Ahmad Muhammad Hassanein, who in 1926 succeeded Nash'at as the king's principal political agent (Nash'at was forced out by the British because of his suspected link to Stack's assassins). The letter writer, who described himself as a "simple fellah," complained of the tyranny of the party system and its "ill effects on the nation, unprecedented in history." It was necessary, he claimed, to liberate "the people" (*sha'b*) from this tyranny and limit politics to the ruling house (*ṣāhat al-qaṣr al-'āmer*) so that all political affairs would be supervised by the elite of the nation (*yanẓuru li-kull al-shu'ūn bi-'ayn al-qawmiyya*). Offering his opinion on the corrupting influence of party politics, the writer went on to say that an individual did not have the right to restrict his thought to his personal preferences, but rather should direct it toward the benefit of the country. The letter concluded by begging pardon for expressing his opinion since he was but a "simple fellah" and not one of those "people of the pen" or "people of politics" (*ahl al-qalam or ahl al-siyāsa*).[51]

The letter underscored how the country's middle stratum viewed itself as representing the very bedrock of Egyptian society and, therefore, in conservative nationalist discourse, also the representatives of "the people." It was no coincidence that the counter-revolution adopted the language of the revolution, claiming to represent the people, while in fact restoring the old order. As the electoral lists indicate, the political order established after 1922 placed the notables under the scrutiny of the bureaucracy, and average Egyptians under the sway of the notables.

In this hierarchical political system, a significant sector of the notables was interested in a government that promised to preserve the system of state patronage that had sustained their local power bases during previous generations. Although the players changed, this political structure remained relatively consistent over the course of the twentieth century and into the twenty-first.

2011: Remnants, Divisions, Forces

At the start of 2011, two broad-based populist movements were afoot: the Taḥrīr "revolutionaries" and the Muslim Brotherhood. The Muslim Brotherhood endorsed the revolutionary demonstrations in Taḥrīr Square on January 28, three days into the revolution, creating an irresistible tide for regime change. Though the army appeared on the scene that same evening, the soldiers did not fire into the crowds. Rather, there was the sense of a people and a people's army united against a corrupt regime. Mubarak stepped down on February 11. A new government was formed of officers and civilian remnants, under the purview of the military council, SCAF.

Pressuring SCAF to enact substantial reforms were a variety of activist groups including the 6 April movement, the 25 January Revolutionary Youth Coalition, labour unions, and the Socialist (*Tagammu'*) Party. Revolutionary demands called for constitutional reform, starting with a constituent assembly that would write a new constitution before any elections were held. Debates over the legitimacy of this agenda pitted the revolutionaries against SCAF. Demonstrations resulted in the military's intervention against protestors in March, resulting in arrests, convictions, and allegations that the military used torture.[52]

To defuse the revolutionary opposition, SCAF appointed a new government and chose the leaders of the Muslim Brotherhood as its instrument on a constitutional committee—an early sign of an alliance between the military and the Brotherhood. In the referendum on constitutional amendments that took place on March 19, 2011, revolutionary groups influenced the vote in Cairo and Alexandria, but the provinces sided overwhelmingly with the proposal of SCAF and the Brothers. As a result, there was no constituent assembly and elections preceded the writing of the constitution. Concurrent attacks on Christians, apparently driven by hard-core Islamists, seemed to be tolerated by the military—yet another sign of plots behind the scenes.[53] It was in this period, the spring of 2011, that Sisi allegedly began to act as the liaison between SCAF and the Muslim Brotherhood.[54]

Ahdaf Soueif's memoir of these events is sympathetic to the revolutionaries and points to the convergence of the military and conservative social forces against the revolution. One notable example: Taḥrīr demonstrators marching to the Ministry of Defense on the anniversary of the July 1952 revolution were crushed after confronting a barricade in the al-'Abbāsiyya quarter of Cairo. A phalanx of security police lined up at the barricade while the regime's "thugs" ranged in alleys and rooftops. The military intervened with tear gas.[55] Soueif noted a change in the public temper: "Again there are people on the balconies, watching us, but now mostly impassive. The street tries to carry on with its life."[56] The social support for the military's actions is testified also by the fact that this confrontation had the air of a street battle between rival youth gangs as though the youth (*shabāb*) of al-'Abbāsiyya were protecting their turf from the *shabāb* of Taḥrīr. The revolutionary demonstrators retreated to Taḥrīr, regrouped, and planned a massive demonstration for July 29. On that day, large numbers of mainstream supporters of the more important Islamist groups—the Muslim Brotherhood and the Salafi—thwarted any revolutionary surge, demanding a constitution that emphasized the Islamic identity of the nation. Soueif observed that it was the marshaling of this Islamist base, the "poor and the provincial," that checked the revolutionaries. She maintained that the Taḥrīr ideal was replaced by the reality of political divisions based on class and regional differences.[57] The fundamental differences, however, were more likely ideological: research has shown that Muslim Brotherhood activists, like the revolutionaries, were drawn from the educated classes dispersed across the country and concentrated in the Cairo region.[58]

SCAF capitalized on these divisions, evident in the military intervention at Taḥrīr on August 1, 2011, when the Taḥrīr revolutionaries were held responsible for the woeful slump in economic activity. Casting protestors as criminals and external agents in a manner characteristic of the tactics of the Mubarak regime, state radio and television made references to "infiltrators," "outside forces," "terror," "civil war" (*fitna*), and Egypt's "image abroad," all of which fostered fears and took a toll on the public mood.[59] When 26 Christian protestors were killed by military personnel at Maspero, the Television Building, in October 2011, their deaths were blamed on revolutionary activists. It demonstrated that state media had rallied around an anti-Christian and anti-revolutionary narrative. In another tactic typical of the old regime, prominent community leaders were co-opted, for instance, Christian priests worked to camouflage by rapid burial the evidence of the military's brutal killings of the slain at Maspero.[60] Some journalists maintained that the "massacre" had required the coordination of SCAF, state media, and the intelligence or police services.[61]

During the elections shortly thereafter, late in 2011, the remnants re-emerged in political parties, competing with revolutionaries and Islamists.[62] State machinery deployed by prominent families and the former New Democratic Party (NDP, the ruling party prior to 2011) made use of less than subtle forms of intimidation. Notables and other powerbrokers did not entirely dominate the elections because the new electoral constituencies allowed for competitive claims. Nevertheless, a myriad of bloc alliances, coupled with the weakness of the leftist revolutionary lists (Egyptian Bloc and the Revolution Continues), meant that the elections were ultimately dominated by the Islamist lists (the Brothers' Freedom and Justice Party and the Salafist al-Nur Party). By the second phase of the elections in December, those sympathetic with the revolution, or at least substantial reform, often found themselves voting for the Freedom and Justice or al-Nur candidates simply because the other parties that were likely to succeed seemed to represent regime restoration.[63] The Islamist lists together took more than 65 percent of the seats in parliament, while the Egyptian Bloc took less than 7 percent and the Revolution Continues, less than 2 percent.

Once the electoral success of the Islamists was self-evident in the first round of parliamentary elections, SCAF tried to check an Islamist-dominated government by revising the constitutional amendments to entrench the military's political powers. In response, the Muslim Brotherhood planned a protest at Taḥrīr on November 18, 2011. At the same time, the revolutionaries mobilized in disparate leftist groups to confront police in battles that proved violent and fruitless at Muhammad Mahmoud Street, off Taḥrīr Square. Warily, the Brothers drew back, focusing instead on the electoral campaign as the best means to defeat the remnants.[64]

Like the Wafd in 1924, by early 2012, the Muslim Brotherhood appeared triumphant. It had rejected the SCAF-sponsored plan to entrench the military's constitutional powers in November 2011. It had won parliamentary elections. The constituent assembly formed to devise the constitution was also controlled by the Islamist bloc. To ensure that constitutional revisions followed an Islamist agenda, liberal voices in the assembly were ignored, meanwhile the Islamist parliament avoided an open confrontation with the military. Instead, state media publicized the revolutionaries' ongoing confrontations with the police, stressing the threat they posed to public security. Meanwhile, the revolutionaries besieged the Islamist parliament and mobilized against the military's tribunals, which were imprisoning suspects without trial. Police pursued protesters mercilessly: at the Port Said football stadium, for instance, the revolution's most militant adherents, the "Ultra football fans," met a brutal police response in February 2012.[65] Such scenes compromised the revolutionaries' standing in the run-up to the presidential elections. Old regime candidates campaigned for law and order, referring to revolutionary thugs, sectarianism, or issues of state sovereignty and nationalist credentials in relation to phantom threats like "foreign agents," Israel, and the CIA. SCAF used these issues to influence the "security calculus" of ordinary Egyptians.[66]

Having exhausted the revolutionary leftists, the military turned to the Muslim Brothers. SCAF reduced the field of presidential candidates to halt Islamist advances. It disbanded the Islamist-dominated parliament in May. At the end of that month, al-ʿAbbāsiyya residents again defended the Ministry of Defense against those protesting the electoral commission's dismissal of Islamist presidential candidates. Many people were astonished to discover that their final electoral choice was between a conservative Muslim Brotherhood candidate, Muhammad Morsi, or a remnant, Ahmad Shafīq.[67]

Shortly after his election at the end of June 2012, Morsi retired the senior military staff of SCAF, which seemed to signal enhanced Islamist strength. In retrospect, however, the fact that Sisi was simultaneously appointed Minister of Defense suggests that Morsi was playing to the puppet master. Allegedly, Sisi covertly backed the revolutionary opposition to Morsi.[68] Morsi provided all the ammunition the revolutionaries needed by forming a cabinet of Brothers and Salafists, stacking the civil administration with members of his organization, and postponing elections, ensuring that the Islamists continued to dominate the constituent assembly, and appropriating legislative powers to the office of the presidency, a measure codified in the presidential decree of November 22, 2012. The capstone was the constitutional revision of December 1, 2012. Although the new document was decidedly Islamist, one article conceded to the military its immunity from civilian oversight.

Islamist access to power had depended upon a bargain with the military, and the Brothers remained deferential to that arrangement. The counter-revolution, too, required a coalition, in this case of revolutionary leftists and the military. Circumstances suggest that from the December 2012 battles at the presidential palace (*Ittiḥādiyya*) to the May 2013 mass rallies under the banner of *Tamarrud* (Revolt), the revolutionary opposition to Morsi had the backing of the military.[69] *Tamarrud* stirred popular forces while also representing the institutional forces that called for regime change. These are the two factors, identified by Hinnebusch, which opened a pathway for authority-building: the mobilizing power of a charismatic movement and the institutional integrity of the "deep state."[70]

By 2013, social scientists studying Egypt had already adjusted their perspective, analyzing the counter-revolutionary trend. Nevertheless, social movement theory remains relevant given that the necessary conditions for revolution persisted: the vulnerability of the government (particularly the question of the state's domestic legitimacy); unequal distribution of resources; and the mobilizing capacity of civil rights activists and labor unions.[71] Political economy is also a key analytical tool, given that the basic structure of state repression and co-optation had not changed fundamentally; it was simply less legitimate and more violent.[72] And yet, after 2013, the regime could claim to represent the revolution.[73]

Conclusion

Revolutionary rhetoric habitually juxtaposes "the revolution" or "the people" to the "regime." However, regimes can be defined more broadly to include constituencies, social-cultural groups, and localized networks.[74] While the political element, in the formal sense of constitutional rights and political institutions, remained weak, the Egyptian government's strength relied on its control of numerous supervisory bureaucracies, some of which oversaw basic services and utilities, the electoral bureaucracy, the media, and the police. Thus, this was a political economy controlled by the "deep state's" agencies, governmental and nongovernmental. Politics entailed seeking access to resources (the scarcity of gas and electricity, for instance, delegitimized the revolution). From 2011 onward, the social forces that arrayed themselves against the revolutionaries were regional and localized, not just the entitled members of the state apparatus (though tied to them through patronage networks).[75] Revolutionary accounts mute these divisions within Egyptian society. Yet it is indicative of the dynamics of contemporary Egypt that the disentitled could confront the state, resist, and even revolt, while at the same time remaining enmeshed in governmental circles of power.

In the period of the 1919 revolution, public office, land, and water were the critical resources to attain. The Wafd's appeal lay in its ability to marshal such resources, both those offered by the government and those localized in the hands of notables and patrons. It gained control of them with the assistance of the bureaucracy, particularly the Ministry of the Interior, where the monarchy also had substantial influence. Turning to the monarchy to destroy their Liberal-Constitutional rivals, the radical revolutionaries of the Wafd underestimated the counter-revolutionary potential of the remnants. When the conservative powerbrokers in the bureaucracy and parliament abandoned it, the Wafd system of control broke down, offering a pathway for the restoration of remnants of the old regime.

The above argument began with Ibn Khaldun's theory that state authority depended on a combination of tribal allegiance and religious charisma; Weber accepted that logic but found in the modern situation that political authority required a combination of the bureaucratic cadre and the populist or ideological party; in 1919 and 2011, these forces were similarly configured, and led to comparable outcomes. The bureaucratic or deep state found a way to absorb popular forces in 2013, just as it was shown that the monarchists were able to mobilize social resources that, if not superseding the Wafd's popularity, provided the momentum for a counter-revolution that toppled a popularly elected government in 1924.

Notes

1. "Egypt's Constitution Gets 98% "'Yes' Vote," *The Guardian* (January 18, 2014), https://www.theguardian.com/world/2014/jan/18/egypt-constitution-yes-vote-mohamed-morsi.
2. For a recent critique of the military in Egypt, see Robert Springborg, *Egypt* (Cambridge: Polity, 2018).
3. "Regime" or *"nizam"* denotes order, with antecedents in Ottoman and earlier Islamic political ideology; "deep state" originally referred to the key power centers in the modern Turkish state: the presidency, security services, and the military.
4. Fund for Peace, "Fragile States Index," Country Dashboard, Egypt, accessed May 1, 2018, http://fundforpeace.org/fsi/country-data/; and Amnesty International, Country Profile: Egypt, accessed May 9, 2018, https://www.amnesty.org/en/countries/middle-east-and-north-africa/egypt/report-egypt/.
5. Shadi Hamid, "The Struggle for Middle East Democracy," *The Cairo Review of Global Affairs* 1, no. 1 (April 26, 2011): 26; Agnieszka Paczynska, "Economic Liberalization and Union Struggles in Cairo," in Diane Singerman, ed., *Cairo Contested: Governance, Urban Space, and Global Modernity* (Cairo: American University in Cairo Press, 2009), 344; and Adhaf Soueif, *Cairo, Memoir of a City Transformed* (London: Bloomsbury, 2014), 196.
6. Joel Beinin, "The Roots of the Egyptian Crisis," *Jacobin* (January 8, 2018), https://jacobinmag.com/2018/01/egypt-robert-springborg-arab-spring.
7. "60,000 Political Prisoners and 1,250 Missing: Welcome to the New Egypt," *Haaretz* (September 11, 2016), https://www.haaretz.com/middle-east-news/.premium-60-000-political-prisoners-and-1,250-missing-welcome-to-the-new-egypt-1.5440308. Some put the figure at 40,000; see Springborg, *Egypt*, 63, 145.
8. "Remnants" or *"fulul"* has the meaning of "the scattered remnants of an army," Hans Wehr, *A Dictionary of Modern Written Arabic*, ed. J.M. Cowan (Ithaca, NY: Spoken Languages Services, 1976).
9. Yezid Sayigh, "Above the State: The Officers Republic in Egypt," *The Carnegie Papers* (Beirut: Carnegie Middle East Centre, August 2012): 1–28, http://carnegieendowment.org/files/officers_republic1.pdf. This interpretation of events seems to have been corroborated by Mohammad Hassanein Heikal, grandee of the Nasserist project, editor of *al-Ahram* through the Nasserist period, and adviser to all following presidents including Sisi. These events, and the strategic thinking attributed to the military, can be followed in David Kirkpatrick's reportage for *The New York Times*. See David Kirkpatrick, "Egypt's New Strongman, Sisi Knows Best," *New York Times* (May 25, 2014), A1. According to Marc Lynch, the Egyptian military planned Morsi's removal from office ahead of his election, see Marc Lynch, *The Arab Uprising: The Unfinished Revolutions of the New Middle East* (New York: Public Affairs, 2012), 88.
10. Thanassis Cambanis, *Once Upon a Revolution: An Egyptian Story* (New York: Simon & Schuster, 2015).

11. Adel Abdel Ghafar, *Egyptians in Revolt: The Political Economy of Labor and Student Mobilizations 1919–2011* (London: Routledge, 2017).
12. Marc Lynch, ed., *The Arab Uprisings Explained: New Contentious Politics in the Middle East* (New York: Columbia University Press, 2014), 114, 135; and Springborg, *Egypt*, 37–38, 62–67.
13. Some of the revolutionary terminology has its origins in the French Revolution: Condorcet coined the term "counter-revolution" in 1796.
14. Raymond Hinnebusch, "A Historical Sociology Approach to Regime Restoration in Post-Arab Uprising MENA," in Marc Lynch, ed., *The Arab Thermidor: The Revenge of the Security State*, POMEPS 11 (February 27, 2015), https://pomeps.org/wp-content/uploads/2015/03/POMEPS_Studies_11_Thermidor_Web.pdf, 10–13.
15. Nader Sorhabi, "Historicizing Revolutions: Constitutional Revolutions in the Ottoman Empire, Iran, and Russia: 1905–1908," *American Journal of Sociology* 100, no. 6 (May 1995): 1383–1447. The study explores institutional and voluntarist factors, with close attention to the stages of revolutions.
16. This intervention by Churchill encouraged old regime remnants: Oriental Secretary Keown Boyd quoted Yakan on the threat posed by revolutionaries in the memorandum, "Situation in Egypt," June 30, 1921, Foreign Office File (hereafter, FO) 371/6301 8283/260/16, National Archives of England. It also resulted in a letter of protest about Churchill from Egyptian lawyers, July 13, 1921, FO371/6301 8409/260/16.
17. Secret Intelligence Service Report, April 11, 1922, "King Fuad, Seconded by Sarwat Pasha, is Becoming Despotic and Talks of Governing with the Whip," FO370/773 3947/1/16.
18. *La Liberté* (July 29, 1922), in Majlis al-Wuzarā' Files (Council of Ministers), Box 1/3/B, Egyptian National Archives (hereafter, ENA). In this article, the monarchist publicist insisted that the king was ignorant of the machinations of the Liberals.
19. Letter, January 1925, unsigned, in Abdin Files (Royal Palace), Box 218, "Review of Parties," ENA.
20. *Egyptian Gazette* (October 18, 1923); and *Egyptian Gazette* (January 12, 1924).
21. Memorandum, "The Power of the King," Kerr to Foreign Office, November 3, 1924, FO371/10022 9549/22/16.
22. Memorandum, "Political Situation in Egypt," 4 January 1923, Appendix B, September 30, 1922, FO371/8972 306/306/16.
23. Memorandum, Allenby to MacDonald, March 29, 1924, FO371/10020 3102/22/16. The issue in this case was the inclusion of the Sudan issue in the speech from the throne, which alienated more radical revolutionaries from the Zaghlūl government.
24. Memorandum, Allenby to Curzon, 23 April 1922, "Egyptian Constitution," FO371/8961 4589/1/16. Memorandum, "Political Situation in Egypt," January 4, 1923, Appendix B, Part 2, October 15, 1922 (original FO file, E11477/1/16), "Remarks by Sarwat Pasha."
25. Zaghlūl's speech can be found in the *Journal Officiel* (January 29, 1924).

26. The language is comparable to Abbé Sieyès, *Qu'est-ce-que le Tiers Etat?* (Paris, 1789).
27. Joel Beinin and Zachary Lockman, *Workers on the Nile: Nationalism, Communism, Islam and the Egyptian Working Class, 1882–1954* (Princeton: Princeton University Press, 1987), 121–137.
28. Memorandum, Allenby to MacDonald, July 14, 1924, FO/371/10021 6081/22/16.
29. Allenby to MacDonald, December 15, 1924, FO371/10046 11296/368/16, noting that British intelligence reports showed that Zaghlūl had inspired "secret terrorist societies and a host of revolutionary students."
30. Kerr to Chamberlain, November 3, 1924, "The Power of the King," FO371/10022 1549/22/16, "Press Reports," FO371/10022 9971/22/16.
31. On Nash'at, see Abdin Files, "Review of Parties," Hizb al-Ittihad, Box 218, a letter dated January 1925. On Badrāwī, as well as other prominent defectors from the Wafd, see FO371/10887 1257/29/16.
32. Report, "Political Developments in Egypt Prior to the Murder of Sir Lee Stack," n.d., FO371/10044 10208/368/16.
33. Memorandum, Allenby to MacDonald, November 2, 1924, FO371/10022 9745/22/16.
34. Speech, Zaghlūl, Majlis al-Wuzarā' Files, Box 6, ENA.
35. Benedict Anderson, *Imagined Communities* (London: Verso, 1983), 12.
36. Report, "Situation in Egypt," FO371/10044 10340/368/16.
37. Memorandum, "Political Murders in Egypt." An independent panel of inquiry into the murder of Sir Lee Stack reported that Shafīq Manṣūr, the lead political assassin in the case, claimed that Nash'at, the king's political agent, had inspired the assassination. Nash'at had been involved in the Wafd's "secret apparatus," its militant wing, before joining the monarchists. FO371/11582 637/25/16 (1926) and FO141 787/27 (1928). Henry Keown-Boyd, *The Lion and the Sphinx: The Rise and Fall of the British in Egypt, 1882–1956* (Spennymoor: The Memoir Club, 2002).
38. The use of political violence for authority-building was evident in the assassination attempt against Gamal 'Abd al-Nasser in 1954, and, in another counter-revolutionary example, the assassination attempt against Napoleon in 1800. In each case, the event distracted the public from the autocracy's ongoing entrenchment and at the same time justified it. Following Sorhabi, "Historicizing Revolutions," 1387, after November 1924, Egypt entered stage three of the revolution following a trajectory like that of the Russian Revolution of 1905.
39. British reactions to the assassination were premised on Wafd responsibility, justifying the fall of Zaghlūl and the revival of old regime remnants. The reaction can be followed in Jayne Gifford, *Britain in Egypt: Egyptian Nationalism and Imperial Strategy 1919–1931* (London: I.B. Tauris, 2020), 129–131, 134–137, 182.
40. Telegram addressed to Nash'at Pasha, "ra'īs al-diwān al-malakī" (July 12, 1925), Abdin Files, Box 218, contained a declaration of loyalty to the king signed by individuals from the Wafd's general membership, as well as former members of the Wafd Central Committee. Report, Egyptian Press, 2 February 1925,

FO371/10887 335/29/16, shows that Stack's assassination in 1924 cost the Wafd Party not only the confidence of the British government but also of a significant sector of Egyptian political society. Parliament was adjourned after Zaghlūl's resignation.

41. Document, "HE, 1926," Sir Robert Allason Furness, Box 3, Folder 1, Middle East Centre, St Antony's, Oxford, GB165-0115. Furness commented in the document on the policy of the British High Commission (HE) in Egypt, "We were considering, not without perplexity, how to re-establish ourselves, when the murder of Sir Lee Stack provided a fortunate opportunity."
42. *Egyptian Gazette* (December 25, 1924).
43. Zaki Fahmī, *Ṣafwat al-ʻAṣr* (Cairo: Maṭbaʻat al-iʻtimād, 1926), 158.
44. Report, "Political Developments in Egypt Prior to the Murder of Sir Lee Stack," FO371/10044 10208/368/16.
45. Telegraph addressed to "ra'īs al-diwan al-maliki," 12 July 1925, Abdin Files, Box 218, ENA.
46. Memorandum, Allenby to Chamberlain, January 9, 1925, FO141/819/17628/1.
47. See Leonard Binder, *In a Moment of Enthusiasm* (Chicago: University of Chicago Press, 1978), for a discussion of the middle stratum's importance in mobilizing popular forces and its influence on Nasser's revolution. See also Robert Springborg, *Family, Power and Politics in Egypt* (Philadelphia: University of Pennsylvania, 1982).
48. *"Dossier al-Ḥukūma al-Malakiyya al-Miṣriyya"* (Report of the royal government of Egypt), n.d., Abdin Files, Box 218, ENA. This dossier includes a telegraph from Damanhur, Beheira, addressed to the "Master of Ceremonies," listing the Ittiḥād Party membership.
49. Memorandum, Henderson to Murray, June 1925, FO371/10888 1898/29/16, which includes the report of Neville Henderson, Acting High Commissioner, on his interview with a *Times* journalist.
50. *Al-Siyasa* (December 12, 1925).
51. Unsigned letter, Giza (n.d.), Abdin Files, Box 219, ENA.
52. Ahdaf Soueif, *Cairo: My City, Our Revolution* (London: Bloomsbury, 2012), 65. At each confrontation, the military arrested the revolutionary protestors, who then disappeared from the streets into the custody of SCAF. There were 6,235 people imprisoned by military tribunal by January 2012, with another 1,225 given suspended sentences.
53. Mariz Tadros, "Sectarianism and its Discontents in Post-Mubarak Egypt," *MERIP* 41, no. 2 (Summer 2011): 26–31.
54. Springborg, *Egypt*, 62.
55. Soueif, *Cairo: My City*, 74.
56. Soueif, *Cairo: My City*, 79.
57. Soueif, *Cairo: My City*, 100–104.
58. Neil Ketchley and Michael Biggs, "Who Actually Died in Egypt's Rābiʻa Massacre," *The Washington Post* (August 14, 2015), https://www.washingtonpost.com/news/monkey-cage/wp/2015/08/14/counting-the-dead-of-egypt's-tiananmen/?utm_term=.ba41002d4c8c. Ironically, Soueif's

characterization of the Islamists as the "poor" and "provincial" replicates the language of Sisi's regime after June 2013.

59. Sayigh, "Above the State," 23.
60. Soueif, *Cairo: Memoir*, 161.
61. Cambanis, *Once Upon a Revolution*, 136.
62. Samuel Tadros, "Egypt's Elections, Why the Islamists Won," *World Affairs* (March/April, 2012), http://www.worldaffairsjournal.org/article/egypt%E2%80%99s-elections-why-islamists-won.
63. Based on interviews with Egyptians at the time of the 2011 parliamentary elections.
64. Cambanis, *Once Upon a Revolution*, 155.
65. Luce Ryzova, "The Second Revolution," *al-Jazeera* (November 29, 2011), https://www.aljazeera.com/indepth/opinion/2011/11/201111288494638419.html.
66. The anti-revolutionary discourses from March 2011 were documented by Steven Heydemann and Reinoud Leenders, "Authoritarian Learning and Counterrevolution," in Marc Lynch, ed., *The Arab Uprisings Explained: New Contentious Politics in the Middle East* (New York: Columbia University Press, 2014), 84. See also Leila Fadel, "Sam LaHood, NGO Worker, Hid in U.S. Embassy in Cairo for Four Weeks under Real Fear of Arrest," *Washington Post* (March 6, 2012), https://www.washingtonpost.com/blogs/blogpost/post/sam-lahood-blames-mubarak-era-minister-with-agenda-of-her-own-for-raid/2012/03/06/gIQA9rwKuR_blog.html?utm_term=.ef2488883725.
67. The candidate list for the first round, heavily vetted by SCAF, included 13 candidates. Morsi took only 25 percent of the votes, but with more votes than the others; he was the candidate in the second round of voting, which again offered voters a choice between an Islamist or a remnant.
68. Springborg, *Egypt*, 63.
69. Cambanis, *Once Upon a Revolution*, 221. Nevertheless, Sisi continued to appear in public with the president until a few days before the June 30 military intervention.
70. Lynch, *The Arab Thermidor*.
71. Charles Tilley, Doug McAdam, and Sidney Tarrow, *The Dynamics of Contentious Politics* (New York: Cambridge University Press, 2004); and Doug McAdam, John D. McCarthy, and Mayer N. Zald, eds., *Comparative Perspectives on Social Movements: Political Opportunities, Mobilizing Structures, and Cultural Framings* (New York: Cambridge University Press, 1996). The application of this theory to the Middle East has focused on the mobilizing potential of the Islamists; see Salwa Musa, "Islamist Movements as Social Movements: Contestation and Identity Frames," *Historical Reflections* 30, no. 3 (2004): 385–402; and Quintan Wilktorwitz, ed., *Islamic Activism: A Social Movement Theory Approach* (Bloomington: Indiana University Press, 2004).
72. Alan Richards and John Waterbury, *A Political Economy of the Middle East* (Boulder: Westview, 3rd ed., 2013).
73. Tom Stevenson, "Sisi's Way," *London Review of Books* 37, no. 4 (February 2015).

74. Ismail Musa, *Political Life in Cairo's New Quarters: Confronting the Everyday State* (Minneapolis: University of Minneapolis, 2006), and Diane Singerman, ed., *Cairo Contested: Governance, Urban Space, and Global Modernity New* (Cairo: American University in Cairo Press, 2009).
75. Richards and Waterbury, *Political Economy*, 423, point to the relatively inclusive character of the Egyptian state at an elite level, as compared to Ben Ali's Tunisia, to account for Egyptian regime persistence.

Selected Bibliography

Abdel Ghafar, Adel, *Egyptians in Revolt: The Political Economy of Labor and Student Mobilizations 1919–2011* (London: Routledge, 2017).

Beinin, Joel, and Lockman Zachary, *Workers on the Nile: Nationalism, Communism, Islam and the Egyptian Working Class, 1882–1954* (Princeton: Princeton University Press, 1987), 121–137.

Gifford, Jayne, *Britain in Egypt: Egyptian Nationalism and Imperial Strategy 1919–1931* (London: I.B. Tauris, 2020).

Lynch, Marc, ed., *The Arab Uprisings Explained: New Contentious Politics in the Middle East* (New York: Columbia University Press, 2014).

Musa, Ismail, *Political Life in Cairo's New Quarters: Confronting the Everyday State* (Minneapolis: University of Minneapolis, 2006).

Paczynska, Agnieszka, "Economic Liberalization and Union Struggles in Cairo," in Diane Singerman, ed., *Cairo Contested: Governance, Urban Space, and Global Modernity* (Cairo: American University in Cairo Press, 2009).

Sayigh, Yezid, "Above the State: The Officers Republic in Egypt," *The Carnegie Papers* (Beirut: Carnegie Middle East Centre, August 2012): 1–28.

Sorhabi, Nader, "Historicizing Revolutions: Constitutional Revolutions in the Ottoman Empire, Iran, and Russia: 1905–1908," *American Journal of Sociology* 100, no. 6 (May 1995): 1383–1447.

Soueif, Adhaf, *Cairo, Memoir of a City Transformed* (London: Bloomsbury, 2014).

Soueif, Ahdaf, *Cairo: My City, Our Revolution* (London: Bloomsbury, 2012).

Wilktorwitz, Quintan, ed., *Islamic Activism: A Social Movement Theory Approach* (Bloomington: Indiana University Press, 2004).

Vertical Versus Horizontal: Egypt's State–Religion Discourse Before and After the 2011 Uprising

Limor Lavie

Introduction

One of the most controversial issues to unsettle Egyptian society in the transition period between President Mubarak's downfall and President Morsi's ouster was the status of Islam in the post-revolutionary state. The public debate on how to define Egypt's identity in the new constitution revealed a deep political and social polarization, of a magnitude not seen before in Egypt. The discourse on state–religion relations since the January 2011 uprising sheds light on the characteristics of this discourse during Mubarak's reign and enables us to re-examine it.

Drawing on education theory, this chapter will contend that under Mubarak, a "vertical discourse" of state–religion relations was implemented. The chapter will demonstrate how Mubarak nationalized the state–religion discourse, hollowed it out, and forced on the public an artificial consensus regarding the model of a civil state, different from the concepts of a secular state or a religious one. Due to Mubarak's intense campaign, most political currents, including Islamists, had to align themselves with the prevalent notion and adjust to the same terminology.

The nature of this discourse has become apparent in light of the post-Mubarak discourse on the status of Islam in Egypt in general, and on the idea of the civil state in particular. The controversy that surrounded the two successive processes of constitution-making from 2011 to 2014, and especially the debate around the drafting of the "identity clauses," reopened an unconstrained public debate over the status of religion. Thus, the transitional period after the 2011 upheaval has witnessed a "horizontal discourse", which encompassed conflicting worldviews, a variety of languages and multiple voices, some of which were not part of the discourse until then, such as those of the Copts and Salafis. The "invisible" nature of the discourse around the 2019 amendment of Article 200, which anchored the "civil-ness of Egypt" and the responsibility of the armed forces to protect it, further illuminates the vertical character of the civil state discourse under Mubarak.

To elucidate these claims, the first section of this chapter will put forward the definitions of vertical versus horizontal discourses. The following section will discuss the state–religion relations discourse under Mubarak, emphasizing how, from the second half of the 1990s, his regime institutionalized the discourse and, aided by intellectuals and the religious establishment, forced its model of a civil state upon its subjects. Finally, the chapter will examine the metamorphoses that the civil state discourse experienced in the aftermath of the Mubarak era. This was manifested during the drafting process of the post-revolutionary constitutions, and highlighted the indoctrinating character that this discourse had acquired under Mubarak.

Vertical Versus Horizontal Discourses—A Theoretical Framework

The existing literature on the Egyptian discourse of state–religion relations rests on various typologies of discourses. While most research on this topic relies on Foucault's perception of discourse as a social construction by means of which power relations are exercised,[1] later studies, mainly within the discipline of education studies, have offered multiple categorizations of discourses.[2] Some studies concentrate on the differentiation between a dominant discourse and secondary discourses or a hegemonic discourse and a counterhegemonic one.[3] Others analyze this discourse along professional or institutional lines (such as religious establishment institutions and the judiciary),[4] or on an ideological basis (left/right, conservative/liberal, etc.).[5] This chapter uses a different typology in examining the discourse of state–religion relations in Egypt, which distinguishes between vertical and horizontal discourses.[6]

Bernstein typifies the horizontal discourse as "common sense" knowledge, because everyone, presently or potentially, has access to it. It corresponds to a differentiated and segmented form of knowledge, and tends to be oral, local, context-dependent, multilayered, and contradictory. A vertical discourse, on the other hand, is "official knowledge." It has the form of a coherent, explicit, and systematically principled structure, organized hierarchically instead of segmentally.

Horizontal knowledge structures are related through the functional relations of segment or context and everyday life, sometimes with no relation to what is acquired in another segment or context. Unlike a horizontal discourse, the integration of a vertical discourse is not at the level of the relation between segments or contexts, but at the level of meanings. A vertical discourse consists not of distinct segments, but of specific symbolic structures of explicit knowledge, in an attempt to integrate knowledge at lower levels, thus showing underlying uniformities across an expanding range of apparently different phenomena.

Maton and Muller find this distinction crucial for understanding how various forms of knowledge are differently distributed in society, shaping social practices, identity, relation, and consciousness. Hierarchical knowledge structures are produced by an "integrating" code, aimed at the development of a theory that is more general and more unifying than previous ones. Horizontal knowledge structures, on the other hand, consist of multiple languages based on different and often opposing assumptions. While the horizontal discourse is an accumulation of languages, perceptions, and ideas, the vertical one is characterized by the subsumption of existing ideas within more overarching propositions.[7]

From the Top Down: The State–Religion Discourse under Mubarak

In the struggle over Egypt's identity, which wavered between religious conservatism and secular Liberalism, the Mubarak regime filled a restraining role, not a leading one, until the 1990s. In the first half of that decade, a profound and relatively free debate developed between liberal intellectuals and centrist Islamist (*Wasaṭīyya*) intellectuals regarding the status of religion in the state.[8] Mubarak allowed a relatively broad field for freedom of expression in the 1980s, estimating that such a policy would enhance the legitimacy he needed at the beginning of his term. Hence, his regime permitted the debate between liberals and conservatives to proceed as long as it posed no political threat.

However, in the first half of the 1990s, the controversy over the place of religion in Egypt heated up and climaxed in the assassination of the liberal intellectual Farag Foda who was one of the vocal proponents of the civil state, by extremists.[9] Sensing that civil society's open discourse regarding the status of religion had gotten out of hand, Mubarak took over and started to direct the discourse from above throughout the second half of his reign.[10]

In effect, Mubarak institutionalized the discourse on the status of Islam by impressing upon it a uniform theme—the notion of a civil state.[11] The institutionalization of the discourse was a process in which a Western, political-social-cultural concept foreign to Islam and traditional Egyptian society was intentionally planted in it by the regime via intellectuals, among other means, in an attempt to control the discourse, direct it, and shape it according to the regime's needs and worldview. The regime's expropriation of the civil state discourse—transferring it from civil society into the hands of the regime and turning the very concept of the civil state into the regime's motto, was part of its effort to curb the Islamization of Egypt's law, constitution, and society, which had begun in Sadat's era.[12]

Mubarak strove to instill from above the idea that Egypt is a civil state—neither a religious state in which Islam dictates all spheres of life nor a secular one that relegates religion solely to the private sphere—but rather, an intermediate model of a progressive state that operates according to modern, Western norms and patterns and that grants Islam a spiritual status, as the source of human values. This understanding of the rather ambiguous notion of a civil state implies that the Mubarak regime intervened in the intellectual controversy and settled it in favor of a non-Islamist interpretation of the concept.

The demand to establish a civil state served as a common denominator for the regime and the secular opposition, and particularly the leftist party, *Tagammu'*, whose interpretation of the civil state was more far-reaching than that of the regime. *Tagammu'* revealed an increasingly secular conception of a civil state, mostly regarding the separation of religion from politics and legislation while emphasizing total civil equality and non-discrimination.[13]

The theoretical message that Egypt was seeking for itself an identity of a civil state was the regime's response to several problems: first was the need to eradicate the terrorism of the radical Islamist organizations, moderate them, and deter them from the path of violence; the second was the delegitimization of the Muslim Brotherhood, who had become a threat to the regime following their performance in the 1992 earthquake and their great achievements in the parliamentary elections of 2000 and 2005; and third was the need to respond to local and international pressures to modernize and respect minority rights and liberties, while continuing to pay lip service to Islam in consideration of the society's traditionalism. Mubarak walked on eggshells in an attempt to coexist with both the liberals and the Islamists, the Muslim majority and the Copts, and simultaneously satisfy pressure from locals and from the United States, following the 9/11 terrorist acts and President Bush's policy of democratization of the Middle East.[14]

In the second half of Mubarak's reign, the use of the term "civil state" became increasingly prevalent in the rhetoric of Mubarak himself as well as of his party's platform.[15] The National Democratic Party functioned as a governmental and presidential mechanism for oppression and indoctrination.[16] It championed the idea of a civil state, which often served as the theme of its annual conferences.[17] Mubarak's son Gamal, who chaired the party, defined the civil state as its chief goal.[18]

The nationalization of the civil state discourse was furthered by the mobilization of numerous state-sponsored intellectuals who helped idealize the concept, portraying it as a state of all its citizens with equal rights and equal duties for all citizens—women and men, Muslims and non-Muslims—regardless of gender, race, ethnicity, religion, school of jurisprudence, and so on. A state of modern institutions and modern patterns of government, which perceives the nation as the source of authority and the relationship between the state and its citizens as a social contract; a state that promotes social justice and encourages reform, development, and science; a state that is not secular and does not revoke religion. The civil state was presented as an Islamic state in which the dominance of Islam does not imply regression and does not hold back progress.[19]

The theorization of the civil state in Mubarak's era was conducted primarily by the Egyptian philosopher Gāber ʻAṣfūr (b. 1944). He was the director of the National Center for Translation and prior to that served as the General Secretary of the Supreme Council for Culture. Following the ouster of Mubarak, ʻAṣfūr was appointed Minister of Culture, then resigned shortly thereafter. He was reappointed in Ibrāhīm Maḥlab's second government, which began in June 2014. His regular column in the *al-Ahram* daily often promotes the idea of a civil state.[20] ʻAṣfūr described the civil state as the fastest and shortest way to realize Egypt's dream of progress, and viewed the calls for a religious state as the gravest danger facing the nation.[21]

From the mid-1990s, the religious establishment—al-'Azhar, the Mufti of Egypt, and the Ministry of Endowment—started supporting the adoption of the civil state into the formal discourse, linking the civil state to Islam and rejecting the idea of a religious state. A most significant contribution toward validating the civil state was made by ʻAbd al-Muʻṭī Bayyūmī (1940–2012), a member of the Academy of Islamic Research of al-'Azhar. He was appointed to the People's Council by Mubarak, serving from 2000–2005. In his book "Islam and the Civil State" (*al-Islām wa-l-Dawla al-Madanīyya,* 2004), Bayyūmī presented the Islamic state as a first-rate civil state.[22] He stressed that the civil state, the origin of modern democracies, had been founded by Muhammad, and that the West had imitated Islam.[23]

In the civil state, wrote Bayyūmī, the Quran has supremacy over the constitution; the constitution is the father of law, while the Quran is the spirit of the constitution. Yet Bayyūmī rejected the demand to implement the Quran as a constitution in modern times, arguing that such calls create a negative image of Islam. Bayyūmī also supported man-made legislation and borrowing solutions from non-Islamic countries, just as solutions were borrowed from the Persians in the Prophet's time.[24] All in all, Bayyūmī sanctioned the concept of the civil state within a broadly interpreted framework that included many patterns of Western, modern government—more than the Sheikh of al-'Azhar, Muhammad Sayyid Ṭanṭāwī, was willing to accept.

Thus, several years later, Ṭanṭāwī adopted a narrower interpretation of the civil state, accepting only some of Bayyūmī's ideas. In a series of articles published in February–March 2007 in the daily *al-Ahram*, he claimed that there is no religious state in Islam, and that it was Islam that established the first civil state. There is no doubt that Islamic Sharīʿa is consistent with the civil state, wrote Ṭanṭāwī, describing it as a civilized state whose sons establish their culture on the basis of the entire corpus of science. Such positive principles accord with Sharīʿa, he explained. After emigrating to al-Madina, Muhammad founded "the honorable civil state, which draws its rules, practices, and organization from the guidance of religion and the direction of the noble Quran." Ṭanṭāwī emphasized the idea of human brotherhood as the basis of the civil state, and explained that this value, too, originated in Islam.[25]

The current Sheikh of al-'Azhar, Ahmad al-Ṭayyib, has also expressed support for the notion that Egypt is an Islamic civil state.[26] Similarly, ʿAlī Gumʿa (b. 1952), the grand mufti of Egypt from 2003–2013, often wrote that the state founded by Muhammad was the first civil state in the world, maintaining that al-Madina enlightened the world with its modern civil government.[27] Muhammad Hamdī Zaqzūq (1933–2020), who served as the Minister of Endowments from 1996 until Mubarak's fall, also adopted the approach that from its outset, the state in Islam has been a civil one rather than a religious one.[28]

Mubarak's intense campaign to unify the discourse affected the discourses of both liberals and Islamists, pushing them to reach a middle ground and to champion the civil state model. During the last decade of his reign, calls to completely cancel the second article of the constitution, which stated that "Islam is the religion of the state," and that "the principles of Islamic Sharīʿa are the primary source of legislation," were rarely voiced in the official media; they came primarily from human rights activists, dissident liberals, and Copts living abroad.[29] This eventually led the Muslim Brotherhood to moderate their tone, silence their call to implement Sharīʿa, and from the 2000s, they officially incorporated the idea of a civil state into their political agenda, after rejecting it for years.[30] Even some of the leaders of the ultra-conservative Salafi al-Gamā'a al-Islāmīyya, such as the head of the organization's Shūrā Council, Karam Zuhdī, began including the idea of civil rule in Islam in his speeches, referring to it in the narrow sense of rejecting the rule of a religious scholar.[31] This shows the extent to which support for the idea of a civil state had become an admission ticket to the realm of consensus, and a path to political and social mobility.

Mubarak succeeded in neutralizing the discourse of state–religion relations and blurring its concepts to the point where it was difficult to distinguish the differences in the positions taken by the political camps. Using coercion and fear, Mubarak created agreement, superficially. But in January 2011, with the fall of his regime, it became clear that the consensus surrounding the civil state model that had prevailed in the final years of his reign, was for appearances only, a result of the artificial unifying measures that he had taken and the vertical discourse he had forced upon society.

The Opening of the State–Religion Discourse after Mubarak's Downfall

Liberated from the domination of the fallen regime, the spokesmen for both the non-Islamist and the Islamist factions began expressing more freely their positions regarding the civil state, exposing the size of the gaps among the parties and the depth of the social polarization. When these disparate political and social forces came together to formulate common principles for Egypt's future, to be embodied in a constitution, it became clear that they were nowhere near a uniform stance supporting a civil state; in fact, it was the very idea of a civil state that prevented them from reaching an agreement.

Civil parties now appeared, championing the establishment of a civil state in Egypt.[32] Among the youths of the revolution, citizen organizations such as the Civil Democratic Coalition emerged, announcing the preservation of the country's civil identity as their primary goal. Campaigns supporting the civil state were launched in social media.[33] More than ever before, the public discourse abounded with calls for the establishment of a secular state and the separation of religion from politics and the state; for the establishment of a liberal democracy; and the annulment of the second article of the constitution.[34] Copt activists also felt more comfortable than before to join in these calls.[35]

At the same time, calls for the implementation of Sharī'a and the restoration of the caliphate were once again voiced. In the publications of some Muslim Brotherhood members, there appeared once again the clear demand to implement Sharī'a and Islamic punishments (*ḥudūd*).[36] If it were not for the negative connotations of the term "religious state," one of these publications explained, nothing would stand in the way of saying that the Islamic state is a religious state, that is, a state in which religion is the starting point for everything else.[37] The heads of the religious establishment, the Sheikh al-'Azhar and the Grand Mufti, too, moved away from their support of the civil state and rejected the possibility that Egypt would be defined as a civil state in the constitution.[38]

As in the state–religion discourse of the 1980s, the Islamists argued that the civil camp was interested in establishing a secular, anti-religious state in Egypt, while the civil camp counter-argued that the Islamists intended to establish in Egypt a religious state governed by Islamic law.[39] This polarization of the state–religion discourse was particularly noticeable with the rise of the Salafi movements, which had not been involved previously in politics; they joined the political game after the 2011 uprising and gained unprecedented success. At the same time, they joined the discourse regarding the status of Islam. Compared with the Muslim Brotherhood, the Salafi movements had a more conservative Islamic ideology that completely and utterly rejected the concept and principles of a civil state, which they regarded as atheistic and blasphemous. During the drafting of the post-revolution 2012 constitution, the Salafi factions were completely unwilling to accept in it any reference to a civil state, while advocating the full enactment of the Sharī'a.[40]

The Salafis steadfastly refused to relinquish their adherence to the concept of God's sovereignty in favor of the people's sovereignty embodied in the civil state, and further refused to be associated with any concept that could be interpreted as a secular state. Countering the youth slogan "Civil, Civil!" (*Madanīyya, Madanīyya!*), the Salafi Islamists unleashed their own motto: "Islamic, Islamic!" (*Islāmīyya, Islāmīyya!*) in mass demonstrations during the second half of 2011, as the Supreme Council of the Armed Forces attempted to anchor Egypt's identity as a civil state in the new constitution.[41]

Public discourse in general became more straightforward in its declarations regarding Egypt's future and identity. Under the influence of the Salafis, the Islamists began attacking secular intellectuals openly, delegitimizing their concept of a civil state and describing it as a secular state identified with the ousted regime.[42] Sheikh Ahmad al-Maḥallāwī (b. 1925), the preacher at al-Qā'ed Ibrāhīm mosque in Alexandria, went so far as to describe those calling for a civil state as heretics and idolaters. These forces, he added, are enemies from within who wish to change Allah's Sharīʿa and to impose the Sharīʿa of idols.[43]

During the Muslim Brotherhood's rule, the state–religion discourse continued to be a horizontal one. The constituent assembly in charge of drafting the constitution did not represent all the voices involved in the state–religion discourse, but these voices were allowed to be heard, and they were expressed in different media outlets and online forums.[44] They included demands to amend the second article to say that Islam is only the religion of the majority.[45] Liberal intellectuals, Copts, and human rights and women's organizations continued to press for appropriate representation of the civil forces in the constituent assembly, and they suggested various formulations of the constitutional articles pertaining to the status of religion.[46]

Following the overthrow of Morsi in a military coup in 2013, a new process of constitution drafting was initiated, culminating in the definition of Egypt as a "state with a civil government (*Ḥukūmatuhā Madanīyya*)" in the preamble to the 2014 constitution.[47] This formula was a compromise that responded to the demand made by secular parties, such as *Tagammu'*, the Free Egyptian party and the Conference (*al-Mu'tamar*) party, human rights organizations, and other civil society initiatives, that the concept of a civil state be explicitly placed in the first article. The compromise was also accepted by al-'Azhar and the Salafi al-Nūr party.[48]

Yet, the civil state discourse during the drafting of the 2014 constitution was less inclusive than the public debate that had accompanied the work of the constituent assembly of the 2012 constitution. While the socio-political segments identified with the coup were voiced vehemently, the Muslim Brotherhood and their supporters were excluded from the discourse. This turn put an end to the horizontal discourse and sets the path for the civil state discourse under al-Sisi's rule.

The Invisible Discourse of the Civil State under al-Sisi

The constitutional amendments ratified in a referendum in April 2019 serve as another litmus test through which we can examine the metamorphoses of the civil state discourse in post-revolutionary Egypt. Upon the initiative of 155 parliament deputies supporting al-Sisi, Article 200 of the 2014 constitution was amended to stipulate that the armed forces are obliged to defend "Egypt's civil-ness" (*madanīyyat al-dawla*).[49] Hence, *de jure*, it is implicit that Egypt's nature as a state is civil and that the army is the guarantor of its non-religious and non-Islamist orientation. The subtext or the unstated conventions are that it is the duty of the military to prevent the resumption of power by Islamist forces, mainly the Muslim Brotherhood, portrayed in the narrative of the June 30, 2013 upheaval's supporters as seeking to lead Egypt in the direction of a religious state. In July 2020, the State Security Law was also amended accordingly, dictating a procedure in case the civil-ness of the state is endangered.[50]

While it could be assumed that these significant constitutional and legislative amendments would be publicly debated or at least accompanied by a vertical discourse that would prepare the public opinion and justify these amendments or explain their meanings and implications, such a debate never took place.[51] While examining whether the discourse of the civil state under al-Sisi from 2014 to the present remains as horizontal as during the transition period or has returned to being vertical as at the end of the Mubarak period, it seems that neither of these two analytical categories is suitable, and that it would be better to describe it as an "invisible discourse," a category also borrowed from education studies.

First coined by James Boyd White, an invisible discourse refers to what is between the lines or "behind the words," that is, "expectations that do not find explicit expression anywhere but are part of the legal culture that the surface language simply assumes." The effects of these expectations "are everywhere but they themselves are invisible."[52] Put differently, the invisible discourse is "the body of knowledge, assumptions, and operating procedures which is left out of the surface of a discourse but which is necessary for understanding and producing it."[53]

Although these amendments were a top–down dictation, they were not bound by a vertical discourse that included the development of an "official knowledge" in a systematic, structured, and organized manner. Unlike Mubarak, who integrated the idea of a civil state into his rhetoric and that of his party, this theme is not at all prominent in al-Sisi's rhetoric or in the way he presents his vision for the future of Egypt.[54] While Mubarak harnessed intellectuals, politicians, and the religious establishment to the theorization and idealization of the civil state concept, under al-Sisi Egyptian publicists hardly paid any attention to this specific amendment of the constitution, and al-'Azhar also did not speak for or against it.[55] While under Mubarak, different segments of Egyptian society had adapted their discourse to the vertically dictated one, under al-Sisi most segments of society did not voice an opinion at all, either out of political exclusion, like the silenced Muslim Brotherhood and civil youth organizations, or out of lack of interest.[56] The process of drafting the amendments did include a "social dialogue" that lasted two weeks during March 2019, in which the public was invited to come to parliament and debate the proposed amendments. However, this dialogue was considered a façade as the discussions were not public and were not allowed to be broadcast.[57]

Exceptions included the "civic democratic movement," which objected to the amendments as a whole rather than to Article 200 specifically and even sought to protest against them but was rejected,[58] and al-Nūr party which vehemently opposed the expression *madanīyyat al-dawla* in Article 200,[59] but ultimately voted in its favor.[60] As Shaimaa Magued observes, the Salafi al-Nūr party, which consistently led the struggle against the idea of a civil state since 2011, succumbed to the regime's imposition of the civil state perception, despite the secular connotation of the phrase, out of the desire to fill the political vacuum left by the Muslim Brotherhood since Morsi's ouster in 2013.[61] This concession came after Egypt's parliament speaker 'Ali 'Abd al-'Āl had clarified for the record that the term *madanīyyat al-dawla* does not imply a secular state.[62] In other words, al-Nūr party, which was the last opponent of the constitutionalization of a civil state, eventually relinquished its oppositional voice and backed the official language.

Conclusion

This chapter suggests that the horizontal nature of the transitional discourse on the role of Islam in post-Mubarak Egypt and the invisible nature of the civil state discourse under al-Sisi, illuminate the vertical character it had acquired from the mid-1990s and until Mubarak's downfall. The pre-revolutionary discourse about the role of religion in the state was systematically structured, principled, and hierarchically organized around the civil state. This was carried out by state agents—political parties, sponsored intellectuals, and the religious establishment—which developed the civil state idea as an integrating code. While his message did not actually integrate the rival segments of society or rival political currents, as was evident once Mubarak stepped down, it did force them to align their discourses with the language of the ostensible integrating code, making the state–religion discourse during the last decade of Mubarak's rule outwardly consensual.

During the transition period, on the other hand, the state–religion discourse enjoyed relative freedom of state interference, revealing contradicting interpretations of the ideal state and the status of Islam within it. All segments of society had access to this public debate, and no one was silenced or forced to adopt a certain view. This is not to say that the process of constitution drafting represented the public wishes or propelled no turbulence. However, political and social groups and individuals were able to publicly express their various views regarding the drafting of the constitution and the redefining of Egypt's orientation. While at times certain groups were more dominant than others, the diversity of opinions was salient.

However, the heterogeneous character that the civil state discourse had acquired during the short transition period in terms of participants, content, and motility of ideas did not last long. Under al-Sisi, the civil state discourse did not revert back to the indoctrinating, top–down character that had prevailed from the middle of the Mubarak era. While the Mubarak regime took pains to conceptualize the notion of the civil state as a seemingly integrating code, turning the discourse of state–religion relations into a monolith, it did not cross the Rubicon of the constitutionalization of the civil state in the 2007 amendments to the constitution. The al-Sisi regime, on the other hand, boldly codified Egypt's civil-ness in the 2019 constitutional amendments, using a language that conceals an excluding code, with no noticeable efforts to propagate a discourse that would legitimize the constitutionalization of the civil state or make it appear widely acceptable.

Notes

1. Michel Foucault, "The Order of Discourse," in Robert Young (ed.), *Untying the Text: A Post-Structuralist Reader* (London: Routledge, 1981), 52.
2. James Paul Gee, "Literacy, Discourse, and Linguistics: Introduction," *Journal of Education* 171, no. 1 (1989), 5–176.
3. See, for example, Meir Hatina, "On the Margins of Consensus: The Call to Separate Religion and State in Modern Egypt," *Middle Eastern Studies* 36, no. 1, 35–67; and Annette Ranko, *The Muslim Brotherhood and Its Quest for Hegemony in Egypt: State-Discourse and Islamist Counter-Discourse* (Hamburg: Springer Fachmedien Wiesbaden, 2015).
4. See, for instance, Jakob Skovgaard-Petersen, *Defining Islam for the Egyptian State: Muftis and Fatwas of the Dār al-Iftā* (Leiden: Brill, 1997), 27–30; and Nathan J. Brown, "Egypt: Cacophony and Consensus in the Twenty-First Century," in Robert W. Hefner (ed.), *Shari'a Politics: Islamic Law and Society in the Modern World* (Bloomington: Indiana University Press, 2011), 94–120.
5. See, for instance, Sagi Polka, "The Centrist Stream in Egypt and its Role in the Public Discourse Surrounding the Shaping of the Country's Cultural Identity," *Middle Eastern Studies* 39, no. 3 (2003), 39–64.
6. Basil Bernstein, "Vertical and Horizontal Discourse: An Essay," *British Journal of Sociology of Education* 20, no. 2 (1999), 157–173.
7. Karl Maton and John Muller, "A Sociology for the Transmission of Knowledge," in Frances Christie and J. R. Martin (eds.), *Language, Knowledge and Pedagogy: Functional Linguistic and Sociological Perspectives* (London: Continuum, 2007), 23–24.
8. On the term *Wasaṭīyya*, see Raymond W. Baker, "The Islamic 'Wasatiyyah' and the Quest for Democracy," *Oriente Moderno*, Nuova serie 87, no. 2 (2007), 327–354.
9. On the writings of Farag Foda, see Meir Hatina, *Identity Politics in the Middle East: Liberal Thought and Islamic Challenge in Egypt* (London: Tauris, 2007), 47–118.
10. Limor Lavie, *The Battle over a Civil State: Egypt's Road to June 30, 2013* (Albany: SUNY Press, 2018), 1–54.
11. For a discussion of the evolution of the civil state concept in Egypt, see Limor Lavie, "The Idea of the Civil State in Egypt: Its Evolution and Political Impact Following the 2011 Revolution," *The Middle East Journal* 71, no. 1 (2017), 23–44.
12. Raymond W. Baker, *Sadat and After: Struggles for Egypt's Political Soul* (London: I.B. Tauris, 1990), 243–254.
13. Farīda al-Naqqāsh, "Dawlat Dīn am Dīn Dawla?" *Al-Hilāl* (January 2006), 64–71; Rif'at al-Sa'īd, "Miṣr wa-l-Dawla al-Madanīyya," *Al-Ahrām* (October 16, 2010); and 'Īd 'Abd al-Ḥalīm, "Al-Dawla al-Madanīyya Hiya al-Ḥall: I'lān Sha'n al-Muwāṭana wa-Ilghā' Maẓāher al-Tamyīz Ḍarūra 'Ājila," *Al-Ahālī* (January 12, 2011).

14. On Bush's pressure for democratic reforms in the Muslim world, see Tom Carothers, "Promoting Democracy and Fighting Terror," *Foreign Policy* (January/February, 2003, reprinted), http://www.esiweb.org/pdf/esi_news_id_6_b.pdf; and Katerina Dalacoura, "US Democracy Promotion in the Arab Middle East since 11 September 2001: A Critique," *International Affairs* 81, no. 5 (2005), 963–979. Regarding internal pressures for democratic reforms in Egypt, see Rabab El-Mahdi, "Enough! Egypt's Quest for Democracy," *Comparative Political Studies* 42, no. 8 (2009), 1011–1039; and Saad Eddin Ibrahim, "Reform and Frustration in Egypt," *Journal of Democracy* 7, no. 4 (1996), 125–135.
15. "Al-Ra'īs fī al-Dhikrā al-37 li-l-Naṣr al-Majīd: Na'malu min ajl Dawla Madanīyya Ḥadītha la Takhliṭu al-Dīn bi-l-Siyāsa wa-Taqifu ma'a al-Fuqarā'," *Al-Ahrām* (October 6, 2010).
16. Alaa Al-Din Arafat, *The Mubarak Leadership and Future of Democracy in Egypt* (New York: Palgrave Macmillan, 2009), 19.
17. Nuhāl Shukrī, "Al-Ḥizb Yaltazimu bi-l-Dawla al-Madanīyya wa-bi-Iḥtirām Ḥuqūq Kull al-Muwāṭinīna," *Al-Ahrām* (October 21, 2009).
18. 'Abdallah Kamāl, "Al-'Uẓamā' al-Thalātha fī Khiṭāb Gamāl," *Rūz al-Yūsuf* (December 28, 2010).
19. For instance, Muhammad Barakāt, "Ru'ya li-l-Mustaqbal Miṣr Dawla Madanīyya Ḥadītha," *Al-Akhbār*, April 8, 2010; Muhammad 'Alī Ibrāhīm, "Tahdīd al-Aqbāṭ qabla al-Intikhābāt—al-Qā'eda wa-l-Dawla al-Dīnīyya," *Al-Gumhūrīyya*, November 4, 2010; Muhammad Kamāl, "Lā Wilāya li-Faqīh fī al-Dawla al-Madanīyya," *Rūz al-Yūsuf*, November 20, 2010; Ḥammād 'Abdallah Ḥammād, "Al-Huwīyya al-Madanīyya li-l-Dawla," *Al-Ahrām*, November 24, 2010; Makram Muhammad Ahmad, "Afkār wa-Ru'ā fī al-Dīn wa-l-'Ilm wa-l-Siyāsa," *Al-Muṣawwar*, November 24, 2010; Waḥīd 'Abd al-Magīd, "Al-Dīn wa-l-Dawla al-Madanīyya fī al-Intikhābāt al-Barlamānīyya," *Al-Ahrām*, November 30, 2010; and 'Abd al-'Āṭī Muhammad, "Thaqāfat al-Dawla al-Madanīyya lā Tazālu Ghā'eba," *Al-Ahrām al-'Arabī*, January 8, 2011.
20. Gāber 'Aṣfūr, *Hawāmish 'alā Daftar al-Tanwīr* (Kuwait: Dār Su'ād al-Ṣabbāḥ, 1994), 219–236, 244–259, 282, 318; Gāber 'Aṣfūr, "Dhākirat al-Dawla al-Madanīyya," *Al-Ahrām*, February 2, 2009; Gāber 'Aṣfūr, "Thawrat 1919 ba'da Tis'īna 'Āmm: al-Aqbāṭ wa-l-Thawra," *Al-Shurūk*, June 18, 2009; Gāber 'Aṣfūr, "Ta'ṣīl Ma'nā al-Dawla al-Madanīyya (2)," *Al-Ahrām*, September 3, 2012; Gāber 'Aṣfūr, "Al-Dawla al-Madanīyya wa-l-Dīn," *Al-Ahrām*, September 13, 2010; and Gāber 'Aṣfūr, *Ḍidda al-Ta'aṣṣub* (Casablanca: Al-Markaz al-Thaqāfī al-'Arabī, 2001), 303.
21. Gāber 'Aṣfūr, "Naḥwa I'tilāf Waṭanī Jadīd,"*Al-Ahrām*, December 20, 2010; Gāber 'Aṣfūr, "Hal Naḥnu Dawla Madanīyya?" *Al-Ahrām*, January 12, 2009; Gāber 'Aṣfūr, "'Aql al-Ṭabaqa al-Wusṭā (2)," *Al-Ahrām*, January 3, 2011; Gāber 'Aṣfūr, "Hal Na'īshu fī Dawla Madanīyya Ḥaqqan?" *Al-Ahrām*, June 26, 2010; Gāber 'Aṣfūr, "Al-Dawla al-Madanīyya Marratan Ukhrā," *Al-Ahrām*, September 6, 2010; Gāber 'Aṣfūr, "Makhāṭer al-Dawla al-Dīnīyya (3)," *Al-Ahrām*, January 29, 2007; and Gāber 'Aṣfūr, "Makhāṭer al-Dawla al-Dīnīyya (4)," *Al-Ahrām*, February 5, 2007.

22. 'Abd al-Mu'ṭī Bayyūmī, *Al-Islām wa-l-Dawla al-Madanīyya* (Cairo: Dār al-Hilāl, 2004), 6–8.
23. Similar ideas were expressed by Bayyūmī in other publications: 'Abd al-Mu'ṭī Bayyūmī, "Al-Sharī'a al-Islāmīyya fī Dawla Madanīyya," *Al-Hilāl*, January 2006, 34–39; and 'Abd al-Mu'ṭī Bayyūmī, "'Alāqat al-Dīn bi-l-Siyāsa: Al-Tafsīr bi-l-Naṣṣ," *Al-Hilāl*, March 2007, 42–50.
24. 'Abd al-Mu'ṭī Bayyūmī, "Al-Sharī'a al-Islāmīyya fī Dawla Madanīyya," *Al-Hilāl*, January 2006, 212.
25. Muhammad Sayyid Ṭanṭāwī, "Lā Wujūd li-l-Dawla al-Dīnīyya fī al-Islām," *Al-Ahrām* (February 21, 2007); and Muhammad Sayyid Ṭanṭāwī, "Al-Dawla al-Madanīyya Assasahā al-Islām," *Al-Ahrām* (March 17, 2007).
26. Interview with Sheikh of al-'Azhar Ahmad al-Ṭayyib, *Al-Muṣawwar* (December 29, 2010).
27. 'Alī Gum'a, "Namūdhaj al-Ta'āyush ma'a al-Ākhar 7/20: Wathīqat al-Madīna wa-Dustūr al-Muwāṭana," *Al-Ahrām* (January 15, 2011); and 'Alī Gum'a, "Namūdhaj al-Ta'āyush ma'a al-Ākhar 8/20: Wathīqat al-Madīna al-Usus wa-l-Mabādi'," *Al-Ahrām* (January 22, 2011).
28. Magdī al-Daqqāq, "Dr. Muhamad Ḥamdī Zaqzūq Wazīr al-Awqāf: al-Islām lā Ya'rifu al-Dawla al-Dīnīyya," *Uktūbir*, August 29, 2010.
29. For instance, in October 2009, the Egyptian author and women's activist, Nawal El Saadawi, initiated meetings of authors who supported the establishment of a secular state and the cancellation of the second article in the constitution; this was part of a worldwide movement called Majmū'at al-Taḍāmun al-Miṣrī min ajl al-Mujtama' al-Madanī.
30. On the transformation of the Muslim Brotherhood's discourse, see Limor Lavie, "The Egyptian Muslim Brothers' Ideal State Model: A Religious State—Out; A Civil State—In," *Middle Eastern Studies* 6 (2017), 996–1012.
31. Interview with Karam Zuhdī, *al-Muṣawwar* (August 8, 2003).
32. 'Amr Ḥamzāwī, "Madanīyyat al-Dawla wa-l-Siyāsa," *Al-Shurūq* April 4, 2011; Shāfiya Mahmud Ma'rūf, "Nurīduhā Dawlatan Madanīyyatan dhāt Marji'īyya Islāmīyya," www.ikhwanonline.com, April 10, 2011.
33. Lavie, *The Battle over a Civil State*, 64.
34. 'Iṣām 'Abdallah, "Al-Dīmuqrāṭīyya al-Lībirālīyya Asās al-Dawla al-Madanīyya," *Rūz al-Yūsuf*, February 16, 2011; Amīra Ibrāhīm, "Aṣwāt Khabītha Tuṭālibu Lajnat Ta'dīlāt al-Dustūr bi-Ilghā' al-Mādda al-Thāniya wa-Naz' Huwīyyat Miṣr al-Islāmīyya," *Al-Liwā' al-Islāmī*, February 24, 2011; and Emad Gad, "January 25 Revolution: Religion is for God, Egypt for Egyptians," *Ahram Online*, March 3, 2011.
35. Midḥat Qilāda, "Al-Dawla al-Madanīyya Thumma al-Dawla al-Madanīyya," *Ahl al-Qur'ān*, February 10, 2011, http://www.ahl-alquran.com/arabic/show_article.php?main_id=7692 (accessed January 14, 2014); Mīnā Badī' 'Abd al-Mālek, "Naḥwa Dawla Madanīyya dhāt Marji'īyya 'Ilmīyya," *Al-Ahrām*, July 8, 2011; Kamāl Zākher Mūsā, "Al-Dawla al-Madanīyya wa-l-Muwāṭana Ru'ya 'Almānīyya 1/2," *Al-Akhbār*, April 30, 2011; and Hānī Labīb, "Lā Aḥad

Yurīdu Daf' Thaman al-Wuṣūl ilayhā: Ḥal Yaqifu al-Jamī' ḍidda al-Dawla al-Madanīyya?" *Rūz al-Yūsuf*, June 4, 2011.

36. Ahmad Ahmad Gādd, "Al-Sharī'a al-Islāmīyya," www.ikhwanonline.com, June 11, 2011.
37. 'Alā' Muhammad 'Abd al-Nabī, "Al-Ḥukūma al-Madanīyya wa-l-Marji'īyya," www.ikhwanonline.com, March 27, 2011.
38. Transcript of an interview with Sheikh of al-'Azhar, Ahmad al-Ṭayyib, to the al-Arabiya Channel from *Al-Liwā' al-Islāmī*, March 10, 2011; Interview with the Mufti 'Alī Gum'a: Khālid Mūsā, "Muftī al-Jumhūrīyya: al-Islām lam Ya'rifu al-Dawla al-Dīnīyya.. wa-l-Dawla dhāt al-Marji'īyya al-Islāmīyya al-Aqrab li-Miṣr (2)," *Al-Shurūq*, August 4, 2011.
39. Anwar Mughīth, "Al-Dawla al-Islāmīyya laysat Madanīyya," *Al-Yawm al-Sābi'*, April 6, 2011; 'Abd al-Mu'ṭī Ḥigāzī, "Lā hiya Madanīyya.. wa-lā hiya Dīmūqrāṭīyya," *Al-Ahrām*, April 20, 2011; 'Abd al-Mu'ṭī Ḥigāzī, "Miṣr hiya Marji'īyyatuna," *Al-Ahrām*, November 9, 2011; Farīda al-Naqqāsh, "Madanīyyat al-Islāmīyyīna al-Zā'ifa," *Al-Ahālī*, March 23, 2011; Nasama Talīma, "Huwīyyat Miṣr Dā'iman.. Dawla Madanīyya Dīmūqrāṭīyya Taḥmī al-Insān wa-l-Ḥurrīyya," *Al-Ahālī*, November 2, 2011; 'Alī Hussein Ḥammād, "Islāmīyya lā Dīnīyya wa-lā Madanīyya," *Al-Ahrām*, February 22, 2012; Fahmī Huwaydī, "Al-Madanīyya Qinā' lā Qīma," *Al-Shurūq*, June 13, 2012; and Muhammad Mukhtār, "Mādhā Yurīdu Naṣārā Miṣr min Muslimīhā," March 12, 2011, http://www.egyig.com (accessed March 12, 2011).
40. Al-Shaykh Muhammad 'Abd al-'Azīz Abū al-Nagā (ed.), *Al-'Almānīyya, al-Lībirālīyya, al-Dīmūqrāṭīyya, al-Dawla al-Madanīyya fī Mīzān al-Islām*, 2nd ed. (Jam'īyyat al-Tartīl li-l-Khidmāt al-Thaqāfīyya wa-l-Dīnīyya, 2011); Ḥātim bin Ḥasan al-Dīb, *Mādhā Ta'rifu 'an hādhihi al-Muṣṭalaḥāt: al-Dawla al-Islāmīyya, al-Dawla al-Madanīyya, al-'Almānīyya, al-Lībirālīyya, al-Dīmuqrāṭīyya, al-Thiyūqrāṭīyya* (Shibin El Kom: Mu'assasat al-Ṣaḥāba li-l-Ṭab' wa-l-Nashr wa-l-Tawzī', 2011); Abū Fahr al-Salafī, *Al-Dawla al-Madanīyya: Mafāhīm wa-Aḥkām* (Cairo: Dār 'Alam al-Nawāder al-'Aṣrīyya li-l-Nashr wa-l-Tawzī', 2011), 27–34; Interview with Yāser Burhāmī: *Al-Ahrām*, November 10, 2011; and 'Ādel 'Afīfī, "Al-Islām lā Ya'rifu al-Dawla al-Dīnīyya al-Thiyūqrāṭīyya," *Al-Miṣrīyyūna*, March 20, 2011.
41. See text of the "supra-constitutional principles document", *Al-Maṣrī al-Yawm*, August 14, 2011, www.almasryalyoum.com/news/details/103142 (accessed November 18, 2020).
42. For instance, Muhammad 'Abd al-Qudūs, "Miṣr al-Madanīyya Tarfuḍu al-'Almānīyya," *Al-Wafd*, March 6, 2011; Ḥilmī Muhammad al-Qa'ūd, "Gāber 'Aṣfūr.. wa-Dimā' al-Shuhadā'," www.ikhwanonline.com, February 23, 2011; and Muhammad 'Alī Dabbūr, "Al-Dawla al-Dīnīyya am al-Dawla al-Islāmīyya?" www.ikhwanonline.com, July 11, 2011.
43. Khāled Badārī, "Al-Maḥallāwī Yaṣifu al-Muṭālibīna bi-l-Dawla al-Madanīyya bi-l-Kafara wa-'Abadat al-Ṭāghūt.. wa-Nushaṭā': Man Yuhājimūhum Kānū Wuqūd al-Thawra," *Al-Badīl*, June 10, 2011.

44. Tofigh Maboudi and Ghazal P. Nadi, "Crowdssourcing the Egyptian Constitution: Social Media, Elites, and the Populace," *Political Research Quarterly* 69, no. 4 (2016), 716–731; and Nathan J. Brown and Clark B. Lombardi, "Contesting Islamic Constitutionalism after the Arab Spring: Islam in Egypt's Post-Mubārak Constitutions," in Rainer Grote and Tilmann J. Röder (eds.), *Constitutionalism, Human Rights, and Islam after the Arab Spring* (Oxford: Oxford University Press, 2016), 245–272.
45. Muhammad Munīr Mujāhed, "Al-Dīn wa-l-Dawla fī al-Dustūr," *Al-Shurūq*, July 15, 2012.
46. ʿAmr Ḥamzāwī, "Al-Dawla wa-l-Muwāṭen wa-l-Dīn fī al-Dustūr al-Jadīd," *Al-Waṭan*, September 3, 2012; Ragab Ramaḍān, "Murquṣ: Kātidrāʾīyyat al-Iskandarīyya Tatamassaku bi-Madanīyyat al-Dawla wa-Mabādiʾ al-Sharīʿa al-Islāmīyya," *Al-Maṣrī al-Yawm*, July 4, 2012; and "Al-Majmaʿ al-Muqaddas al-Qubṭī Yuṣdiru Bayānan li-l-Muṭālaba bi-Dawla Madanīyya min khilāl Dustūr Madanī," March 29, 2012, http://www.linga.org/international-news/MzcxMQ (accessed November 18, 2020).
47. https://www.constituteproject.org/constitution/Egypt_2014.pdf (accessed November 27, 2020).
48. Lavie, *The Battle over a Civil State*, 104–118.
49. The official English translation of the amended article is: "The Armed Forces belong to the People, and their duty is to protect the country, preserve its security and the integrity of its territories and maintain the Constitution, democracy, the basic of civil state as well as the people's gains, rights and freedoms…" https://www.sis.gov.eg/section/10/9418?lang=en-us (accessed November 27, 2020).
50. Ismāʿīl al-Ashwal, "Taʿarraf ʿalā al-Ijrāʾāt al-Jadīda fī Qānūn al-Amn al-Qawmī li-l-Ḥifāẓ ʿalā Madanīyyat wa-Salāmat al-Dawla," *Al-Shurūq*, July 6, 2020.
51. The following are a few examples of the support given by some public figures and publicists to the proposed constitutional amendment, as presented in the Egyptian press: "Baʿda al-Muṭālaba bi-Taʿdīl al-Madda '200' li-Ḥimāyat al-Dawla al-Madanīyya.. Siyāsīyyunā: Al-Takhawwuf min al-Qiwā al-Islāmīyya Hājis Mawjūd, wa-Muwājahatuhā Maʿrakat Fikr wa-Waʿi," *Al-Ahālī*, February 19, 2019; http://alahalygate.com/archives/74619 (accessed November 26, 2020); and ʿAmr al-Khayyāt, "Dustūriyyat Taʿdīl al-Dustūr," *Akhbār al-Yawm*, March 22, 2019. One account pointed to the obscurity of *'Madanīyyat al-Dawla'* and stressed the need to revise the phrasing, in a future permanent constitution: Mahmud al-ʿAlāylī, "Naḥwa Dustūr Dāʾem," *Al-Maṣrī al-Yawm*, April 27, 2019.
52. James Boyd White, "The Invisible Discourse of the Law: Reflections on Legal Literacy and General Education," in Richard W. Bailey and Robin Melanie Fosheim (eds.), *Literacy for Life: The Demands for Reading and Writing* (New York: Modem Language Association, 1983), 146.
53. Deborah Brandt, "Review: Versions of Literacy," *College English* 47, no. 2 (1985), 138.
54. Al-Sisi refers to the notion of a civil state only rarely in his public speeches, see Wisām ʿAbd al-ʿAlīm, "Al-Sīsī li-Wafd al-Kūngris: al-Ḥukūma Multazima bi-Irsāʾ Dawla Madanīyya Dīmuqrāṭīyya Tuʿlī al-Qanūn wa-l-ʿAdāla," *Al-Ahrām*,

November 21, 2015; http://gate.ahram.org.eg/News/812650.aspx (accessed November 26, 2020); and "Al-Sīsī: al-Jaysh Mas'ūl 'an Ḥimāyat Madanīyyat al-Dawla wa-Man' Suqūṭihā," www.aljazeera.net, December 25, 2019.

55. Gāber 'Aṣfūr who was a prominent theorist of the civil state during Mubarāk's reign, now refrained almost completely from speaking about the constitutionalization of the civil state. In the following op-eds, he recalls his stand in previous constitution-drafting processes, with no mention of the latest amendments: Gāber 'Aṣfūr, "Dhikrayāt Dustūr 1," *Al-Ahrām*, June 21, 2020; and Gāber 'Aṣfūr, "Dhikrayāt Dustūr 2," *Al-Ahrām*, June 28, 2020.
56. Gianluca Paolo Parolin, "Drifting Power Relations in the Egyptian Constitution: The 2019 Amendments," Saggi-DPCE online, 2020/3, 3177.
57. "Al-Madanīyya al-Dīmuqrātīyya: al-Ḥiwār al-Mujtama'ī Masraḥīyya Hazlīyya.. wa-sa-Nuqaddimu Ṭalaban li-l-Taẓāhur Rafḍan li-l-Ta'dīlāt al-Dustūrīyya," elsharqtv.org, March 23, 2019.
58. Ibid.
59. Muhammad 'Abd al-Qāder wa-Muhammad Gharīb, "Ḥizb al-Nūr Yarfuḍu al-Ta'dīlāt al-Dustūrīyya I'tirāḍan 'alā 'Madanīyya' fī al-Dustūr," *Al-Maṣrī al-Yawm*, April 16, 2019; and Ḥamdī Rizq, "Li-mādhā Yarfuḍu Ḥizb al-Nūr al-Dawla al-Madanīyya?" *Al-Yawm al-Sābi'*, March 30, 2019.
60. Mahmud Ḥuayn, "'Al-Lā'āt al-Thalātha'.. Sirr Taghyīr Mawqif Ḥizb al-Nūr wa-Muwāfaqatihi 'alā al-Ta'dīlāt al-Dustūrīyya," *Al-Yawm al-Sābi'*, April 16, 2019.
61. Shaimaa Magued, "The Inter-Islamic Competition and the Shift in al-Nur Party Stance Towards Civil State in Egypt," *British Journal of Middle Eastern Studies* (2020).
62. "'Tashrī'īyyat al-Nuwwāb' Tuqirru Ikhtiṣāṣ al-Quwwāt al-Musallaḥa bi-l-Ḥifāẓ 'alā Madanīyyat al-Dawla," *Al-Yawm al-Sābi'*, April 14, 2019.

Selected Bibliography

Baker, Raymond W., "The Islamic 'Wasatiyyah' and the Quest for Democracy," *Oriente Moderno*, Nuova serie 87, no. 2 (2007), 327–354.

Bernstein, Basil, "Vertical and Horizontal Discourse: An Essay," *British Journal of Sociology of Education* 20, no. 2 (1999), 157–173.

Brown, Nathan J., "Egypt: Cacophony and Consensus in the Twenty-First Century," in Robert W. Hefner (ed.), *Sharīʿa Politics: Islamic Law and Society in the Modern World* (Bloomington: Indiana University Press, 2011), 94–120.

Brown, Nathan J., and Clark B. Lombardi, "Contesting Islamic Constitutionalism after the Arab Spring: Islam in Egypt's Post-Mubārak Constitutions," in Rainer Grote and Tilmann J. Röder (eds.), *Constitutionalism, Human Rights, and Islam after the Arab Spring* (Oxford: Oxford University Press, 2016), 245–272.

Hatina, Meir, "On the Margins of Consensus: The Call to Separate Religion and State in Modern Egypt," *Middle Eastern Studies* 36, no. 1, 35– 67.

Lavie, Limor, *The Battle over a Civil State: Egypt's Road to June 30, 2013* (Albany: SUNY Press, 2018), 1–54.

Lavie, Limor, "The Idea of the Civil State in Egypt: Its Evolution and Political Impact Following the 2011 Revolution," *The Middle East Journal* 71, no. 1 (2017), 23–44.

Magued, Shaimaa, "The Inter-Islamic Competition and the Shift in al-Nur Party Stance Towards Civil State in Egypt," *British Journal of Middle Eastern Studies* (2020).

Ranko, Annette, *The Muslim Brotherhood and Its Quest for Hegemony in Egypt: State-Discourse and Islamist Counter-Discourse* (Hamburg: Springer Fachmedien Wiesbaden, 2015).

Skovgaard-Petersen, Jakob, *Defining Islam for the Egyptian State: Muftis and Fatwas of the Dār al-Iftā* (Leiden: Brill, 1997).

The Lonely Minority? Assessing the Modern Story of Egypt's Copts and their "Return to Tradition"

Heather J. Sharkey

Introduction: A Lonely Minority?

In 1963, an American journalist named Edward Wakin published a book called *A Lonely Minority: The Modern Story of Egypt's Copts*. The title referred to Egypt's Christians, who accounted for about 10 percent of the country's population. Wakin described Egypt as a deeply sectarian society where the pan-Arab, socialist regime of Gamal ʻAbd al-Nasser was pushing Copts into the margins while ostensibly promoting what Wakin called "secular patriotism."[1]

Wakin's bleak assessment offers a checkpoint, a decade after the Free Officers' Revolution of 1952, for examining the modern Coptic Orthodox Church and community. During the twentieth century, Coptic morale,[2] and with it the Coptic sense of national belonging, wavered and dipped, even as the Egyptian state claimed to be both Islamic and inclusive. At the same time, the Coptic Orthodox Church became increasingly energetic, to the extent that one leading chronicler suggested that the mid-twentieth century—the same period that Wakin described in terms of Coptic loneliness—started a period of "unprecedented revival" and "unprecedented renaissance" relative to the two thousand years of Coptic history.[3]

In the pages that follow, I aim to explore this tension between Coptic energy and debility. I will start by considering the condition of Copts when Wakin wrote. Then I will discuss how the changes and the revival often associated with the post-1952 church had roots in the eighteenth and nineteenth centuries—the same period when, as Peter Gran argued in his now-classic book, *Islamic Roots of Capitalism: Egypt, 1760–1840*, "modern Egypt emerged out of its own internal dynamic" in the context of the global economy.[4] Coptic history, in this sense, moved in step with Egyptian history and remained integral to it despite many changes, while many Copts saw Copticity as integrally Egyptian. Finally, I will examine how, despite these elements of continuity, the

1960s witnessed important departures that changed Coptic connections to Egypt. Above all, opportunities expanded abroad as countries like the United States and Australia relaxed immigration policies that had deterred entry to people of non-European origin. In response, many Copts seized the chance to leave Egypt. The result is a robust diaspora whose members are becoming integrated into lands of settlement in ways that are fundamentally shifting the Egyptian moorings of Coptic global culture.

A Lonely Minority Revisited: Copts in the 1960s

Writing *The Lonely Minority* in the early 1960s, Edward Wakin described systematic discrimination against Copts in a period often associated with the peak of pan-Arab secularism, when religious differences were theoretically independent of, and mostly irrelevant to, citizenship. As a journalist assigned to the Middle East by a major US media conglomerate (then known as the Scripps-Howard News Service), Wakin had regular access to Egypt. Wakin's son—himself now a journalist for *The New York Times*—observed in an obituary that the senior Wakin had spoken to Copts from different walks of life and then "had to smuggle his notes out of [Egypt] hidden in his luggage" in order to escape Nasser's censors.[5] In other words, Wakin had been acting *sub rosa* in his investigation of Coptic conditions. The secretive mode of his research undoubtedly explains why his oral sources remained anonymous and why his account of Nasserite Egypt stands out for signaling the religious partisanship, or sectarianism, that ran counter to the state's claims of equal citizenship and religious neutrality.

Wakin suggested that Copts in 1963 were still reeling from the revolution of 1952. Their glory days were finished: these had peaked in 1919, when they joined Muslim partners in the anti-colonial, nationalist protests that they collectively hailed as a *thawra*, or revolution. Nasser's nationalization measures struck Coptic businesses hard. So, too, had land reform, which destroyed Coptic elites and, according to Wakin, "benefited Moslems almost exclusively, since local officials [were] all Moslems and [were] left free to guarantee the selection of Moslems" for receiving farmland. Copts felt that discrimination was growing in the public sector, so that even when Coptic students scored higher on exams, Muslims got the government jobs or university places. Making things worse was the Muslim Brotherhood, whose "aim was not annihilation of non-Moslems; it was subjugation [...] and on this point in particular the Brotherhood appealed to the Moslem masses." Wakin concluded by describing Copts as a "lonely minority"—lonely because Europeans had left Egypt after the Suez Crisis of 1956, while Egyptian Jews had either left or were leaving. "Now that Egypt has become a single-minority country, the Copts stand alone, absorbing all the anxieties and frustrations of the dominant majority."[6]

In 2004, almost 40 years after Wakin's book debuted, the French scholar Brigitte Voile published a historical and ethnographic analysis in which she argued that the 1960s marked a Coptic "return to tradition"[7] in Egypt. This return to tradition, which was still driving Coptic communal life in the early twenty-first century, responded to manifold tensions. Despite Nasser's distancing from the Muslim Brotherhood, she wrote, his pan-Arab ideology in this decade was "tainted with Islamism." Her Coptic interlocutors reported, as they had to Wakin, that under the Nasser regime they had faced land seizures disproportionally relative to Muslims, while running into barriers that blocked educational and professional advancement. Adding to the malaise were policy changes that "assisted the Islamization of public life," such as the 1955 law that made Quran study obligatory even for Christians in private schools; accelerated mosque-building (even as long-standing restrictions on church-building continued); wider Quran-lecturing on television; and growing public adherence to Ramadan in ways that changed the public rhythms of life.

Voile's account of Coptic debility echoed the litany of woes that Wakin recited. It also echoed the bleak assessment which the sociologist Saad Eddin Ibrahim made in 1996 when he published a report that emerged from a conference hosted in Cyprus two years earlier.[8] Voile's account differed from those of Wakin and Ibrahim, however, insofar as she aimed to trace the consequences political events had on Coptic devotional culture. Thus, Voile studied phenomena like the resurgent popular interest in saints—holy figures whose past suffering inspired Copts as they struggled with mundane challenges like getting jobs and saving enough money to marry.[9]

In the 1960s, during the tenure of Pope Cyril VI (1959–1971), the Coptic "return to tradition" took other forms, too. Interest in monastic traditions "skyrocketed" as growing numbers of young men—and now also women—pursued religious careers.[10] Church groups more energetically offered Coptic language classes, while some dreamed of turning what had become a "dead" liturgical language into something "living" and spoken again. At the same time, scholars traced Coptic history anew while examining the careers of patriarchs and saints.[11] Exemplifying the last trend was 'Īrīs Ḥabīb al-Miṣrī, who published in 1960 the first installment of a multi-volume chronicle that drew on Coptic ecclesiastical sources, which she had accessed as the personal assistant to Yusāb II (Joseph II), patriarch from 1946–1956.[12]

Of course, many Muslims were feeling a sense of social and economic malaise in the 1960s, too—and this gave rise in the 1970s and 1980s to a full-blown "Islamic Revival," as some scholars now call it. Led by the Muslim Brotherhood and other groups along the Salafi spectrum, this Muslim revival promoted "public performances of piety" such as visually and sartorially enforcing gender segregation, as manifest in Muslim women's fuller coverage of their heads and bodies; and the staging of mass Friday prayers in Cairo's public squares.[13] Instead of providing a foundation for mutual respect through religiosity, however, the Coptic and Islamist movements stood separately. The Islamic Revival, for example, accentuated the cultural differences of Muslims relative to Copts within Egypt by reviving the kind of religious distinctions in dress (especially for women) that had begun to lapse in the mid-nineteenth century.[14] Whether implicitly or explicitly, Islamist groups promoted notions of Muslim supremacy that recalled historical patterns of non-Muslim subordination while undermining the ideals of social parity through citizenship that many Copts had come to embrace. Egypt's Islamic Revival enhanced the Coptic malaise.[15]

For Muslims and Copts alike, the changes of the 1960s and 1970s did not emerge in a vacuum. From the late nineteenth century, many Egyptian Muslim thinkers had assumed that Islam occupied, or should occupy, a central place within the developing Egyptian nationalist movement. As decades passed, these sentiments contributed to what Israel Gershoni and James Jankowski called a "supra-Egyptian nationalism," Muslim in its matrix, which organizations like the Muslim Brotherhood manifested in the 1930s.[16]

Led by Saʿd Zaghlūl, the Wafd Party of the post-World War I period had *not* stressed Egypt's specifically Muslim dimensions. Partly for this reason, the Wafd famously attracted Copts to its cause. The Wafd's manifesto that "religion is for God, but the nation is for all" appealed strongly to Copts because it suggested possibilities for their equal participation in Egypt. At the same time, many Copts felt uneasy about the emphasis on Islam and pan-Islamic solidarity that ran through other strains of the Egyptian nationalist movement and marked the Egyptian Constitution of 1923; it contained language enshrining Islam as a source of Egyptian law with direct consequences for family matters like marriage, where the laws privileged Muslims over Christians.

In short, what seemed natural to many Muslims—asserting Egypt's Muslim cultural values—failed to enthuse many Copts and recalled the centuries-old social, political, and legal order of Islamic statehood that had treated non-Muslims as *dhimmis*, people who were protected by Muslims but socially and legally subordinate to them. Along these lines, Mira Tzoreff argued that while intellectuals like Mustafa Kamel (1874–

1908), leader of the National Party, acknowledged connections between Muslims and Copts in Egypt, he also extolled the unity that bound Egyptian Muslims to foreign Muslims. "Mustafa Kamel's National Party program," she wrote, "caused many previously-supportive Copts to rethink their position, as it positioned the Muslim Iranian, Afghan, and Tunisian on an equal footing with Egyptian Muslims," while placing Copts on a "lower level." From as early as 1900, Tzoreff continued, this tendency on the part of Mustafa Kamel to stress pan-Muslim loyalty prompted Copts to "deviate from their assimilationist pattern of conduct" by calling for Coptic revival.[17]

Of course, some *fin-de-siècle* Coptic intellectuals who aspired to cultural revival perceived their efforts as integrally Coptic and Egyptian, not Coptic alone. Here we can see the continuing ambiguity within "Copticity" as it has stood relative to Egypt and Egyptian nationalism. This ambiguity later found expression in an interview with the Al-Jazeera broadcasting network that Pope Shenouda III (1923–2012; patriarch from 1971 to 2012) gave near the end of his life, when he observed, regarding his Coptic followers, that "Egypt is not a land in which we live, but a nation that lives within us."[18] This notion, articulated in the early twenty-first century, was relevant in the early twentieth century, too. According to this line of thought, if all Coptic culture is intrinsically Egyptian, then all Coptic culture forms part of the Egyptian *patrimoine*—with the French term implying heritage in its noble and national form.

The Eighteenth-Century Roots of Coptic Revival

To understand the history of modern Coptic thought and the mood of revival, we must go back to the eighteenth century to consider antecedents for change that set the mood for Egyptian Coptic Orthodox intellectuals from the mid-nineteenth century through the mid-twentieth.[19]

Despite the tendency of mid-twentieth-century Coptic and Muslim Egyptian thinkers to dismiss the pre-Muhammad Ali (pre-1801) or pre-Napoleonic (pre-1798) period of Egyptian history as either a dark age or a period of torpor, the eighteenth century was a period of ferment in its own right.[20] The people, ideas, and goods that circulated more intensively throughout the Ottoman Empire in this century swept up Copts and changed them, too.

For a start, growing numbers of Catholic missionaries had arrived in the seventeenth century, eager to persuade their Eastern Christian counterparts to recognize Roman papal authority and adopt Catholic doctrines and practices. While these overtures had a pronounced impact in places like Aleppo and Mount Lebanon, they proved significant for Egypt, too, and not only by producing a Coptic Catholic Church.[21] By posing existential challenges to Coptic Orthodoxy—challenges that provoked responses and reforms—the Catholic missionary impetus contributed to what Febe Armanios called a "modest resurgence" in Coptic Orthodox religious and communal life that gained momentum in the eighteenth century.[22] For one example of how missionaries made an impact, consider the influx of books they brought from Catholic sources in Europe. These inspired Coptic Orthodox lay elites, who commissioned new hagiographies—stories about the lives of saints that proved as central to Copts' devotional life in the eighteenth century as they remain today.[23]

The art historian Julien Auber de Lapierre recently argued that we can find further evidence for an eighteenth-century florescence in Coptic icons: paintings of Jesus Christ, the Virgin Mary, and a panoply of saints, which functioned in churches, monasteries, and shrines as devotional aids. Two artists who contributed important innovations were an Armenian named Yuḥanna al-Armanī (d. 1786), who migrated from Jerusalem to Egypt around 1740, and his Egyptian collaborator, Ibrahīm al-Nāsikh (d. 1785). Al-Armanī's icons showed obvious continuities with earlier Byzantine (Greek) and distinctly Coptic (Egyptian) conventions. However, they also portrayed a wider array of biblical scenes than Coptic art had hitherto covered, and featured some distinctly Western pictorial motifs such as angels with wings.[24] Auber de Lapierre connected this change to the influx, again, of Western European and also Armenian Christian books, many of which were printed in Italy and the Netherlands and circulated in Egypt by Franciscan Catholic missionaries. These books contained engravings by artists like Cornelis Bloemaert (1603–1692), of the Dutch Golden Age, which proffered new ideas for illustrations.[25] At the same time, changes in Coptic imagery signaled a growing openness to—and more than that, a keen curiosity in—books and especially Bibles. In nineteenth-century Egypt, Protestant British and American missionaries nurtured these interests by circulating cheap printed Bibles and other Christian tracts, simultaneously promoting literacy among Coptic men and women of all ages and social classes.[26]

Al-Armanī's icons signaled in other ways, too, how the Coptic worldview was changing. For example, al-Armanī painted some saints—even the Virgin Mary herself—on horseback. What Auber de Lapierre calls "*le saint cavalier*"—the knight-saint—was a "fundamental element of the principle of reinvention or renaissance of Egyptian Christian art in the Ottoman period." While images of saints on horseback had appeared in Coptic monasteries from the eighth to thirteenth centuries, they had disappeared during the Mamluk period. In al-Armanī's icons, saints on horseback made a comeback, this time wielding sabers. The change may have had double significance: it reflected the broad appeal of the heroic Ottoman pictorial tradition, but at the same time possibly suggested a Coptic challenge to *dhimmi* subordination, which historically barred non-Muslims from bearing arms and riding horses.[27]

The bottom line is that books, and the texts and illustrations they contained, were shifting Coptic church cultures as the eighteenth century progressed. This claim will come as no surprise to historians like Nelly Hanna, who traced the rise of a broader book-writing culture in the eighteenth-century among middle-class Egyptian Muslim men "who were educated without necessarily being scholarly,"[28] and Ami Ayalon, who assessed the far-reaching cultural impact of the rise of Arabic mass readership during the nineteenth and twentieth centuries when cheap printing methods supplanted manuscript writing.[29] As Marshall McLuhan observed in 1962, the rise of typography enabled readers to "recreate...the world in the image of a global village."[30]

Cultures of reading, writing, and printing certainly energized Coptic thinkers, connected them to people and places farther afield (especially to Christians in Europe, North America, and elsewhere in the Ottoman Empire), and stimulated the mood of reform within their church as in Egypt at large.

The Nineteenth- and Early Twentieth-Century Roots of Coptic Revival

Innovations and reforms in Coptic communal culture continued and accelerated during the nineteenth century and the first decades of the twentieth. Several figures stand out for contributions which were in some cases rhetorical and aspirational, and in other cases material. I will highlight a few of these figures below.

The first was Cyril IV (1816–1861), patriarch from 1854 to 1861. Hailed by Copts as the "Reformer," Cyril IV began to require priests to study the Coptic language (which had become extinct as a spoken language during the early centuries of the Islamic era), and standardized pronunciation in liturgies, which had varied considerably beforehand.[31] Cyril IV also imported a press from Austria and sponsored the printing of books on Coptic topics.[32] Above all, this patriarch opened a modern "Great Coptic School" in Cairo, styled on schools which the German Protestant missionary John Lieder had founded for the British Church Missionary Society (CMS) in mid-nineteenth-century Egypt. Other schools followed for boys and girls, teaching not only subjects like mathematics, but also French, English, Arabic, and "Turkish" (Ottoman Turkish or Osmanli). These schools shaped a generation of Coptic elites including Boutros Ghali (1846–1910), prime minister of Egypt from 1908 to 1910, and instilled among Copts as a whole a belief in education as a means to collective progress.

A second influential individual, who flourished a half century after Cyril IV, was Marcus Simaika (1864–1944). An accountant by training who earned places on both the khedival legislative council and the new Coptic lay communal council (*Al-majlis al-millī*), Simaika was well connected both to British authorities of the post-1882 Occupation and to the French academic establishment in Egypt.[33] He made his greatest contribution to Coptic and Egyptian culture by founding in 1908 the Coptic Museum, which collected and curated Coptic manuscripts, ecclesiastical silverware, architectural elements, and everyday objects. By describing Coptic society in 1897 as awakening after a long slumber, Simeika invoked the *Nahḍa* (revival or renaissance) rhetoric that was central to incipient Arab nationalist thought in this period, and that has continued to inspire some scholars of the Coptic past.[34] By celebrating Egyptian continuities with ancient civilization, Simaika also contributed to a "Pharaonicist" strain in Egyptian nationalist thought.[35] He cemented a deep sense of cultural pride among modern Copts.

A third seminal thinker was Yaʿqūb Nakhla Rufīla, a contemporary of Simaika, who published a book called *Tārīkh al-'Umma al-Qibṭīyya*—"The History of the Coptic People"—in 1897. Rufīla's book "was the inaugural one-volume, comprehensive, indexed, 'scientific' study of the Coptic community to appear in the Arabic language."[36] Writing in straightforward Arabic, Rufīla insisted that Copts needed to know their past, extending back thousands of years, to chart a bright future. He credited Copts with founding the first civilization—Egyptian civilization—which blazed trails for the rest of the world to follow.[37] Rufīla set out to show how Egyptian antiquity and Coptic tradition anchored Egypt and its Copts as they advanced in the modern era. Like Simaika, Rufīla strengthened Copts' belief in the civilizational integrity of their Christian and Egyptian culture.

Two other important reformers were Klūdyūs Labīb (1868–1918) and Tādrus Shanūda al-Manqabbādi (1857–1932). Labīb initiated efforts to revive Coptic as a spoken language, and went so far as to coin new Coptic words for things like "telephone" and "automobile."[38] Al-Manqabbādi, a supporter of the ʿUrābī Revolt, founded the Society for the Preservation of the Coptic Calendar in 1884, nine years after the Egyptian government had replaced this calendar with the Gregorian (western Christian) calendar for its official use. Among other things, this society encouraged the revival of the Nayrouz Festival, historically connected to the onset of Nile flooding, which had evolved into a Christian holiday for recognizing Coptic martyrs killed by the Byzantine emperor Diocletian.[39] They sought to preserve ancient traditions while adapting them to new times.

Ultimately, these Coptic reformers of the nineteenth and early twentieth centuries contributed not just to the revival of traditions, but also to an ideology of revivalism. They fortified a political belief among Copts about their collective capacity for progressive reform and empowerment in the modern age.

We can see the legacies of these thinkers in the chronicles of the historian 'Īrīs Ḥabīb al-Miṣrī (d. 1994), the product of an American mission-school education, who published her first volume on Coptic history in 1960, three years before Wakin's *The Lonely Minority* appeared.[40] Like many other Coptic intellectuals of the twentieth century, 'Īrīs Ḥabīb al-Miṣrī believed that the dismantling of hierarchies which had historically privileged Muslims relative to Christians was a major leap forward for Egypt. She contributed to the strain of thought that portrayed the pre-nineteenth century era as a dark and repressive age in Coptic history, and that hailed the 1919 revolution as a thrilling moment of collaboration with Muslims. She also traced modern Coptic history as a movement from degradation to enlightenment in the first decades of the Muhammad 'Ali dynasty era (1801–1952). She went so far as to call the reforms of the nineteenth century—especially the abolition of the *jizya* (the tax required of Christians and Jews to signal their subordination to Muslims) in the 1850s—as a movement toward Coptic "emancipation," although she blamed the Ottomans, not Egypt's Muslim rulers, for earlier repression.[41]

Yet, it was not just Muhammad 'Ali and his heirs who effected these great changes. Al-Miṣrī too celebrated great Coptic reformers of the nineteenth century, again including Cyril IV. This patriarch, she observed, had welcomed the concept of Copts as equal citizens and reached out to his Muslim counterparts at al-'Azhar. By making such claims, her works on Coptic ecclesiastical history advanced distinctly republican ideas about Muslim–Coptic fraternity and parity in Egypt.[42]

Fast Forward: Ḥabīb Girgis and the Sunday School Movement

Many Coptic Orthodox Christians later hailed Pope Cyril IV's Coptic schools as symbols of enterprise and revival in the mid-nineteenth century, but in fact foreign Catholic and Protestant mission schools were more expansive than their Orthodox counterparts during the late nineteenth century and through the mid-twentieth.[43] Since mission schools enrolled many Muslim youth, too, they offered opportunities for Christians to socialize with Muslims.[44] Thus, mission schools fostered the kind of camaraderie that contributed to shared nationalism, especially among Coptic and Muslim elites, while helping to cultivate a cadre of prosperous laymen, that is, Christian community leaders who did not belong to the clergy and who exerted influence outside of church affairs. Marcus Simaika, who first attended the Great Coptic School before transferring to a French Catholic (Lasallian) institution, exemplified this trend.

Catholic and Protestant schools boosted Coptic social mobility and forged a bigger, more broadly educated Coptic middle class. Nevertheless, because these schools often wooed Copts as potential converts, missionaries and their institutions irked Orthodox leaders even as they spurred them to reform and adapt.

One of the most far-reaching responses to missionary influence was launched in 1918, when a schoolteacher named Ḥabīb Girgis (1875–1951) embraced the Anglo–American Protestant concept of the "Sunday School" and adapted it for an Orthodox congregation in the middle-class Cairo neighborhood of Faggāla. Modeled on programs that American Presbyterians had introduced to Evangelical (Egyptian Presbyterian) churches, Ḥabīb Girgis's Sunday School classes taught Bible, church doctrine, and social ethics for adults and children alike.[45]

Sunday Schools contributed to what historians now call the Coptic "Sunday School Movement" that blossomed in the 1940s. It was a "Movement" with a capital M because it signaled profound changes in its Orthodox supporters' vision of what churches could do. They increasingly saw churches not only as places for prayer and ritual, but also as community centers where people could study religious and non-religious subjects while socializing. In this fashion, churches blended worship, education, and leisure. It is no accident that the Muslim Brotherhood pursued a similar vision: Hasan al-Bannā (1906–1949), who founded the organization in 1928, also copied programmatic elements of the American missions.[46]

The Sunday School Movement inspired a teenager named Naẓir Gayyed, who went to Cairo University and became a high-school English and social studies teacher. He stopped teaching in 1954 in order to join a monastery, eventually entering the Orthodox priesthood. He rose through the ranks until, in 1971, he became patriarch as Shenouda III. A powerful figure who led Copts during the tenure of Egyptian presidents Anwar al-Sadat and Hosni Mubarak, Shenouda III now looms large in accounts of late twentieth- and early twenty-first-century Coptic history. He was a visible product of the Sunday School Movement which continued to inspire the Coptic Orthodox Church and community in the Sadat and Mubarak eras.

In 2003, the Egyptian scholar S.S. Hasan published a riveting account of the Sunday School Movement in which she advanced several persuasive arguments about its impact in the late twentieth century. I will highlight a few of her arguments here.

First, Hasan dated the start of a Coptic sense of malaise to the 1940s—the decade before, not after, the Free Officers' coup. By the time the 1952 revolution occurred, she maintained, pessimism and disillusionment had already set in among Copts, especially among "the first generation of university graduates, a generation that had come of age in a period of secular slogans," who "realized that unlike their Muslim compatriots, who graduated with them…they had no chance to play a significant role in the polity."[47] In the 1940s, the ascension of the Muslim Brotherhood, and the government's tilt toward laws that favored Muslims in schools, places of worship, and laws, compounded the unease.[48]

Second, foreign missions were no longer much of a threat by the 1950s, when decolonization forced missions to contract, but the pro-Muslim policies of the Egyptian government *were* threatening. In this context, the Sunday School Movement was able to respond by making the church into a social welfare institution which played a psychologically palliative role. "The Coptic Orthodox Church," Hasan explained, "took upon itself the role of bolstering the battered self-image of Egyptian Christians as well as of equipping them with the values and skills that would enable them to succeed economically despite discrimination."[49]

Third, the revolution of 1952 and the nationalizations that followed destroyed the old-guard elite of Coptic laymen. Left standing were ecclesiastical leaders (members of the clergy and high-ranking churchmen like bishops) along with members of a socially humbler and more conservative stratum of Egyptian society. While Hasan was not unique in observing this trend (Wakin observed it, too), she went farther than other analysts by describing the shift of power among Copts—from wealthy landowning and professional elites to the middle classes—as a "revolution."[50] She meant revolution not in a metaphorical sense, suggesting grand changes, but in a true political sense: revolution as the destruction and rebuilding of institutions as centers of power. For these reasons, she continued, the Sunday School Movement and Coptic Church did not really guide a return to tradition and the *status quo ante*;

rather, they *refashioned* tradition while enabling churches to respond to the times and to Coptic anxieties.

The result of these anxieties was that Copts flocked to churches after the revolution of 1952. Attendance increased dramatically relative to the 1940s, at least according to the recollections of older people whom Hasan interviewed, as churches became centers not only for worship, but also for the flocking together of a community beset by social, political, and economic anxieties. Attendance remained high in years that followed. By the 1990s, many of the churches that Hasan visited were packed and standing-room only.[51]

The 1960s Revisited: Copts in Egypt and Abroad

By the mid-twentieth century, the Coptic Orthodox Church was thriving despite the growing malaise. It hardly needed "revival." Yet, the 1960s were a decade which many Copts, and scholars who later studied them, have described with exactly this term. What made the 1960s so striking as a decade when Copts rallied to their churches?

One pivotal development, as Wakin suggested, was that Egyptian Jews had left the country, or were leaving. If Copts had already been a minority in Egypt—a claim that many Copts have hotly denied, for reasons I will consider below—then they became in the 1960s a "lonely" one, in the sense of being isolated as non-Muslims. Their isolation led them to pull more closely into churches as centers of community life.

The Arab–Israeli conflict made Coptic exposure worse. Copts fell under closer scrutiny regarding their loyalty to Egyptian and Arab causes. National unity acquired an element of staging. Egyptian authorities expected Copts to *perform* their loyalty, for example, by participating in "unity marches."[52]

Meanwhile, by the 1960s, the Coptic Orthodox Church was becoming more active in international Christian forums. The Coptic Orthodox Church had already joined the mostly-Protestant World Council of Churches (WCC), based in Geneva, as a founding member in 1948. A Coptic delegation made its first appearance at a WCC meeting (held in Illinois) in 1954, and thereafter attended regularly.[53] In 1962, it joined the Near East Christian Council (NECC), which Protestant churches had formed in 1956 from an earlier regional organization of Protestant missions. In 1974, the NECC evolved into the Middle East Council of Churches (MECC), with the Coptic Orthodox Church assuming a prominent role. In 1990, the Middle Eastern Catholic churches—including the Coptic Catholic Church—joined the MECC, too.[54] While it may be tempting to attribute this late twentieth-century solidarity wholly to ecumenical bonhomie on the world stage, conditions in Egypt and the Middle East also played a role, contributing to Christian anxieties that drew together diverse churches whose relations had historically been tense and adversarial. Equally important was the role of one church figure, Bishop Samuel, who later died standing next to Anwar Sadat in 1981—killed by the same assassin. A long-time rival of Shenouda (with whom he had been nominated for the Coptic papacy in 1971), Bishop Samuel was an avid promoter of ecumenical relations, willing to work with Protestants and Catholics both in Egypt, on projects like literacy and vaccination campaigns, and abroad, in countries like Canada and the United States where Copts were beginning to settle.[55]

To be sure, the Coptic Orthodox Church gained a degree of international prestige and prominence by participating in international Christian organizations. After his elevation to the papacy in 1971, Shenouda III became a kind of ecclesiastical statesman, boosting "Coptic aspirations on the road to internationalism."[56] At the same time, global engagements confirmed the ambitions of the Coptic Church abroad. Perhaps the most important sign of this change occurred in 1962 when the Cairo-based Institute of Coptic Studies (itself founded only in 1954[57]) started an African studies department to train Coptic missionaries for countries such as Kenya and Uganda.[58] For centuries, Islamic rule had blocked the Coptic Church from proselytizing, but now, outside Egypt, it was able to evangelize again—signaling another "return to tradition" and recalling the church's legendary founder, St. Mark the Evangelist, who had brought Christianity to Egypt in the first century. So important have such overtures become to the church's self-image that in 2017 the Coptic Orthodox cathedral in Cairo commissioned a new mural, high on a wall where worshippers enter, featuring a map of its missions to Asia, Africa, and the Americas.[59]

For Copts in Egypt during the 1960s, as for Middle Eastern Christians elsewhere, connections to foreign "Christian" powers sometimes became a liability, too.[60] Consider what happened with *Nostra Aetate*, the declaration on "the relation of the [Roman Catholic] church to non-Christian religions," which Pope John XXIII proclaimed at the Second Vatican Council in 1965. The document expressed a sense of fellowship with non-Christian believers in the divine. It specifically cited Muslims, Hindus, Buddhists, and Jews, while referring to "unity and love among men" [sic].[61] In fact, the architects of *Nostra Aetate* had intended the document to signal special warmth toward Jews, 20 years after the end of World War II and with the Holocaust still a fresh memory. Already in 1959, John XXIII had ordered Catholic priests, when delivering Good Friday prayers, to remove the word "*perfidus*"—meaning treacherous—as a descriptor of Jews.[62]

What did Vatican II and *Nostra Aetate* have to do with the Copts? Simply, in Egypt in the mid-1960s, in the context of Arab–Israeli hostility, some Egyptian government officials believed that its references to Jews were too friendly. Not only Egyptian officials but officials from other Middle Eastern countries as well had protested the Vatican's efforts to absolve Jews for crucifying Jesus—a claim that had justified centuries of Christian persecution of Jews in Europe.[63] At the same time, Egyptian authorities advised church leaders to give sermons lambasting Israel and emphasizing Jewish guilt for Christ's death.[64] These details show how messy and mutually entangled the history of Middle Eastern Muslim, Christian, and Jewish people have been; and how the heat generated by Coptic links to foreign Christians (whether perceived, potential, or real) sometimes forced Copts to hustle to prove national loyalty.

The 1960s also comprised an important decade for Copts because it inaugurated a period of heightened migration. Along with other Egyptians, Copts took fixed-term jobs in Arab states where oil riches were flowing, in Libya and the Gulf. Indeed, the Coptic Orthodox Church appointed a bishop to Kuwait in 1963.[65] Even more significantly, Copts left for the United States, Canada, Australia, New Zealand, and anywhere else that offered them opportunity, such as Bolivia and South Africa. Recognizing this trend, the church sent a priest to Toronto in 1964.[66] Tense conditions and limited prospects in Egypt pushed Copts *out*, while congenial conditions abroad pulled Copts *in*.

Foreign immigration policies proved to be critical. In 1965, in the United States, the U.S. Congress passed the Hart-Celler Act, which reversed the Johnson-Reed Act of 1924. Originally intended to block Chinese immigration into the United States at a time of rampant Sinophobia, the Johnson-Reed Act had also barred most migration from the Middle East while favoring entry by European "whites." In its reversal, the Hart-Celler Act of 1965 opened the door to Asian and African immigration in ways that benefitted more Egyptians from the late 1960s onward. Reflecting this trend, the Church authorized the opening of churches (physical buildings with ordained priests) in Los Angeles in 1969 and Jersey City, New Jersey, in 1970—even though Copts had been worshiping informally together in these cities before then.[67] In the mid-1960s, Australia likewise dismantled its "White Australia Policy," which had privileged "white" European immigration while restricting East Asians and other people of color. Copts were thus able to enter Australia, where they established a church in Sydney in 1970. The same decade saw a Coptic community grow in Canada, especially in Toronto and Montreal.[68] These migrations were different from the Arab-state migrations since the English-speaking countries allowed for naturalization. Consequently, many Copts settled and secured citizenship.

In Egypt, during the 1960s, meanwhile, sectarianism was solidifying. Despite or precisely because of the Egyptian government's secular rhetoric, religious bias became unofficial and thus less visible, even as the Egyptian government insisted that its citizenship was egalitarian. The anthropologist Saba Mahmood described this phenomenon, noting that "secular governance…contributed to the exacerbation of religious tensions in postcolonial Egypt, hardening interfaith boundaries and polarizing religious differences." Echoing a claim that S.S. Hasan advanced about Copts and the Sunday School Movement, Mahmood observed the Egyptian state's retraction from social welfare provision during the Sadat and Mubarak eras. While the state "privatized" social services by essentially ceding them to Egyptian Christian and Muslim religious organizations, it remained very intrusive through its surveillance and top–down style of policy making.[69] Meanwhile, Coptic ecclesiastical figures—and above all, the patriarch Shenouda III—effected a "monopolization of political power" in mediating with Egyptian authorities.[70]

In the long run, the very trends that strengthened the church fortified a tendency toward Coptic introspection or self-communalization in Egypt. On a micro level, drawing on fieldwork conducted in Cairo in the 1990s, one anthropologist noted that Copts were reporting how relations with Muslim neighbors had deteriorated from a generation before; people in apartment buildings, for example, were less likely to chat across balconies. Coptic parents were teaching their children to remain silent about their religion as a means to survive in a Muslim-dominated state and society. At the same time, Coptic priests were keeping their flocks close to churches and encouraging worshipers to confess regularly. The priests could then undertake moral surveillance—a kind of monitoring that suggested parallels between the church and the state.[71]

Conclusion: Copts as a Minority and a Diaspora

Wakin dubbed the Copts a "lonely minority" in 1963. This phrase—and the very title of his book—touched a sore point for many Copts in Egypt. No effort to examine his book as a foil for the past century of Coptic history could end without reflecting on the "m-word" (minority) and why so many Egyptian Christians and Muslims have found it repugnant.

What was so bad about being a "minority"? Elizabeth Monier tried to explain the persistent opposition to the term in 2018, in an article on the political mood among Copts after the 2011 overthrow of Hosni Mubarak. "The denial of the minority label by Coptic leaders [in Egypt remains] part of the entrenched strategy of seeking to minimize exclusion." Referring to the sporadic attacks on Coptic people and institutions that began in the 1980s and continued up to and beyond 2011, she added that this strategy on the part of Coptic leaders also entailed an effort "to cooperate with the government by playing down attacks on Copts, often [by] resorting to informal reconciliation meetings to resolve disputes rather than subjecting the problem to the scrutiny of the justice system or public debate."[72]

While many Copts in Egypt have rejected the minority label, Coptic activists in countries like the United States and Canada have seemed more inclined to accept it for their coreligionists still in Egypt, and have sometimes lobbied on their behalf.[73] Suffice it to say that the term "minority" has carried baggage from the late-imperial machinations of Britain and France in the Middle East after World War I.[74] It has implied marginalization and subordination in ways that have edged uncomfortably close to the history of Christians as *dhimmi*s. Use of the term has also threatened a still-potent Coptic dream of social parity and *waḥda waṭanīyya* (national unity), a founding myth of Egyptian nationalism comparable in force to the "self-made man" concept in the USA. Finally, the minority label has endangered an ideal cherished by many Copts in the twentieth and twenty-first centuries: that they are the eponymous Egyptians (the word Copt, or *Qibṭī* in Arabic, traces its roots to the Greek name for Egypt, *Aigyptus*), and as such, that they are central, not marginal, to Egypt.

And yet, the term "minority" undoubtedly captures elements of the Coptic situation in Egypt since the 1960s, if not before: their persistent sense of malaise and vulnerability; the limits they have faced on professional advancement, especially in the public sector; the pressures of majoritarian Muslim culture and Islamization that have confronted them in schools and in the streets; and, since the early Mubarak era, the physical and existential threats that Islamists (and in the case of the 2011 Maspero massacre, the Egyptian security forces) have posed by assaulting or slaughtering Coptic people.

Awareness of the fraught situation facing Copts explains the defensive, sometimes outraged reaction that the term "minority" has sometimes generated among Muslim leaders and intellectuals. Consider the outrage in Egypt that arose in 1994 when Saad Eddin Ibrahim, as leader of the Ibn Khaldun Center for Development Studies in Cairo, proposed to hold a conference on Middle Eastern minorities,

Copts included. Objectors protested so loudly that they forced him both to move the conference from Egypt to Cyprus and to change the word "minorities" (*aqalliyyāt* in Arabic) on the program to "religious communities, sects, and ethnic groups" (*al-milal wal-niḥal wal-aʿrāq*). Likewise, the report that he later published on the subject with the London-based Minority Rights Group International opened what Ami Ayalon called a "Pandora's box" by challenging claims to unity and social parity that had long anchored Egyptian nationalist rhetoric.[75]

In contrast to the Copts within Egypt, Copts in the diaspora—who by 2017 were sustaining more than 500 Coptic Orthodox churches[76]—do not seem encumbered by this "minority" debate. It undoubtedly helps that countries like the United States, Canada, and Australia have majoritarian (yet very diverse) Christian populations, along with traditions of church–state separation, against which Coptic immigrants are unlikely to chafe. It helps, too, that many Copts have prospered abroad, especially the first generation of Coptic migrants who tended to have advanced education,[77] even if many other, newer immigrant Copts scrape by in humble jobs as gas-station attendants or food-truck workers.[78] Also boosting Coptic integration and acceptance may be that some of their churches have been attracting non-Egyptian members from other Christian backgrounds.[79] Likewise, diasporic Copts have faced few restrictions on church-building or job-seeking of the kind that have weighed heavily on Christians in Egypt. The Melbourne community is a case in point. In 2000, its leaders founded Saint Athanasius College as a Coptic theological seminary in Australia. The college recently opened a second campus with a worship hall in the Eporo Tower, a 44-story building which it owns in downtown Melbourne. Its opening ceremony, which was considered so important that Pope Tawadros himself attended it,[80] offers proof that Copts can flourish in a country like Australia and enjoy freedoms that Egypt withholds.

Conditions in Egypt during the 1960s stoked feelings of marginalization among Copts; conditions abroad enabled them to leave. Today, 50 years on, Copts in Egypt remain beleaguered and look to churches as centers of community life, even as growing numbers of Copts prosper abroad. Ultimately, the diaspora raises questions about where Coptic culture will go. The very fact that Coptic culture today is increasingly "happening" in places like New York, Toronto, and Melbourne suggests that Copticity may no longer be automatically or unquestionably Egyptian.[81]

Notes

1. Edward Wakin, *A Lonely Minority: The Modern Story of Egypt's Copts* (New York: William Morrow & Company, 1963).
2. Unless indicated otherwise, when I refer to Coptic churches in this chapter, I will be referring to Coptic Orthodox churches and not to their Egyptian Catholic and Protestant counterparts.
3. Otto F.A. Meinardus, *Two Thousand Years of Coptic Christianity* (Cairo: American University in Cairo Press, 2016), 1, 3.
4. Peter Gran, *Islamic Roots of Capitalism: Egypt, 1760–1840,* New edition, Intro. Afaf Lutfi al-Sayyid Marsot (Syracuse: Syracuse University Press, 1998), xiv.
5. Patrick Verel, "University Mourns Edward Wakin, Former Communications Professor," *Fordham News,* December 9, 2009, https://news.fordham.edu/university-news/university-mourns-edward-wakin-former-communications-professor/.
6. Wakin, *The Lonely Minority*, 48, 74, 168.
7. Brigitte Voile, *Les coptes d'Égypte sous Nasser: Sainteté, miracles, apparitions* (Paris: CNRS Éditions, 2004), 54, 56.
8. Ibrahim also gave statistics and numbers for Coptic debility. He stated, for example, that Copts "lost 75 percent of their work and property" amid Nasser-era nationalizations. Saad Eddin Ibrahim et al, *The Copts of Egypt,* Minority Rights Group International (London: Minority Rights Group, 1996), 16. On the "heat" that this conference generated, see Ami Ayalon, "Egypt's Coptic Pandora's Box," in *Minorities and the State in the Arab World*, ed. Ofra Bengio & Gabriel Ben-Dor (Boulder: Lynne Rienner Publishers, 1999), 53–71.
9. Voile, *Les coptes d'Égypte sous Nasser*, 54–56.
10. Pieternella van Doorn-Harder, *Contemporary Coptic Nuns* (Columbia: University of South Carolina Press, 1995); and Nelly van Doorn-Harder, *Copts in Context: Negotiating Identity, Tradition, and Modernity* (Columbia: University of South Carolina Press, 2017), 11.
11. Voile, *Les coptes d'Égypte sous Nasser*, 57.
12. 'Īrīs Ḥabīb al-Miṣrī, *Qiṣṣat al-kanīsa al-qibṭiyya,* 7 volumes (Cairo, n.p: 1960–1975).
13. Aaron Rock-Singer, "Prayer and the Islamic Revival: A Timely Challenge," *International Journal of Middle East Studies* 48 (2016), 293–312; and Aaron Rock-Singer, "The Salafi Mystique: The Rise of Gender Segregation in 1970s Egypt," *Islamic Law and Society* 23 (2016), 279–305.
14. On the history of clothing distinctions, see Heather J. Sharkey, *A History of Muslims, Christians, and Jews in the Middle East* (Cambridge: Cambridge University Press, 2017); Gudrun Krämer, "Moving Out of Place: Minorities in Middle Eastern Urban Societies, 1800–1914," in *The Urban Social History of the Middle East, 1750–1950,* ed. Peter Sluglett (Syracuse: Syracuse University Press, 2008), 182–223, see especially 218; and *Vivian Ibrahim, The Copts of Egypt: Challenges of Modernization and Identity* (London: Tauris Academic Studies, 2011), 15–16.

15. On the parallel development of the Islamic and Coptic revivals, see Sebastian Elsässer, *The Coptic Question in the Mubarak Era* (New York: Oxford University Press, 2014).
16. Israel Gershoni and James Jankowski, *Redefining the Egyptian Nation, 1930–1945* (Cambridge: Cambridge University Press, 1995).
17. Mira Tzoreff, "The Copts of Egypt: Fully Fledged Citizens or a New Dhimmi?", in *Inglorious Revolutions: State Cohesion in the Middle East after the Arab Spring*, ed. Brandon Friedman and Bruce Maddy-Weitzman (Tel Aviv: The Moshe Dayan Center, 2014), 187.
18. Quoted in Tzoreff, "The Copts of Egypt," 189.
19. Paul Sedra, *From Mission to Modernity: Evangelicals, Reformers and Education in Nineteenth-Century Egypt* (London: I.B. Tauris, 2011). Here and below, see especially 5–9.
20. The Coptic chronicler ʾĪrīs Ḥabīb al-Miṣrī regarded this as a dark age. Muhammad Mustafa Badawi (1925–2012), in his otherwise delightful studies of Arabic literary culture, described it as an age of sterile complacency. M.M. Badawi, *A Critical Introduction to Modern Arabic Poetry* (Cambridge: Cambridge University Press, 1975).
21. Alastair Hamilton, *The Copts and the West, 1439–1822: The European Discovery of the Egyptian Church* (Oxford: Oxford University Press, 2006); and Bernard Heyberger, *Les Chrétiens du Proche-Orient au temps de la Réforme Catholique (Syrie, Liban, Palestine, XVIIe–XVIIIe siècles)* (Rome: École Française de Rome, 1994).
22. Febe Armanios, *Coptic Christianity in Ottoman Egypt* (Oxford: Oxford University Press, 2011).
23. Anthony George Shenoda, "Cultivating Mystery: Miracles and a Coptic Moral Imaginary," PhD diss., Harvard University, 2010.
24. Julien Auber de Lapierre, "Tradition et innovation—la dualité iconographique du peintre Yuhanna al-Armani," in *Études Coptes XIII: Quinzième journée d'études* (Louvain-la-Neuve, 12–14 mai 2011), ed. Anne Boud'hors and Catherine Louis (Paris: Éditions de Boccard, 2015), 27–42, see 35.
25. Auber de Lapierre, "Tradition et innovation," 34.
26. Heather J. Sharkey, "American Missionaries, the Arabic Bible, and Coptic Reform in Late Nineteenth-Century Egypt," in *American Missionaries in the Modern Middle East: Foundational Encounters*, ed. Mehmet Ali Doğan and Heather J. Sharkey (Salt Lake City: University of Utah Press, 2011), 237–259.
27. Auber de Lapierre, "Tradition et innovation," 34–37.
28. Nelly Hanna, *In Praise of Books: A Cultural History of Cairo's Middle Class, Sixteenth to Eighteenth Century* (Syracuse: Syracuse University Press, 2003), 3.
29. Ami Ayalon, *The Arabic Print Revolution: Cultural Production and Mass Readership* (Cambridge: Cambridge University Press, 2016).
30. Marshall McLuhan, *The Gutenberg Galaxy: The Making of Typographic Man* (Toronto: University of Toronto Press, 1962), 31.
31. Hiroko Miyokawa, "The Revival of the Coptic Language and the Formation of Coptic Ethnoreligious Identity in Modern Egypt," in Van Doorn-Harder, *Copts in Context*, 151–152.

32. Sedra, *From Mission to Modernity*, 112.
33. Julien Auber de Lapierre, "Marcus Simaika ou l'inventeur du patrimoine copte." Paper presented at the conference *In Partibus Fidelium*: Missions du Levant et connaissance de l'Orient chrétien (XIX–XXI siècles), École Française de Rome, Rome, November 28, 2017.
34. Again, Meinardus invokes a renaissance discourse in his *Two Thousand Years of Coptic Christianity*.
35. Donald Malcolm Reid, *Whose Pharaohs? Archaeology, Museums, and Egyptian National Identity from Napoleon to World War I* (Berkeley: University of California Press, 2002).
36. Sedra, *From Mission to Modernity*, 8.
37. Ya'qūb Nakhla Rufila, *Kitāb Tārīkh al-'Umma al-Qibṭīyya*, 2nd ed. (Cairo: Maṭba'a at Metropole, 2000), 3.
38. Miyokawa, "The Revival of the Coptic Language," 151–156, see 152.
39. Hiroko Miyokawa, "The Struggle over Egyptianness: A Case Study of the Nayrouz Festival," in *Minorities and the Modern Arab World*, ed. Laura Robson (Syracuse: Syracuse University Press, 2016), 122–139.
40. 'Īrīs Ḥabīb al-Miṣrī attended the American (Presbyterian) Girls' School in Cairo, and later Dropsie College in Philadelphia, the precursor to what is now the Herbert D. Katz Center for Advanced Judaic Studies at the University of Pennsylvania.
41. Iris Habib el-Masri, *The Story of the Copts* (Beirut: Middle East Council of Churches, 1978), 507; and Heather J. Sharkey, "The Ottoman Tanzimat Edict of 1856 and Its Consequences for the Christians of Egypt: The Rashomon Effect in Coptic History," in *Copts in Modernity*, ed. Lisa Agaiby, Nelly van Doorn-Harder, and Mark Swanson (Leiden: Brill, 2021).
42. Sedra, *From Mission to Modernity*, 9, 111.
43. J. Heyworth-Dunne, *An Introduction to the History of Education in Modern Egypt* (London: Luzac & Co., 1938); and Jirjis Salāma, *Tārīkh al-ta'līm al-ajnabī fi Miṣr fi al-qarn al-tāsi' 'ashar wa-al-'ishrīn* (Cairo: al-Majlis al-a'la li-ri'āyat al-funūn wa-al-adab wa-al-'ulūm al-ijtimā'īyya, 1963).
44. Sharkey, *A History of Muslims, Christians, and Jews*, 256–257.
45. (Bishop) Suriel, *Habib Girgis: Coptic Orthodox Educator and a Light in the Darkness* (Yonkers: St. Vladimir's Seminary Press, 2016).
46. Heather Sharkey, *American Evangelicals in Egypt: Missionary Encounters in an Age of Empire* (Princeton: Princeton University Press, 2008), 107.
47. S.S. Hasan, *Christians versus Muslims in Modern Egypt: The Century-Long Struggle for Coptic Equality* (Oxford: Oxford University Press, 2003), 57.
48. Vivian Ibrahim, *The Copts of Egypt*, 87–93.
49. Hasan, *Christians versus Muslims in Modern Egypt*, 3.
50. Ibid., 76.
51. Hasan, *Christians versus Muslims in Modern Egypt*, 12.
52. Wakin, *The Lonely Minority*, 50–51.
53. Aziz S. Atiya, *A History of Eastern Christianity* (London: Methuen & Co., 1968), 120.
54. Paul Nabil El-Sayah, "Middle East Council of Churches (MECC)," *New Catholic Encyclopedia*, accessed October 11, 2018, http://www.encyclopedia.com/

religion/encyclopedias-almanacs-transcripts-and-maps/middle-east-council-churches-mecc; Middle East Council of Churches, "MECC's History," accessed October 11, 2018, https://mecc.org/history/.

55. Michael Akladios, "Ordinary Copts: Ecumenism, Activism, and Belonging in North American Cities, 1954–1992" (PhD diss., York University, 2020); and Hasan, *Christians versus Muslims in Modern Egypt*, 91.
56. Atiya, *A History of Eastern Christianity*, 121.
57. Van Doorn-Harder, *Copts in Context*, 11.
58. Meinardus, *Two Thousand Years of Coptic Christianity*, 135–136.
59. I saw this mural myself when I visited the cathedral in September 2017.
60. On the liability of foreign connections, see Bernard Heyberger, *Les Chrétiens d'Orient* (Paris: Presses universitaires de France, 2017).
61. Paul VI, *Nostra Aetate: Declaration on the Relation of the Church to Non-Christian Religions* (Rome: The Vatican, 1965).
62. Philip A. Cunningham, *Seeking Shalom: The Journey to Right Relationship between Catholics and Jews* (Grand Rapids: William B. Eerdmans Publishing Company, 2015), 145.
63. Ibid.
64. Heather Sharkey, *American Evangelicals in Egypt*, 208–210; Adīb Najīb Salāma, *al-Injīliyyūn wa-al-'amal al-qawmī: dirāsa tawthīqīyya* (Cairo: Dar al-Thaqāfa, 1993). Salāma focused on the Evangelicals (Presbyterians) but discussed many pronouncements on Arab–Israeli and Palestinian affairs, including overtures to the Vatican, that came from the Egyptian Orthodox, Catholic, and Protestant Churches together.
65. Atiya, *A History of Eastern Christianity*, 120.
66. Akladios, "Ordinary Copts."
67. Ibid.
68. Meinardus, *Two Thousand Years of Coptic Christianity* 129; and Michael Akladios, "Coptic History as Shared History: The Immigrants' Church Encounters Uneven Secularization and Arab Associational Life in Central Canada after 1960." Paper presented at the symposium on Modern Coptic History, University of Pennsylvania, March 2, 2018.
69. Saba Mahmood, *Religious Difference in a Secular Age: A Minority Report* (Princeton: Princeton University Press, 2016), 1; Hussein Ali Agrama, *Questioning Secularism: Islam, Sovereignty, and the Rule of Law in Modern Egypt* (Chicago: University of Chicago Press, 2012).
70. Mariz Tadros, *Copts at the Crossroads: The Challenges of Building Inclusive Democracy in Egypt* (Cairo: American University in Cairo Press, 2013), 15; and Van Doorn-Harder, *Copts in Context*, 12.
71. Elizabeth E. Oram, "Constructing Modern Copts: The Production of Coptic Christian Identity in Contemporary Egypt" (PhD diss., Princeton University, 2004), 64 and elsewhere.
72. Elizabeth Monier, "Sectarianism without Borders: Copts and Genocide Recognition," Middle East Institute, April 24, 2018, http://www.mei.edu/content/map/sectarianism-without-borders-copts-and-genocide-recognition.
73. Akladios, "Ordinary Copts."

74. Laura Robson, "Introduction," in *Minorities and the Modern Arab World*, ed. Laura Robson (Syracuse: Syracuse University Press, 2016), 1–16.
75. Ayalon, "Egypt's Pandora's Box."
76. Van Doorn-Harder, *Copts in Context*, 6.
77. Akladios, "Ordinary Copts."
78. Candace Lukasik has been doing research on newer Coptic immigrants in New York and New Jersey, and their connections to Egypt. See, for example, Candace Lukasik, "Land, Migration, and Memory in an Upper Egyptian Village," June 25, 2017, *Coptic Canadian History Project*, https://thecchp.com/2017/06/25/land-migration-and-memory/ (accessed October 29, 2020).
79. Rachel Loewen, "Strategies of Adaptation for Survival: The Introduction of Converts to the Coptic Orthodox Community in the Greater Toronto Area," in Van Doorn-Harder, *Copts in Context*, 124–133.
80. Christian Youth Channel, "Opening Eporo Tower with H.H. Pope Tawadros II, Melbourne, Victoria," September 11, 2017, https://www.youtube.com/watch?v=5d-vfzhLjok (2 hours 57 minutes).
81. One forum for discussing diasporic Copts vis-à-vis Egypt is the Coptic Canadian History Project, which includes oral histories, reflective essays, and interviews, and more. See https://thecchp.com, accessed August 29, 2018.

Selected Bibliography

Armanios, Febe, *Coptic Christianity in Ottoman Egypt* (Oxford: Oxford University Press, 2011).

Ayalon, Ami, "Egypt's Coptic Pandora's Box," in Ofra Bengio & Gabriel Ben-Dor, eds., *Minorities and the State in the Arab World* (Boulder: Lynne Rienner Publishers, 1999), 53–71.

Van Doorn-Harder, Pieternella, *Contemporary Coptic Nuns* (Columbia: University of South Carolina Press, 1995).

Elsässer, Sebastian, *The Coptic Question in the Mubarak Era* (New York: Oxford University Press, 2014).

Hasan, S.S., *Christians versus Muslims in Modern Egypt: The Century-Long Struggle for Coptic Equality* (Oxford: Oxford University Press, 2003).

Ibrahim, Vivian, *The Copts of Egypt: Challenges of Modernization and Identity* (London: Tauris Academic Studies, 2011).

Meinardus, Otto F.A., *Two Thousand Years of Coptic Christianity* (Cairo: American University in Cairo Press, 2016).

Sharkey, Heather J., *A History of Muslims, Christians, and Jews in the Middle East* (Cambridge: Cambridge University Press, 2017).

Sedra, Paul, *From Mission to Modernity: Evangelicals, Reformers and Education in Nineteenth-Century Egypt* (London: I.B. Tauris, 2011).

Suriel, Girgis (Bishop), *Habib: Coptic Orthodox Educator and a Light in the Darkness* (Yonkers: St. Vladimir's Seminary Press, 2016).

Tadros, Mariz, *Copts at the Crossroads: The Challenges of Building Inclusive Democracy in Egypt* (Cairo: American University in Cairo Press, 2013).

Tzoreff, Mira, "The Copts of Egypt: Fully Fledged Citizens or a New Dhimmi?", in Brandon Friedman and Bruce Maddy-Weitzman, eds., *Inglorious Revolutions: State Cohesion in the Middle East after the Arab Spring* (Tel Aviv: The Moshe Dayan Center, 2014).

Voile, Brigitte, *Les coptes d'Égypte sous Nasser: Sainteté, miracles, apparitions* (Paris: CNRS Éditions, 2004).

Wakin, Edward, *A Lonely Minority: The Modern Story of Egypt's Copts* (New York: William Morrow & Company, 1963).

Egypt: The Inevitable Consequences of Inconsistent Socio-Economic Policies

Onn Winckler

Egypt's Current Economic Challenges

Despite the substantial improvement of the Egyptian economic performance following the implementation of some major structural reforms in 2016 (see Fig. 7.1), Egypt's economy continues to confront major challenges even prior to the onset of the coronavirus pandemic: By the fiscal year (FY) 2018/19, Egypt's debt-to-GDP ratio was as high as 90.2 percent;[1] the fiscal deficit amounted to 8.2 percent of the GDP;[2] the inflation rate, although somewhat decreased, amounted to 14.4 percent (see Fig. 7.2); and the unemployment continued to be in double digit figures. In fact, the unemployment rate among the young age group (15–24) and women amounted to as high as 26 percent and 38 percent, respectively.[3] Egypt's non-energy exports remained comprised of a small number of low-added-value products. Even the huge devaluation of the Egyptian pound (LE) in recent years has not lead to a sharp increase in manufactured and high-tech exports. In the FY2019/20, Egypt's total non-oil and gas exports amounted to a mere $16.9 billion,[4] while high-tech products represent less than 1 percent of Egypt's total exports.[5] During the 2011–2019 period, Egypt's per capita GDP increased by a mere 14.2 percent in real terms (see Fig. 7.1). Overall, in 2019, Egypt was ranked 116th among 188 countries listed in the HDI (Human Development Index),[6] declining from the 112 rank in 2012.[7] The only sector that markedly grew in recent years was the tourism industry.

However, the fact is that Egypt has major rental income sources,[8] the most prominent being:

(a) **Socio-demographic rents** in the form of a homogenous population with Arabs constituting the entire of Egypt's population and about 93–95 percent being Sunni-Muslims.[9] In the case of the Arab countries, it appears, none of the ethno-religious heterogeneous countries have succeeded in surviving and all of them, without exception, deteriorated into prolonged civil wars. In Syria, Iraq, Yemen,

Figure 7.1: Egypt's real GDP growth rate, 1961–2019 (%)

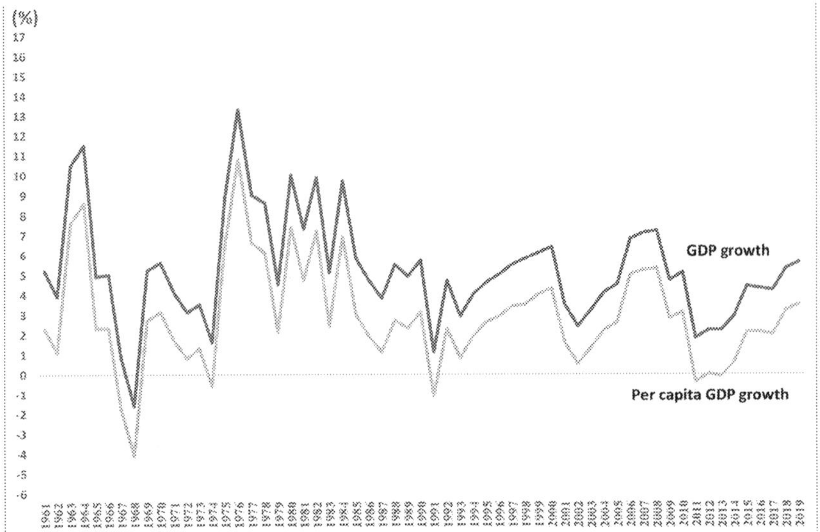

Source: World Bank, *World Development Indicators.*

Figure 7.2: Egypt's inflation rate (consumer prices), 1961–2018 (%)

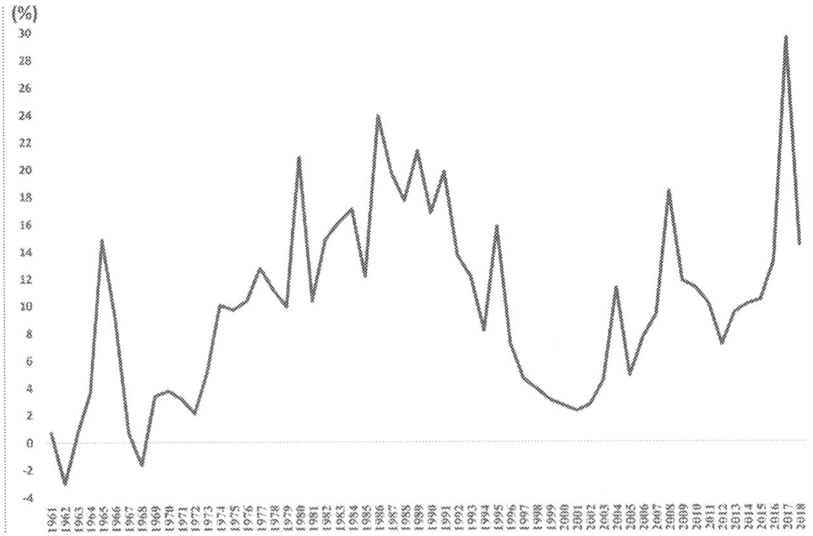

Source: World Bank, *World Development Indicators.*

Bahrain, and Lebanon, religious heterogeneity has constituted the main reason for political instability since their establishment.

(b) **Economic rents** in the form of fossil rent (oil and gas); the Suez Canal; a substantial amount of water from the Nile River; geographical location; and vast numbers of natural tourist attractions. During the 2015–2019 period, Egypt's net revenues from the Suez Canal amounted to $27.2 billion.[10] Egypt's proven hydrocarbon reserves at the end of 2015 stood at 4.4 billion barrels of oil and 77.2 trillion cubic feet (tcf) of natural gas. In 2017, Egypt's petroleum and other liquids production averaged 666,000 b/d (barrel per day).[11]

(c) **Geostrategic rent**. Since the 1950s, Egypt benefited from geostrategic rent in the form of massive foreign aid, first from the Soviet Union and the USA, then later from the Arab oil countries and the USA Since the collapse of Mubarak's regime, the financial aid has come mainly from the Arabian Gulf oil countries and the USA Overall, during the 2011–2019 period, the Arabian Gulf oil countries provided Egypt with $92 billion in the forms of cash grants and loans.[12] In addition, Egypt received massive cash inflows from the USA, amounting to $1.4 billion annually during the 2016–2020 period, approximately 90 percent of which was military aid.[13] Overall, since 1946 and until 2020, the US aid to Egypt amounted to $84.2 billion.[14] Lastly, Egypt received huge loans from the IMF; the latest one, $12 billion, was in November 2016.

What Went Wrong?

If such is the case, what has brought Egypt to its current dismal economic situation?

My basic argument is that since the Nasserist period, the Egyptian authorities chose the right policies, in both the demographic and economic arenas, but failed to implement them effectively. Thus, Egypt's current economic situation is not the result of bad choices or civil wars, as is the case in Syria and Yemen, for example, but due purely to the "soft" nature of all the regimes, including that of al-Sisi. It appears that Gad Gilbar's description of the Nasserist regime as a "soft revolution,"[15] is correct regarding all of his successors as well.

Sadat's cancellation of subsidy cuts on basic food products following the "food riots" of January 1977, and Mubarak's refusal in 1987 to cut food and energy subsidies again were typical of the overall soft nature of their regimes. One explanation for their soft nature may be found in Paul Rivlin's observation that "the [Egyptian] regime did not see economic success as vital to its survival."[16] In retrospect, however, it appears that Mubarak's and Mursi's regimes collapsed precisely on economic grounds. Their collapse was caused neither by the Arab–Israeli conflict, nor by "the conflict with the West"; rather, in both regimes, the cause was, above all, the uprising of the educated and frustrated young middle class.[17]

The following section of this chapter briefly examines Egypt's natalist and macroeconomic policies and their implementation from the Nasserite period until the collapse of Mubarak's regime; next it will focus on al-Sisi policies on these two issues; and will conclude by examining the changes that Egypt must undertake in order to recover from its current severe socio-economic situation.

The Correct but Indecisive Natalist Policy

The first Arab leader to become aware of the devastating long-term consequences of rapid population growth was 'Abd al-Nasser, as early as 1953, with the established a parliamentary committee for population matters.[18] At that time, the new regime began to deal with demography from two directions: first, to encourage emigration of rural population from Egypt to other Arab countries;[19] and second, to establish experimental family planning clinics.[20] Additionally, a voluntary family planning association, the Egyptian Association for Population Studies, was established in 1953.[21]

Despite this awareness, however, Egypt adopted an official national family planning program only 13 years later, in 1966.[22] Meanwhile, Egypt's population increased from 23 million in 1953 to almost 33 million in 1966 (see Fig. 7.3), while the crude birth rate (CBR) remained stable at the rate of 42–43 per 1,000 people. It should be noted, however, that neglecting the family planning issue for such a long period led to a higher natural increase rate (NIR), which increased from 2.3 percent in 1953 to 2.8 percent in 1966, due to the steady decline of the crude death rate (CDR) (see Fig. 7.4).

Indeed, as one can see in Figure 7.4, during the second half of the 1960s and the early 1970s, Egypt's fertility rate went down substantially. However, it appears that this was brought about not by the national family planning program, but by the economic hardships following the June 1967 War, the War of Attrition (1969–1970), and the October 1973 War.[23] Since 1975, with the improvement of the economic and security situations, Egypt's fertility rates increased again to its level prior to the implementation of the national family planning program. By 1979, Egypt's CBR was similar to that of 1966 (see Fig. 7.4).

Figure 7.3: Egypt's population, 1897–2050 (de facto population, thousands)

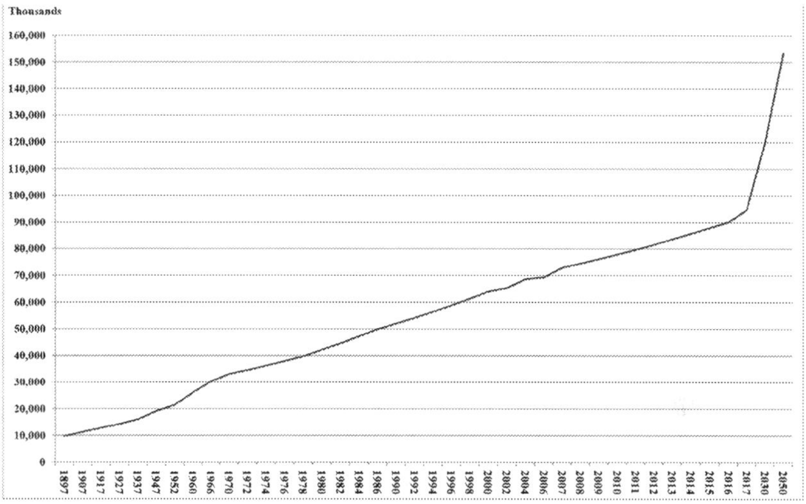

Sources: Egypt, CAPMAS (Central Agency for Public Mobilization and Statistics), *Statistical Yearbook*, various Issues (Cairo); UN, Department of Economic and Social Affairs, Population Division, *World Population Prospects-2019 Revision*.

Figure 7.4: Egypt's natural increase rate, 1907–2019

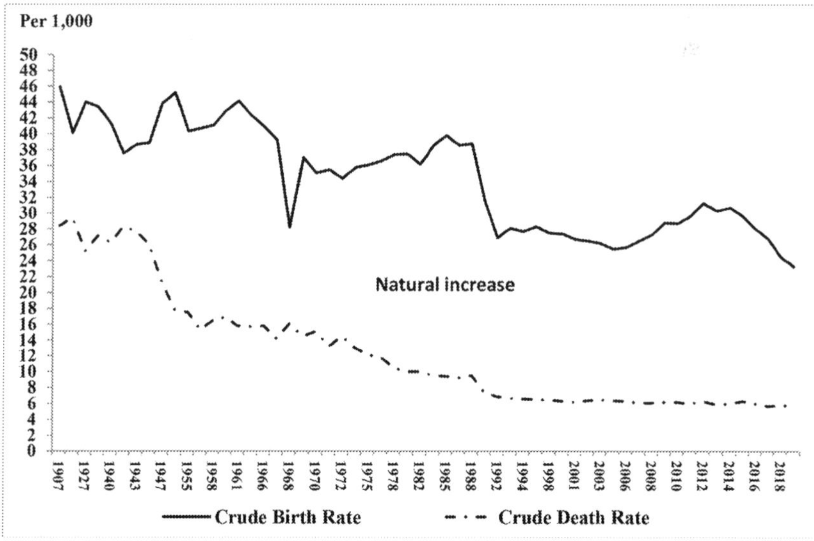

Sources: CAPMAS, *Statistical Yearbook*, various Issues (Cairo); UN, Department of Economic and Social Affairs, *Demographic Yearbook*, various issues (New York); A.M. Abdelghany, "Evaluating the Application of the Stable Population Model of the Population of Egypt", *Population Bulletin of ECWA*, 21 (December 1981), 109, Table 3; Robert Mabro, *The Egyptian Economy, 1952–1972* (Oxford: Clarendon Press, 1974), 29, Table 2.2; and James Coyle and John Parker, *Urbanization and Agricultural Policy in Egypt* (Washington, DC, Agriculture Department, 1981), 8, Table 4.

Although Sadat was fully aware of the devastating consequences of the rapid population growth, "he hardly paid any attention to the [demographic] problem," as noted by Saad Eddin Ibrahim.[24] Thomas Lippman noted that: "Sadat and his prime ministers hardly even gave lip service to birth control."[25] Gilbar explained that Sadat's limited action in the area of family planning stemmed from his fear of confronting the Muslim Brotherhood.[26] Whatever the reason, the result was the same: awareness but no action.

In his first four years in power, Mubarak too did almost nothing to curb the high fertility rate.[27] Thus, in 1985, almost 20 years after the adoption of the first national family planning program and more than three decades after the recognition of the demographic problem, Egypt's NIR peaked at more than 3 percent—higher than ever before (see Fig. 7.4). Only in 1985, with the end of the "oil decade," the National Population Council was established, headed by Mubarak himself. A year later, in 1986, a new family planning program was announced with the aim of reducing the NIR from 2.8 percent in 1986 to 2.1 percent in 2001.[28] In contrast to the previous program, this program was indeed effective: The total fertility rate (TFR) declined from 4.9 children per woman in 1983–1984 to 3.6 in 1993–1995.[29] In November 2001, the Egyptian government adopted a new long-term demographic strategy aiming to reduce the TFR to replacement level by 2017.[30] In retrospect, this policy totally failed. From the mid-1990s until the collapse of Mubarak's regime, Egypt's TFR remained the same: 3.3–3.5 children per woman.

The ascendancy of al-Sisi to power in July 2013 represents a turning point in Egypt's natalist policy. In contrast to his predecessor, Mursi, al-Sisi admitted publically as early as 2014 that: "increasing population is one of Egypt's main problems."[31] In the National Youth Conference, held in Alexandria in July 2017, he declared that: "overpopulation and terrorism are Egypt's real two threats."[32] Indeed, in June 2015, the National Population Strategy for the 2015–2030 period was initiated, aiming to reduce the TFR to 2.4 in 2030.[33] This aim would be achieved through providing governmental financial incentives to keep children in school, expanding family planning services, and boosting public awareness of the benefits of small families.[34] In 2019, Egypt launched a public campaign—"two is enough." In order to convince the population to practice modern contraception, the Egyptian authorities recruited the top religious clerics to the campaign.[35] Indeed, in recent years, Egypt's fertility rate somewhat declined and reached 3.1 in 2018 as compared to 3.5 in 2014.[36] Nominally, the number of births in Egypt declined from the peak of 2.685 million in 2015—higher than ever before—to 2.305 million in 2019.[37]

It should be noted, however, that although under al-Sisi regime the issue of family planning receives much higher attention compared to Mursi period's, it still remains at the "margin" of the overall socio-economic discourse. A prominent sign for the marginality of the issue is that in the IMF reports on Egypt, even in recent years, the demographic issue as a whole and the necessity of reducing the current high fertility rate in particularly was not mentioned at all.[38]

Hence, by 2018, Egypt's CBR was far above the prevailing rate in Turkey, Iran, Brazil, and South Korea; in all of them the CBR had been similar, or even higher, than in Egypt in the early 1960s (see Fig. 7.5). Thus, after almost six decades of national family planning programs, Egypt's fertility rate is still far from the targeted replacement level (2.1 children per woman).

Figure 7.5: CBR of Egypt, Iran, Turkey, Brazil, Mexico, and South Korea, 1960–2018

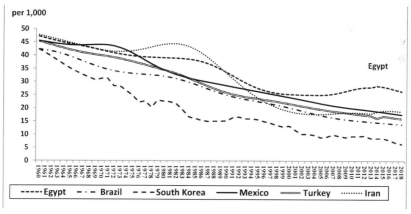

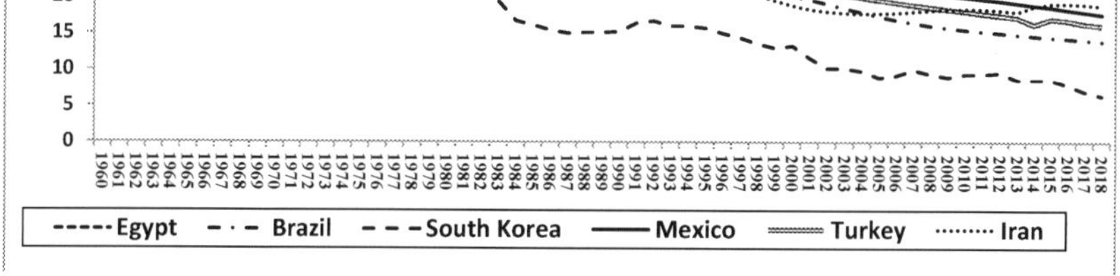

Source: World Bank, *World Development Indicators.*

A prominent characteristic of the low priority of the demographic issue is the lack of enforcement of Egypt's laws regarding the minimum age for women's first marriage (18 years). Thus, marriages of under-aged girls, and consequently births of mothers below the age of 18, are still commonplace in Egypt, mainly in the rural areas. The Minister of Population, Hala Youssef, announced in July 2015 that about 15 percent of all marriages in Egypt are child marriages.[39] It is therefore not surprising that, according to the data revealed in the Egypt Demographic and Health Survey of 2014, the age-specific fertility rate for the age group of 15–19 was 79 per 1,000 women in Upper Egypt's rural areas and 71 in the rural areas of Lower Egypt.[40] Thus, the policy was correct, the laws existed, but the problem was, and still is, the lack of enforcement.

The failure of the Egyptian authorities to curb the high fertility rate led to other economic failures, mainly the inability to lower the country's huge subsidies bill for foodstuff and energy products. By the FY2009/2010, the governmental expenditure on subsidies of energy products alone amounted to $12.3 billion.[41] Overall, during the 2001–2011 years, the subsidies bill on basic energy and foodstuff products accounted for more than 20 percent of total governmental expenditures.[42] However, even this did not suffice to maintain the prices of the basic food and energy products. Although under al-Sisi's regime the subsidies, mainly on energy products, were largely reduced, the subsidy bill continued to be a heavy burden on the governmental budget, amounting to $3.18 billion in the FY2018/19.[43]

The inescapable result was high inflation. By 2006, inflation in Egypt amounted to 7.6 percent; it rose to 9.3 percent in 2007, 18.3 percent in 2008, and fell to 11.8 percent in 2009 due to decreasing oil prices in the first few months of that year. As Hazem Kandil said regarding the decade prior to the collapse of Mubarak's regime, the standard of living for almost all Egyptians was getting progressively worse.[44] This situation only deteriorated since the onset of al-Sisi regime with the inflation rate accelerating and peaking at almost 30 percent in 2017 (see Fig. 7.2).

Erratic Economic Development: Up and Down

With regard to Egypt's economic policies and performances, it seems that the observation of "right policy, poor performance" applies in the same way as in the natalist policy arena. Robert Tignor described Egypt's economic situation on the eve of the Free Officers seizing power as follows:

> Corruption, bad financial policies, and the cotton speculation crisis of 1951–1952 had brought the country to "the shadow of catastrophe." The country had an unparalleled budget deficit [...]. The government's financial reserves were near exhaustion.[45]

The Free Officers' main socio-economic goals were poverty reduction, narrowing the huge economic gaps, and the establishment of an industrial base that could transform Egypt into a modern socialist industrialized country. The only available option to achieve these targets, under the socio-economic-political structure of Egypt at that time, was to adopt a state-led economy. This kind of policy, it should be noted, was very common in developing countries worldwide at that time.[46] The practical expression of the Free Officers' socio-economic policy was the First Five-Year Plan, covering the 1960–1965 period. At first glance, its achievements were impressive: The GDP growth rate skyrocketed during the first half of the 1960s (see Fig. 7.1); more than one million jobs were added;[47] and the healthcare and the educational systems were largely improved, as manifested by the steady decline of the CDR (see Fig. 7.4) and the sharp rise of the literacy rate, especially among the young generation.[48] Overall, it seemed that the Egyptian economy was on the right track.

However, only one year later, in 1966, the Egyptian government proved incapable of implementing the Second Five-Year Plan, 1966–1970, and the economy deteriorated again into a severe recession, which led to a negative per capita growth rate. About this period, Galal Amin noted that: "Egypt witnessed one of the bleakest periods in its modern history."[49] The economic recession continued throughout the late 1960s and early 1970s (see Fig. 7.1).

A major reason for this prolonged recession was Egypt's huge military expenditures, which skyrocketed during the 1964–1974 decade (see Fig. 7.6). Thus, after more than two decades of a revolutionary regime, Egypt was "back to square one" with a severe recession in addition ongoing high fertility rates.

Figure 7.6: Egypt's military expenditures, 1960–2019 (% of GDP)

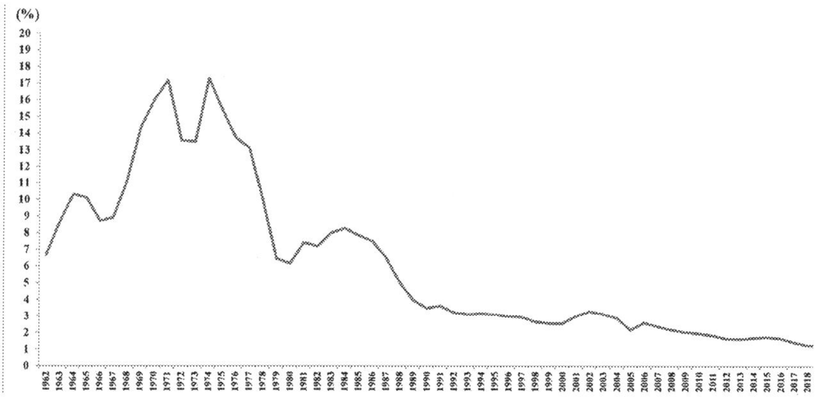

Source: World Bank, *World Development Indicators.*

In October 1974, Sadat initiated a new macroeconomic policy—the *infitāḥ* (the open-door policy)—which was supported by the IMF. Its aim was to attract private investments, both foreign and local, in order to transform Egypt from a state-led economy to a more market-led one. Indeed, the decade ahead was a "bonanza period" for the Egyptian economy, with an average annual GDP growth rate of almost 10 percent (see Fig. 7.1).

However, the rapid expansion of the country's economy during the "bonanza oil decade" was not the result of the *infitāḥ* itself, but rather Egypt's vast rental incomes: workers' remittances, which skyrocketed in the early 1980s,[50] when the number of Egyptian workers in other Arab countries peaked at more than 3 million;[51] the increasing revenues from oil exports, which peaked at more than $3 billion in 1981 as compared to only $45 million in 1972;[52] the high revenues from the Suez Canal, which reopened in 1975; and lastly, massive financial aid from the Arab oil countries until 1978, and since then from the USA.

However, despite the rapid economic expansion, the basic characteristics of the Egyptian economy remained as it had previously been with only limited changes. Hence, despite the adoption of the market-led approach, the public sector remained the major employer of the urban workforce. During the 1976–1986 decade, 44 percent of the new entrants into the workforce were absorbed into the public sector and an additional 19 percent in public enterprises. In the early 1980s, 28 percent of the total Egyptian workforce was employed directly by the public sector,[53] an extremely high percentage considering that 15 percent of the Egyptian workforce at that time was working abroad and another 35 percent was working in agriculture. Thus, in terms of the labor market, the *infitāḥ* did not contribute much to expanding private sector employment.

As regard to foreign investments, in practice, only a small amount actually came through: in mid-1982, almost eight years following the launch of the *infitāḥ* policy, Arab investments in Egypt totaled less than $600 million.[54] This low scale of foreign investments in Egypt at the time can be attributed to the government's lack of encouragement. Khalid Ikram noted that the reason for the low scale foreign investments in Egypt was that only a "few ancillary actions were taken [by the government] to buttress the new approach [...]. There was an absence of policies that would have increased competiveness."[55] Galal Amin commented on Sadat's overall economic performance:

> Sadat left a huge foreign debt, the likes of which Egypt had not seen before, not even in the days of Khedive Ismail [...]. He also left a high rate of inflation, which was unprecedented in Egypt's modern history [...].[56]

Hence, not only did Sadat fail to utilize the "oil decade" to solve at least some of Egypt's major structural macroeconomic problems, he maintained the high subsidies that had existed previously and absorbed an enormous number of new employees in the public sector. An OECD report noted regarding the rapid growth of the Egyptian economy during the "oil decade" that it only "masked Egypt's structural weaknesses."[57]

Indeed, with the sharp decline of oil prices in the mid-1980s,[58] the Egyptian economy again found itself in a severe recession. In early 1987, Egypt's external debt was extremely high—equal to the total GDP—while its current account deficit amounted to 8 percent of the GDP which led, as observed in an IMF report, to "an inability to service external debt obligations."[59]

The economic recession was naturally manifested by higher unemployment. The 1986 census put the unemployment rate at 14 percent,[60] although unofficial estimates put the rate in 1988 as high as 20 percent.[61] Besides the recession, the major factor behind Egypt's unemployment jump-off was the inability of the public sector to continue to absorb a considerable number of young newcomers to the workforce.[62] The socio-economic situation had become unsustainable with stagnation of per capita GDP growth (see Fig. 7.1).

This severe recession confirmed that the Egyptian authorities had missed the opportunity of the "oil decade" to transform the economy from a *rentier*-based one to one based on exports. As Riad El-Ghonemy puts it: "One wonders about the [the Egyptian] government's missed opportunity to use its high share in oil and gas export [...] in order to balance the economy."[63] In sum, the oil decade turned out to be a lost decade in both the demographic and macroeconomic arenas.

Under these conditions, the Egyptian authorities had no choice but to conclude an agreement with the IMF, signed in May 1987, for a new loan. In exchange for a loan of $327 million, the Egyptian authorities were obligated to implement a gradual devaluation of the LE; to lower the subsidies on basic energy and foodstuff products; and to narrow the budgetary deficit.[64] This was the second *infitāḥ*.

Although no doubt crucial, these reforms were not sufficient to revive the Egyptian economy. A close examination of the Egyptian economic structure in the late 1980s reveals that almost nothing changed. Egypt continued to be a *rentier* economy with its major sources of hard currency continuing to be oil exports, workers' remittances, revenues from the Suez Canal, and tourism. However, due to the decline in all of these *rentier* sources as a result of the decline in oil prices, the dependence on loans and foreign aid steadily increased. By the late 1980s, Egypt's current account deficit had reached 8 percent of the GDP, while the inflation rate had exceeded 20 percent.[65] In the mid-1990, Egypt's total external debt amounted to $47.6 billion (in current prices), equivalent to 150 percent of its GDP, making Egypt's external debt burden one of the highest worldwide. In 1991, the budget deficit reached 15.3 percent of the GDP,[66] and the inflation rate amounted to almost 20 percent (see Fig. 7.2).

Again, as in 1987, the Egyptian government had no choice but to adopt a third *infitāḥ*—the Economic and Structural Adjustment Program—which included privatization of 314 public sector factories and enterprises, liberalization of the financial sector, and removal of the governmental price supervision on many goods.[67] The privatization process was accelerated in 1993. These reforms were combined with sizable external assistance, first and foremost new loans from the IMF and the World Bank;[68] debt relief from Arab and Western countries following Egypt's support of the anti-Iraqi coalition in the Kuwaiti crisis of 1990–1991;[69] a massive increase in the number of Egyptian workers in the Arabian Gulf oil countries at the expense of Jordanian, Palestinian, Sudanese, and Yemenite workers;[70] recovery of the tourism industry;[71] and lastly, the overall feeling that the Arab–Israeli conflict, which was considered one of the main barriers for economic prosperity in the whole Middle East, was close to end. The general feeling was that the reforms and the major improvement of the economic environment, the result of the Middle East peace process on the one hand and the substantial fertility decline on the other, would pave a new course for the Egyptian economy. Thus, for example, an IMF report on the Egyptian economy from September 1997 opened as follows:

> Egypt is well embarked on a reform effort aimed at placing the economy on a higher growth trajectory that would durably raise living standards, reverse the rising tide of unemployment, reduce the level of poverty, and facilitate Egypt's accelerated integration in the world economy […]. This effort produced a remarkable turn-around in Egypt's macroeconomic fortunes.[72]

This positive opinion on the performance of the Egyptian economy continued during the early 2000s as well. Thus, for example, Samir Radwan noted in 2003:

> There is a growing consensus in professional circles, as well as in the press, that Egypt's potential for economic take-off has never been better […]. The economic stabilization programs adopted in the early 1990s have achieved most of their objectives, and there has been turn-around in growth performance […].[73]

Indeed, from 1992 until 2010, Egypt succeeded in achieving a solid GDP growth rate, even in per capita terms. By 2010, on the eve of Mubarak's collapse, the Egyptian economy performed better than ever before, with the sole exception of the "bonanza oil decade." Even in 2008 and 2009—at the height of the global recession—the Egyptian economy did not suffer from recession but actually reached a remarkable GDP growth rate of 7.2 percent in 2008 and 4.7 percent in 2009 (see Fig. 7.1).

However, it appeared that the Egyptian youth wanted more than solid growth. They wanted solid employment as well in line with the "authoritarian social bargain" that had ruled the Egyptian politics since the 1960s.[74] And on that particular issue, namely, increasing employment opportunities to the educated young, the Egyptian authorities had largely failed. Thus, as correctly described by the ESCWA report on the Arab middle class:

> [...] opportunities for decent employment were curtailed after the implementation of structural adjustment programs and a general freeze on public sector recruitment in the 1990s. The private sector could not fill this void, leading to the proliferation of informal jobs, mainly in low value-added service sectors.[75]

The reason for the limited scope of private sector employment during the first decade of the twenty-first century was the inefficiency of non-energy related industries. In retrospect, the only period in which these industries achieved high growth rates in Egypt was during the first half of the 1960s. That rapid industrial expansion, however, was due to the public sector industries which enjoyed both governmental protection and large-scale subsidies.

Egypt failed, however, in the second phase of industrialization: to transform its non-energy related industries from ISI (import substitution industrialization) to export-led which would have been capable of competing in international markets. The disconnect between the Egyptian industry and global industrial developments for more than three decades, from the early 1960s until the early 1990s, it appears, led to the creation of a too large technological gap that it could no longer be bridged. Only huge import duties, negative real interest rates, an artificial exchange rate, and above all subsidized energy prices maintained the traditional Egyptian ISI industries, such as transport equipment.[76] These industries, however, as Sabry Aglan pointed out, were "inefficient and internationally uncompetitive, with low-quality products, low productivity of labor, and high costs of production."[77]

The failure of the Egyptian non-oil industries was manifested, first and foremost, by the almost total absence of medium-sized and large competitive-innovative firms producing non-oil related tradable products which could hold their own in international markets.[78] In all the emerging markets worldwide, these companies led to overall economic development. This the case in India, for example, with the high-tech industry; in Romania and Turkey with the automobile industry; and so forth. Lacking these kinds of companies, left the Egyptian economy without any growth engine other than low-tech tourism products and *rentier* sources, mainly workers' remittances and Suez Canal revenues. This is best illustrated by the composition of the Egyptian export: by the FY2009/10, Egypt's non-oil exports totaled only $10 billion.[79]

Moreover, jobs in the service sector remained at the lower end of the value chain, given that Egypt had not kept pace with the development of information technology and financial services.[80] Hence, the Egyptian non-oil related industry had become irrelevant in terms of enhancing macroeconomic development or providing a major source of employment, particularly for the educated young.

The failure of the Egyptian economy to promote export-led sectors other than tourism on the one hand, and the huge number of higher education graduates on the other, created an "alleged middle class." Thus, while in the developed economies the middle class shaped the state's socio-economic and political nature, in Egypt, as in the other Arab countries, the regime "invented" a middle class. This middle class survived as long as the state was able to finance its lifestyle. Hence, while in the emerging and industrial economies the middle class is the largest taxpayer, in Egypt the middle class is the largest consumer of the state budget through public sector employment and subsidies. With a near absence of export-led industries and services, the contribution of the Egyptian middle class to the economic development was marginal.

Consequently, although during the first decade of the twenty-first century the Egyptian economy expanded by as much as 5 percent on annual average (see Fig. 7.1), the fruits of this rapid growth did not "trickle down" to the middle and the lower classes. Thus, Egypt's economic inequality steadily increased and consequently so did the poverty rate which increased from 16.7 percent in 2000 to 25.2 percent in 2011. In the rural areas of Upper Egypt, the poverty rate in 2011 amounted to as high as 60 percent.[81]

The Egyptian Economy Following the Collapse of Mubarak's Regime

The collapse of Mubarak's regime had devastating consequences on the Egyptian economy. As one can see in Figure 7.1, Egypt's GDP growth rate deteriorated from 5.1 percent in 2010 to a little more than 2 percent in the four years that followed, bringing the annual per capita GDP growth rate to less than 1 percent. This severe recession was caused by the deterioration of both the security and the political situations, which harmed the tourism industry—the main engine of the Egyptian economy in the decade prior to Mubarak's ouster. By 2015, the number of tourists in Egypt was 9.3 million, compared to 14.7 million in 2010, a decline of 37 percent.[82] The number of tourist hotel nights went down from 147.4 million to 89.2 million during the corresponding period.[83] The overall tourism revenues decreased from $12.5 billion in 2010[84] to only $3.8 billion in 2016—a mere 2 percent of the GDP.[85]

In 2016, three years after al-Sisi seized power, the Sustainable Development Strategy was adopted, aiming to boost the economic performances. The two paramount long-term aims of the program were to achieve an annual GDP growth of 5.5–6 percent and reduce the unemployment rate to 10–11 percent.[86] Indeed, from 2017 and until the onset of the coronavirus pandemic, the Egyptian economy rapidly recovered due mainly to: the $12.5 billion loan form the IMF; the substantial cut in subsidies, mainly on energy products; the rapid recovery of the tourism sector with revenues of $13 billion in 2019—higher than ever before;[87] and lately, the surge in the number of Egyptian workers abroad which peaked at approximately 10 million (about half of them in the Arabian Gulf oil countries) in early 2020.[88] The GDP increased accordingly, from a mere 2.9 percent in 2014, namely, almost stagnation in per capita terms, to 4.3 percent in 2016 and a peak of 5.6 percent in 2019 (see Fig. 7.1).

The coronavirus pandemic hit the Egyptian economy as all other worldwide economies. Although due to the young age pyramid, the number of deaths in Egypt is thus far very small—7,741 until the end of 2020[89]—the pandemic caused severe economic damages, as it hurt Egypt's three major sources of foreign currency: the tourism industry, the workers' remittances, and the Suez Canal revenues. In the last quarter of the FY2019/20 (April–June 2020), Egypt's GDP shrunk by 8.7 percent.[90] Later, following the emergency response package of LE100 billion (1.7 percent of the GDP), the Egyptian economy somewhat recovered.[91] Overall, according to a preliminary estimate of the *Economist*, Egypt's economy contracted by 3.5 percent in 2020, namely, a decline of more than 5 percent in per capita terms.[92]

Summary and Conclusions: Egypt's Dire Economic Future

According to the September 2017 census, Egypt's (de facto) population measured 94.8 million.[93] By the end of March 2021, Egypt's de facto population numbered 101.7 million, representing a monthly net increase of about 165,000.[94] The current extremely high natural increase rate of more than 2 percent annually indicates a rapid population growth in the near future as well. Hence, Egypt's population is expected to number about 154 million in 2050 (see Fig. 7.3). This means that during the first half of the twenty-first century Egypt's population is expected to increase by more than 80 million!

The most prominent problem of Egypt's demography is that the ideal number of children of the Egyptian women is 3.1—much above the replacement level. Even among women who completed at least a secondary education, the ideal number of children is 3.0.[95] Hence, Egypt's core demographic problem is not insufficient family planning services—which could be overcome by upgrading services—but the attitude of the Egyptian women, even the educated ones, who want a large number of children.

No doubt, Egypt's economic performances have largely improved since the ascendancy of al-Sisi. The question remains, however, "is it enough"? Thus far, since al-Sisi came to power, Egypt's population has witnessed a steadily deteriorating living standard due to accelerated inflation. Also, the unemployment rate has remained extremely high, particularly among the educated young. The political impact of prolonged youth unemployment means an unstable political system. The "huge army" of unemployed educated youth, al-Sisi has to remember, has already defeated two regimes: that of Mubarak and that of Mursi. In November 2017, the IMF staff emphasized that:

> Reducing unemployment, specifically among Egypt's youth, and integrating more women into the labor force are key to Egypt's economic liftoff and are the strongest and most sustainable form of social protection.[96]

Is it not clear that Egypt had to reduce unemployment, "specifically among Egypt's youth"? Is it not clear that Egypt had to "integrate more women into the labor force"? The problem with the IMF and the professionals in Egypt's various ministries as well as the academicians is that they have continued to identify the same problems of the Egyptian economy and to offer the same "solutions." There is nothing new in the demographic arena either. As early as 1936, Wendell Cleland published a book titled *The Population Problem in Egypt*. To declare in the late 2010s that the Egyptian economy must create "sufficient employment opportunities for its educated youth" is like saying to a hungry person, after a close examination and in-depth research the professional conclusion is that you must eat in order to survive. However, there appears to be no answer to the core question of how to get sufficient food for the rapidly growing population; or, in Egypt's case, how to create at least 800,000 new real employment opportunities in the private sector on an annual basis.

Thus far, however, neither the IMF, the World Bank, nor other professional lending groups or academicians have dealt with the basic, long-term problems of the Egyptian economy: its rapid population growth and the technological shortcomings of the non-oil industries and services. Almost without exception, all of the reports on the Egyptian economy concentrated on surface reforms only, namely, the trade regime, the scale of the subsidies, and short-term public sector debt services. Their assumption was, and largely remains until present day, that if the Egyptian economy grows by at least twice the population growth rate it will eventually avoid falling again into a deep recession.

Therefore, the three most prominent indicators used to measure the performance of the Egyptian economy are the GDP growth rate, the scale of subsidies on basic foodstuff and energy products and the share the debt services require of the government's total expenditures. If the Egyptian economy achieves progress in these three areas, its economy is projected to function well. For example, in a 2009 report on the Egyptian economy—at the peak of the global economic recession when the majority of countries worldwide were suffering from negative GDP growth—the IMF projected that Egypt's GDP growth rate would be extremely high, 7.0 percent in the FY2010/11, with only a slight decline to 6.5 percent the following two years.[97] In reality, however, the GDP growth rate during these three years was less than a third of the IMF's forecast.

The 2011 revolution proved beyond any doubt that these three indicators are not enough to preserve a stable regime. The Egyptian economic problems, it appears, are much deeper and its recovery, if possible at all due to the combined results of the rapid population growth and the coronavirus pandemic damages, should be found in areas that have thus far not received attention either from the IMF and other international lending institutions or from the academics.

The real solution to Egypt's socio-economic problems, it seems, lies in enforcing the legal marriage age for girls throughout Egypt in order to reduce the current extremely high fertility rate, particularly in the rural areas. Another important step is to promote gender equality in all aspects of life,[98] first and foremost increasing women's low labor force participation rate.[99] Personal tax revenues should be increased and subsidies should be limited only to those who need them, not to the entire population.[100] The army's involvement in the economy as an independent entity should be stopped, and military expense should be massively reduced. Public sector corruption should be eradicated, and all laws everywhere within the Egyptian territory, including the most remote areas, should be enforced. These uncompromising necessities, however, are nowhere to be found in the current Egyptian plans.

Overstaffing of the public sector was a primary cause of Egypt's failure to bring about real socio-economic change since Sadat's first *infitāḥ*. Because the public sector has become the foundation stone of the revolutionary regime, it has become so bloated that it is currently too big to allow any real reforms. In the FY2015/16, the number of public sector employees was 5.77 million.[101] Nobody can monitor the performance of so many employees. Already Sadat realized that an enormous public sector is a barrier to implement any kind of reforms. However, despite his call in May 1977 for an "administrative revolution" in order to implementing the *infitāḥ* policy,[102] neither Sadat himself nor his successors carried it out. Rather, the Egyptian public sector steadily continued to expand and since the 1970s has become the shock absorber for the surplus urban workforce, first and foremost for the educated young.

Also, in the area of family planning, the foundation of al-Sisi's current policy is the same as it was under Mubarak's regime, namely, a policy that does not include positive or negative economic incentives for small families. Hence, Egypt's natalist policy was and still is very soft despite the fact that the experience of six decades of this kind of policy is that it is not sufficient to bring about radical fertility decline.

Thus, especially following the onset of the coronavirus pandemic, the Egyptian economy is delicate again. The financial assistance of the Arabian Gulf oil countries is expected to decline eventually, or at least not to increase, due to low oil export revenues since 2015. The USA cannot be expected to increase financial assistance to Egypt much, if at all. And last, because the Arabian Gulf oil countries prefer non-Arab workers, the jobs available for Egyptians there are not likely to become more plentiful.

In his famous book, *The Egypt of Nasser and Sadat,* John Waterbury noted about the July 1952 revolution that: "A revolution, like any other form of politics, is made with people. To some degree, Egypt's [July 1952] revolution was made because of too many people."[103] This observation is true also regarding the January 2011 revolution, al-Sisi's *coup d'état* of July 2013, and perhaps the next one too which will come sooner or later if the living standard of the young, educated, and frustratingly unemployed middle class does not substantially improve.

Notes

1. The World Bank, *Egypt's Overview*, October 1, 2020.
2. *Reuters*, July 29, 2020.
3. African Development Bank, *Egypt Economic Outlook-2020*.
4. IMF, *Arab Republic of Egypt*, IMF country report no. 20/271 (September 2020), 13, Table 2a.
5. OECD, *Compact for Economic Governance: Stocktaking Report: Egypt* (Paris, 2019), 24.
6. The HDI is an integrated statistical index that includes many parameters in three categories: health, education, and per capita income (in PPP terms). It aims at ranking countries worldwide according to their socio-economic situation and the quality of life of their citizens. The index was established in 1990. See United Nations Development Programme (UNDP), *Human Development Report-2020* (New York, 2020), 344, Table 1. On the index itself, see Elizabeth A. Stanton, "The Human Development Index: A History", PERI Working Papers Series no. 127 (February 2007).
7. UNDP, *Human Development Report-2013* (New York, 2013), 145, Table 1.
8. The term rental income, drawn by Adam Smith and later further developed by David Ricardo, relates to "income derived from the gift of nature."
9. Minority Rights Group International, "Copts in Egypt" [https://minorityrights.org/minorities/copts].
10. *Reuters*, August 6, 2020.
11. U.S. Energy Information Administration (EIA), *Egypt* [updated May 24, 2018].
12. Michele Dunne, "Egypt: Looking Elsewhere to Meet Bottomless Needs," Carnegie Endowment for International Peace, June 9, 2020.
13. Jeremy M. Sharp, *Egypt: Background and U.S. Relations*, Congressional Research Services (May 27, 2020), 24, Table 2.
14. Current prices, not adjusted for inflation. See Ibid., 29–31, Table A-1.
15. Gad G. Gilbar, "Nasser's Soft Revolution," in his *Population Dilemmas in the Middle East* (London: Frank Cass, 1997), 80–96.
16. Paul Rivlin, *Arab Economies in the Twenty-First Century* (Cambridge: Cambridge University Press, 2009), 126–127.
17. For the definition of the Arab middle class, see ESCWA, *Arab Middle Class: Measurement and Role in Driving Change* (Beirut, 2014), 15, 29–49.
18. Ayman G. Zohry, "Population Policies and Family Planning Program in Egypt: Evolution and Performance," in *CDC 26th Annual Seminar on Population Issues in the Middle East, Africa and Asia-1997* (Cairo, 1997), 194.
19. Azriel Karni, "*Temurot be-Yahas la-Piquah 'al ha-Yeluda ba-Mizrah ha-Tikhon*" [Trends in Fertility Control in the Middle East], *Hamizrah Hehadash* 17 (1967), 231 (Hebrew).
20. J. Mayone Stycos et al., *Community Development and Family Planning: An Egyptian Experiment* (Boulder: Westview Press, 1988), 14.

21. Khalid Ikram, *Egypt: Economic Management in a Period of Transition, A World Bank Country Economic Report* (Baltimore: Johns Hopkins University Press, 1980), 110.
22. On the first Egyptian family planning policy, adopted by the Supreme Council for Family Planning in 1966, see Steven K. Wisensale and Amany A. Khodair, "The Two-Child Family: The Egyptian Model of Family Planning," *Journal of Comparative Family Studies* 29, no. 3 (1998), 505.
23. Gilbar, "Nasser's Soft Revolution," 84–85. See also John Waterbury, *The Egypt of Nasser and Sadat: The Political Economy of Two Regimes* (Princeton: Princeton University Press, 1983), 45.
24. Saad Eddin Ibrahim, "State, Women, and Civil Society: An Evaluation of Egypt's Population Policy," in Carla Makhlouf Obermeyer (ed.), *Family, Gender, and Population in the Middle East: Policies in Context* (Cairo: American University in Cairo Press, 1995), 65.
25. Thomas W. Lippman, *Egypt After Nasser: Sadat, Peace and the Mirage of Prosperity* (New York: Paragon House, 1989), 162.
26. Gilbar, "Nasser's Soft Revolution," 85.
27. Ami Ayalon, "Demographya, Politiqa, ve-Masoret be-Mitzrayim shel Mubarak" [Demography, Politics and Tradition in Mubarak's Egypt] in Ami Ayalon and Gad G. Gilbar (eds.), *Demographya ve-Politiqa be-Medinot 'Arav* [*Demography and Politics in the Arab States*] (Tel Aviv: Hakibbutz Hameuchad, 1995), 32 (Hebrew).
28. Kamran Asdar Ali, *Planning the Family in Egypt: New Bodies, New Selves* (Austin: University of Texas Press, 2002), 33.
29. Egypt, Ministry of Health and Population, *Egypt Demographic and Health Survey-2014* (Cairo, May 2015), 43, Table 4.4.
30. Warren C. Robinson and Fatma H. El-Zanaty, *The Demographic Revolution in Modern Egypt* (Boulder: Lexington Books, 2005), 115.
31. *Ahram Online*, May 1, 2014.
32. *Egypt Today*, July 24, 2017.
33. UNFPA, the [Egyptian] National Population Council and the Egyptian Center for Public Opinion and Research, *Population Situation Analysis-Egypt 2016* (Cairo, December 2016), 49.
34. *Al-Jazeera*, June 9, 2015.
35. USAID, "Strengthening Egypt's Family Planning Program," February 23, 2021, 3–4.
36. UNFPA, Egypt: Family Planning [https://egypt.unfpa.org/en/node/22543].
37. CAPMAS, *Statistical Yearbook-2020*, Table 3-1.
38. See, for example, IMF, *Arab Republic of Egypt: 2014 Article IV Consultation* (February 2015); and IMF, *Arab Republic of Egypt*, IMF country report no. 17/17 (January 2017); and IMF, *Arab Republic of Egypt*, IMF country report no. 20/271 (September 2020).
39. *Egyptian Streets*, August 1, 2015.
40. *Egypt Demographic and Health Survey-2014*, 40, Table 4.1.
41. *MEES*, July 2, 2012.

42. Ahmed Farouk Ghoneim, "The Political Economy of Food Price Policy in Egypt," in Per Pinstrup-Andersen (ed.), *Food Price Policy in an Era of Market Instability: A Political Economy Analysis* (Oxford: Oxford University Press, 2015), 254.
43. *Reuters*, June 24, 2019.
44. Hazem Kandil, "Why did the Egyptian Middle Class March to Tahrir Square?" *Mediterranean Politics* 17, no. 2 (July 2012), 210.
45. Robert L. Tignor, "Foreign Capital, Foreign Communities, and the Egyptian Revolution of 1952," in Shimon Shamir (ed.), *Egypt from Monarchy to Republic: A Reassessment of Revolution and Change* (Boulder: Westview Press, 1995), 105.
46. Waterbury, *The Egypt of Nasser and Sadat*, 57.
47. Moshe Efrat, "Tokhnit ha-'Asor ve-Totzoteha" ("The Decade Plan and its Consequences") in Shimon Shamir (ed.), *Yeridat ha-Nasserism, 1965–1970: Shqi'ata shel Tenu'a Meshikhit* (*The Decline of Nasserism, 1965–1970: The Waning of a Messianic Movement*) (Tel Aviv: The Shiloh Center, 1978), 66 (Hebrew); and Ragui Assaad, "The MENA Paradox: Higher Education but Lower Job Quality," in *Moving Jobs to the Center Stage*, Berlin Workshop Series (Berlin: BMZ, 2013), 33, Fig. 1.
48. By 1967, the enrollment ratio in Egypt at the primary school age amounted to 80 percent as compared to 45 percent in 1952. See Mahmud A. Faksh, "The Consequences of the Introduction and Spread of Modern Education: Education and National Integration in Egypt," *Middle Eastern Studies*, 16 no. 2 (1980), 45.
49. Galal A. Amin, *Egypt's Economic Predicament: A Study in the Interaction of External Pressure, Political Folly and Social Tension in Egypt, 1960–1990* (Leiden: E.J. Brill, 1995), 6.
50. Regarding the scale of the remittances of the Egyptian workers abroad during the oil decade, see Elie Poden and Onn Winckler, "The Boycott that Never Was: Egypt and the Arab System, 1979–1989," *Durham Middle East Papers* 72 (December 2002), 36–39.
51. *MEED*, September 16, 1983, 22; EIU, *Egypt, Country Profile, 1986–87*, 8; and Gil Feiler, "Migration and Recession: Arab Labor Mobility in the Middle East, 1982–1989," *Population and Development Review* 17, no. 1 (1991), 136.
52. Amin, *Egypt's Economic Predicament*, 54, Table 3.7.
53. EIU, QER, *Egypt-Annual Supplement*, 1985, 30.
54. *MEED*, July 2, 1982, 8.
55. Khalid Ikram, *The Egyptian Economy, 1952–2000: Performance, Policies, and Issues* (London: Routledge, 2006), 24.
56. Galal Amin, *Egypt in the Era of Hosni Mubarak, 1981–2011* (Cairo: American University in Cairo Press, 2011), 3.
57. OECD, *Compact for Economic Governance: Stocktaking Report: Egypt*, 20.
58. By June 1986, the price of oil barrel was less than $10 compared to $36 in 1980 (current prices). In constant 1990 prices, oil prices went down from $49.6 in 1981 to $17.1 in 1986 (spot crude prices). See Paul Rivlin, *World Oil and Energy Trends: Strategic Implications for the Middle East* (Tel Aviv: Tel Aviv University, Jaffee Center for Strategic Studies, September 2000), 17, Table 1.

59. IMF, *The Egyptian Stabilization Experience: An Analytical Retrospective*, IMF working paper no. WP/97/105 (September 1997), 7.
60. ESCWA, *Return Migration: Profiles, Impact and Absorption in Home Countries* (New York, 1993), 17.
61. EIU, *Country Report-Egypt*, no. 4 (1988), 10.
62. Assaad, "The MENA Paradox," 31.
63. M. Riad El-Ghonemy, "Development Strategies, 1950–2001: Progress and Challenges for the Twenty-First Century," in M. Riad El-Ghonemy (ed.), *Egypt in the Twenty-First Century: Challenges and Development* (London: Routledge Curzon, 2003), 88.
64. Mahmoud A.T. Elkhafif, *The Egyptian Economy: A Modeling Approach* (Westport: Praeger, 1996), 1.
65. Arvind Subramanian, "Egypt: Poised for Sustained Growth?" *Finance & Development* (December 1997), 44.
66. Ikram, *The Egyptian Economy, 1952–2000*, 60.
67. Ghonemy, "Development Strategies," 80; and Elkhafif, *The Egyptian Economy*, 1.
68. Joseph Licari, *Economic Reform in Egypt in a Changing Global Economy*, OECD Development Centre, working paper no. 129 (December 1997), 14.
69. Egypt's foreign public debt declined from $47.6 billion in mid-1990 to $24 billion in mid-1994, while its foreign currency reserves increased from $3 billion in late 1990 to $17 billion by the end of 1996. See Amin, *Egypt in the Era of Hosni Mubrak*, 58; Subramanian, "Egypt: Poised for Sustained Growth?" 44; and Dieter Weiss and Ulrich Wurzel, *The Economics and Politics of Transition to an Open Market Economy: Egypt* (Paris: Development Centre of the OECD, 1998), 24.
70. According to the December 1996 census, 2.18 million Egyptian citizens migrated abroad temporarily. See CAPMAS, *Statistical Yearbook, 1992–1998*, 11, Table 1–15.
71. The number of tourists in Egypt increased from 2.214 million in 1991 to 3.896 million in 1996. Tourism receipts went up from $2.029 billion to $2.984 billion during the corresponding period. On the development of the Egyptian tourism industry during the 1990s, see Yoel Mansfeld and Onn Winckler, "Options for Viable Economic Development through Tourism among the Non-Oil Arab Countries: The Egyptian Case," *Tourism Economics* 10, no. 4 (December 2004), 376–378.
72. IMF, *The Egyptian Stabilization Experience*, 4–5. An OECD report on the Egyptian economy, published in December 1997, presented a similar optimistic opinion. See Licari, *Economic Reform in Egypt*, 7.
73. Samir Radwan, "Full Employment: The Challenge in the Twenty-First Century," in El-Ghonemy (ed.), *Egypt in the Twenty-First Century*, 111.
74. According to the "authoritarian social contract/bargain," the population, especially the young middle class, exchanged their political participation in return for various socio-economic benefits, primarily public sector employment

(lifetime jobs), free health care and educational services, massive subsidies on basic foodstuff and energy products, and low personal taxation.

75. ESCWA, *Arab Middle Class*, 21.
76. Weiss and Wurzel, *The Economics and Politics of Transition*, 23.
77. Sabry Aglan, "Industrial Development: Progress and Challenges in the Future," in El-Ghonemy (ed.), *Egypt in the Twenty-First Century*, 166.
78. Yusuf, *Middle East Transitions*, 11.
79. Central Bank of Egypt, *Economic Review* 54, no. 4 (2010/2011), 101.
80. ESCWA, *Arab Middle Class*, 16; 56.
81. USAID, "Strengthening Egypt's Family Planning Program" (February 23, 2021), 35. On the development of economic inequality in Egypt, see Paolo Verme et al., *Inside the Inequality in the Arab Republic of Egypt* (Washington, DC: World Bank, 2014).
82. CAPMAS, *Statistical Yearbook-2016*, Table 13-1.
83. Ibid., Table 13-2.
84. *Ahram Online*, January 19, 2016.
85. *MEES*, September 29, 2017.
86. OECD, *Compact for Economic Governance: Stocktaking Report: Egypt*, 26, Box 1.
87. Nihal Samir, "Egypt's Tourism Revenues Decline to $4bn in 2020 from $13.03bn in 2019," *Daily News* (Cairo), January 4, 2021.
88. Michele Dunne, "Egypt: Looking Elsewhere to Meet Bottomless Needs," Carnegie Endowment for International Peace, June 9, 2020.
89. *Al-Jazeera*, January 3, 2021.
90. Egypt, Ministry of Planning and Economic Development, *Impact of COVID-19 on the Egyptian Economy: Economic Sectors, Jobs, and Households*, by Clemens Breisinger, Mariam Raouf, Manfred Wiebelt, Ahmed Kamaly, and Mouchera Karara (Cairo, June 2020), 7.
91. The World Bank, *Egypt's Overview*, October 1, 2020.
92. EIU, *Egypt* [https://country.eiu.com/Egypt].
93. CAPMES, *Al-Ta'dād al-'Amm lil-Sukkān wal-Iskān wal-Munsha'āt-2017* (The Population, Housing and Establishments Census-2017), Cairo, 2017 (Arabic).
94. CAPMAS homepage [https://www.capmas.gov.eg/].
95. Egypt, Ministry of Health and Population, *Egypt Health Issues Survey-2015* (Cairo, October 2015), 88, Table 6.5.
96. IMF, *Press Release* no. 17/431 (November 10, 2017).
97. IMF, *Arab Republic of Egypt: 2008 Article IV Consultation*, IMF country report no. 09/25, January 2009, 22, Table 6.
98. According to the *Global Gender Gap*, in 2019 Egypt ranked 134 out of 153 countries in gender equality. See World Economic Forum, *Global Gender Gap-2020*, 9, Table 1.
99. In 2018, Egypt's female labor force participation rate was as low as 25 percent—one of the lowest worldwide. See Caroline Krafft, Ragui Assaad, and Caitlyn Keo, "The Evolution of Labor Supply in Egypt from 1988–2018," Economic Research Forum, working paper no. 1358 (Cairo, October 2019), 20.

100. Egypt's tax base, particularly the share of the personal income tax, is very narrow due to the large share of the informal sector estimated at between one-third and two-thirds of the total Egyptian economy. In the FY2018/19, the personal income tax contributed a mere 11.8 percent of the total tax revenues. See OECD, *Compact for Economic Governance: Stocktaking Report: Egypt*, 40; 58–59; and IMF, *Arab Republic of Egypt*, IMF country report no. 21/7 (January 2021), 21, Table 3a.
101. CAPMAS, *Annual Bulletin of Employees in Government Sector 2015/2016*, http://www.capmas.gov.eg/Pages/StatisticsOracle.aspx?Oracle_id=814&year=2016& page_id=5104&YearID=22984.
102. Weiss and Wurzel, *The Economics and Politics of Transition*, 31.
103. Waterbury, *The Egypt of Nasser and Sadat*, 41.

Selected Bibliography

Ali, Kamran Asdar, *Planning the Family in Egypt: New Bodies, New Selves* (Austin: University of Texas Press, 2002).

Amin, Galal A., *Egypt's Economic Predicament: A Study in the Interaction of External Pressure, Political Folly and Social Tension in Egypt, 1960–1990* (Leiden: E.J. Brill, 1995).

Ghoneim, Ahmed Farouk, "The Political Economy of Food Price Policy in Egypt," in Per Pinstrup-Andersen, ed., *Food Price Policy in an Era of Market Instability: A Political Economy Analysis* (Oxford: Oxford University Press, 2015).

El-Ghonemy, M. Riad, "Development Strategies, 1950–2001: Progress and Challenges for the Twenty-First Century," in M. Riad El-Ghonemy, ed., *Egypt in the Twenty-First Century: Challenges and Development* (London: Routledge Curzon, 2003).

Gilbar, Gad G., "Nasser's Soft Revolution," in Gad G. Gilbar, *Population Dilemmas in the Middle East* (London: Frank Cass, 1997), 80–96.

Ikram, Khalid, *Egypt: Economic Management in a Period of Transition, A World Bank Country Economic Report* (Baltimore: Johns Hopkins University Press, 1980).

Rivlin, Paul, *Arab Economies in the Twenty-First Century* (Cambridge: Cambridge University Press, 2009).

Robinson, Warren C., and Fatma H. El-Zanaty, *The Demographic Revolution in Modern Egypt* (Boulder: Lexington Books, 2005).

Saad, Eddin Ibrahim, "State, Women, and Civil Society: An Evaluation of Egypt's Population Policy," in Carla Makhlouf Obermeyer, ed., *Family, Gender, and Population in the Middle East: Policies in Context* (Cairo: American University in Cairo Press, 1995).

Stycos, J. Mayone et al., *Community Development and Family Planning: An Egyptian Experiment* (Boulder: Westview Press, 1988).

Waterbury, John, *The Egypt of Nasser and Sadat: The Political Economy of Two Regimes* (Princeton: Princeton University Press, 1983).

From Leader to Partner: Egypt's Declining Role in the Arab System (1952–2020)

Elie Podeh

Introduction

Egypt's Arab identity began to crystallize in the inter-war years (1919–1939) as Egyptians became increasingly aware of their cultural and linguistic affinity with the Arab world. After independence in 1936, Egypt gradually assumed an increasingly central role in the emerging Arab system, and in 1945 Cairo became home to the headquarters of the newly established Arab League. Over the years, Egypt's central position in the Arab system was based on a combination of tangible assets such as military and human resources, and intangible ones such as geo-strategic location, regime legitimacy, domestic stability, pan-Arab ideology, cultural centrality, charismatic leadership, and a self-perception of Arab leadership. These attributes each weighed differently over time, yet their availability, coupled with Egypt's readiness to use them to wield its influence, ensured Egypt's central position in the Arab system.

The fact that Egypt has been playing a major role in the Arab system is, of course, hardly a revelation. Scholars have used a variety of terms to depict Egypt's status—leadership, hegemony, dominance, superiority, preponderance, primacy, *primus inter pares,* etc. The problem is that they have often used these terms interchangeably without explaining the theoretical distinctions between them. This chapter, therefore, offers a typology of Egypt's leadership phenomenon through a comparison of four Egyptian regimes—Nasser (1952–1970); Sadat (1970–1981); Mubarak (1981–2011), and Sisi (2013–present)—using an analytical framework termed here as the preponderance continuum. Because of the centrality of the leadership variable in Third World countries in general, and in Egypt in particular, this categorization seems appropriate.[1]

When discussing a state's aspirations for dominance, realists usually emphasize the importance of hard, or tangible, dimensions of power—

military force, economic resources, GNP, human resources, and size of territory. Indices of such tangible assets serve as a scientific basis for constructing formal rankings in the international system.[2] In Kenneth Waltz's opinion, states are not put at the top of such hierarchies because they excel in one dimension of power; rather, "their rank depends on how they score on *all* of the following items: size of population and territory, resource endowment, economic capability, military strength, political stability and competence."[3]

Over the years, however, evidence has proved that intangible, or soft, dimensions of power are no less important prerequisites for wielding influence in the international arena. Regime legitimacy, charismatic leadership, prestige, moral authority, norms of behavior, ideology, and cultural dominance are some of the variables included in the measurement of preponderance in general. A state's influence also depends on its willingness to use its assets to project power. Without such motivation, high-level capabilities will not translate into influence. Influence may be exerted through non-coercive or soft means such as diplomacy, negotiations, bargaining, persuasion, and side-payments, and more coercive, hard means such as threats, clandestine activities, propaganda, intimidation, sanctions, and military force.[4]

Another factor that affects a state's ability to project power is its own perception of its status. Karl Holsti offers 17 role perceptions in relation to state behavior, including the role of "regional leader," which connotes "duties or special responsibilities that a government perceives for itself in its relation to states in a particular region with which it identifies."[5] Arguably, states with such self-perceptions are more willing to fulfill such duties. No less important are the corresponding perceptions of the other players in the system: How they perceive the role of the aspiring state may affect the latter's behavior, regardless of its actual capabilities.

Based on several theoretical works that offer definitions of the preponderance phenomenon,[6] this study analyzes four Egyptian regimes according to the following continuum of preponderance:

The Preponderance Continuum

Primus inter pares (First among equals)	Leadership	Hegemony	Dominance (Empire)

The drive for power is universal. Though hegemony, leadership and dominance are terms mainly analyzed in relation to the international system, they are equally applicable to regional actors. Since the inception of the Arab system in the 1930s,[7] the quest for hegemony was perhaps its most common feature.[8] In Arab parlance, a distinction is made between "hegemony" (*haymana*) and "leadership" (*za'āma, qiyāda* or *riyāda*). While the former refers to superpower domination and has a negative connotation, the latter traditionally refers to a positive Arab role that is beneficial to the system as a whole. Another common Arab term used to describe Egypt's role in the Arab world is "the Senior Sister" (*al-Shaqīqa al-Kubrā*), which equates the Arab states to a family in which Egypt naturally enjoys a senior position with respect to its members.[9] This term corresponds to the *"primus inter pares"* on the above continuum.

In its quest for regional pre-eminence, Egypt has had various tangible (hard) and intangible (soft) assets at its disposable. Some assets were constant—geo-strategic location, size of territory, cultural-religious centrality, and large population, as well as Egypt's self-perception of leadership. Other assets, such as military, economic and political capabilities, charismatic leadership, internal stability and legitimacy, ideology, and symbolic or moral authority, were more transitory, fluctuating according to historical developments. This chapter will show that the changing nature of these capabilities affected the role Egypt has been playing in the Arab system for the past seven decades, under four regimes.[10]

The Nasser Regime (1952–1970)

Egypt's involvement in Arab affairs was relatively subdued until mid-1954, a result of the power struggle between Nasser and Muhammad Naguib, the two leaders of the military coup, and their preoccupation with Egypt's pressing domestic problems, particularly the negotiations with Britain over its Suez base and the Sudan. The Baghdad Pact (henceforth BP) posed the first major test of Nasser's power in the regional system. In February 1955, Iraq signed a pact with Turkey, which was later extended to include Britain, Iran, and Pakistan. Iraq hoped to leverage the BP to strengthen its position in the Arab world. To thwart the Iraqi aspirations, Nasser employed several tools to prevent other Arab rulers from joining the BP: diplomacy, propaganda, clandestine activities, bribery, and threats. The propaganda apparatus and the intelligence services he had built were important instruments of influence, used to threaten other Arab rulers, compelling them to act according to his wishes. Nasser also made use of symbolic assets including the symbolic power of pan-Arabism, which inadvertently strengthened his commitment to that ideology, and the positive image of the revolution. Finally, Nasser strongly believed in the inevitability of

Egyptian leadership. This image was propagated in his *The Philosophy of the Revolution*, which circulated widely in Egypt and the Arab world. Nasser's successful campaign to block the BP led to Iraq's isolation.[11]

From 1955 to 1958, Nasser's stature in the Arab world reached its zenith as a result of several moves. First, he made his first-ever appearance on the international stage at the conference of the non-aligned countries in Bandung in April 1955. His successful performance there and the image he portrayed as one of the leaders of the emerging non-aligned movement served him well in his future Arab dialogues. Second, the signing of the Czech arms deal in September 1955 strengthened Egypt's military capabilities and boosted Nasser's anti-imperialist image. Though the change in the military balance of power was directed toward the Arab–Israeli arena, Nasser made use of this asset in the Arab system as well. Indeed, in what was an unprecedented move for the Arab system, he sent a token force to Syria in November 1957 in response to a political crisis, primarily to keep Syria within Egypt's sphere of influence. Third, the nationalization of the Suez Canal Company in July 1956 further strengthened Nasser's anti-Western image. Though militarily defeated in the 1956 Suez Crisis, his reputation as a powerful leader was bolstered by the fact that he was able to stand up to the tripartite Western coalition. Finally, Egypt's union with Syria in February 1958 was achieved without coercion: Nasser's popularity, legitimacy, and charisma served as a magnet for the Syrians, who accepted his demands. At this point, Nasser was at the apex of his power as the leader of the Arab nation and the pan-Arab movement, and head of the strongest Arab state—the United Arab Republic (UAR). Within five months, however, the foundations of the union began to crumble. Iraq refused to join it, undermining Nasser's aspirations to expand the UAR and casting doubt on Nasser's ability to lead the entire Arab world. When Syria withdrew from the UAR in September 1961, Nasser experienced his severest setback in the Arab world thus far.[12]

The 1962 military coup in Yemen presented Nasser with an opportunity to recover some of his lost prestige. He demonstrated his initiative by sending military forces to Yemen. This intervention involved 70,000 soldiers at its peak, yet ended in failure after more than five years, mainly because Egyptian forces were unprepared to meet Yemen's harsh topographical and climatic conditions. The entire episode, described by Nasser as his own Vietnam,[13] drained Egypt's economy, soured its relations with the United States, and weakened its position in the Arab system. The intervention demonstrated that Egypt's military superiority in the Arab world rested on a fragile foundation.

Nevertheless, two Ba'thi-led coups in Iraq and Syria, in February and March 1963 respectively, highlighted Nasser's status as leader of the Arab world. In a quest for legitimacy, the new regimes in Iraq and Syria commenced negotiations with Egypt to establish a tripartite federation. The Cairo Declaration of April 17 seemingly heralded the birth of a new Arab entity, but the agreement was never implemented due to ideological, political, and personal reasons.[14] Facing mounting criticism (especially from the Syrian Ba'th) against his ineffectiveness regarding the Israeli menace, Nasser decided to mend fences with his conservative Arab rivals on the basis of ad hoc cooperation. Thus, he initiated the Arab Summit—a new diplomatic mechanism that provided him with the legitimacy he sought and a tool to further Egypt's interests in Arab politics. The Cairo summit, held in January 1964, sanctioned an indefinite postponement of the war against Israel and effectively preserved Nasser's prestige and dignity. The decisions to establish a joint Arab command under Egyptian leadership, to divert the tributaries of the Jordan River, and to establish an organization for the Palestinian people (PLO) under an Egyptian protégé named Ahmad al-Shuqayrī, were evidence of Egypt's dominant position in the Arab world.[15] Nasser enlisted support for these initiatives with little coercion.

Yet, two disastrous military adventures—Yemen (1962–1967) and the Six-Day War (June 1967)—had devastating implications for Egypt and its status in the Arab system in the post-1967 period. Weakened militarily and economically, Egypt found itself increasingly dependent on the support of the Soviet Union and the oil-producing Arab states. In addition, the 1967 war dealt a final blow to Nasser's pan-Arab aspirations. Despite these developments, Nasser's perception of Egypt's place in the Arab system hardly changed, and his image remained virtually unscathed. "Even in defeat," wrote Fouad Ajami, "Nasser was still a pan-Arab hero."[16] Sensing that his political survival and regional pre-eminence depended on resuming hostilities with Israel, Nasser's strategy until his death was based on "increasing military pressure while keeping the door open to international mediation."[17] This strategy may explain why he initiated the War of Attrition against Israel in March 1969, while negotiating with the UN and accepting US Secretary of State William Rogers' peace initiatives.

From 1967 to 1970 Nasser was still setting the Arab agenda, but he was less successful persuading others to follow him. In November 1967, he accepted UN Resolution 242, but none of the other Arab states did (except Jordan). When Nasser asked the Arab leaders at the 1969 Rabat summit to support the struggle against Israel, the oil-producing countries were unwilling to raise their donations above the ceiling determined in the 1967 Khartoum summit. Still, Nasser's success at brokering the Cairo agreement between Lebanon and the PLO in November 1969, and the agreement the following September between Jordan and the PLO after the Civil War ("Black September") confirmed that his leadership was not a thing of the past. And so, as Kerr wrote, "in the public eye at least, he [Nasser] died as a martyr to the cause of Arab brotherhood."[18]

Did Nasser's Egypt ever achieve the status of a hegemonic power in the Arab system? Paul Noble, after analyzing the aggregate power capabilities of states in the Arab system, concluded that after 1955 it was a "highly unbalanced, virtually one-power system, dominated by Egypt."[19] With equal conviction, however, Carl Brown maintained that after World War I "no single state, either from within the area or from outside, was able to establish effective hegemony."[20] A partial reconciliation of these conflicting assessments may be found in Kerr's remarks: "It has been said that Nasser was eager for Egypt to play the role of Prussia, but that he was no Bismarck. This may seem unfair: after all, despite everything, he was undeniably a man of remarkable personal strengths and political skills, and it was not his fault that history placed something less than the Prussian army at his disposal."[21] Kerr was alluding to the growing gap between Nasser's perceptions and capabilities needed to fulfill them. From 1955 to 1961 Egypt enjoyed, in addition to its permanent assets, relative superiority over the other Arab states in terms of its demographic and military capabilities.[22] Nasser had enjoyed more legitimacy and was more charismatic than any other modern Egyptian leader. His country also possessed moral authority as the vanguard of the Arab Revolution, pan-Arabism, and the champion of the Palestinian cause in its struggle against Israel. Cairo became "the Mecca" of the Arab intelligentsia, the hub of cultural and political activity.[23] Egypt's methodology for promoting its influence included persuasion, diplomacy, propaganda, intelligence, espionage, and bribery.[24] Thus, its hard and soft capabilities, coupled with assertive use of means, allowed Nasser to maximize his gains and reach the status of a hegemon during the years 1955–1961 (see Table 8.1). Even at the height of his power, however, he did not reach the dominant position to which he aspired because he lacked sufficient power to dictate his terms to the system's recalcitrant Arab actors.

In the second period, 1962–1970, some of Nasser's intangible assets, such as his legitimacy and moral authority as a revolutionary and pan-Arab leader, were on the decline. In addition, Egypt's political, demographic, military, and economic capabilities had also dwindled as a result of the country's military defeats, economic recession, and population growth. No wonder that it was in this period that Nasser used the military option for the first time to compensate for his loss of influence. To maintain his position in the Arab world, he also increased his dependence on the Soviet Union. It was during this period that the gap between Egyptian perceptions and its capabilities and methods gradually widened. Although Egypt's hegemonic perceptions were not matched by its capabilities in this period, it remained the leader of the Arab world (see Table 8.1).

The Sadat Regime (1970–1981)

Following Nasser's death in 1970, Egypt's role in the Arab world underwent a transformation. The country became dependent on foreign capital investment, markets for exporting manufacturing goods, markets for importing grains, meat and arms, and free access to Arab labor markets.[25] Its increasing dependence on oil-producing Arab states such as Saudi Arabia and Kuwait circumscribed its maneuverability in the Arab system. Consequently, "economic difficulties contributed to the evolution of a more inward-looking and less activist foreign policy."[26]

Egypt's status in the Arab system was also affected by the growing validity and legitimacy accorded to the territorial Arab state—a consequence of the decline of pan-Arabism. In the absence of any competing or attractive supra-state legitimacy and as a result of the consolidation of the states' institutions, the Arab world became a "normal" state system. Consequently, states respected the sovereignty of other Arab members of the system, and intervention in their internal affairs became less acceptable. Barnett concluded that in the post-1967 period, the regional order was secured through "the establishment of relatively stable normative expectations that revolve around sovereignty."[27]

Sadat enjoyed little of Nasser's legitimacy or charisma, at least until the 1973 war. Sadat also held a different perception of Egypt's role in the Arab system, explicitly stating that Egypt did not entertain any "imperial scheme" and that its policy was not "of coercion, pressure or even persuasion." Egypt, he concluded, "is ready to go with any Arab country as far as that country wishes to go."[28] He devised a new concept of inter-Arab relations that "perceived cooperation—including reception of material aid—with any Arab partner conditional on mutual respect for each other's sovereignty."[29] At least until 1973, Sadat maintained a low profile in Arab affairs, concentrating instead on domestic goals: recovery of the territories occupied by Israel in 1967, preferably by negotiation, and the improvement of Egypt's economy, preferably through rapprochement with the USA.

Still, when these diplomatic efforts collapsed, Sadat successfully formed an Arab war coalition by non-coercive means. The token military forces sent by Iraq, Algeria, Jordan, Libya, Morocco, Tunisia, Kuwait, and Sudan to support the war effort in 1973 reinforced the tripartite coalition of Egypt, Syria, and Saudi Arabia. Compared to 1967, the expeditionary Arab forces in 1973 were generally larger and from a greater number of states. The Saudis' use of the oil weapon also demonstrated solidarity with Egypt.[30] The Arab mobilization behind Egypt attested to its centrality in Arab affairs. Daniel Dishon concluded that, although it was not in a position of hegemony, "the centrality of Egypt existed in a real sense." Based on Heikal's terminology, he saw Egypt as the "key country" (*balad al-miftāḥ*) in the Arab system.[31] Yet, Egypt's role in the Arab world had been gradually diminishing since the early 1970s.[32]

Following its first disengagement agreement with Israel of January 1974, Egypt persuaded Syria to sign a similar agreement. Moreover, Sadat persuaded the Arab leaders at the Rabat summit that October to adopt a phased peace strategy regarding Israel, including Arab recognition of the PLO as the sole representative of the Palestinian people.[33] This show of solidarity crumbled, however, when Sadat decided to sign separately a second interim agreement with Israel (September 1975), exposing him to vehement Arab criticism. Arab divisions became wider with Sadat's visit in Jerusalem (November 1977), the Camp David Agreement (September 1978), and the Israeli–Egyptian peace treaty (March 1979). The Baghdad summits in October 1978 and March 1979 threatened to undermine Egypt's leading role, potentially even relegating it to the margins of Arab decision making. A flurry of sanctions threatened to isolate Egypt politically and economically, after its moral authority and legitimacy had been eroded by the signing of the peace treaty with Israel. In fact, the boycott was an attempt to delegitimize Egypt and allowed Iraq to pose a credible claim to Arab leadership, which had eluded it for many years. As a result, the Arab League headquarters moved from Cairo to Tunis and many Arab countries severed their diplomatic relations with Egypt.[34]

Structurally, the Arab system underwent significant changes in the 1970s. Dessouki asserted that "oil has created a new cleavage between Arab states based on economic status. It has altered the balance of power in favor of the rich, who are not only subsidizing the poor but also attracting their trained manpower."[35] The Arab world moved into an era of polycentrism, multiple centers of influence, and dispersed capabilities and sharing of power. He concluded, therefore, that "the days in which one country could exert its leadership over the Arab world are gone." Egyptian influence declined and no other Arab state was powerful enough take its place.[36] The leadership vacuum was evident in the absence of any viable Arab alternative to Sadat's peaceful approach.[37] Yet, the formation of the 1973 war coalition and its self-perceived glorious results consolidated Sadat's legitimacy and strengthened Egypt's leadership in the system, which was based on mutual interests and persuasion, and relied on some tangible and intangible resources, rather than coercion. While Egypt could no longer serve as the moral authority for the Arabs due to the negotiations and subsequent peace treaty with Israel, and although it was formally discredited and officially isolated, in practice Egypt continued playing an important role in the Arab system as *primus inter pares* (see Table 8.1).[38] Its permanent assets, its self-perception of leadership, massive US support, and the lack of any other potential Arab leader were all crucial in maintaining this role.

Table 8.1: Egypt's Role in the Arab System (1952–2018)

Primus Inter Pares	**Leadership**	**Hegemony**	**Dominance**
Naguib/Nasser (1952–1954)	Nasser (1962–1970)	Nasser (1955–1961)	—
Sadat(1971–1973)	Sadat (1974–Nov. 1977)	—	—
Sadat (Nov. 1977–1981)	Mubarak (1990–2011)	—	—
Mubarak (Oct. 1981–1989)	—	—	—

The Mubarak Regime (1981–2011)

When Hosni Mubarak succeeded Sadat in 1981, he inherited a set of economic and political problems that would affect Egypt's place in the Arab system throughout his presidency. In terms of Egypt's regional standing, Mubarak's era can be divided into two periods, divided by the 1990 Iraqi invasion of Kuwait. The first was characterized by Egypt's struggle against the Arab boycott, while the second was marked by its efforts to reassert its leadership role despite formidable domestic economic challenges and the divisions in the Arab world. Mubarak enjoyed more legitimacy than Sadat because he was not associated personally with the peace treaty, though he strongly supported it.

Mubarak also shared with his predecessors the self-perception of Egypt's leadership role in the Arab world.

The Arab boycott threatened to erode Egypt's remaining influence. However, the 1979 Iranian Revolution and the consequent Iran–Iraq war undermined Iraq's pretensions for Arab leadership and opened the door for Egypt's return to the Arab world. The fact that Iraq—the state that led the boycott—initiated a rapprochement with Egypt in pursuit of arms and labor, indirectly conferred legitimacy on the peace treaty itself. Moreover, an in-depth analysis of Egypt's status in the Arab system in the 1980s shows that the boycott existed only formally; in fact, Egypt's economic and political ties with Arab countries remained strong and, in certain cases, even increased.[39]

In the early 1980s, Kerr believed that Egypt would continue playing a central role in the new Arab order despite the boycott.[40] An in-depth analysis of Egypt's activity tends to confirm Kerr's conclusion. The quantitative data for the years 1985–1990 clearly show that Egypt dropped in world and regional ranking of military expenditure and GNP. Despite this development, Egypt succeeded in playing a modest leading role. In light of Iraq's protracted war with Iran, Egypt even offered to send military forces to the Gulf to defend the oil monarchies,[41] and its political capabilities and particularly its special relations with the USA allowed it to play a leading role in the peace process and the Jordanian–Palestinian dialogue. The Arab states—most of them grudgingly, some indifferently, and a few enthusiastically—acquiesced, though they attempted to conceal their support for Egypt's leadership because of its peace treaty with Israel. Thus, in a system that was more polycentric and divided than ever, Egypt's role until 1989 was tantamount to a *primus inter pares*, based on its modest tangible capabilities and some intangible assets.

Egypt's leading role became more visible following its readmission into the Arab League in May 1989. On the eve of the Casablanca summit, celebrating Egypt's return, the influential weekly magazine *al-Muṣawwar* published an editorial—undoubtedly reflecting the official view—analyzing Egypt's new role in the Arab system. It stated that Mubarak's Egypt was not interested in the kind of role that characterized Nasser's Egypt. "It is inconceivable," it declared, "that there can be a submission by the Arab countries to a single center of power. This is now a thing of the past." Rather, a new kind of distribution of burdens was suggested, which "will correspond to the existing balances of power in the Arab world." Egypt would seek a role that "respects the right of diversity and multiplicity, and that calls for coordination and integration before unity. It is a role that is in harmony with all roles, without dictation or hegemony."[42] In many ways, this was a continuation of Sadat's policy.

The disintegration of the Soviet Union in 1989 and Iraq's invasion of Kuwait in 1990 launched a new era in Arab politics and created an opportunity for Egypt to reassert its leadership in the Arab system. Opposed to the Iraqi bid for pre-eminence, Egypt had the blessing of the USA to convene an emergency summit in Cairo, which condemned Iraq and called for its withdrawal from Kuwait. In addition, together with Syria, Egypt sent a military force to Saudi Arabia, providing an Arab umbrella for the US-led international force. Egypt's role in the crisis paid off nicely: the USA, Europe, Japan, and the Arab states erased almost half of its $40 billion foreign debt.

Mubarak also hoped to reap some political-strategic dividends from the crisis and translate his military presence in the Gulf to tangible assets in the Arab system. Putting Egypt at the center of the system, wrote Raymond Hinnebusch, "would give greater leverage over the US and establish Cairo as a partner, rather than a client, in the New World Order."[43] Thus, the Damascus Declaration, issued on March 6, 1991, by Egypt, Syria, and the six GCC members, outlined a new vision for the Arab regional order. It stated that the Egyptian-Syrian force in the Gulf "represents a nucleus for an Arab peace force which would safeguard the security and integrity of Arab countries in the Gulf region and constitute a model that would ensure the effectiveness of the comprehensive Arab defense system." The declaration also spelled out the norms of Arab politics to be preserved: commitment to territorial integrity, respect of sovereignty, inadmissibility of the acquisition of territory by force, nonintervention in internal affairs, and the settlement of disputes by peaceful means.[44] However, only two months later, the international forces withdrew from the Gulf: the GCC countries preferred an "over-the-horizon" US presence. The Damascus Declaration was meant to solidify Egypt's leadership status in the Gulf, and hence in the entire Arab system, but the GCC countries decided that the political and economic price of the Egyptian-Syrian military presence was too high.[45]

The containment of Egypt's influence in the Gulf pushed Mubarak to concentrate on advancing the peace process. Clearly, a settlement of the Arab–Israeli conflict was bound to reinforce Egypt's legitimacy and leadership in the Arab system, creating a congenial atmosphere for foreign and Arab investments. Here, Mubarak was relying on an important Egyptian asset: its "supposed indispensability in the peace process, as the only Arab state at peace with Israel."[46] Indeed, the Madrid conference, which convened in October 1991, and the peace process that followed in the years 1992–1993, accentuated Egypt's pioneering role in the efforts to achieve peace in the Middle East, paving the way for other Arab states and the PLO. As the result of its unique position, Egypt played the role of a double broker or mediator: between Israel and the Arab states, and between the latter and the USA. Moreover, Mubarak participated in the secret negotiations between Israel and the PLO that led to the signing of the Oslo Accords in September 1993. In its aftermath, Cairo became the main venue for the Israeli–Palestinian negotiations that culminated in the Gaza and Jericho agreement, signed in Cairo in May 1994.

Progress in the resolution of the Arab–Israeli conflict, however, posed a serious dilemma and challenge for the Egyptian decision-makers as well as intellectuals. On the positive side, progress toward peace could grant access to Western and Israeli technology and know-how, which would benefit the less developed Arab economies. This kind of thinking led to the convening of the Middle East and North African (MENA) economic conferences in Casablanca, Amman, Cairo, and Doha from 1993 to 1997. On the negative side, it renewed Egyptian fears of Israeli expansionism. Moreover, the concept of "Middle Easternism" (*al-sharq awsaṭīyya*) threatened to further erode Egypt's regional influence in view of Israel's powerful economic and military capabilities. Recognition of Israel's status in the region (as well as that of Turkey and Iran) might mean that a new Middle Eastern system could replace the old Arab system as the natural economic and political arena for the Arab states. Thus, dialectically, the effects of the peace process might also be detrimental to Egypt's regional aspirations.[47]

In the second half of Mubarak's rule, a series of domestic problems hampered Egypt's ability to assume a leadership role in the Arab world. First, Mubarak was compelled to devote increasing resources after 1992 to contain the Islamic menace whose terrorist activities threatened to undermine the regime's stability. Second, in the early 1990s, Egypt embarked on a series of successful structural reforms based on the recommendations of the International Monetary Fund (IMF) and the World Bank (WB), and consequently received financial support from these institutions. Finally, Mubarak was the first Egyptian president to institute drastic measures to curb the country's rapid population growth.[48] These developments on the home front reduced the resources Egypt could devote to foreign interventions, thereby hindering Egypt's ability to be a leader of the Arab world.

The deterioration in the Israeli–Palestinian conflict following the assassination of the Israeli Prime Minister Yitzhak Rabin in November 1995 also threatened to undermine regional and domestic stability. Egypt found itself in the role of stabilizer, attempting to relieve Israeli–Palestinian tensions. Iraq, Egypt's main rival for Arab pre-eminence, offered no competition; it was embroiled at the time in a protracted war in the Persian Gulf. Hence, Egypt became the most important Arab actor—militarily, politically, and culturally. Statistics for the 1990s confirm that Egypt rose in world and regional rankings in terms of its military expenditure and GNP, in contrast to the contemporaneous decline in Iraqi and Syrian military and economic capabilities.

The escalation of Israeli–Palestinian relations after October 2000 prompted Egypt to renew its mediation efforts. Mubarak, however, failed to put an end to the Second Intifada, and he watched enviously as Saudi Crown Prince ʿAbdullah's peace initiative was approved with certain modifications by the Beirut Arab summit in March 2002.[49] But Mubarak's concerns were dispelled when it emerged that Israel rejected the Arab Peace Initiative (API), and therefore Saudi Arabia was not able to use it to assert its leadership in the Arab system. Moreover, as a result of the US occupation of Iraq in April 2003, the Arab summits that were originally scheduled to take place in Bahrain and Tunisia in 2003 and 2004, respectively, were relocated and held in Cairo.

What kind of role, then, did Egypt play in the Arab system in the three decades of the Mubarak era? In the first period, which lasted until the Gulf War in 1990, Egypt played the role of *primus inter pares* (see Table 8.1). In contrast to conventional wisdom, Egypt was not marginalized by the Arab boycott and, despite the sanctions imposed on it, continued to interact with most Arab states politically and economically. Regarding its material capabilities, Egypt enjoyed some military advantages but these were offset by its domestic economic and demographic challenges. In terms of non-material assets, Mubarak enjoyed greater legitimacy than Sadat though he still suffered from the stigma of having supported the peace treaty with Israel. These deficiencies were compensated by a strong determination to reassert Egypt's regional influence, primarily through diplomacy. From 1990, Egypt was firmly reinstated as the leader of the Arab world, based on its renewed military capabilities and a strong self-image of regional preponderance. Egypt also profited from the fact that Iraq, its traditional rival, was isolated and ostracized. In addition, the fact that Egypt was considered the major Arab ally of the US superpower served as an additional non-material asset in the eyes of most regional players.

The al-Sisi Regime (2013–)

The January 2011 revolution, known as the Arab Spring, ousted the Mubarak regime and, after a short upheaval, led to the election of Muhammad Morsi, representing the Muslim Brotherhood, in June

2012. Before a year had elapsed, Morsi was deposed by a military coup led by ʻAbd al-Fattah al-Sisi, the Minister of Defense, who was elected president in May 2014 and re-elected in January 2018.

The internal problems following the Arab Spring led to the "domestication of Egypt's foreign policy."[50] Indeed, on the occasion of the fifth anniversary of the June 30, 2013 Revolution (deposing Morsi), Sisi emphasized Egypt's main challenges: "the absence of security and political stability, the prevalence of terrorism and armed violence and the collapse of the economy."[51] Yet, in spite of these formidable challenges, Sisi did not abandon the foreign field and made many foreign visits. According to official statements, their purpose was to establish a "balanced" international position and promote "Egypt's openness to all."[52] Indeed, when Egypt's Vision 2030 was outlined in February 2016, one of its stated objectives was "strengthening Egypt's position and leadership at the regional and international levels."[53] Yet, this lofty aim could not conceal the fact that Sisi's regional foreign policy record has been poor. True, he proposed the formation of a Joint Arab Force to deal with the Gulf crisis, but the project quickly failed. Also, Egypt was hardly involved in the numerous conflicts in the region. When Saudi Arabia and the UAE established a coalition against the pro-Iranian Houthis in Yemen, Egypt sent only four combat ships. This token force stood in sharp contrast to Egypt's extensive heavy military involvement in Yemen in the 1960s. Moreover, Egypt never became involved in the Syrian civil war, and its involvement in the neighboring Libyan civil war was limited. The only regional conflicts in which Egypt actively participated were neighboring conflicts with Hamas in Gaza and with Ethiopia regarding the construction of its Renaissance Dam. This "hands-off" approach was expressed by Foreign Minister Sameh Shoukri in a statement to parliament in May 2016, that "Egypt is not seeking leadership (*riyāda*), and we do not want to be a leader of anyone…We want to be partners, in a way that preserves common interests."[54]

Interestingly, however, Egypt continues to build its military capabilities beyond its domestic needs. Since 2011, Egypt's spending has risen dramatically, and costly arms deals have been signed with France, Germany, and the Soviet Union, making Egypt the twelfth largest military power in the world, the first in the Arab world, and the sixth strongest navy in the world. Moreover, from 2014 to 2017, Egypt participated in military exercises with Saudi Arabia, UAE, Bahrain, Kuwait, Russia, and Greece.[55] No less important, Egypt's foreign policy underwent a process of "militarization," as the two new defense institutions established under the new constitution—the National Security Council and the National Council for Combating Terrorism and

Extremism—play an important role in the execution of Egypt's foreign policy.[56] Egypt's increasing militarism may be motivated by Sisi's desire to appease the army and enlist its support both to reinforce his own position and extend assistance in addressing domestic terror (including the banned Muslim Brotherhood). It is nevertheless plausible that in the absence of any effective economic tools, Sisi may be developing Egypt's military capabilities to enhance his country's regional status.

Egypt's main lack of leadership assets lies in its economic sphere, which deteriorated following the Arab Spring: As a result of the failure to stem population growth (2.4–2.6 percent, which means that annual population growth is 2.3 million), 35 percent of the country's 104 million residents (July 2020) are believed to live below the national poverty line ($45 per month). Dwindling foreign reserves, which dropped to $17 billion in 2016, compelled Egypt to take a $12 billion loan from the IMF and agree to the introduction of broad reforms, including reduced subsidies for energy, the introduction of a sales tax, and a 50 percent devaluation of the Egyptian pound. In addition, the Gulf countries of Saudi Arabia, UAE, and Kuwait contributed an unverified sum of billions of dollars to alleviate the economic crisis.[57] The huge project of widening the Suez Canal, reopened in 2015, was aimed at acquiring additional revenues. However, despite some improvement in the economy by 2020 (e.g., foreign reserves increased to $38.245 billion[58]), rising inflation, soaring prices, and growing unemployment meant that domestic issues—the economy and the fight against terrorism—will probably remain Egypt's main priority and hinder its ability to project power beyond its borders.[59]

Nonetheless, Egyptians continue to speak of its leadership of the Arab world. For example, former Foreign Minister Nabil Fahmy predicted in 2016 that Egypt is "ready to play a leading role *(dawr qiyādī)*" in the region.[60] A former assistant to the foreign minister assessed that Sisi's foreign policy "has scored successes, restoring Egypt's influence, and I dare say, leadership."[61] Eman Ragab, an expert on security at al-Ahram Center wrote that "if Egypt continues on this path during al-Sisi's expected second term in office, then there will be many positive outcomes, such as Egypt's becoming a major regional partner steering the region to a safer and more secure future,"[62] and another writer wondered whether Egypt or Saudi Arabia was leading the Arab world.[63] Contradicting assessments have also been voiced, such as the comment by an Egyptian-born Palestinian thinker, who opined that "Arabs must stop waiting for Egypt, rid themselves of this irrational nostalgia for its past role and start looking at the future."[64] Indeed, several Arab scholars acknowledged Egypt's diminished role, which dovetailed the growing role of non-Arab regional powers—Israel, Turkey, and Iran—and the rise of Saudi Arabia as a potential Arab leader.[65]

Some of these assessments seem to be more wishful thinking than sober analyses of reality. Despite its growing military capabilities, Egypt is not involved in the major regional conflicts except those at its doorstep, which potentially can affect its national security interests. Moreover, Sisi does not possess sufficient attributes of soft power—legitimacy, charisma, and attractive ideology—to serve as a beacon for the Arab world. Therefore, Egypt's current position does not seem to fit neatly into any of the categories on the proposed preponderance continuum. For the first time in its modern history, Egypt is not functioning in any leadership capacity.

Ayellet Yehiav, a leading expert on Egypt in the Israeli Foreign Office, who tragically passed away two weeks after participating in the conference leading to this volume, offered me, in a private conversation, the term "indispensable leadership" to describe Egypt's position. In his *Philosophy of the Revolution*, ʻAbd al-Nasser wrote that "within the Arab circle there is a role wandering aimlessly in search of a hero."[66] It seems that this role continues to wander in the Arab world. Today, Saudi Arabia is the only relevant contender for this role, but Egypt's indispensability to the Arab world—based on its history, culture, and military capabilities—may yet bring it back to a leading Arab position in the future.

Notes

1. Nael Shama, *Egyptian Foreign Policy from Mubarak to Morsi* (London: Routledge, 2014), 239. See also 'Abd al-Mun'im al-Mashāṭ (ed.), *al-Dawr al-Iqlīmī li-Maṣr fi al-Sharq al-'Awsaṭ* (Cairo: 1995).
2. See Joseph S. Nye, Jr., *Bound to Lead: The Changing Nature of American Power* (New York: Basic Books, 1990), 26–29; and Hans J. Morgenthau, *Politics among Nations: The Struggle for Power and Peace*, 5th ed. (New York: Alfred Knopf, 1978), 117–155.
3. Kenneth N. Waltz, *Theory of International Politics* (Reading, MA: Addison-Wesley Publishing, 1979), 131.
4. On the distinction between "soft" and "hard" power, see Nye, Jr., *Bound to Lead*, 32.
5. K.J. Holsti, "National Role Conceptions in the Study of Foreign Policy," in Stephan G. Walker (ed.), *Role Theory and Foreign Policy Analysis* (Durham: Duke University Press, 1987), 21.
6. Charles Kindleberger, "Dominance and Leadership in the International Economy," *International Organization* 35, no. 2 (June 1981), 243; and Hedley Bull, *The Anarchical Society: A Study of Order in World Politics* (New York: Columbia University Press, 1977), 214–215.
7. On the beginning of the Arab system, see Elie Podeh, "The Emergence of the Arab State System Reconsidered," *Diplomacy and Statecraft* 9 (1998), 50–82.
8. Elie Podeh, *The Quest for Hegemony in the Arab World: The Struggle over the Baghdad Pact* (Leiden: E, J. Brill, 1995).
9. Haggai Erlich, *Egypt—The Older Sister* (Tel Aviv: The Open University, 2003), 13 (Hebrew).
10. On Egypt's foreign policy, see Ali E. Hillal Dessouki, "The Primacy of Economics: The Foreign Policy of Egypt," in Bahgat Korany and Ali E. Hillal Dessouki (eds.), *The Foreign Policies of Arab States* (Cairo: American University in Cairo Press, 1984), 119–146; and Raymond Hinnebusch, "The Foreign Policy of Egypt," in Raymond Hinnebusch and Anoushiravan Ehteshami (eds.), *The Foreign Policies of Middle East States* (Boulder: Lynne Rienner, 2002), 91–114.
11. Podeh, *The Quest for Hegemony in the Arab World*, 126–242.
12. On the UAR, see Elie Podeh, *The Decline of Arab Unity: The Rise and Fall of the United Arab Republic* (Brighton: Sussex Academic Press, 1999).
13. Quoted in A.I. Dawisha, "Intervention in the Yemen: An Analysis of Egyptian Perceptions and Policies," *Middle East Journal* 29 (1975), 55.
14. On the tripartite talks, see Elie Podeh, "To Unite or Not to Unite: That Is *Not* the Question—The 1963 Tripartite Unity Talks Reassessed," *Middle Eastern Studies* 39, no. 1 (2003), 150–185.
15. Avraham Sela, *The Decline of the Arab–Israeli Conflict* (Albany: SUNY Press, 1998), 57–61.
16. "The End of Pan-Arabism," *Foreign Affairs* 57, no. 2 (1978), 358.
17. Sela, *The Decline of the Arab–Israeli Conflict*, 111.

18. Malcolm Kerr, *The Arab Cold War: Gamal 'Abd al-Nasser and His Rivals*, 3rd ed. (London: Oxford University Press, 1971), 155.
19. Paul C. Noble, "The Arab System: Opportunities, Constraints and Pressures," in Bahgat Korany and Ali E. Hillal Dessouki (eds.), *The Foreign Policies of Arab States* (Cairo: The American University in Cairo Press, 1984), 104.
20. Carl Brown, *International Politics and the Middle East* (London: I.B. Tauris, 1984), 88.
21. Kerr, *The Arab Cold War*, 154–155.
22. For data, see Noble, "The Arab System," 52–55, 58–60.
23. In this connection, see various articles in Elie Podeh and Onn Winckler (eds.), *Rethinking Nasserism: Revolution and Historical Memory in Modern Egypt* (Gainesville: University Press of Florida, 2004).
24. On these methods, see Adeed Dawisha, *Egypt in the Arab World: The Elements of Foreign Policy* (London: Macmillan, 1976), 160–179.
25. John Waterbury, "Egypt: The Wages of Dependency," in A.L. Udovitch (ed.), *The Middle East: Oil, Conflict and Hope* (Lexington: Lexington Books, 1976), 342–343.
26. Dessouki, "Primacy of Economics," 124–126.
27. *Dialogues in Arab Politics: Negotiations in Regional Order* (New York: Columbia University Press, 1998), 263.
28. Anwar al-Sadat, "Where Egypt Stands," *Foreign Affairs* 51, no. 1 (1972), 117.
29. Sela, *The Decline of the Arab–Israeli Conflict*, 140. See also Dessouki, "The Primacy of Economics," 129.
30. For more about the road to the war and the Arab conduct during it, see Sela, *The Decline of the Arab–Israeli Conflict*, 140–150.
31. "Inter-Arab Relations," in Itamar Rabinovich and Haim Shaked (eds.), *From June to October: The Middle East between 1967 and 1973* (New Brunswick, NJ: Transaction Books, 1978), 167–168.
32. Bruce Maddy-Weitzman, *A Century of Arab Politics: From the Arab Revolt to the Arab Spring* (Lanham: Rowman and Littlefield, 2016), 109–129.
33. Sela, *The Decline of the Arab–Israeli Conflict*, 155–157.
34. Ibid., 201–213. Regarding the boycott, see Elie Podeh and Onn Winckler, *The Boycott That Never Was: Egypt in the Arab World, 1979–1989*, Durham Middle East Papers, no. 72 (Durham, 2002).
35. Ali E. Hillal Dessouki, "The New Arab Political Order: Implications for the 1980s," in Malcolm H. Kerr and El Sayed Yassin (eds.), *Rich and Poor States in the Middle East: Egypt and the New Arab Order* (Boulder: Westview, 1982), 319.
36. Ibid., 329.
37. Ibid., 343.
38. See Podeh and Winckler, *The Boycott That Never Was*.
39. For an analysis of this phenomenon, see Podeh and Winckler, *The Boycott That Never Was*.
40. Malcolm H. Kerr, "Introduction: Egypt in the Shadow of the Gulf," *Rich and Poor States, in the Middle East*, 6, 11–12.

41. In terms of military expenditure, Egypt ranked third in the Arab world; in terms of size of its armed forces, it was ranked second, after Iraq. See Shlomo Gazit (ed.), *The Middle East Military Balance 1988–1989* (Boulder: Westview, 1989), 151–152, 174, 277, 308–309, 311.
42. Makram Muhammad Ahmad, *al-Muṣawwar*, May 19, 1989.
43. "Egypt, Syria and the Arab System in the New World Order," in Haifaa A. Jawad (ed.), *The Middle East in the New World Order* (London: Routledge, 2nd ed., 1997), 171.
44. For the full text, see *Journal of Palestine Studies* 20, no. 2 (Winter 1991), 161–163.
45. Bruce Maddy-Weitzman, "A New Arab Order? Regional Security after the Gulf War," *Orient* 34, no. 2 (1993), 224–225.
46. Hinnebusch, "Egypt, Syrian and the Arab System," 171.
47. On this concept and the debate in Egypt, see Sela, *The Decline of the Arab–Israeli Conflict*, 339–340.
48. See, in this connection, Galal Amin, *Egypt in the Era of Hosni Mubarak, 1981–2011* (Cairo: American University of Cairo Press, 2011).
49. Elie Podeh, "Israel and the Arab Peace Imitative, 2002–2014—A Plausible Missed Opportunity?" *Middle East Journal* 68 (2014), 584–603.
50. Eric Trager, "The Domestication of Sisi's Foreign Policy," *Caravan*, Hoover Institute (March 8, 2017), see https://www.hoover.org/research/sisis-domesticated-foreign-policy.
51. For the text, see http://sis.gov.eg/Story/132112?lang=en-us, July 2, 2018.
52. Eman Ragab, "New Foreign Policy Thinking," *al-Ahram Weekly* 1328 (January 2017): 19–25.
53. "Egypt's Vision 2030," https://mped.gov.eg/EgyptVision?lang=en.
54. Quoted in Mohamed Kamal, "The Middle East according to Egypt," *The Cairo Review of Global Affairs* (Spring 2018).
55. Yagil Henkin, "The Egyptian Military Buildup: An Enigma," The Jerusalem Institute for Strategic Studies (January 7, 2018); Nael Sham, "Egypt's Power Game: Why Cairo Boosting its Military Power," *Jadaliyya* (September 6, 2017); and Eman Ragab, "The National Security Components of Egyptian Foreign Policy," *Ahram Online* (May 10, 2018).
56. Ibid.
57. According to one report, only Saudi Arabia gave Egypt until 2016, $25 billion, see http://nesannews.org/?id=58158. The original article was published in *Huffington Post* but I did not find it.
58. "Egypt's Foreign Reserves Record $38.425B by End of September," *Egypt Today*, October 7, 2000, https://www.egypttoday.com/Article/3/92812/Egypt%E2%80%99s-foreign-reserves-record-38-425B-by-end-of-September.
59. Paul Rivlin, "The Egyptian Economy: The Plot Thickens," *Iqtisadi* 7, no. 2 (February 23, 2017); "Egypt's Economy: Turning the Corner, Standing Still or in Retreat?" *Iqtisadi* 8, no. 2 (February 26, 2018); and Stephan Roll, "'Flash-in-the-Pan' Development in Egypt?" SWP Comment 31 (July 2018).
60. Interview, *al-Shorouk* (January 20, 2016).

61. Hussein Haridy, "One Year Later," *al-Ahram Weekly*, 1250 (November 4, 2017).
62. Eman Ragab, "The National Security Components of Egyptian Foreign Policy," *Ahram Online* (May 10, 2018).
63. ʻAbdallah al-Sināwī, "Miṣr wal-Suʻudīyya: Liman Qiyādat al-ʻĀlam al-ʻArabī?" *al-Shorouk* (December 11, 2015).
64. Basheer Nafi, "Egypt Is No Longer the Heart of the Arab World," *Middle East Eye* (May 13, 2017).
65. Khayr al-Dīn Ḥasīb, "al-ʻArab… 'Ila 'Ayna? Naḥwa Khuṭṭat Ṭarīq lil-Khurūj min al-Ma'ziq al-ʻArabī al-Rāhen," *al-Mustaqbal al-ʻArabī* (January 2016), 120; and ʻAlī al-Dīn Hilāl, "Ḥāl al-'Umma al-ʻArabīyya, 2016–2015," *al-Mustaqbal al-ʻArabī* (May 2016), 18.
66. Premier Gamal Abdul Nasser, *Egypt's Liberation: The Philosophy of the Revolution* (Washington: Public Affairs Press, 1955), 87–88.

Selected Bibliography

Amin, Galal, *Egypt in the Era of Hosni Mubarak, 1981–2011* (Cairo: American University of Cairo Press, 2011).

Hinnebusch, Raymond, "The Foreign Policy of Egypt," in Raymond Hinnebusch and Anoushiravan Ehteshami, eds., *The Foreign Policies of Middle East States* (Boulder: Lynne Rienner, 2002), 91–114.

Maddy-Weitzman, Bruce, *A Century of Arab Politics: From the Arab Revolt to the Arab Spring* (Lanham: Rowman and Littlefield, 2016).

Podeh, Elie, *The Quest for Hegemony in the Arab World: The Struggle over the Baghdad Pact* (Leiden: E, J. Brill, 1995).

Podeh, Elie, "To Unite or Not to Unite: That Is Not the Question—The 1963 Tripartite Unity Talks Reassessed," *Middle Eastern Studies* 39, no. 1 (2003), 150–185.

Shama, Nael, *Egyptian Foreign Policy from Mubarak to Morsi* (London: Routledge, 2014).

HOW SHOULD A REVOLUTION BE REMEMBERED? HEGEMONIC COLLECTIVE MEMORY VERSUS COUNTER-COLLECTIVE MEMORIES

State Efforts to Establish Museums for the 1952 Revolution in Egypt

Joyce van de Bildt-de Jong

The Free Officers revolution of July 1952 was a major turning point in the modern history of Egypt: it marked the beginning of the elimination of foreign hegemony. Dramatically stated, it was the first time in two millennia that Egypt was being governed by Egyptians. The revolution put an end to the monarchy and what was perceived as the corrupt, ineffective governance of the palace. Most importantly, it was felt that the revolution returned a sense of dignity to the Egyptian people. Its reforms fundamentally changed Egyptian society, among other things with its policies regarding land redistribution, free education, and nationalization of banks and companies. At the same time, the perceived shortcomings of the revolution, especially its abiding lack of democracy, weak economy, and failure to attain social justice, continue to have an impact today. Nevertheless, as the country's central historical event in the twentieth century, the memory of the revolution has been vital in forming the Egyptian national identity.

The 1952 revolution marked the beginning of a new era for Egypt and represented a sharp break with the past. For the Egyptian state, the 1952 revolution became the "founding national narrative" of the republic. It symbolized the break with the monarchic and colonized past and defined Egypt as a sovereign nation, hence legitimizing the new ruling elite's position in power.[1] Gamal ʿAbd al-Nasser's regime sought to implant the revolutionary narrative in the public through commemorative ceremonies, history writing, school curricula, street naming, revolutionary trials, publication of stamps, and the institution of new public holidays.[2] During the Sadat and Mubarak years, the 1952 revolution remained an important part of the state's master narrative as well. Though both leaders distanced themselves from policies associated with the revolutionary reforms of the Nasser era, they adapted the narrative of the revolution in a way that benefited their policies and their image in order to maintain the legitimacy they derived from the revolutionary legacy.

In spite of the centrality of the event in Egyptian history and its potential function of boosting the regime's legitimacy, the state has constantly delayed the establishment of an official museum for the revolution. This is particularly noticeable given the fact that the state's narrative of the revolution has been constantly challenged by various groups within Egyptian society. Its meaning, its achievements, its desired orientation, and its shortcomings have remained the topic of intense debate since its outbreak. The memory of the revolution as well as the narrative of its events remain highly contested. Over time, the revolution became subject to the "politics of memory" as groups within society exploited selected elements of the revolutionary legacy to serve their political goals of the moment. In light of this situation, it is striking that the Egyptian government for a long time failed to capitalize on the possibility of establishing a state museum where it could demonstrate its own narrative of the revolution. Timothy Luke describes the potential of museums as "subtle agencies of political persuasion"—invoking powerful symbols that can evoke ideals, recast realities, and manufacture meanings.[3] Moreover, Eric Davis has argued that states can use museums to strengthen their power and authority. As such, museums can serve as an instrument for social control, using the representation of the past to promote well-defined ideological messages to the populace at large, and glorifying historical episodes for the purpose of boosting the government's legitimacy.[4] Although the government first announced its intention for the establishment of an official museum of the revolution in 1996, it has taken at least 25 years to materialize these plans and to open the museum to the public.

In 1996, the Egyptian government made its first effort to establish a museum for the 1952 revolution. President Hosni Mubarak issued Presidential Decree No. 204 to transform the former headquarters of the Revolutionary Command Council (RCC) into a Museum of the Leaders of the 1952 revolution.[5] For symbolic reasons, the former RCC headquarters, located on Gezira Island in Cairo, were designated as the location for the envisioned museum. Several historic decisions had been issued here, including the agrarian reform law and the abolition of political parties.[6] The establishment of the republic was proclaimed from this building, and the first president of the republic, Mohammed Naguib, had his office on the third floor.[7] During the Suez Crisis in 1956, Nasser used the building as his place of lodging and command, reportedly remaining there without leaving for ten days in a row.[8] The building housed Nasser's former office, too, and his funeral cortege departed from the site on October 1, 1970. Moreover, the building witnessed several court cases, including the revolutionary trials (*muḥākamāt al-thawra*) of feudal lords, members of the royal family, and politicians. It was the venue of the famous trial of the Muslim Brotherhood, charged with the assassination attempt of Nasser in al-Manshiya Square in Alexandria; the trial of Field Marshal 'Abd al-Ḥakīm 'Amr and dozens of other officers, who supposedly had intended to overthrow the government and isolate Nasser after the Six-Day War defeat in 1967; and the trials of the "centers of power" following Anwar al-Sadat's Corrective Revolution in 1971.[9] When these trials ended, President Sadat used the building as the headquarters of his personal secretariat since it was close to his home in Giza.[10] Allegedly, the idea to turn the building into a museum was first proposed during the Nasser era; preparations for its opening were underway until the project came to a halt with the outbreak of the 1967 war. The project has remained unfinished ever since.[11]

The Museum of the Leaders of the Revolution envisioned by the Mubarak administration clearly served the purpose of promoting the official memory of 1952. The preliminary narrative for the museum, outlined by the state in the early 2000s, was to focus on the three presidents of the republic—Naguib, Nasser, and Sadat—and to highlight important decisions made by the RCC.[12] Discrete sections would be dedicated to each of the three presidents and feature some of their most important holdings.[13] A portrait of every president would be accompanied by a sentence to illustrate his main contributions to Egypt. Thus, Naguib would be noted for "The liquidation of the monarchy and liberation from the English"; Nasser for "The High Dam, nationalization of the Canal and the Revolution"; and Anwar al-Sadat as "Hero of War and Peace." Hosni Mubarak's picture was to be included, too, accompanied by the caption: "Prosperity of the state in all areas, guaranteeing Arab Unity and completion of the liberation of Sinai."[14]

Other sections of the museum were to be devoted to the remaining members of the RCC, showcasing rare objects such as jewelry, personal weapons, and items of furniture and other antiques, and documents related to the revolution.[15] The building, which consists of several wings, has a garage where the curators planned to display a number of vintage cars, among them Nasser's personal car and the one he used for his popular rounds. One of these, Nasser's small black Austin, was donated to the museum by his daughter, Hoda 'Abd al-Nasser, in 2005 together with his collection of medals.[16] The curators also intended to display the tank used to besiege the palace of King Farouq during the revolution.[17] The exhibition was planned to include the microphone from which President Sadat broadcast the first statement of the revolution; the first flag raised on the Sinai after the Egyptians' crossing in 1973; pictures and busts of Nasser and Sadat; photographs from when the building functioned as the RCC headquarters; gifts presented to Sadat on various occasions; and a set of commemorative stamps issued from 1952 to 1960 to commemorate the anniversary of the revolution.[18] Artists were invited to paint murals of historical events related to the revolution, such as the nationalization of the Suez Canal and the Suez Crisis of 1956. In addition, a panorama depicting the events and leading figures of the revolution was envisioned in the building's tower overlooking the Nile.[19]

Interestingly, a story that was to be left out of the museum's narrative was the building's pre-revolutionary function. Its construction, originally ordered by King Farouq in 1949 for the Royal Navy fleet, was completed in 1951. Initially, it served as an anchorage for royal yachts, and later as a vacation residence for the royal family.[20] The building contained several secret escape routes, one of them leading to the Nile. It is likely that these fortifications made the building attractive to the RCC as headquarters.[21] During the renovations, an enormous structure of stainless steel representing an eagle, symbol of the republic, was built on the roof of the building—a concept that emerged after the discovery of many pictures of eagles adorning the inner and outer walls of the building. The eagle on the roof is supported by pillars bearing the three slogans of the revolution: *Ḥurrīyya, ishtirākīyya, waḥda* (freedom, socialism, unity). A laser beam, introduced in Egypt for the first time, was installed to reflect the eagle and the three slogans in the sky above the museum every year on the night of July 23, for all the public to see.[22]

The opening of the museum was initially planned to take place a few months after the start of construction activities.[23] However, the project was indefinitely delayed. After work on the museum stopped in 2001, supposedly due to a lack of funds, the parliament's Cultural Committee requested an additional 20 million pounds to complete the museum.[24] The opening was postponed until July 2002—the fiftieth, "golden" jubilee of the revolution—but the museum was by no means ready by then.[25] In 2009, after years without progress, the RCC building was placed under the supervision of the Egyptian Supreme Council of Antiquities and added to the list of Islamic and Coptic monuments.[26] The Council's Secretary General Zāhi Ḥawwās was put in charge of implementing the museum project, as well as releasing the first documentary about the revolution.[27] Ḥawwās announced that he would be inviting intellectuals and scholars of contemporary history to participate in the establishment of the July Revolution Museum. In 2009, the Arab Contractors Company won a new tender to carry out the restoration work. By this time, some progress had been made with the construction of the large roof-top eagle. After the January 2011 Revolution, the Ministry of Culture announced that work on the museum would resume, and proposed devoting a hall to the January 25th Revolution.[28] During the short-lived presidency of Muhammad Morsi, the government expressed its intention to convert it into a Museum for All Egyptian Revolutions, not just the July Revolution, and a new committee was appointed to this task. The government of President ʻAbd al-Fattah al-Sisi also promised it would resume renovations, but again the project was stalled. In April 2017, the president issued Decree No. 153, annexing the RCC building to the presidential palaces. Ultimately, in May 2018, the government charged the Ministry of Culture with the task of completing the museum within 15 months. The museum was close to opening by the end of 2020.[29]

The delay of this government project begs for an explanation. One reason could be that government bureaucracy impeded the implementation of the project. Among other things, the initiative reportedly remained "stuck" between departmental sectors of the Ministry of Culture.[30] Others cited corruption, asking where the millions of Egyptian pounds went that had been earmarked for the renovation of the building and turning it into a museum. Egyptian journalist and poet Farouq Gouida noted that the building is not very big; its 40 rooms or so could have been renovated quickly, pointedly remarking that "even the construction of the Aswan High Dam did not take this long."[31]

Nevertheless, explanations such as these fail to answer the question: Why did many other museum projects successfully established in the Mubarak era not face similar problems? During Mubarak's regime, the Ministry of Culture under Farouq Hosny and the Egyptian Supreme Council of Antiquities headed by Egyptologist Dr. Zāhi Ḥawwās led a conscious, clear government effort to preserve Egyptian history in museums. In 2006, the ministry announced that it had placed Egypt's museums at the top of its priorities and that 2006 would be "a revolutionary year for Egypt's museums and museology."[32] That year indeed witnessed the inauguration of more than five new museums and the reopening of three others following restoration and development.[33] Among the museums that received special attention over the past two decades were the Egyptian National Museum, the Library of Alexandria, the Graeco-Roman Museum, the Coptic Museum, and the all-new Nubian Museum. The same period saw the founding of museums honoring historic personalities: the Mustafa Kamel Museum, for instance, was opened in the beginning of 2001, after major restorations had been made to his mausoleum. This museum narrates the history of four famous political leaders of the pre-revolutionary era: Mustafa Kaeil, Muhammad Farid, ʻAbd al-Raḥmān al-Rāfeʻī, and Fatḥī Raḍwan.[34] Its establishment came in the framework of Minister of Culture Hosny's plan "to build several such museums to commemorate and honor renowned Egyptian personalities who played an important role in the national, artistic, cultural and political fields," including the poet Ahmad Shawqī, singers Umm Kulthum and ʻAbd al-Wahhāb, writer Ṭaha Hussein, and artist Mahmud Khalīl.[35] Further plans were announced to build a museum in Cairo honoring Egyptian writer Naguib Mahfouz. In 2003, Saʻd Zaghlūl's former home, known as *Bayt Al-Umma* (House of the Nation), opened its doors to the public. The house had functioned both as Zaghlūl's residence and as a meeting place for intellectuals and political activists in the inter-war period.[36] In light of these numerous achievements, it seems unlikely that the Ministry of Culture did not manage to establish a museum dedicated to the 1952 revolution because of bureaucratic or budgetary reasons.

It is certain that the lack of reliable historic documentation has complicated the process. President Mubarak appointed a history committee, headed by historian Yūnān Labīb Rizq and consisting of history professors from Egyptian universities as well as officials from the Department of Museums in the Ministry of Culture.[37] The committee was instructed to collect the testimonies of the remaining members of the RCC, interview family members of the ones who were already deceased, and gathering relevant items belonging to leaders of the revolution. Most of the committee's meetings with the witnesses of the revolution took place in the former headquarters itself.

Rizq's goal for the museum project was to finally record the complete history of the revolution. Thus, he envisioned part of the museum as a "library" of documents related to the revolution, part of an "attempt to approach the truth" about the history of 1952. He stated: "It will offer researchers and historians the opportunity to study the testimonies and provide a real insight into the events and the history of the revolution."[38] This was his response to the problems that emerged from the individual testimonies about the revolution that had flooded the Egyptian market and media since the 1970s. In his opinion, "the majority of them was not accurate" and could mislead researchers and the public. He concluded that "the writing about the revolution turned into a political activity instead of a historical and scientific endeavor."[39] In 2005, Hoda ʻAbd al-Nasser joined the museum committee. As head of the 'Egyptian Revolution Research Unit' at the Ahram Center for Political and Strategic Studies until then, she had been engaged in a similar history writing initiative. From 1996 to 2002, she led efforts to collect and organize documents related to the 1952 revolution and mainly about ʻAbd al-Nasser, to make them available to researchers and the public.[40]

It is known that the museum's history committee ran into significant difficulties while gathering the key documentation and items related to the revolution. This led to a debate over the disappearance of many revolutionary documents, their inaccessibility, and the chaotic state of their preservation. Farouq Gouida argued that the lack of access to these documents was the reason that historians had been reluctant or unsuccessful in writing the revolution's history.[41] Indeed, public access to information and state archives in Egypt historically has been impeded seriously by security institutions, while the archives themselves have suffered from mismanagement and officials have been accused of purposely destroying documents.[42] According to the Egyptian historian Sharīf Yūnis, during the Nasser years, many documents that contradicted the official narrative of the 1952 events simply disappeared.[43] Muhammad Ṣabr ʻArab, who served as the Director of the National Archives from 1999 to 2005, maintains that the archives do not contain any documents related to the revolution. "What is potentially worse," he wrote, "is that no one, no institution—public or private—has a register of what 'documents of the Revolution' there are, or where they are. This leaves ample room for loss and destruction of archives."[44] As an example, he cited the lacuna of documents pertaining to the Aswan High Dam project, which the National Archives attempted to acquire—to no avail—from the ministries of Agriculture, Irrigation, and Electricity, and from the High Dam Authority itself. The museum committee had been equally challenged when it tried to obtain documents and objects related to Naguib.[45]

While the RCC museum project was apparently on hold, part of the work of its history committee was published elsewhere, stimulating new discussions about the 1952 revolution. First of all, Farouq Gouida, who was involved in some of the personal interviews that the committee had conducted, published some of these testimonies together with his own observations about the history of the 1952 revolution in a series of articles in *al-Ahram* from May 23 to July 18, 1999. Among these was a rare interview with Zakārīyya Muḥyī al-Dīn, who had not written a memoir; this was the first time he had been interviewed since he left the political scene in 1968.[46] Gouida eventually turned his findings into a book titled *Man yaktubu tārīkh thawrat yūlyū?* (*Who Will Write the History of the July Revolution?*). In 2010, Gouida wondered aloud where the museum for the revolution was. He advocated for its importance, saying it is:

> not just an issue of restoring the building and establishing a museum of the July Revolution, but a fundamental issue linked to the history of the Egyptian people, and to make sure that its

> memory won't be lost [...] it concerns an ordeal of history in a country that is said to be the cradle of civilizations and the first to make history... [...] is this what we want for our future generations, to have no memory? Do we want a people with no past?[47]

Another response to the aborted development of the RCC museum came from Sāmī Sharaf. Sharaf, a politician of the Nasserist era, was imprisoned during Sadat's Corrective Revolution and released in May 1981. The idea for the RCC museum led him to promote the idea of turning Nasser's house into a museum. According to Sharaf, in a letter dated October 21, 1970, the state had promised that the house would be allocated "as a museum and a shrine commemorating the late leader."[48] In 1990, the family of Nasser wrote to Mubarak about the idea, and in 1999 Sharaf sought attention for the issue in *al-Ahram*.[49] Finally in 2005, the Ministry of Culture decided to turn Nasser's former house into a museum, which was eventually launched in October 2016.[50] One floor of it is dedicated to an historic overview of important events from the 1952 revolution until Nasser's death in 1970, including the nationalization of the Suez Canal, the 1956 and 1967 wars, and the union with Syria. The museum displays some of the rooms of Nasser's house in their original state, including his office and bedroom suite, as well as various personal belongings such as his camera, eyeglasses, and hand-written drafts of speeches. Notably, the museum's document collection includes some of the original decisions of the RCC, which supposedly should have been included in the RCC museum.

Indeed, the longer the opening of the RCC museum was postponed, the more items related to the revolution were transferred to other Egyptian museums, among them the museums for the three presidents in the "Pharaonic Village" entertainment park.[51] Most of the museums' holdings came from the families of these leaders, who may have otherwise donated them to the Museum for the Leaders of the Revolution. One can argue that perhaps Pharaonic Village "accomplished" what the RCC museum had been intended to do: it became the venue for various anniversaries, such as the birthday and commemoration day of ʻAbd al-Nasser, as well as October 6 celebrations, which are attended by family members and officials. *Al-Ahram* news editor Hanān Haggāg argued that the Ministry of Culture neglected its task of collecting and preserving items from the families for the benefit of the RCC museum, and consequently these rare collectibles were now "for sale" to private museums. She argued that since they concern the history of the country, they should have been the responsibility of the state.[52]

One might wonder why it was possible to erect individual museums for each president, but not one for all the leaders of the revolution jointly. Indeed, one must ask whether the reasons cited for the museum project's failure, such as the lack of documentation discussed above, adequately explain the absence of such a museum. An inescapable conclusion is that the failure to establish it was due as much to political obstacles as to bureaucratic ones: It would be very difficult, if not impossible, to accommodate all the nation's presidents as "Leaders of the Revolution" in a single commemorative site without remarking upon the stark contradictions between them. Considering the divergent views of the revolution's history and the political dissension it causes to this day, a presentation of the various presidencies in one museum could hardly produce a consistent narrative of the revolution that would satisfy a significant number of people. Evidently, then, the solution was to establish separate museums for each president, but not conjoined in one place.

The 25 January Revolution of 2011 and the events of June 30, 2013, have further complicated the formation of a representative narrative of the 1952 revolution and its meaning. Comparisons between the 1952 revolution and the 2011 revolution have been used to promote contradictory interpretations of contemporary developments.[53] On the one hand, there were those who linked the slogans and goals of the 2011 revolution to that of the Free Officers' Revolution of 1952 because of their common call for change, freedom, social justice, and dignity.[54] They argued that the 2011 protests reiterated the original agenda of the 1952 revolution. On the other hand, there were those who claimed that the 2011 revolution came to correct the 1952 revolution and to eliminate, finally, the regime that had ruled Egypt ever since.[55] In yet another comparison in the aftermath of July 3, 2013, some claimed that the army's intervention saved the country from the Muslim Brotherhood as Nasser supposedly had done after 1954.[56] Others believed that, once again, the country had chosen military dictatorship over democracy, as was the case in the 1950s.[57] Thus, although it is still too early to assess the influence of the 2011 revolution and its place in the Egyptian collective memory, it is clear that its events sparked new struggles over the national past.

As for the state, since July 2013, the government led by Sisi has developed a special interest in highlighting the legacy of the 1952 revolution, primarily to cultivate a renewed emphasis on patriotism and the nation's military tradition.[58] According to the current state narrative, the army's move to depose the president in 2011 was a response to the aspirations of the Egyptian people, just like the army acted as the people's vanguard in July 1952. Similarly, this narrative stresses that, just as the 23 July Revolution was constantly confronted by enemies seeking to overthrow it, so the current Egyptian state faces an "existential challenge against a scheme to undermine the state."[59] Moreover, Sisi encouraged a trend in which he was often compared to Nasser.[60]

Sisi's relationship to the 2011 revolution is ambiguous, and the question of who speaks for the 2011 revolution remains a major point of contention within Egyptian society. Since commemoration is an intensely political activity, it is currently more comfortable for the Egyptian state to evade the topic of a museum for the 2011 revolution. Instead, the president has focused on other commemorative projects. He opened a new museum honoring Nasser, for example, and revived several other major projects, such as the National Museum of Egyptian Civilization and the Grand Egyptian Museum. In 2017, he opened a new military base named after Muhammed Naguib, which also housed a museum.

Conclusion

The difficulty in establishing a museum for the 1952 revolution is derived largely from the challenge of collecting key historical records and, perhaps even more, of telling a balanced narrative of the events, its personalities, and their impact. Typically, "museums remain the commanding heights of many ongoing battles over what is accepted as reality."[61] It can be said, in fact, that, "in selecting what to collect, [museums] define what is or is not history."[62] Hence, the museum's establishment has been complicated by the fact that the one definitive history of the 1952 revolution has not been written so far.

At the same time, the museum's envisioned narrative has been subject to much scrutiny during a period when museums worldwide and in Egypt, too, are increasingly evolving into democratic cultural platforms that seek to engage the community, address contemporary issues, and appeal to a wide audience.[63] Some Egyptian intellectuals such as Gouida believed the museum could ultimately contribute to resolving the differences of opinion about the revolution. On the contrary, however, ever since its outbreak, the revolution's contested legacy has encumbered the establishment of the museum. This is a prime example of how museums are the setting for "an ongoing conflict between the construction of meanings that support an authorized collective memory [...] and an ambition to act as places of pluralism and inclusion" of non-state narratives.[64] This challenge has proved far more profound than the bureaucratic obstacles and corruption that have taken the blame for the museum's delay. Indeed, these reasons do not explain why many other museum projects were successfully established according to plan during the Mubarak era. The narrative of the 1952 revolution, as potentially presented by the envisioned museum, has been put under a magnifying glass even more since the revolutions of 2011 and 2013; they not only caused the 1952 revolution to be viewed increasingly through the lens of the present, but also added an urgent need to heed the voice of the Egyptian public. Egypt's difficulty in navigating these waters underscores how fundamentally important the 1952 revolution remains in the minds of Egyptians, how relevant its effects are considered to this day, and how its legacy is perceived to define contemporary Egypt, one way or another, more than 65 years after the event.

Notes

1. Laurie Brand, *Official Stories: Politics and National Narratives in Egypt and Algeria* (Redwood City: Stanford University Press, 2014), 14.
2. Israel Gershoni and James P. Jankowski, *Commemorating the Nation: Collective Memory, Public Commemoration, and National Identity in Twentieth-Century Egypt* (Chicago: Middle East Documentation Center, 2004), 257–279; Elie Podeh, *The Politics of National Celebrations in the Arab Middle East* (Cambridge: Cambridge University Press, 2011), 72–78; Yoav Di-Capua, *Gatekeepers of the Arab Past: Historians and History Writing in Twentieth-Century Egypt* (Berkeley: University of California Press, 2009), 248–281; Yoav Di-Capua, "Embodiment of the Revolutionary Spirit: The Mustafa Kamil Mausoleum in Cairo," *History & Memory* 13, no. 1 (2001): 85–113; Yoram Meital, "Central Cairo: Street Naming and the Struggle over Historical Representation," *Middle Eastern Studies* 43, no. 6 (November 2008): 857–878; Yoram Meital, "School Textbooks and Assembling the Puzzle of the Past in Revolutionary Egypt," *Middle Eastern Studies* 42, no. 2 (March 2006): 255–270; Yoram Meital, "The Aswan High Dam and Revolutionary Symbolism," in *The Nile: Histories, Cultures, Myths*, ed. Hagai Erlikh and Israel Gershoni (Lynne Rienner Publishers, 2000), 219–226; Yoram Meital, *Revolutionary Justice: Special Courts and the Formation of Republican Egypt* (Oxford: Oxford University Press, 2016); and Donald Reid, "Egyptian History Through Stamps," *The Muslim World* 62, no. 3 (1967): 209–229.
3. Timothy Luke, *Museum Politics: Power Plays at the Exhibition* (Minneapolis: University of Minnesota Press, 2002), xix–xiv.
4. Eric Davis, "The Museum and the Politics of Social Control in Iraq," in *Commemorations: The Politics of National Identity*, ed. John R. Gillis (Princeton: Princeton University Press, 1994), 90–104.
5. "Matḥaf Zuʿamā' al-Thawra," website of the Egyptian State Information Service (June 18, 2013), http://www.sis.gov.eg/Story/70596?lang=ar.
6. "Mabnā 'Qiyādat al-Thawra'.. 'Marsā al-Mulūk' Alladhī Taḥawwala 'ilā 'Kharāba,'" *al-Waṭan* (October 12, 2015).
7. Wagīh al-Saqr, "Bad' 'Iqāmat Matḥaf Zuʿamā' al-Thawra," *al-Ahrām*, July 26, 2002, 33.
8. ʿĀtef ʿAbd al-Ghanī, "Aṣrār al-Mabnā Alladhī Kāna Yaḥkumu Miṣr," *October*, July 28, 1996, 48–49.
9. "Mabnā 'Qiyādat al-Thawra'.. 'Marsā al-Mulūk' Alladhī Taḥawwala 'ilā 'Kharāba,'" *al-Waṭan* (October 12, 2015).
10. ʿAbd al-Ghanī, "Aṣrār al-Mabnā Alladhī Kāna Yaḥkumu Miṣr."
11. "A Day like No Other," *Al-Ahram Weekly* (June 5, 2008), http://weekly.ahram.org.eg/Archive/2008/900/fe01.htm.
12. Ola El-Saket, "Egypt's Museums: The Revolutionary Command Council Museum," *Egypt Independent* (August 3, 2011), https://www.egyptindependent.com/egypts-museums-revolutionary-command-council-museum/.
13. Ṭaha Muhammad, "'Ibnat ʿAbd al-Nāṣer Tuhdī Sayyāratahu al-Khāṣṣa 'ilā Matḥaf Zuʿamā' al-Thawra," *al-Jazirah* (May 14, 2005).

14. Al-Saqr, "Bad' 'Iqāmat Matḥaf Zu'amā' al-Thawra."
15. "Da'm 'Ājel li-Matḥaf Zu'amā' al-Thawra," *al-Sharq al-Awsaṭ* (October 5, 2001).
16. Muhammad, "'Ibnat 'Abd al-Nāṣer Tuhdī Sayyāratahu al-Khāṣṣa 'ilā Matḥaf Zu'amā' al-Thawra."
17. Al-Saqr, "Bad' 'Iqāmat Matḥaf Zu'amā' al-Thawra."
18. "Matḥaf Zu'amā' al-Thawra," Egyptian State Information Service (June 18, 2013).
19. Al-Saqr, "Bad' 'Iqāmat Matḥaf Zu'amā' al-Thawra."
20. 'Abd al-Ghanī, "Aṣrār al-Mabnā Alladhī Kāna Yaḥkumu Miṣr."
21. Ibid.
22. Al-Saqr, "Bad' 'Iqāmat Matḥaf Zu'amā' al-Thawra."
23. "Matḥaf Zu'amā' al-Thawra," Egyptian State Information Service (June 18, 2013). 'Abd al-Ghanī, "Aṣrār al-Mabnā Alladhī Kāna Yaḥkumu Miṣr."
24. "Da'm 'Ājel li-Matḥaf Zu'amā' al-Thawra."
25. Al-Saqr, "Bad' 'Iqāmat Matḥaf Zu'amā' al-Thawra."
26. Fatḥīyya al-Dakhākhnī, "Al-Āthār Tabda'u fī 'Inshā' Matḥaf Thawrat 23 Yūlyū bi-Mabnā Qiyādat al-Thawra bi-l-Qāhera," *al-Maṣrī al-Yawm* (December 22, 2009). As such, the RCC building became subject to the law of the protection of monuments and archaeological sites, which gave the building the status of having "historical and archaeological value."
27. Al-Dakhākhnī, Al-Āthār Tabda'u fī 'Inshā' Matḥaf Thawrat 23 Yūlyū."
28. El-Saket, "Egypt's Museums: The Revolutionary Command Council Museum."
29. "Matḥaf Qiyādat al-Thawra Jāhiz Li-l-'Iftitāḥ," *Al-Wafd* (July 23, 2020), https://alwafd.news/article/3095094; and "Museum of the Revolutionary Command Council," Presidential YouTube Channel (November 18, 2002), https://www.youtube.com/watch?v=ZqF2xnlFk8s&list=UUPYussIbK8uihMZcpDIXgwg&index=14.
30. Dīnā 'Abd al-'Alīm, "Mabnā 'Qiyādat al-Thawra' 'Tā'eh' bayna Qitā'āt al-Thaqāfa," *al-Yawm al-Sabe'* (January 4, 2010).
31. Farouq Gouida, "'Ayna Matḥaf Thawrat Yūlyū?," *al-Ahrām* (August 27, 2010).
32. Nevine El-Aref, "New Museums for All," *Al-Ahram Weekly* (January 10, 2006).
33. Ibid.
34. Nevine El-Aref, "Memorabilia of the Nation," *Al-Ahram Weekly* (March 8, 2001).
35. Nevine El-Aref, "House of the Nation," *Al-Ahram Weekly* (February 27, 2003).
36. Ibid.
37. Farouq Gouida, "Man Yaktubu Tārīkh Thawrat Yūlyū? Wa-liqā' ma'a Ḥusayn al-Shāfe'ī," *al-Ahrām* (June 6, 1999).
38. "Al-Dhikrā[alif maqsura] al-47 li-Thawrat 23 Yūlyū: Ḥarb al-Mudhākkirāt 'Athārat As'ila Akhtar mimma Ṭaraḥat 'Ajwiba," *al-Bayān* (July 23, 1999).
39. Ibid.
40. Gamal Nkrumah, "Chasing the Paper Trail," *Al-Ahram Weekly* (July 26, 2007).
41. Gouida, "'Ayna Matḥaf Thawrat Yūlyū?"
42. For a discussion, see Amina Elbendary, "Places of Memory," *Al-Ahram Weekly* (August 2, 2001).
43. El-Saket, "Egypt's Museums: The Revolutionary Command Council Museum."

44. Amina Elbendary, "Recapturing the Revolution," *Al-Ahram Weekly* (July 25, 2002).
45. "Da'm 'jil li-mathaf zu'ama al-thawra."
46. Farouq Gouida, "Man Yaktubu Tārīkh Thawrat Yūlyū? Wa-liqā' ma'a Ḥusayn al-Shāfe'ī," *al-Ahrām* (May 30, 1999).
47. Gouida, "'Ayna Matḥaf Thawrat Yūlyū?"
48. Sharaf, "Sāmī Sharaf [...]: Matḥaf 'Abd al-Nāṣer Takrīm li-Miṣr wa-tārīkhha," *al-Maṣrī al-Yawm* (January 12, 2008).
49. Ibid. The issue came up again during the revolution's Jubilee celebrations in 2002.
50. Nevine El-Aref, "Nasser Museum Opens," *Al-Ahram Weekly* (October 6, 2016).
51. For information about the museums' collections, see Shīrīn Sulṭān, "Al-Qarya al-Fir'awnīyya Tukarrim Nagīb wa-'Abd al-Nāṣir wa-l-Sādāt wa-Tatajāhalu Mubarak," *al-Murāqib* (July 14, 2014).
52. Hanān Haggāg, "Bayna al-'ihdā' wa-l-bay': Matḥaf Qiyādat al-Thawra... Bilā Muqtanayāt," *al-Ahrām* (November 9, 2010).
53. "Ayman Nour: 23 Yūlyū 'Inqilāb'...," CNN Arabic (July 24, 2016), https://arabic.cnn.com/middleeast/2016/07/24/egypt-23-july-1952-anniversary.
54. Ahmed al-Tonsi, "Nasser and Egypt's Two Revolutions." *Al-Ahram Weekly* (September 29, 2011), http://weekly.ahram.org.eg/2011/1066/focus.htm.
55. Abdel Moneim Said Aly, "State and Revolution in Egypt: The Paradox of Change and Politics" Crown Essay 2 (Crown Center for Middle East Studies, Brandeis University), January 2012), 21, http://www.brandeis.edu/crown/publications/ce/CE2.pdf; Rana Mamdouh, "Egypt Revolutions: Erasing History," *al-Akhbar* (July 23, 2012), http://english.al-akhbar.com/node/10193; and Ahmad Shokr, "Reflections on Two Revolutions," MERIP 42 (Winter 2012), https://www.merip.org/mer/mer265/reflections-two-revolutions.
56. Dina Ezzat, "Who is the Field Marshal?," *Al-Ahram Weekly* (April 24-30, 2014); http://weekly.ahram.org.eg/News/6035/17/Who-is--the-Field-Marshal-.aspx.
57. Omar Ashour, "Disarming Egypt's Militarized State," *Brookings* (July 18, 2013), https://www.brookings.edu/opinions/disarming-egypts-militarized-state/; and Mohamed Soffar, "Does History Repeat Itself in Egypt?" *al-Jazeera* (December 25, 2013), https://www.aljazeera.com/indepth/opinion/2013/12/does-history -repeat-itself-egypt-201312231332463333996.html.
58. "Al-Ra'īs 'Adlī Manṣūr: 'Uqba Thawra 23 Yūlyū Waqa'at Akhtā' Nudinuhā... wa-Lākinnahā la Tubarriru al-Intiqām min al-Māḍi," *Al-Ahrām* (July 22, 2013), http://gate.ahram.org.eg/News/375214.aspx; and "Egypt's President Hails Ex-Military Presidents on 1952 Revolution Anniversary," *Ahram Online* (July 22, 2013), http://bit.ly/1JlTDP0.
59. "Sisi: Egyptian Army Took Part in July 23 Revolution to Meet People's Aspirations," Egypt's State Information Service News Archive (July 24, 2014), http://www.us.sis.gov.eg/En/Templates/Articles/tmpArticleNews.aspx?ArtID=78894.

60. Dina Ezzat, "Nostalgic Confusion: el-Sisi as Nasser," *Ahram Online* (July 25, 2014), http://english.ahram.org.eg/NewsContent/1/64/107039/EgyptPolitics-/Nostalgic-confusion-ElSisi-as-Nasser.aspx; and Lubna Abdel Aziz, "Catch the Sisi-mania," (September 19, 2013), http://weekly.ahram.org.eg/News/4103.aspx.
61. Luke, *Museum Politics*, xviii.
62. Graham Black, "Museums, Memory and History," *Cultural and Social History* 8, no. 3 (2011), 415.
63. Mohammed Gamal Rashed, "The Museums of Egypt after the 2011 Revolution," *Museum International* 67 (2015), 1–4, 125–131.
64. Black, "Museums, Memory and History," 415.

Selected Bibliography

Brand, Laurie, *Official Stories: Politics and National Narratives in Egypt and Algeria* (Redwood City: Stanford University Press, 2014).

Di-Capua, Yoav, "Embodiment of the Revolutionary Spirit: The Mustafa Kamil Mausoleum in Cairo," *History & Memory* 13, no. 1 (2001): 85–113.

Gershoni, Israel, and James P. Jankowski, *Commemorating the Nation: Collective Memory, Public Commemoration, and National Identity in Twentieth-Century Egypt* (Chicago: Middle East Documentation Center, 2004).

Luke, Timothy, *Museum Politics: Power Plays at the Exhibition* (Minneapolis: University of Minnesota Press, 2002).

Meital, Yoram, "Central Cairo: Street Naming and the Struggle over Historical Representation," *Middle Eastern Studies* 43, no. 6 (November 2008): 857–878.

Podeh, Elie, *The Politics of National Celebrations in the Arab Middle East* (Cambridge: Cambridge University Press, 2011).

The Jubilee Celebrations of Egypt's 1952 Revolution and the Construction of Collective Memory

Alon Tam

Introduction

At the end of July 2002, the 1952 Free Officers' Revolution in Egypt, commonly known as the July Revolution, celebrated its Golden Jubilee. While this anniversary was commemorated annually, the 2002 celebrations were larger in scale and included a greater variety of events than usual. Official ceremonies were attended by President Hosni Mubarak, foreign dignitaries, and other state leaders; pundits in academia and the media debated the revolution and its heritage; and pageants, displays, exhibitions, colloquia, special radio and television broadcasts, commemorative editions of newspaper and magazines, and public rallies were all dedicated to the memory of the revolution. Notably, the Egyptian government was the dominant force behind the ceremonies. Its minister of culture and chair of the governmental celebration committee, Farouk Hosny, stressed that the festivities were intended to "connect past and present, revive the national memory—especially that of the younger generation—and inspire confidence in the Egyptian people that it can overcome all difficulties and challenges."[1] The organizers' and participants' keen awareness that the Jubilee celebrations constituted a public commemorative act is an invitation to examine them as expressions of collective memory and commemoration, subjects that have generated much interest in the past few decades among historians, sociologists, anthropologists, and scholars of literature and culture.[2]

This chapter takes a historical approach to the 2002 Jubilee celebrations by contextualizing them within their specific time and place, social setting, cultural environment, and political power structure. As many historians, among them Schwartz, Sherman, Ben-Amos, and Zerubavel have shown, commemorative rituals allow their participants to reshape the collective memory of the past according to the exigencies and agendas of the present.[3] Other historians further emphasized how different groups within a single society can develop different and competing memories, which often vie for hegemony in the collective memory and seek to marginalize, or even erase, their rivals from it.[4] Those groups whose narrative(s) of the past become official usually occupy the cultural, social, and political center, while counter-memory or counter-commemoration are often the purview of marginalized groups such as minorities, younger generations, or political opposition groups. Indeed, studies have identified the state and its institutions as the primary choreographers of national commemorations that produce what historian John Bodnar termed "official memory": these exist alongside alternative cultures of commemoration, which produce what Bodnar famously called "vernacular memory." He also argued that the "official" and the "vernacular" do not necessarily oppose each other, but often come into contact and influence one another. This is because, on a practical level, any group that wishes to promote a certain kind of collective memory has to recruit supporters, create political alliances, and raise funds from public and private sources in order to execute its commemorative agenda.[5] Finally, many historical studies have also examined the nexus between collective memory, commemoration, and the formation of national identity, highlighting the role of nationalism as one of the most powerful agents shaping the collective memory of an imagined national community.[6] Egypt has proven to be a particularly fruitful case study for such theories in memory studies. Elie Podeh, for example, discussed the different kinds of national celebrations that successive Egyptian regimes enacted during the twentieth century, while Gershoni and Jankowski offered a more rounded view of the struggles surrounding those public commemorations. These authors all emphasized the centrality of the July celebrations in the efforts of every Egyptian regime, since the 1952 revolution, to build its political legitimacy and broadcast its ideology and achievements.[7]

This chapter, therefore, discusses the various aspects of the 2002 Jubilee celebrations and traces their commemorative narratives. It identifies which events, heroes, and political or ideological values were remembered, and which were ignored or forgotten. More specifically, it aims to answer the following questions: Who were the major players in the commemoration celebrations? How did their various narratives serve the interests of different groups? What were the broader political, social, and cultural contexts of the Jubilee celebrations? And finally, how were these commemorations received by the audiences for whom they were intended? By examining such issues, this study will evaluate how, and to what extent, the commemorations of the July Revolution succeeded in providing the Egyptian polity with a cogent explanation for the political, social, and cultural realities of 2002, or how it legitimized them. This issue was perhaps best captured by a question raised in one of the most prominent public debates surrounding the celebrations: "Is the revolution alive or dead?"

The July Revolution Jubilee Celebrations

The Egyptian government produced three major official events in conjunction with the Jubilee: the military academy graduation ceremonies, attended by President Mubarak, senior officials, and foreign dignitaries; the central celebration, which was also attended by the president and the first lady; as well as a large commemorative exhibition on the July Revolution.

The governmental planning committee had decided that the celebrations would continue for a year, from July 2002 to July 2003, and that during this year landmark events in the history of the revolution (primarily during President Nasser's time in office) would be marked. These included such occasions as the day the land reform laws were introduced; the Bandung Conference; the Egyptian–Syrian unification; and the 1973 October War. The committee also considered a long list of additional projects: launching a museum in Cairo dedicated to the revolution's leadership; the production of documentary films about the revolution, including testimony from surviving members of the revolutionary Command Council (RCC); publication of a comprehensive bibliography of all works and manuscripts written on the revolution in Arabic and other languages; translations of selected academic works into Arabic; and reproducing selected theater plays from the 1950s and 1960s.[8]

The graduation ceremonies of the military academy, covered extensively in the Egyptian media, turned into a colorful pageant commemorating the revolution, during which President Mubarak awarded honorary medals to the cousins Zakarīya and Khāled Muḥyī al-Dīn, two of the most senior members of the RCC who were still alive. The guest of honor was the Libyan leader Muʿammar Qadhafi, who considered himself the keeper of the Nasserite legacy, and whose presence was meant to reaffirm the pan-Arab aspect of the revolution. The military ceremony emphasized the special connection between the army and the revolution and between the army and the Egyptian people.[9] Defense Minister Tantawi stated that, "the revolution is one of the most prominent achievements of the army."

President Mubarak's speech at this event introduced the major themes of the government's commemorative narrative. Mubarak emphasized the revolution's contribution to the nation's liberation from the yoke of British occupation, as well as the changed realities of life in Egypt, both in political terms and in social and economic ones. Mubarak also praised President Nasser's contribution to the revolution and President Sadat's reformation of the revolution's path. Finally, Mubarak outlined the main characteristics of what he called "the current phase" of the revolution under his own leadership: democratization and the establishment of an appropriate form of multi-party political system, as well as the development of the economy according to free market and globalizing ideologies.[10]

While the president's speech at the graduation revealed these major themes, the official pageant that he and the first lady attended on the eve of National Revolution Day (July 22, 2002) introduced the official timeline of the revolutionary story. The show, which was broadcast repeatedly on different Egyptian television channels, was produced by the Cairo Opera House and featured performances from several noted musical and theatrical groups, including the Cairo Symphony Orchestra. Its musical program, theatrical re-enactments, and audio-visual segments presented the history of the revolution in three acts. The first, "The Leader," covered the years 1952–1970 under President Nasser's leadership (while omitting Naguib's presidency, which did not fit the Jubilee's new narrative). The second act, "Sadat—War and Peace," examined Egypt under Sadat, 1970–1981. The third and final act, "Mubarak—Development and Prosperity," elaborated the achievements of Mubarak's presidency.[11]

This periodization, which tried to capture the *zeitgeist* of every period, also attempted to draw a direct, continuous line from the leaders and heroes of the past to the current president, Mubarak. It was not, however, readily accepted, attracting criticism mainly from Nasserite opposition groups who put forward a counter-narrative of the revolution. This counter-narrative raises an important question: To what extent was the memory of the revolution's previous leaders favorable enough to bestow any degree of legitimacy on Mubarak's presidency?

Another special Jubilee event organized by the Ministry of Culture was an intensive, three-week series of cultural, artistic, political, and academic exhibitions and conferences in the Cairo Citadel, starting in the end of July 2002. Launched by President Mubarak and his wife with a photographic exhibition about the revolution's achievements, this series of events featured a book fair of monographs and publications about the revolution and its leaders, with the participation of 1,300 publishers from more than 40 countries. The series also included an exhibition of documents about the revolution sponsored by The National Library and Archives; performances by the Cairo Opera

House, the Cairo Symphony Orchestra, and several other theater, music, and folklore groups; as well as a number of conferences and colloquia open to the public that hosted discussions and debates among Egyptian and foreign scholars concerning the revolution's heritage and significance. The events also included political figures, who discussed their personal experiences as part of the revolution's history.[12]

Although the fair was organized by the Ministry of Culture, the conferences and colloquia also featured political and civil organizations that did not wholly subscribe to the government's version of the revolutionary narrative. For example, the socialist-Nasserite National Progressive Unionist Party (*Ḥizb al-Tagammu'*), a loyal opposition to Mubarak's regime, held a large conference during the fair in honor of its leader, Khāled Muḥyī al-Dīn.[13] A leader of the July Revolution, Muḥyī al-Dīn elaborated on his autobiography and his role in the revolution, emphasizing his tireless support for democracy.[14] A series of other conferences were also hosted throughout Egypt's major cities by organizations such as the Press Association, the General Workers Union, and the culture club of Cairo's affluent *Al-Ma'ādi* quarter.[15] One conference that received much media attention was organized by the Western and Central Delta County Association for Culture in Alexandria; its keynote speaker was Dr. Hodā 'Abd al-Nasser, the daughter of President Nasser and a renowned political scientist, who was greeted with a thundering ovation. When asked what the legacy of the revolution was, she mentioned the republican regime, the freedom and dignity that the revolution gave to ordinary Egyptians, and pan-Arab solidarity. She emphasized the popular support for the Nasserite Revolution, manifested by the images of Nasser still being hoisted in protests around Egypt and the Arab world. However, she also sharply criticized the capitalist-inspired counter-revolution that exacerbated social inequalities, citing examples such as the exorbitant tuitions demanded for education, and the expensive villas on Alexandria's coast that stood empty in the winter while too many Egyptians were slipping back into poverty.[16]

The grand fair's unique form of national commemoration—artistic festivities coupled with scholarly and political debates—was mirrored by the way the Egyptian mass media was involved in these celebrations. Toward the end of July 2002, television channels for the first time began broadcasting rare musical recordings, recitals, and popular shows from the 1950s and 1960s, uncensored. These special broadcasts were explicitly aimed at acquainting the younger generation with the national musical culture that emerged following the revolution (specifically during Nasser's presidency), in order to praise the achievements of the revolution.[17] Television channels also broadcast some of Nasser's famous speeches, documentaries about him, and several feature films that had been made in recent years about the revolution and its leaders, including the influential drama *Nasser '56*.

The main staple of television broadcasting during the Jubilee celebrations, however, was a series of talk shows and televised debates with panels of professional historians, scholars, intellectuals, commentators, and politicians. These broadcasts featured debates about the revolution and its legacy, as well as personal interviews with surviving leaders and officials from the period. Some of the participants subscribed to the government's commemorative narrative, while others offered counter-narratives promoted by Liberals, Leftists, Nasserites, and Islamists. These included, for example, al-Damardāsh al-ʿAqāli, a leader in the "secret organization" of the Muslim Brotherhood, and actor and television host Samīr Ṣabri, who was criticized for being "more monarchist than the monarch himself."[18] Egyptian radio followed suit with a varietiy of interviews and panel debates.[19] The printed press, with its different political and ideological affiliations, joined too, publishing special issues and long series of sensational investigative pieces, political commentaries, historical articles, and debates over the revolution and its legacy, as well as commentary on the Jubilee celebrations themselves. Although the long hand of governmental censorship was always present,[20] the television and radio broadcasts, and certainly the press and the many public conferences, allowed different historical narratives of the revolution to compete in shaping its collective memory.[21]

Major Aspects of the Public Discourse about the Revolution's Legacy

The Revolution's Achievements and Failures

The revolution's legacy, especially of its Nasserite phase, served simultaneously as a major topic of debate, as well as a framework for the whole public discourse about the revolution. What was left of the revolution in 2002? Was it still relevant to the daily realities of life in Egypt, and if so, how? Could it be a road map or compass for the future? Is the revolution still alive? These were the most frequently asked questions, and most of the participants in these debates followed the same strategy: drawing a balance between the achievements and the failures of the revolution, and of President Nasser personally. Participants passed their final judgments according to their own worldviews and political agendas, generally utilizing the same list of pros and cons.

On the positive side, speakers usually mentioned the termination of British occupation; the abolition of the monarchy and the corrupt political system that supported it; the nationalization of the Suez Canal; the construction of the Aswan High Dam; the drive toward industrialization; the redistributive land reform; overall improvements in the standard of living; increased social mobility; better social conditions for workers and farmers; free universal education; and Egypt's leading role in the Arab world and in the non-aligned movement.[22] On the negative side, participants in the public debates, mainly liberals and Islamists, stressed the suppression of political, civic, and personal freedoms; the lack of democracy; the "age of arrests"; and the defeat (*al-Naksa*) in the 1967 war.[23] Far less common were criticisms that originated in President Sadat's de-Nasserization efforts of the 1970s, such as claims that Nasser's drive toward pan-Arabism was an adventurous policy that ultimately damaged Egypt; or claims that Nasser-era social and economic reforms did not yield significant results. These arguments were present, but largely between the lines, primarily because Nasserites still constantly engaged with them, directly or indirectly.[24] Though they could not deny those "failures" and "mistakes" outright, they usually justified them by citing "difficult circumstances." Summarizing the issues, many set forth a decidedly mixed review.[25] Those closer to the government's political agenda, who aimed to create a positive collective memory of the revolution, placed increased emphasis on its achievements, portraying Nasser as a "tragic hero," while the avowed Nasserites praised him, expressing their wish for his return as some sort of savior.[26]

Beyond listing, or balancing, its achievements and failures, many commentators focused on the values of the revolution and their relevance to the realities of Egypt in 2002. Nasserite politicians and intellectuals claimed that the revolution's principal ideals were still pertinent.[27] These included the revolution's social sensitivity, in contrast to the prevailing policy of privatization, rampant capitalism, and surrender to global trends; the importance of Egypt's reassuming its role as a leading Arab power, particularly regarding assistance to the Palestinians;[28] opposition to the new American quest for hegemony in the Middle East;[29] and the importance of reinforcing democratic life in Egypt. At the same time, the proponents of this view were well aware of the need to formulate new ways to implement those values in accord with the changing internal, regional, and international circumstances facing Egypt.[30] In sum, at least for one part of the Egyptian polity, the memory of the revolution indeed constituted a will to be fulfilled, a roadmap for the future.

The Democratization Process under Mubarak

Democracy constituted yet another central theme in the public discourse around the Jubilee celebrations. As mentioned above, the lack of democracy during Nasser's rule was at the heart of the negative assessment of the revolutionary legacy. Mubarak-era critics particularly emphasized the suspension of the party system and of parliamentary life after the revolution, the subsequent rule of a single party (the Arab Socialist Union), the suppression of civil rights, and the rise in political oppression during the Nasser years. The public discourse abounded with stories, personal testimonies, historical accounts, and political commentary on the "era of the prison camps," and on the "rule of the security organizations" under Nasser. Political figures reminisced about the ways Nasser drove them out of political life and into exile or prison for opposing his policies; they recounted examples of state censorship, and recalled how Nasser prohibited journalists, writers, and intellectuals from publishing their own views.[31]

There were also widely published historical accounts of the political strife in March 1954 between President Naguib and a few of his supporters, on the one hand, and the majority of the RCC, headed by Nasser, on the other. The clash between the two flared up over the issue of reinstating parliamentary life, and it led to the abrupt termination of Naguib's presidency only a few months later. Accounts of the clashes between Nasser and the Muslim Brotherhood and the Communists also featured prominently in this discourse.[32] In fact, in 2002, the only story the Islamists told about the revolution was their memory of political and religious oppression. Otherwise, they seem to have ignored the revolution's fiftieth anniversary altogether.[33] Finally, against the backdrop of Nasser-era political repression, many government supporters were quick to highlight President Mubarak's efforts to democratize the political system.[34]

In the face of such critiques, even the Nasserites had to admit that this was not the revolution's finest hour, especially since criticizing the reinstatement of parliamentary life would endanger their very political existence. Nevertheless, they tried to justify the post-revolution suspension of parliamentary life by claiming that the political and social circumstances of the day did not permit its reinstatement, that parliamentary life under the monarchy was neither democratic nor representative, and that the Arab Socialist Union (ASU) made possible, for the first time, the participation of the Egyptian masses in political life.[35] Hitherto unpublished protocols of meetings between the leadership of the ASU and President Nasser were published to demonstrate his efforts at reforming the ASU by eradicating its bureaucratic culture, eliminating corruption, and rendering it more participatory and politically active.[36]

Indeed, criticizing Nasser's "dictatorship" was nothing new: Sadat had invoked it as a main tool for building his own political power and legitimacy as early as 1973.[37] Moreover, President Mubarak's decision to reinstate multi-party parliamentary life, and his emphasis on democracy as a legitimizing tool for his own presidency, dated back to the mid-1980s. In fact, by 2002, there was mounting public criticism of the slow pace and limited breadth of that democratization process. Therefore, the prevalence of democracy as a theme in the revolution's commemorations suggests that it constituted a response to the growing public demand for accelerated and deeper democratization. This demand became clearer in light of two contemporaneous developments: American President George Bush's launch in 2002 of the Middle East Peace Initiative (MEPI), aimed at encouraging democratization in the Middle East; and the public uproar prompted by the United Nations' Arab Human Development Report from that same year, which cited the lack of democracy as one of the major reasons for the lack of human development in the Arab world. Thus, the emphasis on the need to restore both parliamentary life and democracy, as a lesson learned from the memory of the revolution, was Mubarak government's response to both internal and external political pressures.

The Socio-Economic Legacy of the Revolution

Another major theme in the public debate regarding the revolution's legacy was the socio-economic situation. Nearly all the actors in the Jubilee celebrations—both the government and almost all opposition groups, whether Nasserites, socialists, or liberals—agreed that the revolution tried, at the very least, to improve the social and economic circumstances of Egyptian workers and *fellahin*. The Islamist opposition, which championed a social and economic agenda, was the only one that remained silent on this issue. Once again, a mix of personal testimonies, memoirs, and public history writing highlighted the revolution's achievements in the socio-economic sphere: increased social mobility, improvements in education and industrialization, and a drive toward economic independence.

Moreover, the Nasserite and socialist opposition to Mubarak attacked what they described as the abandonment of the revolution's social values under his rule. In particular, they repeatedly attacked his privatization policies and what they called "the surrender to globalization." These policies, according to those critics, hurt Egyptian workers and farmers, and ultimately led to the loss of economic and political independence and their replacement by American economic and political hegemony.[38] The government's supporters, on the other hand, emphasized President Mubarak's unprecedented efforts for economic and social development. They underscored his work to rehabilitate the educational, health, welfare, communications, industrial, and economic infrastructures, which were crumbling when he assumed power. His supporters also emphasized that President Mubarak ensured the implementation of the revolutionary land reforms, implying that they had not been properly carried out by previous leaders.[39]

Commemorating the Heroes of the Revolution

During the Jubilee celebrations, much attention was devoted to commemorating the heroes and leaders of the revolution. The way each player chose to highlight or minimize certain personalities and not others was a function of certain political, cultural, or social agendas. A prominent example: the rehabilitation of the memory of Muhammad Naguib, the republic's first president. This was accomplished through the publication of historiographical pieces by professional historians, personal testimonies and recollections, and the release of relevant historical documents and photographs.[40] Notably, Naguib's involvement in the initial stages of the revolution was emphasized in these accounts; stories abounded about how Nasser and the Free Officers made him privy to the revolutionary plan months before its execution; others stressed his influence on the timing of the actual military takeover; or his actions in the first few days after it, particularly his involvement in the king's deposition and expulsion. Other stories pointed out how Naguib's popularity was instrumental in winning support for the revolution from the people and army.[41] Naguib's modesty, integrity, and personable demeanor were also noted, a subtle jab at the vileness and guile of his rivals, led by Nasser. [42] The subsequent "injustice" inflicted upon Naguib by Nasser—his removal from office, long house arrest and maltreatment, and the omission of his name from official histories—were also underlined.[43] This commemoration of Naguib, unprecedented in scope, was meant to challenge the usual focus on Nasser as the revolution's first and foremost leader.[44]

The way that Naguib's memory was reconstructed served the aim of Mubarak's regime to stress the democratization theme during the revolution Jubilee. Highlighting Naguib's 1954 attempt to restore democracy helped show that the revolution and its republican regime were not inherently averse to democracy, and it painted the Nasser years as an aberration in this respect. As the revolution was running out of unblemished heroes, the government tried to polish its image in Egypt's collective memory by invoking the memory of the democratic, kind, beloved, and almost martyred Naguib.

Several other key figures from the early years of the revolution were similarly rehabilitated. Chief among them was Yūsuf Ṣiddīq, a leading figure in the Free Officers' Movement and a hero of the revolution. One of Naguib's sole allies in the RCC, Ṣiddīq supported the latter's attempts to return the army to its barracks. With Nasser's victory over Naguib and his supporters, Ṣiddīq was exiled, placed under house arrest upon his return to Egypt, and eventually forgotten.[45] Khāled Muḥyī al-Dīn, who was awarded a special medal by President Mubarak during the Jubilee, also used his party's official weekly to recount his personal support for Naguib and for democracy, a standpoint that had led to his dismissal and exile too, at the hands of Nasser.[46]

Thus, Nasser's own place in the commemorative discourse during the Jubilee was complicated. On the one hand, there was extensive coverage of Nasser the individual: his personality, humility, work ethic, and dedication to both the Egyptian people and to the revolution.[47] The Nasserite press exaggerated this image, heaping praise on him with fervent nostalgia for his leadership.[48] He figured widely in television broadcasts during the Jubilee, and his image appeared on billboards throughout the country.[49] The intensity of this preoccupation surprised at least one observer, who openly wondered whether, after so many years in which Nasser had been forgotten, the government was signaling a return to Nasserism.[50]

But on the other hand, Nasser's memory was also challenged by the discussion of his "mistakes," by his depiction as a fallible human being, even a "tragic hero." His memory also suffered from the emphasis on other leaders and heroes of the revolution, and more significantly, from the insistence of some observers and intellectuals, led by Muhammad Hasanayn Haykal, that the revolution was a bigger historical event than Nasser the man.[51] This distinction between Nasser and the revolution enabled Mubarak's government to refute the widespread argument that the revolution died with Nasser, and demonstrate that it still enjoyed a measure of popular support.[52] In a way, Mubarak's government, which had been trying to achieve what sociologist Saad Eddin Ibrahim called "eudaimonic legitimacy"—that is, a legitimacy based on prosperity and a feeling of well-being[53]—also tried to ride the coat-tails of the revolution's traditional legitimacy by divorcing it from the charismatic memory of Gamal ʿAbd al-Nasser.

King Farouk was another major character who drew serious attention in the July Revolution's commemorative discourse. In anniversaries of the revolution before 2002, all references to the king had been extremely negative, emphasizing the ancien régime's corruption and despotism, which legitimized the revolution. This was the dominant commemorative narrative during the Jubilee as well. The press was filled with so-called revelations and historical accounts—often in sensationalist and vitriolic language—of the royal court's excesses and corruption, which had brought disgrace upon Egypt's image. These accounts stressed the king's detachment from Egyptian reality and his ineptitude in ruling the country.[54]

However, a few such pieces were marked by surprisingly respectful and inoffensive language, even compassion, regarding King Farouk. One example, by Jamāl Ḥammād, a leader of the Free Officers' Movement and historian of the revolution, detailed the king's abdication and journey into exile, based on the memoirs of the last commander of the royal fleet of yachts, Jalāl ʿAlūba.[55] Other reports cautiously recounted some redeeming stories about the king, intended to cast his image in a more positive light.[56] Furthermore, several monographs published around the time of the Jubilee seemed to treat the king favorably, prompting vicious criticism from Nasserite quarters.[57] This particular counter-memory might be considered the start of the wave of nostalgia for the monarchic period, which represented values such as Egyptian territorial nationalism, a liberal multi-party system, and a Westernized, cosmopolitan political culture. This nostalgia later evolved into a sharp critique of the social realities under Mubarak.

Finally, it should be noted that in 2002, pan-Arab nationalism was almost absent from the commemorative discourse on the revolution. No significant voice called for a full return to pan-Arabism; even Nasserites spoke only about the need for Egypt, as a distinct nation and state, to recover a leading role in Arab, African, and Third World affairs.[58] Opposition Nasserites were also the ones who criticized what they saw as the Americanization of Egyptian culture, economy, and society, which for them signified a kind of subservience counter to the revolution's legacy.[59]

Vernacular Commemorations

In addition to the prevailing discourse on the revolution's legacy and memory, varied as it was, it is worthwhile examining *vernacular commemorations* of the July revolution, borrowing historian John Bodnar's terminology.[60] Such an examination will shed light on the manner in which the government and non-governmental, civil society groups negotiated the shaping of the collective memory of the Revolution in public spaces. Two examples of such negotiations, which took place in the summer of 2002, may illuminate the interplay between *official* commemoration and unofficial grassroots, political pressures against the official agenda—in other words: vernacular commemoration.

The first case, as Joyce van de Bildt-de Jong elaborates elsewhere in this volume,[61] involved public criticism of the government's procrastination regarding its own decisions during the 1990s to open a museum commemorating the revolution's leadership.[62] Similarly, the weekly *Al-'Arabī*, the mouthpiece of the opposition Nasserite Democratic Arab Party, decried the government's failure to implement a 1970 parliamentary decision to transform Nasser's private home into a museum following his death.[63] This tug of war between the government and other, non-governmental groups, led by a Nasserite opposition, around the opening of museum(s) dealing with the revolution, reveals, on the one hand, the extent to which Nasser's memory, as well as permanent forms of commemoration, made the Mubarak government uneasy. On the other hand, a critique of that situation shows that opposition groups were fully aware of the official commemorative agendas, which prevented them from fully expressing their own political identity; it also indicates the significant place that Nasser's memory still held at that time in some parts of the Egyptian polity. Indeed, Nasserite critics had been complaining for a long time about a deliberate, official eradication of Nasser from the collective memory, lamenting the lack of statues, squares, or streets in Nasser's honor, and pointing out that those commemorations that did exist, such as Nasser's image on the Aswan Dam, had been removed, renamed, or replaced.[64]

Another case involved the heated debate about the erection of a statue of King Fuad in June, 2002, in one of the central squares of the town of Port Fuad. The press reported how local authorities had decided to retrieve the statue—which had been stored in a local warehouse, presumably since the 1952 revolution—and return it to its original pedestal in one of the town's main squares.[65] The mainstream-liberal weekly *Al-Qāhira* colorfully recounted how King Fuad's statue was mounted on its pedestal in the stealth of the night, and then, only 48 hours later, removed in an equally furtive manner after Nasserite critiques and popular outrage caught the attention of parliament.[66]

More interesting, however, were the responses and rebuttals to *Al-Qāhira*'s and other reports. In a letter to *Al-Qāhira*, one William Qosa, self-described as a resident of Port Fuad, contradicted its account of a swift, clandestine installation and then removal of the statue. According to Qosa, the statue was put back in its place in broad daylight and remained in the square for ten days (rather than 48 hours), much to the approval of the people of Port Fuad. He also insisted that King Fuad's statue was re-erected in commemoration of the seventy-fifth anniversary of a ceremony in which he himself had laid the town's cornerstone, that is, not as part of the Revolution Jubilee at all. More importantly, Qosa took offense at the claim that the townspeople were unpatriotic, or had supported the British-controlled monarchy rather than Nasser, the national liberator. There was, Qosa noted, no intrinsic aversion in Port Fuad to commemorating Nasser, but such an idea was never put forward. Moreover, he stressed, the king was as much a part of Port Fuad's history as Nasser was. Moreover, Qosa argued that even if the king was a problematic figure, the streets and squares of Egypt's cities were replete with commemorative monuments to dubious characters who, nonetheless, constitute a valid part of Egypt's history.[67] Criticizing the statue's removal, another commentator remarked that politically insensitive as its retrieval was, it was nonetheless morally wrong to discard commemorative monuments of one historical era in favor of another. The removal of the statue, therefore, constituted nothing short of "an attack on history, and a falsification of collective memory." Besides, this commentator noted, the general public cared little about the historical significance of the king's statue, focusing instead on its contribution to the aesthetics of the town square.[68]

This incident clarifies the intricate interplay over the memory of the revolution, both between and within governmental and non-governmental forces. It also demonstrates a nascent struggle, still limited at the time, between the memory of the revolution and that of the monarchy, perhaps the ultimate counter-memories. The same pro-Nasserite group that complained about the fading memories of Nasser perceived the commemoration of King Fuad as a direct challenge to the memory of the revolution. That King Fuad's statue was rescued from warehouse oblivion by Port Fuad local authorities, with the support of at least some of the townspeople, must have added insult to injury. It is also interesting to note the subtle power play among various governmental authorities over this commemorative act: the Port Fuad municipality reinstated the statue; parliament officials heeded the pro-Nasserite protest and intervened to remove it; and the weekly *Al-Qāhira*, considered very close to Minister of Culture Farouk Hosny, lent its pages to the debate about the matter. Also notable is the fact that some residents of Port Fuad—the primary, everyday consumers of this monument—were indifferent to its significance, suggesting that both the monarchy and the Nasser years bore little relevance to the realities of life in 2002 Egypt, or to its national identity.

Public Reception of the Revolution's Commemoration

How, then, were the celebrations of the revolution's Jubilee received by the public? How, and to what extent, have the various commemoration efforts influenced and shaped Egypt's collective memory concerning the revolution? It is difficult to answer these questions with much certainty, but several cases may point to possible answers. The heightened awareness of the various commemorative agendas in the public discourse and the general effort to reach the younger generation propelled the media to probe the public's response to the Jubilee. Reporters from the mainstream weekly *October* were disheartened when a random street poll they conducted among high school, college, and university students revealed their limited knowledge of basic historical facts about the revolution. Some students told interviewers that they had read a bit about the revolution in history textbooks,[69] but had forgotten all the material after their exams; their teachers had told them not to believe the textbooks anyway, as they were full of "government talk."[70] Other students, however, were able to recount the basic narrative of the revolution's balance of achievements and failures. The feature film *Nasser '56* and the songs of 'Abd al-Ḥalīm Ḥāfeẓ and Umm Kulthum praising Nasser and the revolution's achievements, repeatedly broadcast during the Jubilee festivities, also proved to be instrumental in shaping those students' collective memory of the revolution.[71]

In another street poll, this one conducted by the socialist opposition weekly *Al-Ahālī*, factory and small business workers leveled their grievances against the government's economic and social policies and presented them as deviations from the revolution's ideals.[72] Another news report quoted internet talkbacks about the revolution from the BBC website. Posted by users from Egypt, the Arab world, Europe, and the USA, these comments dealt with the revolution's (specifically, Nasser's) balance of achievements and failures. Despite the commenters' efforts to be impartial, negative judgments seemed to prevail.[73]

Another indication of the reception accorded the Jubilee celebrations may be found in the public scandal that arose from some disparaging comments by the popular singer 'Amr Dhiyāb about those songs of Ḥafeẓ and Umm Kulthum. While the songs generated a considerable amount of nostalgia among older generations, who were delighted that younger people finally had the opportunity to become acquainted with this forgotten piece of Egyptian popular culture,[74] the influential Dhiyāb ridiculed the revolutionary songs ("They wrote a song in honor of a dam," he said, referring to Umm Kulthum's famous song "The

Story of the Dam"), and cynically remarked that Ḥafeẓ was "a singer without a message," while Umm Kulthum "sang for gays."[75]

Finally, several members of the public who wrote letters to newspaper editors explicitly concluded that the revolution's legacy no longer inspired any interest, especially among youth, and that it was not relevant to modern Egyptian life. Some even called on the government to cease its "excessive rambling" about the revolution.[76] Moreover, many commentators, observers, intellectuals, and even apologetic editorialists drew attention to the public's weariness about the debate over the revolution's place in the Egyptian collective memory: The debate, they said, was hackneyed, recycled, uninteresting and irrelevant.[77] Such examples of the general public's lack of interest underscore the failure of the commemorative efforts to shape a living, relevant collective memory of the revolution.

Conclusion

The Jubilee celebrations of the 1952 revolution in Egypt were an extensive, intentional attempt to shape Egypt's collective memory on a scale that made observers ponder its motives and effects.[78] Different actors participated, or not, in commemorative acts in different ways, producing various commemorative narratives that supported their own political, social, or cultural agendas. The government took the leading role, using its power and funds to exploit whatever legitimacy the July Revolution still had; at the same time, it tried to graft its own emphasis on democratization onto the memory of the revolution.[79] The Nasserite loyal opposition seized this opportunity to further its ideology and political plans, while critiquing current policies and realities.[80] The very real opposition embodied by the Muslim Brotherhood largely ignored the event, a silence that reverberated loudly in the general hubbub of the Jubilee. These organized and powerful efforts to shape the memory of the revolution interacted with more vernacular acts of commemoration by non-state actors. Perhaps the most noteworthy characteristic of all these efforts was their own great awareness of their value as acts that might shape not only a collective memory, but also an active legacy that could guide political and social policies.

With that in mind, it is instructive to examine the debate that raged around the extensive use of ego-documents during the Jubilee. A plethora of autobiographies, memoirs, "eyewitness" accounts, and other testimonials were being published or broadcast at the time.[81] Theoretically, such forms of commemoration are indeed an indicator of relevance and of grassroot public interest in the meanings of the event being commemorated, especially as they are ostensibly not controlled by hegemonic powers in the remembering society. However, the case of the 1952 revolution's Jubilee in Egypt somewhat belies this notion. The "memoir wars" were the subject of much criticism: They were so rampant, it was claimed, that they lost any influence in shaping the collective memory of the revolution, let alone any influence on social and political agendas.[82] Furthermore, these "memoir wars" led politicians, scholars, and intellectuals to call for a professionally written account of the revolution's history, one that would objectively adjudicate between the memoirs and corroborate them with relevant documentation.[83] To that end, many professional historians called on the government to release official documents from the revolutionary period and deplored having to rely on American and British archives while the Egyptian records remained sealed in the National Archives, or languishing in private hands.[84] Scholars therefore also pressed political figures and former officials from the early revolutionary era (the Naguib and Nasser period) to hand over to the state, or make available otherwise, any documents they held privately.

In this context, it is significant that the politically and intellectually engaged circles in Egypt called for the manufacture of a standardized collective memory of the revolution, rather than the existing cacophony of personal, "raw" memories. This attests to a moment of detachment: The memory of the revolution in 2002 had less and less immediate impact on Egyptians' everyday lives. Tellingly, the "memory wars" really concerned a shrinking circle of old-guard intellectuals and political figures. It was therefore possible for them to demand a final historical verdict on the revolution, an official standard history, based on hard evidence such as original documents, which would put the visceral, highly personal memory wars to rest. On the other hand, this moment of detachment, or the birth of a historical perspective, was coupled with the public's general disinterest in the subject, or even suspicion of official narratives. To answer a question that many Egyptian observers asked at the time: It seems that if the revolution was not yet dead, it was certainly on its deathbed.

Notes

1. Translated from the Arabic, *Al-Qāhira* 114 (June 18, 2002), 1.
2. Kerwin Lee Klein, "On the Emergence of Memory in Historical Discourse," *Representations* 69 (Winter, 2000), 127–150.
3. Avner Ben-Amos, *Funerals, Politics, and Memory in Modern France, 1789–1996* (Oxford: Oxford University Press, 2000); Daniel J. Sherman, "Art, Commerce and the Production of Memory in France After World War 1," in John R. Gillis (ed.), *Commemorations: The Politics of National Identity* (Princeton, 1994); Barry Schwartz, "The Social Context of Commemoration: A Study in Collective Memory," *Social Forces* 61, no. 2 (December 1982); and Yael Zerubavel, *Recovered Roots: Collective Memory and the Making of Israeli National Tradition* (Chicago: University of Chicago Press, 1995).
4. Ehud. R. Toledano, "Forgetting Egypt's Ottoman Past," in Jayne L. Warner (ed.), *Cultural Horizon: A Festschrift in Honor of Talat S. Halman* (Syracuse, NY: Syracuse University Press, 2001), 150–167.
5. John Bodnar, *Remaking America: Public Memory, Commemoration, and Patriotism in the Twentieth Century* (Princeton: Princeton University Press, 1992).
6. Jeffrey K. Olick, "Collective Memory: The Two Cultures," *Sociological Theory* 17, no. 3 (November 1999), 333–348; and Jan Assmann (translated by John Czaplicka), "Collective Memory and Cultural Identity," *New German Critique* 65, Cultural History / Cultural Studies, (Spring–Summer, 1995), 125–133.
7. Elie Podeh, *The Politics of National Celebrations in the Arab Middle East* (Cambridge: Cambridge University Press, 2011), especially 55–108; and Israel Gershoni and James P. Jankowski, *Commemorating the Nation: Collective Memory, Public Commemoration, and National Identity in Twentieth-Century Egypt* (Chicago: Middle East Documentation Center, 2004).
8. *Al-Qāhira* 114 (June 18, 2002), 1; and *October* 1342 (July 14, 2002), 4.
9. Muḥammad Khalaf-Allah, "Mubarak: The July Revolution is the Apogee of the Egyptian People's Struggle," *October* 1344 (July 28, 2002), 18.
10. *Al-Muṣawwar* 4059 (July 26, 2002), 4.
11. *Al-Qāhira* 118 (July 16, 2002), 1.
12. *Al-Qāhira* 114 (June 18, 2002), 1; *Al-Qāhira* 117 (July 9, 2002), 1; *Al-Qāhira* 118 (July 16, 2002), 1; and *Al-'Arabī* 819 (July 28, 2002), 12.
13. *Ḥizb al-Tagammu' al-Taqaddumi al-Waḥdawi* (The National Progressive Unionist Party) was established in 1977 by Khāled Muḥyī al-Dīn, a Free Officer, as the left-wing faction of the ruling Arab Socialist Union (ASU), consisting of Marxists and Nasserites. It has seen itself since then as a guardian of the socialist legacy of the 1952 revolution.
14. *Al-Ahāli* 1089 (August 15, 2002), 9.
15. On the Press Association's convention, see the report in *Al-'Arabī* 819 (July 28, 2002), 13; on the Workers Union three-day convention at the Workers University in Madīnat Naṣr, see *Al-'Arabī* 818 (July 21, 2002), 20; and on the *al-Ma'ādi* culture club conference, see *Al-Ahāli* 1084 (July 10, 2002), 11.

16. *October* 1345 (August 4, 2002), 25; and *Al-'Arabī* 819 (July 28, 2002), 9, 13.
17. Muḥammad Qābīl, "The Song is the July Revolution's *Diwan*," part 1, *October* 1344 (July 28, 2002), 71; and part 2, *October* 1345 (August 4, 2002), 61.
18. See Madīḥa 'Amāra report, *Al-'Arabī* 819 (July 28, 2002), 6. See also *Al-Aḥrār* (July 23, 2002), 11; and Ibrāhīm Adam, "Tāreq Ḥabīb and his Secret Files," *October* 1342 (July 14, 2002), 22–23.
19. *Al-Qāhira* 118 (July 16, 2002), 1; and *Al-Aḥrār*, ibid.
20. The head of the broadcasting authority's news division was laid off by the minister of communications for allegedly not censoring adequately one of the talk show panels; see *Al-Qāhira* 117 (July 9, 2002), 1. Another incident that generated some public debate in the press was the resignation of Dr. Hudā 'Abd al-Nasser from her post as director of the Revolution Studies Program in the Center for Strategic Studies at *Al-Ahram* publishing house, after accusing *Al-Ahram*'s chief editor, Ibrāhīm Nafe' (considered to be very close to President Mubarak), of editing the title of one of her articles without her approval in order to portray her father as more amenable to American pressure: *Al-'Arabī* 818 (July 21, 2002), 1; and *Al-'Arabī* 819 (July 28, 2002), 9.
21. For a description and commentary on the televised panel debates that presented opposing viewpoints, see Adam, "Tāreq Ḥabīb and his Secret Files," 22–23.
22. See the special issue dedicated to this subject, *Al-'Arabī* 818 (July 21, 2002). See also Ismā'īl Muntaṣar, "Its Biggest Achievement Is Me!" *October* 1344 (July 28, 2002), 19; and "After 50 Years: What Do the Youth Know about the July Revolution?," *October* 1342 (July 14, 2002), 10–12.
23. Jalāl al-Dīn, "What is Left of His Revolution?," *Al-'Arabī* 791 (January 13, 2002), 9; and Ṣalāḥ Muntaṣar, "The July Revolution as Everybody Sees It," *October* 1345 (August 4, 2002), 74. Readers writing on the revolution, *Ṣawt al-Umma* 84 (July 8, 2002), 3.
24. See Maḥmūd Aḥmad Sa'īd's commentary on the Revolution's detractors, *Al-'Arabī* 819 (July 28, 2002), 12; and "The Political Salon," *Al-Aḥrār* (July 29, 2002), 8.
25. S.D.S. Muḥammad, "The 23rd of July Revolution between Achievements and Failures," *Al-Aḥrār* (July 23, 2002), 4; and Rif'at al-Sa'īd, "Nasserism: Legend and Reality," *Al-Ahāli*, 1086 (July 24, 2002), 6.
26. See editorial, "The July Revolution in the Memory of the Nation" in the special issue titled "The Revolution's Album," *October* 1343 (July 21, 2002), 21. See also the editorial preface to Maḥmūd 'Abd al-Raḥīm's interview with Khāled Muḥyī al-Dīn, "The Revolution Did Not End with the Death of 'Abd al-Nasser," ibid., 24–25. On Nasser as a tragic figure, see Rajab al-Bannā, "Haykal and 'Abd al-Nasser in his Final Days," *October* 1345 (August 4, 2002), 10–13; and also a short story by Muṣṭafā al-Barri, "An Image," *October* 1344 (July 28, 2002), 68. See also Layla al-Jabāli, "'Abd al-Nasser and the Fine Times," *Al-Arabi* 791 (January 13, 2002), 13; the special issue of *Al-Arabi* 814 (June 23, 2002); Ḍiyā' al-Dīn Da'ūd, "The Revolution Is the Dream for the Future," *Al-Arabi* 818 (July 21, 2002), 1; 'Abd al-Ghaffār Shukr, *Al-'Arabī* 820 (August 4, 2002), 12; Ṣāfīnāz Kāẓem, "The

One Who Lost his Life in Dreams," *Ṣawt al-Umma* 84 (July 8, 2002), 9; and "An Interview with Muhammad Hasnayn Haykal," *Al-Muṣawwar* 4057 (July 12, 2002), 24–30, 70–71.

27. See the interviews with Khāled Muḥyī al-Dīn, *October* 1343 (July 21, 2002), 24–25; *October* 1345 (August 4, 2002), 22–24. Asked whether the revolution had died with Nasser, Muḥyī al-Dīn denied that, insisting that it was still alive in people's hearts and that even President Mubarak declares his allegiance to it and to its ideals. Aḥmad al-Jamāl, "Issues," *Al-'Arabī* 791 (January 13, 2002), 10; Muḥammad al-Khawli, "A Call for a Salvation Front on the Leader's Birthday: The Nation Is at Risk," ibid.; Fārūq al-'Asharī, "Why Did Nasser Refuse to Surrender to American Hegemony?," ibid.; Ḍiyā' al-Dīn Da'ūd, "The 23rd of July Revolution Is our Civilizational Roadmap," *Al-'Arabī* 812 (June 9, 2002), 13; Fārūq al-'Asharī, "Nasserism Is the Solution," ibid.; Muḥammad Badr al-Dīn, "Gamal 'Abd al-Nasser and Jamal Hamdan Discuss and Interpret the 50th Anniversary of the Revolution," *Al-'Arabī* 818 (July 21, 2002), 14; Majdi Riyāḍ, "Is It Inevitable that Nasserism Will Renew Itself?," ibid., 17; Abd al-Ghaffār Shukr, "The Road to the Renewal of Nasser's Program," ibid., 19.
28. During the Jubilee celebration in 2002, the Palestinian uprising known as *Intifāḍat al-Aqṣā* was at its height, which prompted wide popular calls for the Egyptian government to intervene by force.
29. During the Jubilee celebrations in 2002, the American preparations for the war in Iraq were at their zenith.
30. See Husām Abd al-Qāder's report "Hudā 'Abd al-Nasser in an Alexandria Convention," *October* 1345 (August 22, 2002), 25. See the debate over the viability of Nasserite economic policies: *Al-Ahāli* 1084 (July 10, 2002), 11.
31. Maḥmūd 'Abd al-Shakkūr, "When the Bells of Revolutionary Wrath Rang: Three Articles that Displeased 'Abd al-Nasser," *October* 1347 (August 18, 2002), 22–23; 'Āṭef 'Abd al-Ghani, "Al-Ḥakīm Influenced Nasser's Character Molding," *October* 1345, (August 4, 2002), 26–27; 'Āṭef 'Abd al-Ghani, "Naguib Mahfouz, What Did He Say before Nasser's Throne and Deathbed?," *October* 1344 (July 28, 2002), 32–33; Maḥmūd 'Abd al-Shakkūr, "The Men of Letters and the July Revolution," *October* 1342 (July 14), 36–37; the reports on the famous writer Tharwat Abāẓa's death, *Al-Muṣawwar* 4041 (March 22, 2002), 52–53.
32. See the series "Behind the Scenes of the Revolution and the Brotherhood," in *Al-Aḥrār* (July 16, 2002), 5; (July 17, 2002), 5; (July 18, 2002), 5; (July 19, 2002), 9; (July 21, 2002), 5; (July 22, 2002), 5; (July 23, 2002), 5. See also Aḥmad Ḥamrūsh, "The Revolution and Its War on Religious Extremism," *Rūz al-Yūsuf* 3870, (August 10–16, 2002), 67; Muḥammad 'Awda, "The Revolution and the Muslim Brotherhood," *Al-Muṣawwar* 4057 (July 12, 2002), 55–57. On the left and communists, see Ismā'īl Ṣabri 'Abdallah, "'Abd al-Nasser and the Left," *Al-Muṣawwar* 4057 (July 12, 2002), 52–54.
33. See the Islamist weekly, *Al-Liwā' al-Islāmi* 1070 (July 25, 2002), which reported nothing on the Revolution or its anniversary except for a small congratulatory note to the president on its front page. See also Mamdūḥ Ismā'īl al-Muḥāmi, "The Islamists and the 23rd of July," *Al-Aḥrār* (July 22, 2002), 9.

34. See the report on the chairman of the parliament, Srūr's speech to students at Cairo University, *Al-Aḥrār* (July 31, 2002), 7.
35. See special issue dedicated to this question, *Al-'Arabī* 817 (July 14, 2002). See also *Al-'Arabī* 819 (July 28, 2002), 7; and Maḥmūd al-Zalāqi, "Jamal 'Abd al-Nasser, the Jailer of the Masses and their Prisoner," *Ṣawt al-Umma* 60 (January 21, 2002), 12.
36. *Al-Ahāli* 1084 (July 10, 2002), 7; 1085 (July 17, 2002), 9; 1086 (July 24, 2002), 7; 1087 (July 31, 2002), 7; 1088 (August 7, 2002), 7; 1089 (August 14, 2002), 6. See also "The Admissions of the Hurting Leader," *Al-'Arabī* 817 (July 14, 2002), 12–13.
37. Shimon Shamir (ed.), *The Decline of Nasserism, 1965–1970* (Tel-Aviv: The Shiloah Center for Middle Eastern and African Studies, Tel Aviv University, 1978), 1–60.
38. Khālid al-Qushayri, "The Lost Balance," *Al-Aḥrār* (July 31, 2002), 7; "Was [the Revolution] Socialist?," *Al-Ahāli* 1085 (July 17, 2002), 8; and "What Is Left to the *Fallāḥīn* from the Revolution?," *Al-Ahāli* 1085 (July 17, 2002), 10.
39. Sa'īd Tawfīq, "The Fallāḥīn [who were supposed to benefit from Nasser's] Land Reforms Gained [a sense of] Security in their Property Only during the Times of Ḥosni Mubarak," *Al-Muṣawwar* 4059 (July 26, 2002), 34–35; "Education in Mubarak's Era," *Al-Muṣawwar* 406 (August 9, 2002), 36–37; "Mubarak's Giving in *Asyūt* Saturates the July Tree," *Al-Muṣawwar* 4060 (August 2, 2002), 62–63; Muḥammad Khāled, "The Workers and the Revolution," *October* 1345 (August 4, 2002), 29.
40. See Yāsir Al-Zayyāt article on Naguib, *Ṣawt al-Umma* 85 (July 15, 2002), 10–11.
41. See the series of historical articles by Jamāl Ḥammād, titled "Who Will Lead the Revolution: Fu'ād Ṣādeq or Mohamed Naguib?," *October* 1346 (August 11, 2002), 20–21; 1347 (August 18, 2002), 20–21; 1348 (August 25, 2002), 20–21; 1349 (September 1, 2002), 24–25. See also Jamāl Ḥammād's historical series on the king's deposition and expulsion: "Farouk Gives in to the Ultimatum and *al-Maḥrūsa* Sails with Him to Exile," *October* 1342 (July 14, 2002), 20–21; "The Reasons that Led to the Delay in King Farouk's Deposition," *October* 1343 (July 21, 2002), 22–23; and "How Farouk Contemplated his Flight from Egypt from the Morning of July 23, 1952," *October* 1344 (July 28, 2002), 24–25.
42. Jalāl Amīn, "What Is Left from his Revolution?," *Al-'Arabī*, 791 (January 13, 2002), 9.
43. Jamāl Ḥammād, "Who Will Lead the Revolution: Fu'ād Ṣādeq or Mohamed Naguib?," *October* 1348 (August 25, 2002), 20–21; and Muḥammad 'Abd al-Shakkūr, "Revolutionaries and Civilians in the Revolution's First Governmental Offices," *October* 1344 (July 28, 2002), 26–27.
44. See the spontaneous question about the debate over the place of Nasser and Naguib in Egyptians' collective memory in Ḥamdi Muṣṭafa and Maḥmūd 'Abd al-Raḥīm's report, "On Its 50th anniversary, the Young Generation Does Not Know Anything about the Revolution," *October* 1343 (July 21, 2002), 25–26.
45. Muḥammad Abd al-Shakkūr, "Yūsuf Ṣiddīq, the Hero Who Saved the Revolution," *October* 1343 (July 21, 2002), 26–27. See also the interview by

Maḥmūd Fawzi with 'Alīyya Tawfīq, Yūsuf Ṣiddīq's widow, "I Do Not Hate Nasser, in Spite of the Fact that He Renounced My Husband and Threw Me in Jail," *October* 1344 (July 28, 2002), 28–29.

46. See Maḥmūd Fawzi's extensive interview with Muḥyī al-Dīn, "The Hero Khāled Muḥyī al-Dīn: The Decision on the Revolution Was an Adventure; Our Readiness for It Did Not Surpass 60%," *October* 1345 (August 4, 2002), 22–24.
47. On Nasser's dedication despite his illness, see Rajab al-Bannā, "Haykal and 'Abd al-Nasser in His Final Days," 10–13. See also the special Nasser photo album that depicts his life sympathetically, from cradle to grave: *October* 1343 (July 21, 2002), 29–31. See also Ibrāhīm 'Ayyād al-Marāghi, "What About 'Abd al-Nasser's Home?," *October* 1341 (July 7, 2002), 17. See Dr. Jamāl Shaqra, the first historian to be allowed access to the archives at al-Manshiya al-Kubra, on President's Nasser's "Secret Mail" *Al-'Arabī* 815 (June 30, 2002), 9–12, and *Al-'Arabī* 816 (July 7, 2002), 9–11. On Nasser's concern for children's welfare, see Maḥmūd Aḥmad Sa'īd, "The Dignity of Childhood," *Al-'Arabī* 791 (January 13, 2002), 13. On his concern for "the little man," see Ibrāhīm Mus'id Tawfīq, "The Day 'Abd al-Nasser Told Me: At Your Service, Mr. Ibrahim," *Al-'Arabī* 812 (June 9, 2002), 9.
48. See *Al-'Arabī* 791 (January 13, 2002), 6; and *Al-'Arabī* 819 (July 28, 2002), 6. See also a short story by Muṣṭafa al-Barri titled "An Image," *October* 1344 (July 28, 2002), 68.
49. Aḥmad Sa'īd, "Why Are the Images of Nasser Carried in All Arab Demonstrations Nowadays?" *Al-'Arabī* 818 (July 21, 2002), 15.
50. 'Āṭef al-Bīli, "Allah Will Set It Right," *Al-Aḥrār* (July 22, 2002), 9.
51. On Nasser as a tragic figure, see Rajab al-Bannā, "Haykal and 'Abd al-Nasser in His Final Days," 10–13. For accounts and memoirs depicting the events of the revolution as a haphazard adventure in which Nasser did not play a central part, see Muḥammad Khalaf-Allah, "'Ali Khalīl, the Broadcasting Authority's Dynamo on the Night of July 23, 1952," *October* 1344 (July 28, 2002), 30–31. See also Rajab al-Bannā, "The Secrets of Haykal and Nasser," ibid., 12–17; Maḥmūd 'Abd al-Shakkūr, "New Reading of the July Literature: Three Documents of the Revolution," *October* (July 7, 2002), 36–37. On Nasser as a flesh-and-blood human being, see Amīn Haydi, "Keys to the Personality of 'Abd al-Nasser," *Al-'Arabī* 818 (July 21, 2002), 8; and Nabīl 'Amr, "Gamal 'Abd al-Nasser and the Distance between the Leader and the *Fir'awn*," *Ṣawt al-Umma* 60 (January 21, 2002), 12.
52. Rajab al-Bannā, "'Abd al-Nasser's Revolution or the People's Revolution?" *October* 1343 (July 21, 2002), 10–12. See interview with former vice-president 'Ali Ṣabri, *Al-'Arabī* 818 (July 21, 2002), 4.
53. See Saad Eddin Ibrahim, *Egypt, Islam, and Democracy: Critical Essays, with a New Postscript* (Cairo: American University in Cairo Press, 2002).
54. See the special issue dedicated to the negative memory of King Farouk, *Al-'Arabī* 813 (June 16, 2002). See also Maḥmūd 'Abd al-Shakkūr, "All the King's Men," *October* 1345 (August 4, 2002), 28–29; Jamāl Ḥammād, "How Farouk

Contemplated his Flight from Egypt from the Morning of the July 23, 1952," *October* 1344 (July 28, 2002), 24–25; and *Ṣawt al-Umma* 83 (July 1, 2002), 10.

55. Jamāl Ḥammād, "Farouk's Last Journey on *al-Maḥrūsa*," *October* 1345 (August 4, 2002), 20–21. Wā'il 'Abd al-Fattāḥ, "The Struggle of the Servants and the Agents in the Last King's Court," *Ṣawt al-Umma* 84 (July 8, 2002), 10; and Muḥammad al-Bāzz, "The Nights of Farouk in Exile," *Ṣawt al-Umma* 86 (July 22, 2002), 10–11.
56. These reports revealed, for example, that it was the king himself who had fabricated some of the accounts of his excesses, namely, his love affairs, while still others recalled that the young king had actually enjoyed the favor of the Egyptian public when he ascended the throne, and that his descent into despotism and corruption began only because of a personal crisis coupled with a corrupt, guileful entourage. See Jamāl Ḥammād, "Between the First and Last Hours of Farouk's Reign," *October* 1341 (July 7, 2002), 20–21.
57. Ḥilmi Sālem, "A Prisoner of Panderers," *Al-'Arabī* 813 (June 16, 2002), 11; see also Maḥfūẓ 'Abd al-Raḥmān's fictional story on the return of King Farouk, *Al-'Arabī* 818 (July 21, 2002), 7.
58. Ḥusām 'Abd al-Qāder, "Hudā 'Abd al-Nasser in the Alexandria Convention: Mubarak Restored our Relations with the Arabs and Africa," *October* 1345 (August 4, 2002), 25.
59. Yūsuf al-Qa'īd, The Last Meter of Egypt's Awakening," *Al-'Arabī* 791 (January 13, 2002), 10.
60. Bodnar, *Remaking America.*
61. See Joyce van de Bildt-de Jong's chapter in this volume, 161–176.
62. 'Āṭef 'Abd al-Ghani, "The Revolution Museum Is Still Papers in the Drawers of the Minister of Culture," *October* 1343 (July 21, 2002), 32–33; Ibrāhīm 'Ayyād al-Marāghi, "What about Nasser's Home?" *October* 1341 (July 7, 2002), 17; Aḥmad Nawwār, "Open Letter to the Editor: The Revolutionary Leaders' Museum Is in Great Shape," *October* 1345 (August 4, 2002), 54.
63. Ibtisām al-Rawbi, "The Deserted House of 'Abd al-Nasser in Alexandria," *Al-'Arabī* 791 (January 13, 2002), 11; and Shafīq Aḥmad 'Ali, "The House of 'Abd al-Nasser Is Still Deserted, So the Americans Will Not Be Angered," *Al-'Arabī* 818 (July 21, 2002), 13.
64. Ibid. See also Rajab al-Bannā, "After 50 Years: Where Is the Statue of the Revolution's Leader?" *October* 1341 (July 7, 2002), 11.
65. Qāsim Mus'id 'Alīwa, "Why Is a Statue to King Fuad Being Erected in Port Said while Abd al-Nasser Is Ignored?" *Al-Qāhira* 121 (August 6, 2002), 21. *Al-Qāhira* was a mainstream liberal, intellectually oriented weekly, considered to be under the influence of the minister of culture, Farouk Hosny.
66. Ibid.
67. William Qosa, "What Is Shameful about Erecting a Statue to King Fuad and to Jamal 'Abd al-Nasser Too?," *Al-Qāhira* 125 (September 3, 2002), 21.
68. Al-Sayyid Zard, "The Erection of a Statue Is Symbolic, and that Is Why It was Removed," *Al-Qāhira* 125 (September 3, 2002), 21.

69. Ḥamdi Muṣṭafa and Muṣṭafā ʻAbd al-Raḥīm, "On Its 50th Anniversary."
70. Ibid., 10–12.
71. Ibid. Muḥammad ʻAbd al-Dā'im, ʻAli al-Fātiḥ, and ʻAmr al-Jundī, "Why Does the Regime Celebrate a Revolution against Which It Executed a Counter-Revolution?" *Al-ʻArabī* 819 (July 28, 2002), 9. On the film *Nasser '56,* see Joel Gordon, "Film, Fame and Public Memory: Egyptian Biopics from *Muṣṭafā Kāmel* to *Nasser '56,*" *International Journal of Middle Eastern Studies,* 31 (1999), 61–79.
72. *Al-Ahāli* 1086 (July 24, 2002), 9.
73. Ṣalāḥ Muntaṣar, "The July Revolution as Everybody Sees It," *October* 1345 (August 4, 2002), 74.
74. Muḥammad Qābīl, "Singing is the Revolution's *Diwan,*" *October* 1344 (July 28, 2002), 71; *October* 1345 (August 4, 2002), 61; ʻAbd al-Ḥamīd Yūnus, "In the Course of a Day," *October* 1345 (August 4, 2002), 35; and Tāriq al-Shanāwi, "The Radio Sings and Cheers for ʻAbd al-Nasser," *Rūz al-Yūsuf* 3864 (June 29–July 5, 2002), 84.
75. Ayman al-Ḥakīm, "Four Causes of ʻAmr Dhiyāb's Revolution against the July Revolution," *Al-Qāhira* 114 (June 18, 2002), 3.
76. See the letter to the editor of Hishām ʻAbduh, an Arabic teacher from *Madinat Naṣr,* "Please Close the Revolution's File," *Ṣawt al-Umma* 87 (July 29, 2002), 2; and another Letter to the Editor, *Ṣawt al-Umma* 82 (June 24, 2002), 2.
77. Adam, "Tāreq Ḥabīb and His Secret Files," 22–23; also the editorial, "Half a Century to the Boiling Point in Egypt, 1952–2002," *Ṣawt al-Umma* 83 (July 1, 2002), 10; ʻĀdel Ḥammūda, "Haykal Speaks: If Only Nasser Were Alive," *Ṣawt al-Umma* 84 (July 8, 2002), 3; *Ṣawt al-Umma* 86 (July 22, 2002), 1; and ʻĀdel al-Jūjrī, "The July Revolution and the Fight against Corruption," *Al-Aḥrār* (July 21, 2002), 4.
78. Muḥammad ʻAbd al-Dā'im, ʻAli al-Fātiḥ, and ʻAmr al-Jundī, "Why Does the Regime Celebrate?" 9, 12; Kamāl al-Qalash, "The Birth of the July Celebrations," *Al-ʻArabī* 820 (August 4, 2002), 13; and Aḥmad Taher, "Why Do We Celebrate the July Revolution?" *Al-Qāhira* 122 (August 13, 2002), 17.
79. Rajab al-Bannā, "In One Way," *October* 1344 (July 28, 2002), 11; Ismāʻīl Muntaṣar, "Its Biggest Achievement," 19; Rajab al-Bannā, "After 50 Years," 11; Yūnān Labīb Rizq, "July 23rd, between Revolution and State," *Al-Muṣawwar* 4057 (July 12, 2002), 48–50; Muḥammad Shūmān, "The July Revolution and the Future," *Al-Aḥrār* (July 26, 2002), 4; and Makram Muḥammad Aḥmad, "The Legitimacy of July after 50 Years since the Revolution," *Al-Muṣawwar* 4057 (July 12, 2002), 4–6.
80. Maḥmūd ʻAbd al-Shakkūr, "Between Abd al-Nasser and al-Sadat: Years of Revolution and Change," *October* 1346 (August 11, 2002), 22–23; Bahā' Tāher, "The Meaning of Abd al-Nasser," *Al-ʻArabī* 818 (July 21, 2002), 17; Kamāl al-Qalash, "The Birth of the July Celebrations," 13; Huda ʻAbd al-Nāṣṣer, "A Re-Evalution of the July Revolution," *Al-ʻArabī* 821 (August 11, 2002), 11; and Sharīf Ḥatāta, "They Want to Privatize the July Revolution," *Al-Ahāli* 1085 (July 17, 2002), 11.

81. See, for example, the memoir series of Aḥmad Ḥamrūsh, one of the first Free Officers, a renowned journalist, and a leftist-socialist-Nasserite political figure, in *Al-Ahāli* 1083 (July 3, 2002), 5; 1084 (July 10, 2002), 5; 1085 (July 17, 2002), 5; 1086 (July 24, 2002), 5; 1087 (July 31, 2002), 5; 1088 (August 7, 2002), 5; 1089 (August 14, 2002), 7; 1090 (August 21, 2002), 5. See also Al-Sayyid Ghaḍbān, "The Turning Point," *Al-'Arabī* 791 (January 13, 2002), 12; Maḥfūẓ 'Abd al-Raḥmān, "The 9th and 10th of June Were the Turning Point in My Life," *Al-'Arabī* 812 (June 9, 2002), 9; and an interview with 'Āṭef Naṣṣār, Alexandria's governor, in the first weeks after the revolution, on the forgotten events of *Kafr al-Dawwār*, *Al-Qāhira* 124 (August 27, 2002), 20.
82. Maḥmūd 'Abd al-Shakkūr, "Revolutionaries and Civilians in the First Governmental Offices of the Revolution," *October* 1344 (July 28, 2002), 26–27; Adam, "Tāreq Ḥabīb and His Secret Files," 22–23; see also interview with Jamāl Manṣūr by Maḥmūd Fawzi, "I Wrote the First Free Officers Manifesto, but Was Not Notified of the Revolution's Date," *October* 1342 (July 14, 2002), 38–39. In this interview, another in a series of memoir interviews, Manṣūr, one of the early leaders of clandestine organizations in the Egyptian army, was complaining about some in the RCC who worked deliberately to obliterate the part played by others (in this case, the cavalry corps) in the revolution. On other forgotten heroes of the revolution, see Ḥasan 'Āmer, "Nasser's Quiet Friend Who Lit the Revolution outside Egypt," *Sawt al-Umma* 86 (July 22, 2002), 12.
83. See Khāled Muḥyī al-Dīn, "The Revolution Did Not End with 'Abd al-Nasser," *October* 1343 (July 21, 2002), 24–25.
84. See the call made by Hudā 'Abd al-Nasser in Ḥusām 'Abd al-Qāder's report "Dr. Hudā 'Abd al-Nasser at an Alexandria Convention," *October* 1345 (August 4, 2002), 25. See also "The July Documents Are Hidden in Closets?," *Al-'Arabī* 815 (June 30, 2002), 12; *Al-Aḥrār* (July 22, 2002), 8; and (July 29, 2002), 8.

Selected Bibliography

Gillis, John R., ed., *Commemorations: The Politics of National Identity* (Princeton : Princeton University Press, 1994).

Gordon, Joel, "Film, Fame and Public Memory: Egyptian Biopics from Muṣṭafā Kāmel to Nasser '56," *International Journal of Middle Eastern Studies* 31 (1999), 61–79.

Ibrahim, Saad Eddin, *Egypt, Islam, and Democracy: Critical Essays, with a New Postscript* (Cairo: American University in Cairo Press, 2002).

Schwartz, Barry, "The Social Context of Commemoration: A Study in Collective Memory," *Social Forces* 61, no. 2 (December 1982) , 374–402.

Zerubavel, Yael, *Recovered Roots: Collective Memory and the Making of Israeli National Tradition* (Chicago: Chicago University Press, 1995).

Language, Humor, and Revolution in Contemporary Egypt*

Gabriel M. Rosenbaum

Introduction

The aim of this chapter is to discuss, in the context of the relationship between the 2011 revolution in Egypt and the events that followed it, the linguistic revolution in Egyptian culture in recent years, especially in the last two decades, and the verbal and visual humor that became one of the identifying marks of the 2011 revolution and subsequent events. It is impossible to completely grasp the full picture of the political revolution without understanding the linguistic one and the role that humor played in it.

The Linguistic Situation in Contemporary Egypt and the Language Revolution

In recent decades, colloquial Arabic (*ʿĀmmīyya*; in Egypt: Colloquial Egyptian Arabic, or CEA) has developed as a written and literary language alongside standard Arabic (*Fuṣḥā*, Modern Standard Arabic, MSA, and also classical Arabic). This is a unique, revolutionary change in mainstream Egyptian culture in particular as well as in Arab culture in general.

---

* This chapter is based on my study of Egyptian humor and popular culture (in preparation); the lexicographical research was supported by THE ISRAEL SCIENCE FOUNDATION (grant No. 849/18). The transliterations represent both Modern Standard Arabic (MSA) and Colloquial Egyptian Arabic (CEA); the differences in transliteration represent the difference in pronunciation between these two language varieties.

The chapter contains 30 images. I took several of the photos; the rest came from internet sites and social networks. I received several of the images from Egyptians via email and WhatsApp, without credits. Though I made a great effort to find the images online in order to document their references, several of them were no longer available, so I had to find other sources. In all cases, however, only one source is quoted.

All images, taken from the internet or social networks, have been cropped, so they do not appear here in full.

I wish to thank Dr. Yona Sheffer for his help in arranging the references for the last version of this chapter.

The state language in modern Egypt is Arabic. Egyptian society, like other Arabic-speaking societies, is in a state of diglossia, a case of bilingualism in which two languages, or two variations of a language, are used for different purposes. The two languages (or language varieties) used in Arabic-speaking societies are *Fuṣḥā* and *'Āmmīyya*. Traditionally, *Fuṣḥā* has served as the language of writing, literature, study, and formal communication, while *'Āmmīyya* has been used as the language of speech and everyday communication.

The term *Fuṣḥā* may refer to classical Arabic as well as to Modern Standard Arabic (MSA); the latter is more or less uniform across the Arabic-speaking world (with some vocabulary differences). *'Āmmīyya*, whose status is traditionally lower than that of *Fuṣḥā*, differs according to the countries and regions in which it is spoken. Sometimes these differences make communication difficult, or almost impossible, among speakers from different countries or even regions. In Egypt, however, the differences among the various dialects inside the country do not prevent communication or understanding among their speakers. The most prestigious dialect in Egypt is that of Cairo ("Cairene Arabic"), which is the main vehicle of written and literary *'Āmmīyya*. Cairene Arabic is the Middle East's most widely understood Arabic dialect because of the strong influence of Egyptian music, film, literature, and other media, leading many Arabs in the Middle East to maintain that Egyptian Arabic is the "most beautiful" Arabic dialect.

Traditionally, Arabic literature has been, and still is, written in the standard language—the language of the Quran and other holy texts as well as classical poetry. Arabs (and also non-Arab Muslims) regard it as the most perfect, sublime, and eloquent language. For fourteen hundred years, colloquial Arabic has been looked down upon as inferior, a corrupted version of *Fuṣḥā* not fit for use as a vehicle of serious literature.

Arab societies, therefore, do not recognize their mother tongues as respectable language and refuse to designate them national languages. Opposition to using *'Āmmīyya* as a language of literature has deep roots in Arab culture, Egypt included. In modern Arabic-speaking societies, there is a constant fear of losing contact with Arab and Islamic heritage (whose texts are written in standard, classical Arabic) once *'Āmmīyya* becomes a written language. Today, there is also a fear of political fragmentation if the various dialects were to become written and national languages.

Despite the opposition to the use of CEA, from time to time, some writers have sporadically written in *'Āmmīyya* or included *'Āmmīyya* in their texts. Such texts, however, were not recognized as worthwhile literature and remained at the margins of literature.

In modern Egypt, the pressure to write in *'Āmmīyya* has been stronger, arising from several directions: the impact of realism in Western literature; and the flourishing of theater in Egypt and the consequent proliferation of dramatic works for onstage performance. Plays in MSA are not easily comprehensible to a large segment of the audience, which until today prefers performances in CEA. Many young writers are no longer bothered by the old norms of writing, and some (though not many) would like to detach themselves culturally from the Arab world at large and emphasize Egypt's unique local identity.

Although texts in colloquial Arabic are being written in other places in the Arabic-speaking world, this has been happening on a large scale only in Egypt, where the spoken variety has become a second written language used in poetry, prose, and drama, as well as in nonfiction. In recent years, CEA has been extensively used on the internet and in other electronic means of communication. The influence of English on Egyptian Arabic also increased during this period, and many lexical items derived from English have found their way into CEA, pushing aside words of Arabic or foreign, mainly French, origin.[1]

Hundreds of books written entirely in CEA or in a variety of mixtures of MSA and CEA have been published in Egypt—and nowhere else—in the last two decades. Egyptian Arabic, as a written language, has penetrated all genres and forms of literary and non-literary texts, and can be found in books, in the press, and on billboards on city streets and highways. Magazines written entirely or almost entirely in CEA have appeared, and comics (graphic novels) for adults, written in CEA, have become another legitimate genre in Egypt. Some books of the latter type are based on the events of the 2011 revolution (see below).

In literary and semi-literary writing, new techniques and styles have evolved. A unique style, which I have named *Fuṣḥāmmiyya*,[2] makes alternating use of both MSA and CEA, in assorted combinations. Here, both types are used intentionally and deliberately, and they enjoy equal status (unlike their use in mixed oral discourse). This style has accelerated the legitimacy of CEA as a literary and written language because of the equal status it is accorded alongside MSA.

Fuṣḥāmmiyya also gave rise to stylistic devices such as parallelism[3] and hendiadys,[4] which employ both MSA and CEA. In *Fuṣḥāmmiyya*, CEA is often used to help change the literary point of view (the position or angle from which the events of a story are observed and presented to the readers).[5] All these devices, which were rarely used before the mid-1990s, have become common and have completely changed the nature of writing in Egypt.

Language, Revolution, and Humor

When the 2011 revolution broke out, CEA was already in common use in Egypt in print and on the internet by many, including young and new writers and readers. It was thus no wonder that it became a major vehicle of expression during the January 2011 Revolution and subsequent events. CEA was dominant in the revolution's slogans and was often employed in texts related to the revolution and subsequent political and social events. In such texts, both MSA and CEA were sometimes employed alternately. CEA could also be seen in the graffiti that flourished during the January Revolution and afterwards, next to MSA and sometimes English, but it was less dominant in this vehicle of expression, which was more visual than verbal.[6]

The 2011 revolution and the events that followed it also led to the creation of new vocabulary in Egyptian Arabic, both Standard and Colloquial. Some examples of such linguistic innovations appear below.

Egyptians as a nation and as individuals have the reputation of possessing a highly developed sense of humor and an inclination to create jokes. This was reflected in the many jokes and cartoons that appeared before, during, and after the 2011 revolution, as well as in many of the revolution's slogans. A few typical ones from the early days of the revolution will be quoted, as well as some representative jokes and cartoons of a satirical nature which reflect the atmosphere in Egypt in the pre-revolutionary period; jokes that refer to incidents that took place during the revolution; and some that reflect the changes that occurred in Egypt after the revolution. All of these deliver clear-cut messages, succinctly conveying the atmosphere in Egypt and the public's attitudes toward political and social issues.[7]

In his *Ordinary Egyptians*,[8] Fahmy describes the relations between language, revolution, and humor in modern Egypt up to 1919. The linguistic circumstances at that time, however, differed from those in 2011. At the beginning of the twentieth century (when a large part of the population was illiterate), CEA was not regarded as a legitimate tool for "serious" writing, and its status in official Egyptian (and Arab) culture was low as opposed to the prestigious MSA. In the meantime, however, the status of CEA in Egypt has changed dramatically and, by the beginning of the twenty-first century, it was already de facto a second written and literary language in use by a large part of the populace, many of whom took an active part in spreading the ideas of the 2011 revolution via humoristic messages posted as graffiti, on billboards, and, to a larger extent, on social media.

Revolution, Colloquial Arabic, and the New Vocabulary

Egypt went through several revolutions and uprisings in its modern history. Until 2011, slogans on the street were often shouted in CEA though most of the oral and written documentation of them that exists in Egypt was in Standard Arabic. This changed in the 2011 revolution.

The language revolution in Egypt is not a by-product of the political one. By the time the events of January 2011 transpired, the language revolution had already made tremendous achievements and paved the way for a revolution that, in linguistic terms, differed significantly from its predecessors.

Many lexical innovations have been introduced into Egyptian Arabic during and since the 2011 revolution. New words and phrases were invented, and old words and phrases received new meanings. Many of these words and phrases are used in both CEA and in the Egyptian version of MSA. A number of books report in detail the events of the 2011 revolution and those following it. ʻAbd al-ʻAzīz's *Mawsūʻat thawrat yanāyir* (*Encyclopedia of the January Revolution*),[9] an encyclopedic lexicon, describes and explains in punctilious detail the terminology that was created during the 2011 revolution (so far only the first volume has been published). Ḥāmid's *Thawrat 25 yanāyir laḥẓa bilaḥẓa* (*The January 25 Revolution Moment by Moment*)[10] is a historiographic work with minute descriptions of the events that took place in Egypt during the 18 days from January 25 to February 11. Many revolutionary linguistic innovations appeared in these and other publications, fiction and nonfiction. The following are just a few examples of the revolution's terminology:

فل (*fill*), pl. فلول (*filūl, fulūl*, usually used in the plural, also for the singular): 1. (*Fuṣḥā*: *fulūl*) Scattered remnants of a defeated army; 2. In post-2011 revolution's terminology: a derogatory nickname for members or supporters of the old regime who have retained their old ideology and try to damage the revolution's achievements.

رابعة (*rabʻa*): 1. (In CEA: *ir-rabʻa*, in the feminine, with the definite article, as opposed to *al-rābiʻa* in MSA): "The fourth" (ordinal number); 2. A shortened name for the Rābiʻa al-ʻAdawīyya Mosque in Cairo, named for a famous saint and Sufi woman who lived in the eighth century; 3. "*rabʻa*," "four" (based on meanings (1) and (2), a sign made with four stretched and one bent finger by users of public transportation, informing the driver that their destination is the Rābiʻa al-ʻAdawīyya Mosque or its vicinity; 4. "*rabʻa*," "four," a reference to a member or supporter of the Muslim Brotherhood (after the name of the mosque where members of the Muslim Brotherhood and their supporters took cover and clashed with the security forces following the ousting of the

Brotherhood's President Morsi); 5. *"rab'a,"* "four," a sign as in definition (3) above, indicating that one belongs to or supports the Muslim Brotherhood.

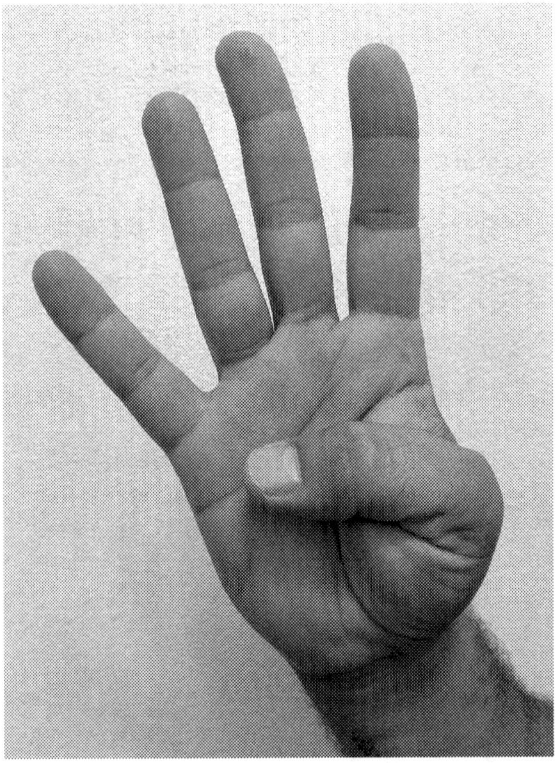

Figure 11.1: *Rab'a,* a sign made with the fingers. (Photo by the author)

Another word derived from the mosque's name is ربعاوي (*rab'āwī*): A member or supporter of the Muslim Brotherhood. Similarly, the term سيساوي (*sisāwi*) denotes a supporter of President Sisi.

نزل (*nizil*): (lit. go down, come down): "To go to Taḥrīr Square to demonstrate and protest." A more recent variation of this term was used in al-Sisi's last election campaign (see below).

أخونة (*akhwana*: noun); أخون, إتأخون (*akhwin, it'akhwin*: verbs): "Brotherhoodization" [of Egypt], making Egypt a MB state."

الجيش والشعب إيد واحدة (*il-gēsh wish-sha'b-i īd waḥda*): "The army and the people are one hand" (i.e., united). This slogan reflects the belief that the Egyptian army would not harm the people demonstrating and protesting.

مليونية (*milyonīyya*): "Demonstration or public protest held with a huge number of participants" (with the aspiration of boasting one million people). Launched in January 2011 in Taḥrīr Square, this became the sobriquet for any subsequent huge demonstration. For example, the following is the *milyonīyya* manifesto of May 27, 2011, which I received in Taḥrīr Square the night before the demonstration began (just a few lines are quoted and translated):

مليونية يوم الجمعة ٢٧ مــايو
هنــزل عشــان مش حــاسس بالتـغيير، إخواتي في السجن والمخلوع في شرم

يا شعب مصر اللى سابقة ضحكته غضبه.. يا مخلي ألف احتلال ينزل على ركبه
سايق عليك النبي ما تقول كده كفاية.. الثورة دى بداية زى الهجرة والميلاد
الثورة دى بسملة كمل بقى الآية

أولا: <u>المطالب الاقتصادية</u>
وضع حد ادنــى وأقصــى للأجور.
إعادة توزيع الثروات لإنقاذ البلاد من الأزمة الاقتصادية.
التحكم في الأسعار.
فرض الضريبة التصاعدية.
محاكمة كافة رجال الأعمال الفاسدين ومصادرة الأموال التي اكتسبوها بشكل غير شرعي.

ثانيا: <u>المطالب السياسية</u>
عودة الأمن بشكل مكثف.
تقديم مبارك للمحاكمة بتهمة الخيانة العظمى، على اثر اعتراف المشير باعطاء مبارك الأمر للقوات المسلحة بقتل المتظاهرين.
إشراف قضائي وحقوقي على جهاز الأمن الوطني ومحاكمة كل الضباط المتورطين في قتل المتظاهرين وتعذيبهم.
حل المجالس المحلية.
حل جهاز الأمن المركزي أو إدماجه في الجيش.
التاكيد علي حقوق المصريين في الخارج في الانتخابات.
إقالة يحيى الجمل ومحاكمة عمر سليمان.

ثالثا: <u>الحريات</u>
إلغاء إحالة المدنيين إلى قضاء عسكري.
إعادة محاكمة كل المحكوم عليهم بأحكام عسكرية بعد تحويلهم إلى المحاكم المدنية.
حظر فض الاعتصامات بالقوة بشكل كامل.
تطهير الإعلام، نريد إعلاما ثوريا معبرا عن صوت الشعب وليس صوت الحاكم أيا من كان.

انــزل وهــات خمســة معــاك
الجدع جدع والجبان جبــان و إحنا يا جدع راجعين للميدان

Figure 11.2: The *milyonīyya* manifesto, Friday, May 27, 2011[11]

مليونية يوم الجمعة 27 مـايو
هنـزل عشـان مش حاسس بالتغيير، إخواتي في السجن والمخلوع في شـرم
[. . .]
أولا: المطالب الاقتصادية:
[. . .]
ثانيا: المطالب السياسية:
[. . .]
ثالثا: الحريات:
[. . .]
انـزل وهـات خمسـة معـاك
الجدع جدع والجبان جبـان و إحنا يا جدع راجعين للميـدان

The *milyonīyya* of May 27

I shall go out [to demonstrate in Taḥrīr Square] because I don't feel a change: my brothers are in jail while the *makhlū'* (see below) is in Sharm [al-Shēkh]
[…]
First: Economic demands
[…]
Second: Political demands
[…]
Third: Freedoms
[…]
Go out [to Taḥrīr Square] and bring five with you
A man is a man and a coward is a coward and we, oh man, are going back to the Square

بلطجي (*balṭagī*), pl. بلطجية (*balṭagīyya*): 1. (CEA) "Thug" (especially one who terrifies a certain neighborhood; a word of Turkish origin). 2. (Since January 2011) "thug, bully," who has been sent by the old regime and its supporters to terrify protestors and demonstrators against the regime.

إستبن (*istibn*): 1. "Spare wheel, spare tire" (apparently after "Stepney," the brand name of the first spare wheels and tires produced in the UK; 2. A derogatory nickname for President Morsi, who was chosen by the Muslim Brotherhood to be Khayrat al-Shāṭer's substitute candidate for president after al-Shāṭer himself was disqualified; thus, this term compared him to a "spare tire."

موقعة الجمل (*mawqi'at al-gamal*): 1. In Islamic history, "The Battle of the Camel," a nickname for a battle in 655/656 CE between 'Alī, the fourth Caliph and Mu'āwiya, the governor of Syria, so called because

'Ā'isha, the Prophet's widow, was riding a camel during the fight and encouraging the army of Mu'āwiya. 2. In the January 2011 Revolution (also موقعة الجحش [*mawqi'at al-gaḥsh*]), "The Battle of the Young Donkey": A nickname for the incidents of February 2, in which the regime's supporters sent thugs (*balṭagiyya*), riding camels, horses, and donkeys, to try to dissolve the crowd in Taḥrīr Square using cold steel and Molotov cocktails.

خرفان (*khirfān*): "Sheep," an epithet for the Muslim Brothers (who follow their leaders like a flock of sheep).

المخلوع (*il-makhlū'*): "The dismissed," passive participle of the verb خلع (*khala'*), a derogatory nickname for President Mubarak.

المعزول (*il-ma'zūl*), sometimes also *il-makhlū'* as above: "the removed," passive participle of the verb عزل (*'azal*), a derogatory nickname for President Morsi.

The verb خلع (*khala'*) also means "to extract a tooth," and is the basis for the pun on the following board:

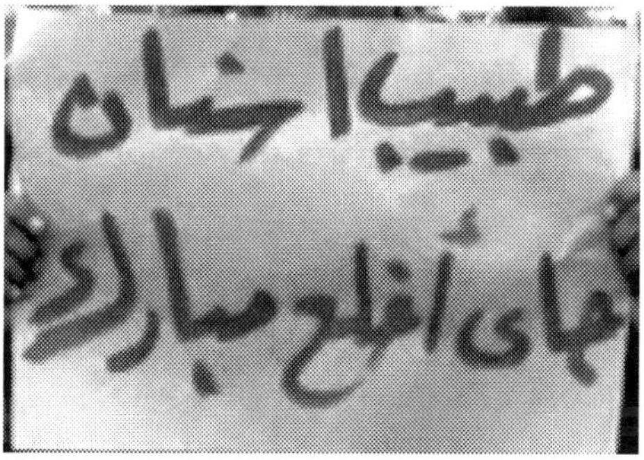

Figure 11.3: The dentist.[12]

طبيب اسنان (*Ṭabīb asnān*)
جاي أخلع مبارك (*Gayy-i 'akhla' Mubārak*)

[I am a] dentist
I have come to "extract" [i.e., remove] Mubarak.

The last example in this short list is the famous slogan shouted by the demonstrators in Egypt and other Arab countries (and therefore called out in MSA) during the Arab Spring:

الشعب يريد إسقاط النظام (*al-sha'b yurīd isqāṭ al-niẓām*): "The people wants to topple the regime."

Not surprisingly, the Egyptians created humorous alternatives to this slogan; the following are two versions, a joke and a sign:

مبارك شوهد يهتف للمتظاهرين: مبارك يريد تغيير الشعب.

Mubārak shūhida yahtifu lil-mutaẓāhirīn: Mubārak yurīd taghyīr al-sha'b.
Mubarak was seen shouting at the demonstrators: Mubarak wants to replace the people.[13]

The same slogan appears on a sign:

Figure 11.4: Mubarak wants to replace the people.[14]

Humor and Satire

Introduction

During and following the January 2011 Revolution, the demonstrators were often at risk of injury and even death, and were sometimes sprayed with tear gas by the police. Still, they retained the cheerful Egyptian spirit reflected in many, or even most, of the slogans they shouted and displayed, slogans that contained humorous elements.

Egyptians, as well as many non-Egyptian Arabic speakers, regard humor as a national trait. Indeed, the production of humor, both written and oral, in Egyptian society is extensive, traditionally produced, more often than not, in colloquial Egyptian Arabic. This Egyptian characteristic is often noted by writers and scholars. The following is one typical statement of many, taken from a book about Egyptian humor:

من أهم ما يميز المصريين في عصرهم الحديث روح الفكاهة المنبثة في أحاديثهم، فهم مشغوفون بالنكتة على كل شخص وكل شيئ. وفي أحرج المواقف وأدقها لا تلبث بارقة الفكاهة أن تلمع وتتألق وترتسم على الأفواه والشفاه.

A prominent characteristic of modern Egyptians is the spirit of humor that infuses their conversations. They will

> joke enthusiastically about any person or thing. Even in the most embarrassing and sensitive situations, humor still shines and gleams and appears on mouths and lips.[15]

A more recent comment on this issue also alludes to the 2011 revolution:

> المصري معروف بخفة ظله وحبه للنكتة (إحنا شعب ابن نكتة اصلاً) لا جديد فيما أقوله ولكن الجديد أن تجد خفة الظل هذه في شعب يثور ! !
>
> The Egyptian is known to have a cheerful disposition and a love for jokes (actually we are a nation fond of jokes). There is nothing new in what I am saying, but what is new is that you find this merry spirit in a nation that rebels![16]

Lane referred to Egyptian humor and satire more than a century and a half ago while remarking upon criticism of the country's rulers:

> The Egyptians are particularly prone to satire; and often display considerable wit in their jeers and jests. Their language affords them great facilities for punning and for ambiguous conversation, in which they very frequently indulge. The lower order sometimes lampoon their rulers in songs, and ridicule those enactments of the government by which they themselves most suffer. I was once much amused with a song which I found to be very popular in the town and district of Aswan, on the southern frontier of Egypt: its burden was a plain invocation to the plague to take their tyrannical governor and his Copt clerk. Another song, which was popular throughout Egypt during my first visit to this country, and which was composed on the occasion of an increase of the income-tax called *firdeh*, began thus: "You who have [nothing on your head but] a *libdeh*! sell it, and pay the *firdeh*." The *libdeh*, I have before mentioned, is a felt cap, which is worn under, or instead of, the turban; and the man must be very poor who has no other covering than this for his head.[17]

Humor and satire are difficult to define, which is why there are so many definitions of both, and so many theories that try to explain them.[18] Here are a few short, accepted definitions.

According to the *Concise Oxford Dictionary*, humor is "the quality of being amusing, especially as expressed in literature or speech," and "the ability to appreciate or express humour."[19]

Satire is "a mode of writing that exposes the failings of individuals, institutions or societies to ridicule and scorn."[20] According to Petro,[21] the two generally undisputed essentials of satire are *criticism* and *humor* of the widest possible variety.

In short, jokes are generally meant to amuse, while satire aims at criticizing, punishing, and changing the world. It should be noted that satire often tends to exaggerate, highlighting weaknesses and negative traits.

Highet says that there are two types of satirists and two different views of the purpose of satire: "The optimist writes in order to heal, the pessimist in order to punish."[22] Through my many conversations with Egyptian satirists and my reading abundant Egyptian satirical works, I have concluded that most Egyptian satirists belong to both types simultaneously.

Verbal and Visual Humor of the Revolution

Most of the revolution's slogans ridiculing the regime and the president (Mubarak) that we shall see here were meant, to a large extent, to amuse, whereas the jokes and some of the cartoons that I have chosen to quote below, while amusing, are more satirical in nature. These jokes succinctly convey the atmosphere in Egypt at the time and public attitudes toward political and social issues, and they deliver clear-cut messages.

It is noticeable that most of the slogans shouted and the signs on display during the 2011 revolution were phrased in CEA, and that the most serious messages were often presented humorously. This was quickly observed by the media and several scholars, and resulted in many articles in print and electronic media, along with some scholarly studies. Among the first studies of this revolutionary humor are those by Zack,[23] and Salem and Taira.[24] Several descriptions in Arabic of the humor of the revolution, sometimes accompanied by black and white images from Taḥrīr Square, were published in Egypt. Among the other authors who collected the revolution's slogans are Bakr[25] (who included a chapter with jokes), Fahmi,[26] al-Gamal,[27] al-Ḥafnāwi[28] (who published a study of the humorous slogans), Munīr,[29] and Sirāj.[30] Some articles on the revolution's humor that appeared on the internet are by Elnamoury,[31] Harutyunyan,[32] Williams,[33] and Sussman.[34] Books by Gröndahl and Mohyeldin[35] and Khalil,[36] both published by the American University in Cairo Press, contain high-quality color images from Taḥrīr Square. Many other collections of the revolution's jokes appeared in print, such as the books by al-Faqī,[37] Gābir,[38] Ḥimāya,[39] and Ibn Bashshār.[40] Chapter 4 in al-Shammā''s book[41] contains a discussion and many examples of the revolution's jokes. Baheyeldin and numerous others presented collections of revolutionary jokes and slogans on the internet.[42]

Humorous Slogans from Taḥrīr Square

Much has been written already on the humorous slogans of the revolution; hence, I shall concentrate here on several variations of what was probably the most prominent slogan of them all. The original, both shouted and written, was the one-word phrase ارحل (*irḥal*): Leave! Go away!—the demonstrators directly demanding that the president resign and leave.[43]

Figure 11.5: *Irḥal* (Leave!)[44]

On a few occasions, the verb *irḥal* was replaced by إمشي (*imshi*): Go! At other times the verb was changed to إنجز (*ingiz*): Hurry up!

While the one-word phrase *irḥal*, written or shouted aloud, reflected a serious tone, it had more humorous overtones in longer slogans written on boards. Following are some common, well-known examples: ارحل إيدي وجعتني (*irḥal īdi waga'itni*): Leave! My hand hurts! [from carrying this sign for such a long time], or ارحل بقى إيدي وجعتني (*irḥal ba'a īdi waga'itni*): Just leave! My hand hurts! The added word *ba'a* here intensifies the verb preceding it.

Figure 11.6: Just leave! My hand hurts![45]

إرحل كتفي وجعني (*irḥal kitfi waga'ni*): Leave! My shoulder hurts!

Figure 11.7: Leave! My shoulder hurts![46]

ارحل مراتي بتولد والولد مش عايز يشوفك (*irḥal mirāti bitiwlid wil-walad mish ʻāyiz yishūfak*): Leave! My wife is about to give birth, and the child doesn't want to see you!

ارحل مراتي وحشتني متزوج منذ 20 يوم (*irḥal mirāti waḥashitni mutazawwig mundhu 20 yōm*): Leave! I miss my wife; I am married for 20 days! (This is written in a mixed style of CEA and MSA.)

Figure 11.8: Leave! I miss my wife…[47]

During the time, Mubarak took to internalize the situation and respond to the demonstrators' *irḥal* demand, another group of funny slogans referring to this issue were created, still with *irḥal* as their leitmotif. One such slogan was based on the popular reputation of the *ṣaʻīdī*s (*ṣaʻāyda*, the inhabitants of Upper Egypt) as tough and strong people, thus the warning here was meant to "frighten" the president:

ارحل قبل ما الصعايدة يوصلوا (*irḥal abl-i ma-ṣ-ṣaʻāyda yiwṣalu*): Leave, before the *ṣaʻīdī*s arrive! The following version, on a board carried by a *ṣaʻīdī*, was accompanied by a monologue in the *ṣaʻīdī* accent by its carrier. It went viral on the internet:

ارحل, قبل الصعايدة ما ياجو (*irḥal, gabl-i-ṣ-ṣaʻāyda ma yaju*): Leave, before the *ṣaʻīdī*s come![48]

Figure 11.9: The *ṣaʻīdi* with his *irḥal* board.[49]

Another group of boards referred to Mubarak's supposed inability to understand the word *irḥal* and grasp its message. In these boards, the protestors tried to "help" the president understand the message. The following are three variations on this theme:

يمكن يفهم بالمقلوب (*i-r-ḥ-l yimkin yifham bil-ma'lūb*): Leave [in mirror writing]; maybe he'll understand the opposite way!

Figure 11.10: *irḥal* in mirror writing[50]

إ ر ح ل بالهيروغليفي يمكن تفهم يا فرعون (*irḥal bil-hiroghlīfi yimkin tifham ya far'ōn*): "Leave," in hieroglyphics; maybe you'll understand, you Pharaoh. There is also a pun here, since the word Pharaoh also means "tyrant."

Figure 11.11: Leave (in hieroglyphics).[51]

לעזוב—ارحل بلغة حبايبك (*LA'AZOV, irḥal bilughit ḥabāybak*): [TO] LEAVE, leave, in the language of your dear ones [i.e., the Israelis]. Here the word *irḥal* is translated into Hebrew in the infinitive, and then repeated in Arabic. The implied message: the president cooperates with the Israelis.

Figure 11.12: Leave (in Hebrew).[52]

The following two slogans use *imshi* and *ingiz* as substitutes for *irḥal*: امشي بقة أنا بردان *(imshi ba'a ana bardān)*: Just go!! I am freezing!

Figure 11.13: Go! I am freezing![53]

هاتمشي.. هاتمشي	[Hatimshi, hatimshi]	You'll go, you'll go!
انجز	[ingiz]	Hurry up
عشان أحلق	['ashān aḥla']	So I'll be able to get a haircut.

Figure 11.14: *Hatimshi* and *ingiz* (Go and hurry up!).[54]

Allusions to Famous Songs

In oral communication as well as in literary texts, Egyptians like to refer to famous Egyptian songs.[55] The following board, signed by "An Egyptian citizen," is a variation on the *irḥal* motif in an allusion to the well-known song *Ya misahharni* ("Oh, you who have been keeping me awake") performed by Umm Kulthum.[56] While in the original text the singer complains that her beloved doesn't pay attention to her, in the following text the anonymous Egyptian citizen demands President Mubarak to resign (*tirhal*) as he doesn't care for his people, ignores their misery, and keeps them hungry, but the president doesn't even consider resigning!

Figure 11.15: Even for one day...[57]

It is not surprising that the Egyptians continued joking even when their goal had been achieved. Once the president responded to the demonstrators' demand, some of them could not resist the temptation to create humor after their victory, too:

إرجع يا ريس, كنا بنهزر معاك الكاميرا الخفية	*Irga' ya rayyis, kunna binhazzar ma'āk il-kamira il-khafiyya*

Come back, President! We were joking with you!
Candid camera.

Figure 11.16: Come back again, President.[58]

Apologizing to President Mubarak

It must be said that there were also Egyptians who sympathized with President Mubarak during and after the revolution. A Facebook site titled *asfīn yā rayyis* (We are sorry, President [Mubarak]; we apologize President [Mubarak]) was launched to express this sympathy. When Mubarak was hospitalized at the armed forces hospital, his supporters would gather under his window to greet him. Several times I heard expressions of sympathy and repentance from ordinary Egyptians, which increased when the Muslim Brotherhood was in power. Still, the manifestation of joy when Mubarak left was much stronger, and it was very obvious that Egyptians were proud of what they had accomplished. The phrase *irfa' rāsak inta maṣrī* (Raise your head, you are Egyptian) was not merely a slogan; I actually heard it from proud Egyptians.

MSA and Egyptian Heritage

To conclude this section, I would like to show one of the photos of graffiti that I took in Cairo in 2011. It quotes a famous phrase by the national leader Muṣṭafā Kāmel (1874–1908):

> لو لم أكن / أولد مصريا لوددت أن أكون مصريا
>
> *Law lam akun/ūlad miṣrīyyan lawadadtu*[59] *an akūna miṣrīyyan.*
>
> If I had not been [in another version: born] Egyptian, I would like to have been Egyptian.

Most Egyptians are familiar with this phrase, written in elevated *Fuṣḥā*, since it is taught in Egyptian schools and occasionally used when one wants to express patriotism and love for Egypt.[60] No wonder, then, that it was revived several times during the 2011 revolution, as in the following inscription on a wall, in which each line appears in one of the three colors of the Egyptian flag: red, white, and black (shown on the right and on the left):

Figure 11.17: I would like to have been Egyptian.[61]

Satirical Jokes

As George Orwell so aptly noted, every joke is a tiny revolution.[62] This section focuses on representative jokes of a satirical nature that reflect the atmosphere in Egypt during the 2011 revolution and the pre- and post-revolutionary periods.

All these jokes are popular in Egypt; they have been told orally, shared on the internet, and quoted in many printed books. Most of them appear in several versions with slight changes.

The Revolution's Background: The Economy

It was well known in Egypt that Mubarak's sons, Gamāl and 'Alā', were involved in state affairs. While it was clear that Gamāl was meant to be his father's successor, many Egyptians believed that 'Alā' was deeply involved in Egypt's economy and took control of practically all its companies and businesses. Many Egyptians were annoyed by that, as can be seen in the following joke, which exaggerates the scope of 'Alā''s control of the Egyptian economy by claiming that he is involved in even the smallest businesses:

> مرة واحد ركب تاكسي ولقى السواق معلق في العربية صور جمال عبد الناصر وانور السادات وحسني مبارك. الراجل استغرب سأل السواق مين اللي انت معلقهم صورهم عندك. قاله دا جمال عبد الناصر الزعيم المصري الراحل ودا انور السادات قائد حركة السلام والامن في البلد ودا حسني مبارك أبو علاء شريكي في التاكسي.
>
> Once a man was riding in a taxi and noticed that the taxi driver had hung pictures of Gamal 'Abd al-Nasser, Anwar al-Sadat, and Hosni Mubarak in the car. The man wondered and asked the driver: "Who are these people whose pictures you have hanging here?" He [the driver] told him: This is Gamal 'Abd al-Nasser, the late Egyptian leader, and this is Anwar al-Sadat, the leader of the peace and security movement in our country, and this is Hosni Mubarak, father of 'Alā' who is my partner in this taxi.[63]

A mocking reference in rhyme to "Abū 'Alā'" ("father of 'Alā'," i.e., Mubarak) also appeared on the following board:

اللهم ارفع عنا الغلاء	Oh, God, take from us the high prices
والبلاء	And the distress
والوباء	And the epidemic
وأبو علاء	And Abū 'Alā' ('Alā''s father).

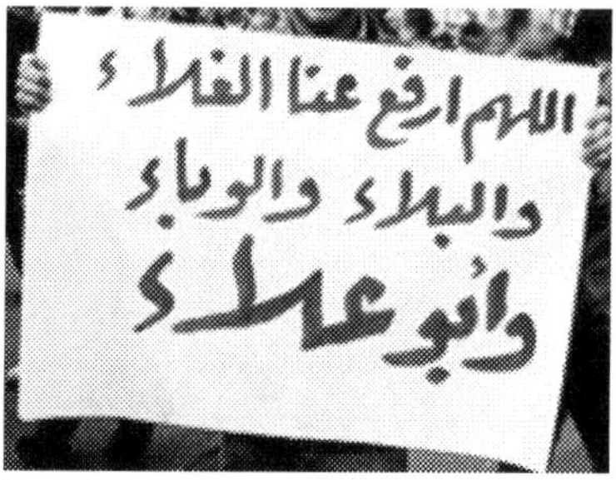

Figure 11.18: Take from us… 'Alā''s father.[64]

Mubarak's Long Rule

The long-term presidency of the seemingly irreplaceable Mubarak was a constant topic of conversation and criticism, augmented by the accepted assumption that Gamāl, Mubarak's son, had been designated as his father's successor, and therefore was disparagingly nicknamed *al-warīth* ("the successor"). Since nobody thought of revolting, Egyptians despaired of finding an opportunity to replace Mubarak, as reflected in the following joke:

> مواطن قبطى سأل مبارك هل يجوز أن يتولى مسيحى الحكم، فرد مبارك: ولا مسلم وحياتك.
>
> A Coptic citizen asked Mubarak: "Is it permissible for a Christian to get the reins of power?" Mubarak answered: "Come on, not even for a Muslim!"[65]

The following joke also refers to the "eternity" of Mubarak's rule:

> مواطن مصري أهدى الرئيس مبارك سلحفاة وقال له: هذه السلحفاة تعيش 400 سنة.. فقال له الرئيس: هنشوف!!
>
> An Egyptian citizen gave the president a turtle as a gift and told him: "This turtle will live for four hundred years." The president said to him: "We'll see!!"[66]

The Weapons of the Egyptian Revolution

Many Egyptians believe, until today, that Nasser died because he was poisoned. Sadat, Nasser's successor, was shot while standing on the podium during the October 6 celebration army parade. The following joke tells about the new deadly weapon that caused the end of the next president, Mubarak:

> مبارك بعد ما مات قابل السادات وعبد الناصر سألوه: سم ولا منصة.. قال: فيس بوك.
>
> Mubarak, after he died, met Sadat and ʻAbd al-Nasser. They asked him: "Poison or podium"? He replied: "Facebook."[67]

This joke also appeared on a board during the demonstrations:

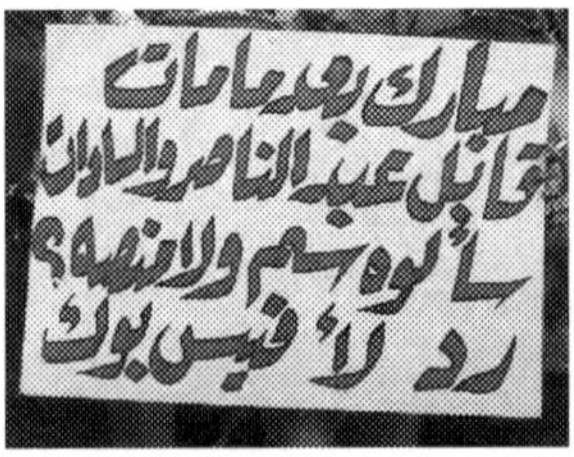

Figure 11.19: Poison, podium, and Facebook.[68]

The rise of the social networks as influential and effective weapons against the regime and its supporters,[69] who were using old-fashioned weapons, is reflected in the following joke and cartoon. The new weapon here is Bluetooth technology:

> بلطجي سألوه: إنتو ليه بترموا مولوتوف على الشباب.. فرد وقال: العيال دول بيرموا علينا قنابل «بلوتوث».
>
> A *balṭagi* was asked: "Why do you throw Molotov [cocktails] on the youngsters?" So he replied and said: "These kids are throwing Bluetooth bombs at us."[70]

The Indifference of President Mubarak

The following joke mocking the president's indifference and imperviousness was one of the very first jokes of the revolution. I heard it, in a shorter version, at the outset of the revolution, just one or two days after the January 25 demonstration in Taḥrīr Square (the following is a printed version):

> حسني مبارك وعمر سليمان كانوا ماشيين في ميدان التحرير.. مبارك قال: هم الناس متجمعين كده ليه هو فيه إيه؟ رد عمر سليمان وقال: مجتمعين عشان يودعوك يا ريس.. مبارك قال: ليه؟ هم رايحين فين؟!
>
> Hosni Mubarak and Omar Sulayman[71] were walking in Taḥrīr Square. Mubarak said: "Why have the people gathered like that? What is the matter?" Omar Sulayman replied and said: They have gathered because they want to say farewell to you, President." Mubarak said: "Why? Where are they going?"[72]

In some other versions of this joke Mubarak asks: هوّ الشعب رايح فين؟ ("Where are the people going?").

Mocking the Fundamentalists

Many anti-Muslim Brotherhood jokes were created in Egypt after the Brothers came to power and after their fall. The following one shows how exasperated average Egyptians were with them:

> واحد اخوان متعصب ركب تاكسى قام قال للسواق: هو على أيام الرسول كان فى راديو؟.. السواق قاله: لأ، قاله: خلاص لازم تطفى الراديو، السواق قفلوا شويه و راح الأخوانجى قايلوا ايام الرسول كان فى سجاير السواق قالوا لاء قالوا يبقى تطفى السجاره اتحمق السواق وضرب فرامل وقاله: هو على أيام الرسول كان فى تاكسى؟ قاله: لأ، قاله: يبقى تنزل تشوفلك قافله ملاكى قريش من قوافل الكفار توصلك.

One fanatic Muslim Brother was riding in a taxi, and then asked the driver: "Was there a radio in the days of the Prophet?" The driver said to him: "No." He told him: "You have to turn off the radio." The driver turned it off. After a short while, the Muslim Brother said to him: "Were there cigarettes in the days of the Prophet?" The driver said: "No." So he told him: "Then you have to put out the cigarette." The driver became angry, abruptly stopped the car and said to him: "Was there a taxi in the days of the Prophet?" He said to him: "No." The driver told him: "Then get out and find yourself a private caravan of infidels with a Quraysh[73] license number that will take you."[74]

The following joke refers to the emergence of Salafīsm, the fundamentalist movement, on the Egyptian political scene, and to the rivalry between them and the Muslim Brothers. In this joke, a Salafi describes the Brothers as evil creatures:

بيسألوا واحد سلفى هوا صحيح الاخوان مذكورين فى القرأن فرد وقالهم طبعا قالولو فى انهى ايه قل اعوذ برب الفلق من شر ما خلق.

A Salafi is asked: "Is it true that the Muslim Brothers are mentioned in the Quran?" He replied and said: "Of course." So they asked him: "In which verse?" [He said:] "'Say, I seek refuge in the Lord of the daybreak/From the evil of what He has created" (or: "Against the harm of what He has created") (Q113/*Al-Falaq*).[75]

Post-Revolution Satirical and Non-Satirical Cartoons

President Morsi is depicted sitting on the presidential throne, holding a chessboard in his hand, saying:

أحرك عسكري ولا أشيل وزير؟ هو ليه مفيش زهر في البتاعة دي!!
aḥarrak ʿaskarī walla ashīl wazīr? huwwa lēh mafīsh zahr-i fi -l-bitāʿa di?

Shall I move a pawn [also: a soldier] or shall I remove the queen [also: a government minister]? Why are there no dice in this thing?

Using the terminology of chess, this cartoon makes use of double-meanings that are obvious in Egyptian Arabic.

Morsi, here depicted as a small person, is sitting on the presidential throne; because it is too big for him, his feet are hanging in the air, conveying the idea that he is not adequate for this job. He is holding a chessboard in his hand, and behind him we see an hourglass and the date, June 30. The message: fast decisions must be taken while there is still time [both for the chess game and the coming events of June 30, 2013]. Morsi, who is unable to make a decision, is talking to himself, with double meanings, hesitating to move a pawn [or a soldier], that is, to order the army to move, or to remove the queen [or a government minister], that is, to remove al-Sisi, the defense minister, from his post. Incapable of making a decision, Morsi asks himself in sorrow why there are no dice in chess (as in backgammon), which could save him from the burden of decision-making). Obviously, he would have preferred to simply throw the dice.

This cartoon makes it clear that the presidency of Egypt is a position far beyond Morsi's qualifications; though he knows what will happen on June 30, he cannot prevent what will be known later as the June 30 Revolution.

I was in Cairo during that week and left on the 29. Conversing with ordinary Egyptians, I heard the following message: "We shall go to Taḥrīr Square, we shall remove Morsi, and the army will protect us." If I was hearing that message, Morsi must have heard it, too, but as the cartoon makes clear, he could not prevent the revolution. The demonstrations that broke out on June 30, supported by the army, indeed led to the removal of President Morsi on July 3 and naturally paved the way for many jokes and cartoons mocking the Muslim Brothers.

The June 30 Revolution that toppled President Morsi and the Muslim Brotherhood's regime resuscitated some slogans of the January 2011 Revolution, such as *irḥal* (leave), now directed against Morsi. The new terminology of the 2013 revolution is also used in a board that was published in one of the blogs: the term *khirfān* (sheep), a disparaging nickname for the Muslim Brothers, is implied without being mentioned explicitly. The board shows a bleating sheep (the inscription *mā'* represents the sound of bleating) while The inscription on top says: *Makānak iz-zirība* (Your place is in the sheep-pen). The import is clear: the Brothers must leave the reins of power and return to the squalid place where they belong.

In a cartoon out of many others a Muslim Brotherhood member, identified by his appearance and the *rab'a* sign on his chest, symbolizes for the Egyptian citizen the June 30 Revolution with the cliché, *ḥarām* (forbidden), a term often used by the Muslim Brothers: ثورة 30 يونيو حرام أصلا (*Thawrat 30 yūnyū ḥarām aṣlan*; The June 30 Revolution is actually forbidden). The Egyptian citizen, unaffected by the Muslim Brother's words, is depicted as tall and happy, while the Muslim Brother is small and miserable. It is quite obvious here that the message of the Muslim Brothers should be totally ignored.[76]

Some cartoons are neither humorous nor satirical, but rather deliver a positive social or political message. One of them reflects the feelings of optimism which arose among many Egyptians after al-Sisi's rise to power, focusing on the president's struggle against corruption which was one of the main reasons for the 2011 revolution. In this cartoon, President al-Sisi stands near by a garbage can of corruption (مزبلة الفساد—*Mazbalat al-fasād*) cleaning Egypt (الرئيس بينظف مصر—*Ir-ra'īs binaḍḍaf maṣr*). Furthermore, al-Sisi is clearly depicted with a *zibība* (lit. raisin) on his forehead, a nickname for the mark created on the forehead of a religious Muslim as a result of its touching the ground during the prayer for many years. The message here is that, one does not have to be a Muslim Brother in order to be a true believer.[77]

The *fakka* Campaign

President al-Sisi is known for his campaigns to collect money from the public for the benefit of Egypt in general and the poor in particular. In one of the campaigns, he asked the public to donate the small change that they receive:

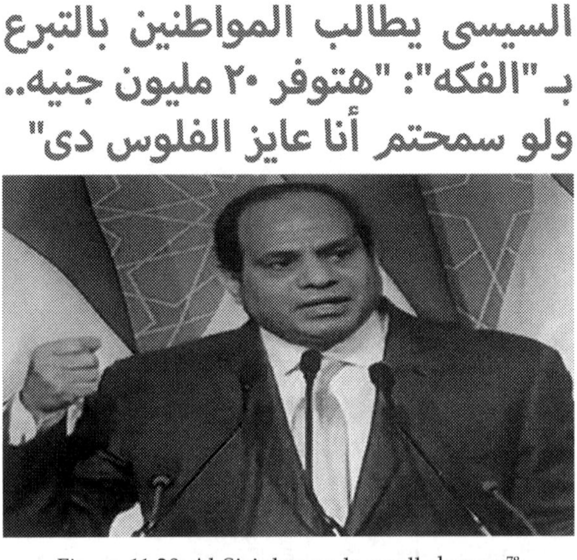

Figure 11.20: Al-Sisi demands small change.[78]

The photo shows President al-Sisi delivering a speech. The caption that accompanies it says:

السيسي يطالب المواطنين التبرع ب «الفكة»: «هتوفر 20 مليون جنيه.. ولو سمحتم أنا عايز الفلوس دي».

> Sisi demands that citizens donate their small change (*fakka*): "It will supply 20 million [Egyptian] pounds, and with your permission I want this money."

Egyptians typically responded to al-Sisi with the following satirical image. Above the photo appears al-Sisi's demand for 20 million pounds. Below it, a citizen says: *Allāh yiḥannin ʿalēk* (May God make people kind to you). This is the Egyptian phrase used as a polite refusal to beggars who ask for money; its use here denotes that Egyptians will not cooperate with the president's aspirations (on *fakka,* see also below).

Figure 11.21: Sorry, I can't give you money.[79]

Connecting the Old and New Egyptian Revolutions

The common CEA phrase *mafīsh fayda* (There is no point, there is no hope, it is a hopeless case) was announced in despair by the national leader Saʿd Zaghlūl (often nicknamed Saʿd-i bāsha, Saʿd Pasha), referring to the prospect of the British ever leaving Egypt. Until today, the phrase *Saʿd-i bāsha 'āl 'ēh? mafīsh fayda!* (What did Saʿd Pasha say? There is no hope!) is said figuratively in Egyptian Arabic when talking about something that has no chance of coming true.

The following image refers to the prospect of collecting small change from Egyptian citizens by alluding to Saʿd Zaghlūl and his famous saying. It shows the well-known figure of Sa'd Zaghlūl with the caption *mafīsh fakka* (there is no small change); the word *fakka* (small change, i.e., money) replaces *fayda*. The message of this vivid image is imparted through bisociation (see tnote 19), referring at one and the same time to both Sa'd Zaghlūl's saying and al-Sisi's demand for spare change from the people, again making it clear that the latter has no chance of fulfilling his aspirations.

Figure 11.22: [Sa'd Zaghlūl:] There is no change.[80]

A link between the Egyptain revolutions, January 2011 and June 2013, that brought President al-Sisi to power is made through a term coined during the Taḥrīr Square demonstrations. As mentioned above, the verb *nizil* (lit. go down or come down) has been used to mean "to go to Taḥrīr Square to demonstrate and protest." Here it appears on a billboard on the street in the imperative: "Go down and participate with your vote," obviously alluding to the 2011 term as used in 2011, and conveying the message that participating in the elections and voting for al-Sisi is as important as participation in the January 2011 Revolution was:

إنزل	Go down
وشارك بصوتك	And participate with your vote
مصر محتاجة صوتك	Egypt needs your vote
من أجل مستقبل أفضل	For the sake of a better future
مع تحيات الحاج أشرف كامل	With greetings from ḥāgg Ashraf Kāmil
منسق حملة من أجل مصر	Coordinator of the "For Egypt's sake" campaign

Figure 11.23: *Inzil* in al-Sisi's election campaign (a).[81]

Another version says:

انزل وشارك	Go down and participate
مصر تناديك	Egypt is calling you.
مع تحيات	With greetings from
رجب هلال حميدة	Ragab Hilāl Ḥimēda

Figure 11.24: *Inzil* in al-Sisi's election campaign (b).[82]

Finally, I would like to discuss the following (non-humorous) banner recently photographed in Cairo (2017). It was hung in the street by an Egyptian citizen (a common practice in Egypt) on the occasion of the October 6 celebration.

This banner summarizes Egyptian presidential history since Nasser, and is reminiscent of the joke about the taxi driver who displayed pictures of three presidents in his car. It is telling to note which presidents do not appear in the banner, not merely those who do.

The three presidents depicted are: Nasser, Sadat, and al-Sisi. Below each figure is a caption. Nasser: *baṭal thawrat 23 yūlyū* (Hero of the July 23 Revolution); Al-Sisi: *baṭal thawrat 30 yūnyū* [*sic.*: *yūlyū*] (Hero of the June [*sic.*: "July"] 30 Revolution); and Sadat: *baṭal al-ḥarb wal-salām* (Hero of war and peace). In addition to Mohamed Naguib, the first president of Egypt, who has been almost forgotten by the Egyptian public, the two presidents who preceeded al-Sisi do not appear here: Mubarak, who represents the corrupt old regime, and Morsi, who represents the unwelcome and outlawed Muslim Brotherhood movement. The presidents do not appear on the banner in chronological order; al-Sisi is in the middle, which may ascribe to him more importance than to the other two.

Bearing in mind the joke about the taxi driver and the three presidents, in this banner al-Sisi has replaced Mubarak, while Morsi is not considered significant enough to be included in the list of Egypt's top presidents.

Figure 11.25: Three Egyptian presidents.[83]

A Comment on Revolution and the Terminology of the Revolution in Egyptian Literature Since 2011

The January 2011 Revolution and the political turnabouts that followed it have inspired literary, semi-literary, and nonfiction writing in Egypt. Dozens of books depicting the revolution and documenting its events, slogans, and verbal and visual humor appeared after the revolution, including prose and poetry, much of which was written in or with CEA. The following are just some examples: Muḥammad Fatḥi's novel *Kān fīh marra thawra* (*Once Upon a Time There Was a Revolution*, 2011)[84] and Amānī al-Tūnisī's novel *Amāni bint.. min midān it-taḥrīr* (*Amāni, A Girl from Taḥrīr Square*, 2011)[85] are written in CEA, while Hishām al-Khashin's novel *7 Ayyām fī al-taḥrīr* (*Seven Days in Taḥrīr [Square]*, 2011)[86] is written in MSA with quotations of the slogans of the revolution in CEA. One book of poetry that refers to a famous pre-revolution prose work is Fāṭima 'Abd al-Mun'im's collection, *Shaklaha it'addilit* (*It Seems that It Became Right*, 2011);[87] the book's title is an allusion to 'Umar Ṭāher's book *Shaklaha bāẓit* (*It Seems that It Went Wrong*, 2005),[88] implying that after the 2011 revolution things in Egypt improved and were corrected. Ibrāhīm ʿAbd al-Magīd, in *Likull arḍ milād: ayyām al-taḥrīr* (*Every Land Has its Birth: The Days of Taḥrīr,* 2011),[89] writes his impressions of the events in Taḥrīr Square, interspersed with selections from his Facebook posts and the reactions to them. Many of the books inspired by the revolution were written by young writers of the new generation; they write in CEA, often upload posts to the internet, and use the new communications terminology. An exceptional book in its attitude is Tāmer ʿAbd al-Munʿim's *Muḏakkirāt filūl* (*Memoirs of a Filūl,* 2018),[90] written from the point of view of a supporter of the old Mubarak regime; this novel mentions the revolution's events and contains terminology of the revolution.

In recent years, there has also been a noticeable increase in the publication of comics for adults (now more accurately called "graphic novels" or "sequential art").[91] The main language used in these is CEA; sometimes sections are written in English, too. Some of these publications begin life on the internet, while others appear first in print and then are uploaded, partly or fully, to the internet. Often these graphic novels are the result of cooperation by several writers and artists. The following are two examples of this type of literature, which are set against the 2011 revolution: *ʿIbiyya;*[92] and *al-Saʿīd and Ḥāzem.*[93]

The short passage below is from one of the post-revolution's books, *Daftar al-ghaḍab* (*Notebook of Anger*) by Al-Shāyib,[94] which contains selections from a diary and from Facebook posts regarding the events in Egypt from January 25, 2011 to November 27, 2012. This paragraph reflects the feelings of many Egyptians after the revolution was accomplished:

> للمرة الأولى منذ ثلاثين عامًا أستيقظ على مصر بدون مبارك. مصر بدون الحيزبون. مصر بدون الوريث، وبدون سرور وصفوت ونظيف وعز وباقي عصابة اللصوص. للمرة الأولى أستيقظ على مصر الجديدة. مصر الكرامة والحرية والعدالة. فتحت عيني، ورأيت نور الصباح يملأ الغرفة. وجدت رغبة قوية في ممارسة تمارين الصباح. حركة الجسم تعني الحياة، وقوة الجسم تعني قوة العقل وقوة النفس، وفي الثورة يحتاج الإنسان لمجموع قواه.
>
> For the first time in thirty years, I wake up in Egypt without Mubarak. Egypt without the evil-looking old hag,[95] Egypt without the heir,[96] and without Surūr,[97] and Ṣafwat,[98] and Naẓīf,[99] and ʿIzz,[100] and the rest of the gang of thieves. For the first time, I wake up in a New Egypt. An Egypt of dignity, freedom, and justice. I opened my eyes and saw the morning light filling the room. I felt a strong desire to perform morning exercises. The movement of the

> body means life, and the strength of the body means the power of reason and the strength of the soul, and in the revolution a person needs all his powers.[101]

Conclusion

In these pages we have seen just a few examples of Colloquial Egyptian Arabic as it was used in the 2011 revolution, an event that was documented in the various media and social networks as it was unfolding.[102] CEA was used overwhelmingly in this revolution as a major language of communication. This is not surprising because by January 2011 CEA, for the first time in the history of Arab culture, had already become a second written and literary language in Egypt (though so far only in Egypt).

This rise of CEA also facilitated the use of humor in the messages conveyed during the revolution. Humor is considered a national trait of the Egyptians, and a significant amount of it has been created traditionally in Egyptian Arabic. Furthermore, the availability of CEA as a written language paved the way for humor to be used as an instrument of expression in the service of the revolution, and perhaps even encouraged it.

Humor, of course, was not used only during the revolution (or revolutions). It is in constant use in Egypt, and currently more than ever because of the flourishing of the internet and the social media, which have become major distribution channels for humor. Before the era of digital and electronic media, jokes were transmitted orally and cartoons were distributed in newspapers; now they are distributed faster and to larger audiences through the new means of communication.

Sa'd Zaghlūl's saying, *Mafīsh fayda* (There is no hope), quoted above, eventually proved wrong: the British did leave Egypt. So perhaps there is hope for positive outcomes of the 2011 and 2013 revolutions. Despite the descriptions above, al-Sisi may yet succeed in getting metaphorical "change" from the people, which is to say he may ultimately fulfill the ambitious social and economic goals that would lead Egypt to a better future. So, conceivably, there may still be *fayda* (hope).

Notes

1. Gabriel M. Rosenbaum, "The Growing Influence of English on Egyptian Arabic," in Olivier Durand, Angela Diana Langone, and Giuliano Mion (eds.), *Alf Lahğa wa-lahğa: Proceedings of the 9th AIDA Conference (Neue Beihefte zur Wiener Zeitschrift für die Kunde des Morgenlandes)* (Vienna: LIT Verlag, 2014), 377–385.
2. Gabriel M. Rosenbaum, "*Fuṣḥāmmiyya*: Alternating Style in Egyptian Prose," *Zeitschrift für arabische Linguistik* 38 (2000), 68–87.
3. Parallelism is "the arrangement of similarly constructed clauses, sentences, or verse lines in a pairing or other sequence suggesting some correspondence between them. The effect of parallelism is usually one of balanced arrangement achieved through repetition of the same syntactic forms." Chris Baldick, *The Concise Oxford Dictionary of Literary Terms*, 2nd ed. (Oxford: Oxford University Press, 2001), 183.
4. Hendiadys is "a figure of speech described in traditional rhetoric as the expression of a single idea by means of two nouns joined by the conjunction 'and' (e.g., 'house and home' or 'law and order'), rather than by a noun qualified by an adjective. The commonest English examples, though, combine two adjectives ('nice and juicy') or verbs ('come and get it')" (Baldick, *Concise Oxford Dictionary of Literary Terms*, 111).
5. Gabriel M. Rosenbaum, "Mixing Colloquial and Literary Arabic in Modern Egyptian Prose through the Use of Free Indirect Style and Interior Monologue," Jérôme Lentin and Jacques Grand Henry (eds.), *Moyen arabe et variétés moyennes de l'arabe à travers l'histoire (Actes du premier colloque international)* (Louvain-la-Neuve: Université catholique de Louvain, Institut orientaliste de Louvain, 2008), 391–404; Rosenbaum, "Mixed Arabic and Stylistic Choices in Contemporary Egyptian Writing," *Quaderni di Semitistica* [*QuSem*] 28 (2012), 291–306.
6. On the graffiti of the revolution, see Mia Gröndahl, *Revolution Graffiti: Street Art of the New Egypt* (Cairo: American University in Cairo Press, 2012); Aḥmad Salīm Aḥmad Sālim, *Grāfiti: shāhid 'alā al-thawra* (Cairo: Akhbār al-Yawm, 2013); Sharīf Bur'ī (ed.), Māya Guwaylī (photography, with contributions from Magi Usāma, et al.), *al-Gudrān tahtif: grāfītī al-thawra al-miṣrīyya* ([Cairo]: Zaytūna, 2012); This book is published in a bilingual edition, in Arabic and in English. Details in English: Sherif Boraïe (ed.), Maya Gowaily (photography, with contributions from Maggie Osama, et al.), *Wall Talk: Graffiti of the Egyptian Revolution* ([Cairo]: Zeitouna, 2012).
7. CEA is the language of jokes, both orally and written; in most cases, cartoon captions are written traditionally in CEA.
8. Ziad Fahmy, *Ordinary Egyptians* (Stanford: Stanford University Press, 2011).
9. Hishām 'Abd al-'Azīz, *Mawsū'at thawrat yanāyir* (Cairo: Al-Hay'a al-miṣrīyya al-'āmma lil-kitāb 1, 2012).
10. Ḥasan Ḥāmid, *Thawrat 25 yanāyir laḥẓa bilaḥẓa* (Cairo: Al-Hay'a al-miṣrīyya al-'āmma lil-kitāb 2012).

11. Manifesto received and scanned by the author.
12. Ghāda Ghālib, "93 *Lāfita kūmīdiyya khilāl thawrat yanāyir: ''Ingiz ba'a 'āyiz aḥla'.. irḥal is-sitt 'āyza tiwlid',"* *al-Miṣri al-yawm* (January 25, 2015), https://lite.almasryalyoum.com/lists/38977/.
13. Usāma Muḥammad Muṣṭafā al-Faqī, "*al-Nukta al-miṣrīyya fī al-thawra al-sha'bīyya: thawrat 25 yanāyir*" (Cairo: Maktabat zahrā' al-sharq, 2011), 120.
14. http://www.yafeta.com/a/131/مبارك-يريد-تغيير-الشعب/ (accessed October 11, 2019).
15. Shawqī Ḍayf, *al-Fukāha fī Miṣr* (Cairo: Dār al-ma'āref, 1985), 5.
16. Ḥamdī Ghālib, *Shāhid 'iyān awi* (Cairo: Al-Riwāq, 2011), 15.
17. Edward William Lane, *An Account of the Manners and Customs of the Modern Egyptians* (Cairo: American University in Cairo Press, 2003), 305–306.
18. Regarding early attempts to arrive at understanding humor, see Aristotle's *Poetics*, in *The Poetics: Aristotle's Theory of Poetry and Fine Art with a Critical Text of the Poetics*, 4th ed., translation and critical notes by S.H. Butcher (New York: Dover Publications, 1951). Three major influential theories have been suggested more recently. On the social aspects of humor, see Henri Bergson, "Laughter," in *Comedy*, ed. Wylie Sypher (Baltimore: Johns Hopkins University Press, 1980) 59–190. Sigmund Freud discusses humor in light of his psychological theories primarily in his book *The Joke and its Relation to the Unconscious*, trans. Joyce Crick (London: Penguin Books, 2002). Arthur Koestler's *The Act of Creation* (London: Pan Books, 1970) posits the concept of *bisociation*: "the mental association of an idea or object with two separate fields that are ordinarily seen as unrelated" (Salvatore Attardo, ed., *Encyclopedia of Humor Studies* (Los Angeles: Sage Reference, 2014), vol. 1, 83. As yet, there is no single theory that covers all aspects of humor, a fact which encourages scholars to devise new theories.
19. *Concise Oxford English Dictionary*, 12th ed. (Oxford: Oxford University Press, 2011), s.v. "Humour." CD Rom.
20. Baldick, *Literary* Terms, 228.
21. Peter Petro, *Modern Satire: Four Studies* (Berlin: Mouton Publishers, 1982), 8.
22. Gilbert Highet, *The Anatomy of Satire* (Princeton: Princeton University Press, 1962), 237.
23. Liesbeth Zack, "'Leave, I Want to have a Shower!' The Use of Humour on the Signs and Banners Seen During the Demonstration in Tahrir Square," in R. Genis, E. de Haard, J. Kalsbeek, E. Keizer, and J. Stelleman (eds.), *Between West and East: Festschrift for Wim Honselaar on the Occasion of His 65th birthday* (Amsterdam: Pegasus, 2012), 711–729.
24. Heba Salem and Kantaro Taira, "Al-Thawra al-daHika: The Challenges of Translating Revolutionary Humor," in Samia Mehrez (ed.), *Translating Egypt's Revolution: The Language of Tahrir* (Cairo: American University in Cairo Press, 2012), 183–211; this is a collection of studies on the January Revolution done within the framework of translation studies.
25. Sharīf Bakr (ed.), *al-Sha'b yurīd*, 2nd ed. (Cairo: Al-'Arabī, 2011).

26. Khāled Fahmi, "*Mu'gam shi'ārāt al-thawra: khazīnat al-ḥikma wal-wa'i,*" *al-Mukhtār al-islāmī* 343 (February 19, 2011), 41–45.
27. Kamāl 'Alī al-Gamal, *Shi'ārāt waṣuwar thawrat 25 yanāyir* (Cairo: Maktabat gazīrat al-ward, n.d).
28. Samīr al-Ḥafnāwi, *al-Shi'arāt wal-hutāfāt al-fukāhiyya fī al-thawra al-miṣriyya* (Cairo: Maktabat gazīrat al-ward, 2011).
29. 'Amr 'Abd al-'Azīz Munīr, *Thawrāt miṣr al-sha'bīyya* (Cairo: Al-Hay'a al-miṣrīyya al-'āmma lil-kitāb, 2015). Chapter 6 (287–352) contains a description of mocking the authorities and the slogans used during Egyptian revolutions and protests, concluding with the 2011 revolution and some examples of its jokes.
30. Nādir Sirāj, *Miṣr al-thawra wa-shi'ārāt shabābihā: dirāsa lisāniyya fī 'afawīyyat al-ta'bīr* (Doha: Al-Markaz al-'arabī lil-abḥāth wa-dirāsat al-siyāsāt, 2014).
31. Mona Elnamoury, "When Is Revolution Untranslatable? When It's Fast and Funny," *Arablit* (November 16, 2012), https://arablit.org/2012/11/16/when-is-revolution-untranslatable-when-it's-fast-and-funny/.
32. Satenik Harutyunyan, "Humor: Egypt's Revolutionary Ally," *Prospect: Journal of International Affairs at UCSD* (July 30, 2012), https://prospectjournal.org/2012/07/30/humor-egypts-revolutionary-ally-2/.
33. Maren Williams, "Egyptian Humor Fuels Revolution" (August 15, 2012), http://cbldf.org/2012/08/egyptian-humor-fuels-revolution/.
34. Anna Louie Sussman, "Laugh, O Revolution: Humor in the Egyptian Uprising," *The Atlantic* (February 24, 2011), http://www.theatlantic.com/international/archive/2011/02/laugh-o-revolution-humor-in-the-egyptian-uprising/71530/.
35. Mia Gröndahl and Ayman Mohyeldin, *Tahrir Square: The Heart of the Egyptian Revolution* (Cairo: American University in Cairo Press, 2011).
36. Karima Khalil (ed.), *Messages from Tahrir: Signs from Egypt's Revolution* (Cairo: American University in Cairo Press, 2011).
37. Al-Faqī, *al-Nukta al-miṣrīyya.*
38. Muntaṣir Gābir, *Iḍḥak 'alā al-ra'īs: kayfa asqaṭa al-miṣrīyyūn niẓām al-ḥukm bil-tankīt* (Cairo: Al-Dār, 2014).
39. Yāsir Ḥimāya, *Iḍḥakī yā thawra* (Cairo: Kunūz, 2011).
40. Ibn Bashshār (ed.), *Agmal nukat al-thawra* (Cairo: Maktabat gazīrat al-ward, 2011).
41. Muḥammad al-Shammā', *Ayyām al-ḥurrīyya fī maydān al-taḥrīr: thamāniyata 'ashara yawman ghayyarat wagh miṣr* (Cairo: Shams, 2011), 117–134.
42. Khalid Baheyeldin, "Jokes from the Egyptian Revolution/*nukat min thawrat maṣr*" (March 8, 2011), https://baheyeldin.com/places/egypt/jokes-egyptian-revolution-نكت-من-ثورة-مصر.html. On Egyptian political humor, see, for example, 'Ādel Ḥammūda, *al-Nukta al-siyāsīyya: kayfa yaskharu al-miṣrīyyūn min ḥukkāmihim,* (Cairo: Sfinkis, 1990); on Egyptian political humor and satire in Ottoman Egypt, see Sayyid 'Ashmāwī, *Sukhrīyyat al-rafḍ watahakkum al-iḥtijāj: 'awwām ahl miṣr wata'assuf wa'anṭazat al-atrāk—miṣr al-'uthmānīyya: 1517–1914* (Cairo: Gāmi'at al-qāhira—kulīyyat al-ādāb, 2003); and on Arab political humor, see Khalid Kishtainy, *Arab Political Humour* (London: Quartet Books, 1985).

43. For a detailed discussion of the *irḥal* slogan, in Egypt and other Arab countries, see Sirāj, *Miṣr al-thawra*, 183–225.
44. http://forums.banatmasr.net/msryat399749/ (accessed October 11, 2019).
45. https://www6.mashy.com/jokes/funny-pictures-from-tahrir/list/ارحل-بقى-ايدى-وجعتنى (accessed October 11, 2019).
46. Gh. Ghālib, "93 Lāfita."
47. http://embed.scribblelive.com/Embed/v5.aspx?Id=21972&Page=99&ThemeId=817 (accessed October 11, 2019).
48. See https://www.youtube.com/watch?v=smtASznnnpg (accessed August 12, 2019).
49. Screenshot from https://www.youtube.com/watch?v=smtASznnnpg (accessed October 11, 2019).
50. Gh. Ghālib, "93 Lāfita."
51. "*Khiffat dam al-sha'b al-miṣrī fī al-muẓāharāt*," *albawaba*, February 7, 2011, https://www.albawaba.com/ar/خفة-دم-الشعب-المصري-في-المظاهرات.
52. Gh. Ghālib, "93 Lāfita."
53. Īmān Maḥgūb, "*Shi'ārāt thawrat yanāyir al-sākhira.. khiffat dam al-miṣrīyyīn fī 18 yawman (ṣuwar)*," *Ṣawt al-umma* (January 28, 2018), http://www.soutalomma.com/Article/750327/شعارات-ثورة-يناير-الساخرة-خفة-دم-المصريين-في-18-يوما.
54. Ibid.
55. Gabriel M. Rosenbaum, "Allusions to Popular Songs in Modern Egyptian Drama," in Joe Cremona, Clive Holes, and Geoffrey Khan (eds.), *Proceedings of the 2nd International Conference of l'Association Internationale de Dialectologie Arabe (AIDA)* (Cambridge: University Publications Centre, 1995), 197–206; and Gabriel M. Rosenbaum, "Nasser and Nasserism as Perceived in Modern Egyptian Literature through Allusions to Popular Songs," in Elie Podeh and Onn Winckler (eds.), *Rethinking Nasserism* (Gainesville: Florida University Press, 2004), 324–342.
56. Lyrics by Aḥmad Rāmī, music by Sayyid Mikkāwi (who also performed this song, although the better-known version is sung by Umm Kulthum, the diva of Egyptian singers).
57. Maḥgūb, "Shi'ārāt."
58. Ibid.
59. In standard Arabic this verb is conjugated *wadidtu* in the first person singular. Egyptians, however, tend to pronounce it *wadadtu*.
60. Even this phrase is sometimes a subject of mockery; see, for example, "*Law lam akun miṣrīyyan lartaḥtu nafsīyyan*," *al-Miṣri al-yawm* (Egypt Independent) (February 13, 2010), http://www.almasryalyoum.com/news/details/13747.
61. Photo taken by the author.
62. George Orwell, "Funny, But Not Vulgar," in *Funny, But Not Vulgar and Other Selected Essays and Journalism* (London: The Folio Society, 1998), 119.
63. https://www.alwatanvoice.com/arabic/comments/show/1581805.html (accessed August 14, 2019); for a printed version, see al-Faqī, *al-Nukta al-miṣrīyya*, 50.

64. "*Al-Thawra fī alf nukta wa-nukta,*" *al-Shurūq* (January 29, 2012), http://www.shorouknews.com/news/view.aspx?cdate=29012012&id=68d7a968-d98d-4450-aa17-9e4ee3f23cef.
65. https://ar-ar.facebook.com/ElWatanNews/posts/457763667581240 (accessed August 14, 2019).
66. Samīr al-Gamal, *Thawrat al-taḥrīr taḍḥak: 'abqarīyyat al-miṣrīyyīn* (Cairo: Kitāb al-gumhūrīyya, 2017), 57.
67. Ibn Bashshār, *Agmal nukat*, 10.
68. Gh. Ghālib, "93 Lāfita."
69. For a concise description of the role played by social media in the Arab Spring, see Pavica Sheldon, *Social Media: Principles and Applications* (Lanham, MD: Lexington Books, 2015), 65–68.
70. Al-Faqī, *al-Nukta al-miṣrīyya*, 121.
71. Sulayman was an army general, intelligence officer, politician, and vice-president during the last days of Mubarak's rule.
72. Ibn Bashshār, *Agmal nukat*, 12.
73. The tribe from Mecca to which the Prophet Muḥammad belonged.
74. *100 Nukta 'an al-ikhwān* (November 21, 2012), http://e5wanjokes.blogspot.com/2012/11/.
75. https://www.facebook.com/SudanChangeNow/posts/1006995546011030/ (accessed August 14, 2019).
76. "*Ākhir takhārīf 'al-irhābīyya': Thawrat 30 yūnyū ḥarām.. bikārīkātēr al-Yawm al-sābi',*" *al-Yawm al-sābi'* (July 2, 2017), https://www.youm7.com/story/2017/7/2/آخر-تخاريف-الإرهابية-ثورة-30-يونيو-حرام-بكاريكاتير-اليوم-السابع/ .
77. http://www.al3asma.com/59110 (no longer accessible; for a slightly trimmed version, see http://www.akhbarak.net/articles/21479608-المقال-من-المصدر-حصاد-الكاريكاتير-السيسى; [accessed October 11, 2019]).
78. "*Al-Sīsī yuṭālib al-muwāṭinīn bil-tabarru' bil-'fakka': 'Hatwaffar 20 milyūn Genēh.. walaw samaḥtum ana 'āyiz il-fulūs di',*" *Barlamāni* (September 26, 2016), http://parlmany.youm7.com/News/4/125271/السيسى-يطالب-المواطنين-بالتبرع-بـ-الفكه-هتوفر-20-مليون-جنيه. For a video of this demand, see https://www.youtube.com/watch?v=f-Xpt6-re2g (accessed August 16, 2019).
79. https://www.nmisr.com/wp-content/uploads/2016/09/3فكة.jpg (accessed January 3, 2018; no longer accessible).
80. "*Abraz al-Komiks al-sākhir min muṭālabat al-Sīsī al-tabarru' bil-fakka... ta'arraf 'alayhā,*" *Raṣd* (September 26, 2016), http://rassd.com/193836.htm.
81. Photo by the author.
82. Photo by the author.
83. Photo by the author.
84. Muḥammad Fatḥi, *Kān fīh marra thawra* (Cairo: Oktob, 2011).
85. Amānī al-Tūnisī, *Amāni bint.. min midān it-taḥrīr* (Cairo: Shabāb buks [Shabab Books], 2011).
86. Hishām al-Khashin, *7 Ayyām fī al-taḥrīr* (Cairo: Al-Dār al-miṣriyya al-lubnāniyya, 2011).

87. Fāṭima 'Abd al-Mun'im, *Shaklaha it'addilit* (Cairo: Dār kiyān, 2011). For a concise description of Egyptian colloquial poetry of 2011, see "Postscript: Egyptian Colloquial Poetry Blooms in the Arab Spring," in Noha M. Radwan, *Egyptian Colloquial Poetry in the Modern Arabic Canon: New Readings of Shi'r al-'Āmmīyya* (New York: Palgrave Macmillan, 2012), 205–211.
88. 'Umar Ṭāher, *Shaklaha bāẓit: albūm igtimā'i sākhir* (Cairo: Aṭlas, 2005).
89. Ibrāhīm 'Abd al-Magīd, *Likull arḍ milād: ayyām al-taḥrīr* (Cairo: Akhbār al-yawm, 2011).
90. Tāmer 'Abd al-Mun'im, *Mudhakkirāt filūl* (Cairo: Samā, 2018).
91. See the entry, "graphic narrative," in M.H. Abrams and Geoffrey Galt Harpham, *A Glossary of Literary Terms*, 11th ed. (Stamford, CT: Cengage Learning, 2015), 153–154. The parallel French term is *bande dessinée* (lit. "drawn strip"), a term that is quite well known outside the francophone countries and regions (where it is extremely popular).
92. Muḥammad Hishām 'Ibīyya, scenario and dialogues, and **Ḥanān al-Karārgī**, illustrations, *18 Yawman: riwāyah muṣawwara* **(**Cairo: Dār al-Miṣrī, 2011).
93. Dīnā Sa'īd and 'Abd al-Raḥmān Ḥāzem, *Lamma al-sha'b: shufna bi'enēna... wukatabna wurasamna bi'idēna, min midān al-taḥrīr* (Cairo: Kitābī, 2011). This book is published in a dual-language edition, in Arabic and in English translation. The details of the English translation: Dina Said and Abd Elrahman Hazem, *When the People: We Have Seen with Our Own Eyes, Written and Drawn with Our Own Hands, from Tahrir Square*, trans. Mariam Khaled (Cairo: Kitaby, 2011). On earlier Egyptian comics, see Allen Douglas and Fedwa Malti-Douglas, *Arab Comic Strips: Politics of an Emerging Mass Culture* (Bloomington: Indiana University Press, 1994).
94. Galāl Al-Shāyib, *Daftar al-ghaḍab: yawmīyyāt shakhṣ 'ādī shāraka fī al-thawra 2010–2012* (Cairo: Dār Nahḍat miṣr, 2013), 178.
95. Suzan, President Mubarak's wife.
96. Gamāl, President Mubarak's son, who was regarded as his successor.
97. Fatḥi Surūr, speaker of the People's Assembly.
98. Ṣafwat al-Sharīf, a politician who served, among other jobs, as the secretary-general of the National Democratic Party.
99. Aḥmad Naẓīf, prime minister of Egypt until January 29, 2011.
100. Aḥmad 'Izz, businessman and politician, owner of the 'Izz Steel Company.
101. Al-Shāyib, *Daftar al-ghaḍab*, 178.
102. See, for example, Nadia Idle and Alex Nunns (eds.), *Tweets from Tahrir: Egypt's Revolution as It Unfolded, in the Words of the People Who Made It* (New York: Or Books, 2011), on the use of Twitter during the revolution; many tweets are quoted.

Selected Bibliography

Attardo, Salvatore, ed., *Encyclopedia of Humor Studies* (Los Angeles: Sage Reference, 2014).

Boraïe, Sherif, ed., *Wall Talk: Graffiti of the Egyptian Revolution* ([Cairo]: Zeitouna, 2012).

Fahmy, Ziad, *Ordinary Egyptians* (Stanford: Stanford University Press, 2011).

Gröndahl, Mia, *Revolution Graffiti: Street Art of the New Egypt* (Cairo: American University in Cairo Press, 2012).

Highet, Gilbert, *The Anatomy of Satire* (Princeton: Princeton University Press, 1962).

Khalil, Karima, ed., *Messages from Tahrir: Signs from Egypt's Revolution* (Cairo: American University in Cairo Press, 2011).

Lane, Edward William, *An Account of the Manners and Customs of the Modern Egyptians* (Cairo: American University in Cairo Press, 2003).

Mehrez, Samia, ed., *Translating Egypt's Revolution: The Language of Tahrir* (Cairo: American University in Cairo Press, 2012).

Petro, Peter, *Modern Satire: Four Studies* (Berlin: Mouton Publishers, 1982).

Radwan, Noha M., *Colloquial Poetry in the Modern Arabic Canon: New Readings of Shi'r al-'Āmmīyya* (New York: Palgrave Macmillan, 2012).

Rosenbaum, Gabriel M., "Fuṣḥāmmiyya: Alternating Style in Egyptian Prose," *Zeitschrift für arabische Linguistik* 38 (2000), 68–87.

Young Egyptians Conquer the Public Sphere of Taḥrīr Square, Reshaping Egyptian Collective Memory and Identity through Graffiti

Mira Tzoreff

From the mid-nineteenth century until the outbreak of the Arab Spring revolution on January 25, 2011, Egypt's autocratic rulers dominated the public and particularly the urban spheres of their country. Moreover, they designed the public space in their own image for personal benefit and glorification while excluding elements that could threaten or undermine their regimes. This chapter explores the resistance of young Egyptian revolutionaries to this policy of control and their determination to realize what Henri Lefebvre called their "right to the city," namely, to conquer the urban public space and liberate it from the total domination of its rulers. These young revolutionaries used their takeover of the public sphere both to document the revolution, its heroes, and its martyrs, and to reconstruct the Egyptian collective identity and memory.

Taḥrīr Square: A Sphere Denying the "Right to the City"

The history of Taḥrīr Square in Cairo from the second half of the nineteenth century until the outbreak of the Lotus Revolution[1] on January 25, 2011, confirms that public spheres, particularly urban ones, mirror the aspirations, tendencies, and even the whims of their political rulers. Indeed, the public sphere is not neutral, it is both political and ideological since hegemonic political and social groups use their strength and power to colonize the streets and impose values and meanings on those who live in the cities. The designers of the public and urban spheres throughout this period were architects recruited to serve the will of the current ruler, and they willingly complied. Their work represented the hegemonic values and meanings which were imposed on those who lived in the cities. An obvious gap existed between the regime's social and political perspective and that of nonestablishment individuals and groups. This disparity aroused feelings of dissatisfaction, alienation, and exclusion among the public. Moreover, many city inhabitants experienced a sense of fear, discrimination, and oppression.[2] Public spheres became contested battlegrounds.

The administration of Taḥrīr Square accommodated the aims and concerns of the autocratic ruler. As of October 1981, new emergency laws enabled the authorities to abolish "the right to the city,"[3] namely, the right to inhabit the public sphere and the freedom to make daily use of it, that is, to live, work, represent and be represented, characterize, possess, or move within it as well as using it as a sphere of resistance to oppression. The sociologist Richard Sennett, who examines social ties and the effects of urban living in the modern world, defines the public sphere as a place where strangers meet. Here, Sennett explains, people interact daily with those whose personal histories, opinions, and innermost desires are not known to them.[4] By walking around the city and strolling through it, the city's pedestrians—walkers and strollers alike—unravel the urban sphere, then reweave or redesign it. In that manner, Michel de Certeau maintains, they notice things generally hidden from view. "The experience of strolling makes it possible to read the city in a personal and blurred manner, and in contrast to the clear urban order to which the planners aspire."[5] The literary and social critic and philosopher Walter Benjamin also discusses the phenomenon of strolling. Like de Certeau, he believes that strolling allows us to become familiar with urban spheres and with the marginal, invisible, forgotten past that is intentionally unrepresented in them. Benjamin introduces the story of a past that has been suppressed and shunted aside. The *flâneur*, according to Benjamin, is the one who compiles the hidden past from street names, from passers-by coincidently strolling the streets and snatches of their conversations. However, the "great reminiscences, the historical frissons—these are all so much junk to the *flâneur*, who is happy to leave them to the tourist."[6]

The right to own the city is an egalitarian and spatial worldview that affirms that every resident of a city, regardless of socio-economic status, class, or gender, has the right to use its spaces. The right to the city also means the privilege of participating in the decision-making process that determines the use of urban space. For Lefebvre, appropriation of the public space denotes a transformation of the power balance in a specific space as well as in its function and meaning; it then becomes not only a location but also a means of struggle. He claims that the right to the city also implies the ability to change it according to a common need or will. There is a distinct correlation between the right to shape the character of a city and a sense of belonging.[7] In Egypt, however, the authorities appropriated the public's right to demonstrate, protest, and even to congregate; any gathering of more than five people was seen as undermining the public order. By restricting access to the open spaces of the city, the authorities were in fact excluding the public from the public sphere.

Realizing a Dream, Liberating the Square

The youth who surged into Taḥrīr Square on January 25, 2011, were among those excluded from the urban spheres. The public arena, however, was only one of three realms that were inaccessible to this young generation. First, Egyptian youth, mainly those who were highly educated, found themselves unemployed as they failed to find jobs appropriate to their professional skills. Their academic diplomas and titles were therefore totally worthless. Among the ranks of the unemployed were 27 percent of Egyptian youth. Of these, 83 percent were men and women aged 15 to 29, about 95 percent of whom were high school or university graduates.[8] This social phenomenon came to be known in Egypt from the 1930s onwards as the "crisis of the educated" (*azmat al-muta'allimīn*).

The exclusion of these young Egyptians from the labor market led to their exclusion from married life, too. The traditional or neo-patriarchal patterns of marriage, dubbed "living room marriages" (*zawāg ṣālonāt*), in which a young groom was required to buy a home for his spouse and pay the bride's parents a high dowry (*mahr*), are deeply rooted throughout Egyptian society. This forced unemployed youths and low-salaried workers into prolonged bachelorhood (till their mid-thirties), and potential brides into spinsterhood (till their late twenties). Sociologist Diane Singerman argues that delaying marriage means postponing maturity, which creates, in her words, a long period of "waithood." Moreover, as marriage was the only ticket to adulthood in this society, young people became trapped and dependent on their parents.

This "marriage crisis" (*azmat al-zawāg*), which permeated almost all social classes, led to the third realm of exclusion, the political sphere. Having internalized the authorities' message of exclusion and their own formative, almost traumatic experiences with the security forces (*amn al-dawla*), young people generally avoided political involvement. Wael Ghonim, the hero, initiator, and organizer of the January 25 revolution, describes this attitude in his autobiography as follows:

> "I'm not into politics." ... it is the result of a deeply rooted culture of fear. Anyone who dared meddle in politics, in opposition to the ruling National Democratic Party (NDP), took a risk, most of

> us shied away, believing that we could not do anything to change the status quo.[9]

In order to avoid clashes with Egyptian security forces, young people escaped into alternative spaces beyond the reach of the long arm of the rulers, the police, and the censors. The most prominent of these was the virtual realm of the social networks, a liminal space that hovered between the privacy of home and public and global realities. Through digital discourse, young Egyptians documented their frustrations, aspirations, and dreams. Ultimately, an organized revolutionary community was born.

The turning point came on January 25, 2011, when hundreds of thousands of young men and women flowed into Taḥrīr Square, determined to hold onto it until their demands for political and social justice were met. In a well-orchestrated move, they conquered the urban sphere, challenged the regime, and demanded the removal of the president. They had a sound argument for toppling the regime; their press statements were polished, and they were able to stage a whole repertoire of street marches, demonstrations, and other public gatherings. Their actions were concrete and public proof of the feasibility and desirability of their revolutionary goals. It was the struggle for the privatization of the public sphere which represented for the young revolutionaries "the other Egypt." By disobeying the security forces, people were expressing their right to the city. For the first time in decades, they assembled publicly to demonstrate, share ideas, and display their creative talents as painters and singers without the interference of the authorities.

In the mid-1980s, under Mubarak's rule, the park surrounding the Egyptian Museum and adjacent to Taḥrīr Square had been expropriated for the official purpose of building a parking lot for tourists visiting the museum. In fact, the authorities were trying to limit public gatherings in the square, which had become a symbol of power and authority. In light of those actions, it is not surprising that the revolution broke out here. From the first days of protest until President Mubarak's removal from power, the demonstrators held on to the square with a resolve that amazed locals and foreigners alike. Though they were determined, Taḥrīr youths were not violent; following Gandhi's legacy, they declared "our revolution is peaceful" (*thawratuna silmīyya*), convinced that patience, perseverance (*ṣabr*), and steadfastness (*ṣumūd*) would allow them to hold on to the square until they achieved their goals.

In contrast, the internal security forces adopted a shoot-to-kill policy against the demonstrators, who were ready to risk their lives for the sake of a new Egypt. The latter's operational orders, disseminated via the social networks from the eve of the revolution and throughout it, confirm that the goal of the operation was to conquer the square. A heading in one of their online posts titled "Where to Assemble?" lists the city center, the television building, and the broadcasting authority. Demonstrators were instructed to "surround the building on all sides, and to infiltrate the building, to take over the broadcasts and to declare control of the television building by the people (*ahl al-balad*) and its liberation from tyrannical dictatorship (*dīktātūrīyya mustabidda*). Similarly, the revolutionaries thought they should lay siege to the presidential palace and the entire *Maṣr el-Gidīda* district. They provided the crowds with a detailed map showing the preferred routes to assembly sites. For other areas of the city, the instructions were to lay "a non-violent siege to all organizations connected with the corrupt regime, but at the same time, refrain from causing destruction (*takhrīb*) or devastation (*tadmīr*)."[10] Demonstrators were told to bring, "on the recommendation of our brethren, the Tunisian revolutionaries," comfortable shoes; light food and drinking water; medicines and first aid, plus a scarf (*kūfīyya*), hooded jacket, and protective goggles against tear gas; gloves to prevent burns from tear gas containers; the lid of a pot as a "shield when the State Security beats you or shoots rubber bullets at you"; and Coca-Cola™ to neutralize the effects of tear gas. Lastly, the revolutionaries asked the protestors to bring "a rose so we can show that we can do what we should and convene in the most peaceful way (*silmīyya*) possible."[11] The recommendation was to start the revolution after Friday prayers at the mosques.

> We should go out onto the streets in rows, with roses and lilies in our hands, without posters or slogans. We should make sure that everyone joins us in the streets in order to create large concentrations of people. If we run into internal security forces (*amn al-dawla*) and they try to prevent us from continuing to march toward the square, we should respond with slogans like: "Long live Egypt!" "Down with the Oppression (*ẓulm*) and the Corruption (*al-fasād*)!" and "Egyptian Independence Day!" (*'Īd Taḥrīr Maṣr!*).

Lastly, organizers stressed that there was "no need to destroy or break things," and that "saving our friends and comrades is infinitely more important than beating up members of the security forces."[12]

The daily-life management of Taḥrīr Square was a form of protest on the one hand but also allowed for a stronger hold on the square on the other. Both Michel de Certeau and Steve Pile, a contemporary geographer who explores the relationship between space and power, argue that if individuals take over the management of the urban public sphere, it becomes an expropriated, counter-hegemonic space. Thus, city squares become empowered arenas for radical, transformative social practices. Taḥrīr Square came to be known as "the independent republic of Taḥrīr." Protesters erected boundaries and checkpoints around it, ensuring the safety of those inside, such as the *flâneurs*, who wished to loiter freely without harassment. To accommodate the thousands of people, speaker podiums, makeshift clinics, and restrooms were set up, as well as a nursery for the children who accompanied their parents. The revolutionaries also organized a lost-and-found area, an artists' corner, and a reading wall for news updates as well as a map of the square and contingency plans for dealing with hired thugs who tried to attack the protesters. Muhammad al-Asad, a Jordanian architect who observed the young revolutionaries at work, commented that it "was really fascinating how people took control and ownership of it. I mean you had a group of people who would collect garbage and recycle it, you had a pharmacy, you had a childcare center… it was truly a public space and people took ownership of it."[13] *Midān al-Taḥrīr,* Taḥrīr Square, was no longer a point of discord but a place of harmony; no more a temporary site of protest but a permanent symbol of the people's will; not a war zone but a liberated space, a sanctuary, and a pilgrimage site.[14]

This generation would no longer tolerate exclusion; they were fighting for their right to use the public sphere. Cairo's urban spaces in general, and Taḥrīr Square in particular, became what socio-cultural anthropologist James Holston calls "spaces of insurgent citizenship."[15] The insurgence was manifest in its scathing anti-establishment slogans, displayed in Arabic for local audiences and in English for the Western world, which had always imagined these youth as passive, politically indifferent, escapist, submissive, and frightened of the regime. One young Egyptian woman carried a sign saying, "Yes, we can too!" as if to confirm that the impossible had happened not only in the United States; in Egypt, revolutionaries were turning the patriarchal pyramid on its head. No longer passive citizens, they now dictated the public agenda themselves. Their wide range of revolutionary slogans utilized recognizable, familiar discourse, such as verses from well-known songs, the famous words of public figures, and slogans from formative events in the recent past. Poets drew inspiration from the events. One of them was Gamāl Bakhīt, whose outstanding poem "Raise Your Head up High, You Are an Egyptian" (*Irfa' ra'sak fo' inta Maṣrī*) was set to music and became the revolutionary anthem. In his poem, Bakhit praises the Egyptian revolutionaries for overcoming their fears, bringing their homeland to the heights and bequeathing justice to their nation. Thus, he urges them to hold their "heads high with pride" and "begin to soar," as they "deserve the glory of victors."[16]

Not only had the patriarchal order collapsed, but gender norms were broken too. Young Egyptian women usually confined by norms of honor and modesty became leaders of the protest. Some wore traditional robes, their hair hidden by a veil, while others dressed in modern outfits without head coverings. Though they raised their voices at the public assemblies, their honor remained intact, and that of their families as well. These hybrid women unraveled the binary approach imposed upon them by "outsiders" and constructed a model that amalgamated their religiosity with a liberal, pluralistic worldview. They navigated their way to personal and gender empowerment within the framework of religion and tradition. Wearing the hijab, the symbol of cultural authenticity, the observant Muslim women promoted liberal views and were no less politically aware and involved than their secular peers.[17]

Graffiti slogans pushed Egyptian woman to "Express [your] rage!" (*ighḍabi!*), and praised the women of Taḥrīr for their courage and activism. "The fact that I could sleep on the street and take part in a revolution against an unjust ruler was an amazing experience," says 28-year-old Asmā' Sheḥāta, a female member of the Muslim Brotherhood who holds a degree in mass communications.[18] Dressed in a brown tunic and a headscarf that covers her shoulders and chest, she recalls, "We, the girls, spoke to the media, arranged protests, slept in Taḥrīr Square, and some of us got detained. So we experienced everything our brothers went through."[19] This spectacle of young Egyptian women flooding the square, shouting slogans denouncing President Mubarak, and mobilizing groups of young men who echoed their chants shattered the belief that Arab and Muslim women could preserve their honor only by remaining at home. This was a new phenomenon. A famous example of the new revolutionary female hybridity was the young, veiled Egyptian woman who earned the title "The Bravest Girl in Egypt" for leading a chorus of male youths and shouting anti-government slogans in Taḥrīr Square: "Down, down with Hosni Mubarak, down, down with all the Mubaraks!" She also nicknamed the military officers "disgusting bunch," the security forces as "the curse of the state…" and the government ministers, ʿAdlī, and Ḥabīb, "ministers of torture" and "traitors head to toe."[20]

Adhering to her religious beliefs, she keeps her traditional Muslim dress; yet this young woman is assertive and dedicated to the goal of toppling the regime. Another courageous woman was 24-year-old Gīgī Ibrāhīm, a prominent activist who was shot in the back in Taḥrīr Square but did not evacuate. "I was more determined... I believe that this fact contributed to the success of the revolution, as hundreds of people were prepared to die for it."[21] Ibrāhīm was rushing from one television network/broadcast to another, speaking on behalf of her comrades who were fighting for a better future for Egypt and the Egyptian people. She was also constantly updating supporters on Facebook and Twitter. Ibrāhīm not only played an active role in the overthrow of the regime, but also contributed to a significant change in attitudes toward Egyptian women both in the home and in public.

While challenging prevailing gender attitudes, Taḥrīr youths also promoted religious solidarity. The revolution started shortly after the attack on the Coptic Christian al-Qadīsayn (The Two Saints) Church in Alexandria on January 1, 2011, in which 21 people were killed. Protest signs in Taḥrīr Square proclaimed "Muslim and Christian unite, the mosque and the church go hand in hand!" (*Al-Muslimūn wa-l-Aqbāṭ ittaḥidū Wa-l-masjid wa-l-kanīsa yad wāḥida.*) This was the revolutionaries' way of asserting that, beneath the animosity and hatred provoked by the regime, Egyptian society was essentially united.

Owning the square meant managing it on a day-to-day basis. The committees organized by the Taḥrīr youths corresponded to various municipal services. Some policed the square in order to facilitate access and prevent traffic jams (Cairo police usually fail to prevent serious traffic congestion and consequent air pollution). While Cairo is infamous for the dirt and grime of its city streets and alleyways, Taḥrīr youths manifested concern for the cleanliness of the city in general, and of the square in particular. Given the separation between different parts of the city, wealthy neighborhoods, which received proper municipal services, were off-limits to most of the Egyptian public while the urban spaces of the hoi polloi, and even tourism sites, were neglected. Lacking a sense of ownership of the public spheres, Cairo residents habitually littered the streets. Once the revolutionaries conquered the urban space, however, they worked to restore a sense of belonging, commitment, and responsibility to the city. Contrary to a "scorched earth policy," they served as sanitation workers when necessary, setting an excellent example for the rest of the city. Taḥrīr youths even volunteered to guard the ancient treasures of the Egyptian Museum, which had been looted during the revolution. A prominent component of Egyptian identity is the Pharaonic golden age, which positioned Egypt as a light among the peoples of the region—a vision that still resonates with many Egyptians. Hence, guarding the museum was akin to guarding the Egyptian collective identity.

Through their daily administration and rehabilitation of urban spheres, the revolutionaries were transforming them into an important resource. Their non-hierarchal network was very different from the notorious power structures of the regime. Novelist 'Alā' Al-Aswāni, author of the best-selling novel, *The Yacoubian Building* (*'Imārat Ya'qūbyān*), commented on this extraordinary phenomenon:

> One night in Taḥrīr Square, during the revolution, I lit a cigarette and threw the empty pack on the floor. An elderly lady came up and greeted me warmly. She identified herself as one of my readers and complimented my writing. I thanked her, but suddenly she stared at me and said, "Please pick the box up off the floor." I was embarrassed. I bent down and picked up the empty box. "Throw it where the garbage belongs," she continued. I did as she said, and when I returned to her, like a guilty child, she smiled and said, "We're now building [a new] Egypt. It has to be clean."[22]

The 2011 battle for the appropriation of the urban sphere reached new heights when young couples renounced luxurious, air-conditioned receptions to marry in the open air of Taḥrīr Square, showing their contempt for the regime that had failed to ameliorate the national marriage crisis.

The "Street Art Spring": From Subculture to Counter-Culture

The "right to the city" also refers to the license to affect urban planning, which can breathe new life to myths or memorial sites, lending them visibility and tangibility, or condemn them to oblivion. Henri Lefebvre argues that there is a constant tension between "representational spaces," that reflect the views of artists, writers, and the public who experience and use them, and "representations of space" that serve the designers of public space, that is, the shapers of the hegemonic narrative. For Michel Foucault, the public sphere is the site of a never-ending battle for power and exclusion. Michel de Certeau asserts that those who make use of it create in fact a counter-narrative to the hegemonic one.[23] For the most part, the aesthetic dimensions of a city are shaped by the hegemonic group, and sometimes by the hegemon himself, through "cultural engineers" such as authors, poets, painters, sculptors, publicists, and journalists. These recruits provide cultural products that further the political agenda. President Gamal 'Abd al-Nasser, who established the Ministry of Culture in 1958, assigned it the task of tracing and reinforcing the collective, pan-Arabic identity of Egyptian citizens through politicized art and the culture industry. Anwar al-Sadat closed the Ministry of Culture as part of his de-Nasserization project; his heir, Hosni Mubarak, brought it back to life. During all this time, Egyptian culture, serving the regime, was subsidized. Whenever it failed to reflect the political agenda, it was censored.

The January 2011 revolution put an end to the control of culture. As Egyptian artists and creators liberated themselves from the regime's financial support, bureaucratic supervision, and censorship, the authorities were powerless to promote their cultural agenda or suppress new subcultures like street art and hip-hop music. Their monopoly endangered; they disparaged these new artistic genres as "youth cultures," that is, trivial and immature manifestations of youthful folly. As far as the regime was concerned, this was simply a form of vandalism, anti-social behavior, and even civil dissent (*fitna*) that would lead to anarchy. For the Egyptian artists struggling to shape their own space, counter-culture, and identity, street art and graffiti were natural choices for expression and commemoration. Graffiti can be defined as a means to communicate a range of ideas, perspectives, and opinions through artistic work, to challenge the status quo by making passers-by think, smile, or cry, to create alternative discourses that encourage lively debate, and to ensure a more egalitarian use of the city. Graffiti can certainly be defined as the right to the city for those who write and paint the city.[24]

In the days of the Greek and Roman empires and in ancient Egypt, political and social issues were debated on city walls; public art was accessible to all and immune to censorship.[25] Street art belongs by definition to pedestrians, who are the first to encounter and absorb it as they pass by. Pure and unedited, circumventing censorship, graffiti is conveyed immediately, almost simultaneously, from the artist to the audience; it is an invaluable medium for social communication among strangers. According to Cairo graffiti artist Karīm Ghūda, it is "a message in the street. It reaches the poor, the rich, the trash collector, the taxi driver [...] Most of these people are away from the internet and the social networking world so it is a way to reach them."[26] Graffiti also creates an alternative and fluid urban geography of resistance: it maps out demonstration sites, the streets where the families of martyrs live, and the political orientation of certain neighborhoods. Muṣṭafa Shawqī, an Egyptian specialist on graffiti, adopted Yoav Litvin's terminology identifying street art as a form of "artivism" or artistic demonstration.[27] The prominent Egyptian graffiti artist Muhammad Fahmī, known as Ganzīr, defines graffiti as a "counter-discourse."[28] While the sovereign power stakes its claim to exclusive ownership of urban space through street signs and directions, rules and regulations regarding conduct and movement in public, and plans for the development of urban sites, street art helps citizens reclaim agency, assert identity, and create historical narrative. Graffiti reiterates the civil right to use the power of imagination within the urban sphere. It is, as Linā Khaṭīb explains, "a visible marker of the citizen."[29] Graffiti art also spawns an imagined community based on a common language, common formative experiences, and the myth of a shared common destiny.[30] Thus, the slogan, "The people want to bring down the regime!" was replaced in February 2011 by "The people want to commemorate the revolution!" Above all, the revolutionaries of 2011 took upon themselves to construct the collective memory of the revolution. According to Khaled Fahmy, one of Egypt's most outstanding contemporary historians, this is a

> collective memory by the people, for the people—with no state functionaries around to curate what is remembered or forgotten.... It is people who make history, not generals or leaders.... But if it is the people who make history, then they should be the ones who write it and read it as well.[31]

During President Mubarak's regime, graffiti was nonexistent; instead, posters of the president, and later of his son, appeared on every corner. The public was discouraged from establishing its presence in the public arena. ʿOmar Hishām, an Egyptian art student, recalls that "before the January 25th Revolution, whenever we would attempt to write graffiti of a political nature, we would do so in groups of three: two would write graffiti and the third would look out for the police."[32] Members of the "April 6th Youth Movement," who employed graffiti to disseminate their anti-establishment messages, were indeed harassed by the security forces.

The Arab Spring revolution made it possible for artists to express themselves any time and everywhere. The streets belonged to the people, and graffiti artists were taking control of walls and façades. Urban public space became an outdoor art gallery, transforming "underground art" into "subversive art." Taḥrīr revolutionaries and graffiti artists saw themselves as a "commemorating community"; representing the marginalized public, they replaced the existing national meta-narrative with their own. It reflected specific interests of the revolutionary group but corresponded with national interests.[33] Graffiti flourished on the streets of Cairo, especially near the Faculty of Fine Arts at the Helwan University in Zamālek. Beside the revolutionary slogans, there were paintings depicting the young martyrs (*shuhadā'*). Graffiti also appeared on the walls of many public buildings, among them the Ministry of the Interior, the Supreme Court, and the American University in Cairo. The artists used bold colors to attract attention to their messages of criticism and protest. Their techniques, some indelible, were diverse, ranging from stencils and sprays to acrylic drawings. Having broken their barriers of fear of the authorities, they drew blatant anti-establishment slogans, clearly proclaiming their revolutionary goals and mocking rulers and the regime. In one depiction, President Mubarak is dressed in the red uniform of death row, a rope around his neck, muttering, "I understand you..." (echoing the last words uttered by Tunisian President Zayn al-ʿābidīn bin ʿAlī as he boarded the plane headed to his exile in Saudi Arabia). Other inscriptions prompted Egyptian men and women to "Go down to the street!" In one instance, the written command emanates from a television screen, a subtle criticism of those who preferred to sit at home and view the protest on television. One bout of black humor generated a painting of a police officer seized by demonstrators as he aims his gun toward them; the caption urges the viewer to identify the precise target. Another picture displays a man in a suit with an Egyptian flag in his hand. The inscription, "I am a bully" (*ana Balṭagī*), slams the infamous internal security people (*Amnal-dawla*), who had described the Taḥrīr revolutionaries as bullies. The Egyptian graffiti artists were creative, using quotes from movies, plays, and famous songs, like the inscription that quotes a line from Egyptian singer Umm Kulthum's famous song "Patience Has Limits" (*Li-l-ṣabr Ḥudūd*).[34] On the wall of the Franciscan School for Nuns in Luxor, graffiti artists wrote a verse by the popular Egyptian poet ʿAbd al-Raḥmān al-Abnūdy, accompanied by a drawing of the deposed Minister of the Interior Ḥabīb al-ʿAdlī, who was known for his brutality. The lines exalt the brave martyrs of the revolution:

> The revolution is not a monopoly… It is neither yours nor mine...
> It is the revolution of he, [sic] who faced the bayonet with his chest...
> And of he [sic] whose eye was gouged by the bullet and he did cry...[35]

The most impressive displays of street art in Egypt's Arab Spring were the commemorations of male and female martyrs (*shāhidat*). The young revolutionaries sought to reconstruct the memory of the revolution in order to prevent its appropriation or possibly erasure by the state. Through this privatization and individualization of memory, artists ensured that the martyrs would not be condemned to the margins of national history or, even worse, to oblivion. Moreover, this process represented a shift from victimization to empowerment and agency; it was a bottom–up commemorative action. The artists gave visual and physical shape to the memory of those who had sacrificed their lives to realize the revolutionary vision. The images were personalized. A typical example is that of 28-year-old Khāled Saʿīd, who in June 2010 was beaten to death by Egyptian police after posting a video of police officers selling drugs. The Facebook page, "We are all Khaled Sa'id,"[36] presents him as a symbol of collective victimhood.[37] Ganzīr claims that the memorial sites (*lieux de mémoire*) dedicated to the *shuhadā'* guarantee that people strolling these streets will not forget those who died a heroic death for a free Egypt.[38] His most impressive work is the wall painting in the colors of the Egyptian flag, depicting the men and women killed during the revolution. These portraits of collective grief reflect the desire, above all, to commemorate the martyrs in the public spaces where they died.

These commemorations touched many. One of Cairo's main avenues, Muhammad Maḥmūd Street, was renamed "Street of the *Shuhadā'*" (*Shāri' al-Shuhadā'*) because of its art. At one point, four youths walking down this street encountered graffiti artist 'Ammār Abu Bakr as he was painting the portrait of the 19-year-old *shahīd* Muhammad Muṣṭafā. The four youths happened to be returning from Muṣṭafā's funeral. They burst into tears, deeply moved by this memorial to their dead comrade.[39]

Foreign graffiti artists also commented on the potency of Egyptian graffiti. Don Karl, a German graffiti artist and co-author of "Walls of Freedom," wondered: "Where have you seen mothers cry in front of the graffiti murals of their sons; where have you seen men pray in front of the portraits of their friends?"[40] In honoring the young *shuhadā'*, artists such as 'Ammār Abu Bakr, Muhammad Faḥmī, and their peers forced members of parliament and other Egyptian politicians and leaders to commemorate them too. Egyptian President-Elect Mohamed Morsi saluted the *shuhadā'* in his first public speech, acknowledging the alternative commemoration created by the street artists, and adding that the martyrs had "made a great sacrifice and with their pure blood [had] watered the tree of liberty."[41]

Renaming city streets, boulevards, and squares was an integral part of the conquest of the city and the square as well; it lent cultural and ideological meaning to the urban public space and indicated control. The usual hierarchy of these commemorations—who is commemorated and where, whether on a main avenue, a side street, or a major boulevard—confirms that street naming is part of the geopolitics of public memory in the urban sphere;[42] furthermore, it facilitates the assimilation of the hegemonic national narrative, highlighting its formative events and mythological heroes. Dictated by the elites, it determines what elements of the shared past should be retained, what significance they should have, and how they are to be remembered. Renaming streets in the midst of a revolution is not solely a geographical act but a political drama, an attempt by marginal groups formerly excluded from urban space to undermine the hegemonic narrative and replace it with a counter-narrative of their own. By invalidating the old regime's acts of commemoration, they suppress their concomitant historical and ideological legacies. According to Henri Lefebvre, "A revolution that does not produce a new space has not realized its full potential [...] A social transformation, to be truly revolutionary in character, must manifest a creative capacity in its effects on daily life, on language and on space—though its impact need not occur at the same rate, or with equal force, in each of these areas."[43]

Renaming public sites in Egypt was not a new phenomenon, but up to this point it had been the prerogative of the regime. The renaming of Muhammad Maḥmūd Street during the January 25 revolution, in contrast, was an act of the people. Appointed prime minister on May 25, 1928, Maḥmūd had been harshly criticized for having collaborated with the British, dissolving the parliament, suspending the constitution, prohibiting students from organizing or participating in demonstrations, reinstituting the censorship law, and enforcing punishment of inciters. His negative reputation, as the ruler who put an end to the liberal era of the 1920s, undoubtedly reminded the revolutionaries of President Mubarak, whom they had just deposed for shattering their hopes for transparent, democratic, and well-organized elections.

Constructing Egyptian Collective Memory and Identity through Grafitti: Commemorating through Amalgamation of Islam and Neo-Pharaonism

According to Asef Bayat, outdoor public spaces where revolutions take place are "not only where people express grievances, but also where they forge identities, enlarge solidarities, and extend their protest beyond their immediate circles to include the unknown, the strangers."[44] Street art, Bayat claims, is a reflection of the political street, which denotes the collective sentiments, shared feelings and public opinions of ordinary people in their daily utterances and practices, broadly expressed in public spaces.[45] Indeed, the graffiti of Egypt's 2011 revolution can be read not as a mere archive of events, but also as a means to reconstruct symbols of national identity and self-representation in times of political turmoil and change.

Shuhadā' Street and its immediate vicinity became one of the revolution's central arenas of memorialization. Commemorative drawings appeared on public buildings like the American University in Cairo, where artists' depictions of the fallen heroes' ascension to paradise were inspired by ancient Egyptian hieroglyphics and Pharaonic burial structures; they were influenced by Pharaonic traditions associating the commemoration of the dead with the hope for resurrection. Graffiti interspersed with Pharaonic motifs began to surface in Egyptian urban spaces toward the end of the revolution's first year. In addition to commemorating the *shuhadā'*, graffiti artists sought to combine Islamic, Pharaonic, and Coptic facets of Egyptian collective identity. In Shuhadā' Street, for example, they chose to amalgamate these components by drawing the image of one of the martyrs side by side with the Pharaonic evil snake, *Apep* (*Apophis*),[46] dressed in military uniform, with three human heads. Linking the martyr and the humanized, evil snake was meant to emphasize the military's responsibility for the deaths of the young martyrs during the revolution. A variation showed the Pharaonic snake leaning on the head of Suzanne Mubarak, the wife of the deposed president, who was wearing army boots. The militarization of President Mubarak's wife intended to point out that even the first lady, who was expected to care for the welfare of ordinary Egyptian citizens, instead joined the army in fighting against them. Other interpretations show the snake with the faces of senior members of Egypt's Supreme Military Council (the de facto ruling entity after the revolution). Although Pharaonic mythology does not depict the snake with the head of a human being, it can be assumed that the artists chose to personify the snake, the symbol of ultimate evil during the golden age of the Pharaohs, in order to dehumanize the members of the Supreme Military Council—the ultimate evil of the present—standing in the way of the revolutionaries.

'Alā' 'Awaḍ is one of the Egyptian graffiti artists who chose to work on Shuhadā' Street, where he interwove Pharaonic, Islamic, and contemporary artistic trends as testimony to "Egypt's rich history." His work features the image of *al-Burāq*,[47] the mythological creature that, according to the Quran, carried the prophet Muhammad through his night journey (*Isrā'*) and thence to heaven (*Mi'rāj*)."[48] According to Islamic tradition, *al-Burāq* symbolizes the borderline between the earthly and heavenly spheres, between the *jāhilīyya*, the "ignorance of divine guidance" of Mecca, and the monotheism of Jerusalem; it is therefore the symbol of liberation from servitude. *Al-Burāq* also signifies enlightenment and, in other contexts, vision and dream. 'Awaḍ highlighted in his graffiti that like *al-Burāq*, who symbolizes the liberation from ignorance and darkness, the revolution represented personal and collective freedom from the shackles of the autocratic regime; hence, it was the link between the Egypt of yesterday and the new Egypt of tomorrow, despite the political uncertainty Egyptians were experiencing during the revolution's heyday.

ʿAwaḍ also painted violent clashes between the army and the revolutionaries. On one wall, he depicted the Taḥrīr youth as Pharaonic soldiers and horsemen preparing for another attack against the army. In the center, ʿAwaḍ drew a boy with white wings and clothing, a symbol of the young revolutionary. The boy stands on the back of *al-Burāq*, who is accompanied by black panthers, the protectors of the revolution. A carriage resembling a prison cell stands nearby; it carries an army officer who was jailed for participating in the demonstration against the Supreme Military Council on April 8, 2011. The painting implies that the Supreme Military Council does not represent the whole army: some army officers bravely sided with the revolutionaries, risking imprisonment on charges of treason. In a similar style, ʿAwaḍ painted another work in green (the color of Islam), in which *al-Burāq* has the head of a woman with disheveled hair and a body that is part mule and part horse, with three front and two rear legs. Surrounded by staring faces and protective black panthers above it, *al-Burāq* stands in the midst of a battlefield looking back toward her protectors. It looks as though she hesitated, deciding whether to withdraw, surrender, or move forward. Here, *al-Buraq* may well represent Taḥrīr Square's young female revolutionaries, who were subjected to frequent humiliations, virginity tests, and sexual harassment;[49] Graffiti Ḥarīmī, a newly established group of artists, took advantage of the momentum and started a campaign for the active participation of female graffiti artists in public spheres. In early 2013, it launched "Women on Walls," a project that explored sexual harassment and the mutilation of female genitals. Cairo's downtown walls were covered with portraits of Umm Kulthum and lyrics from her hit song, "Patience has its Limits," which tells the story of a battered woman who refuses to tolerate any more empty promises, honeyed words and vows, and clearly declares that "patience has its limits."[50]

The street artist ʿAmmār Abu Bakr employed *al-Burāq* as a signifier of Egypt's villagers, who perhaps best embody the Egyptian personality (*al-shakhṣiyya al-Miṣriyya*) and the authentic prototype of Egyptian nationalism. In his graffiti paintings on Muhammed Maḥmūd Street, a sky-blue, white-faced female *al-Burāq* gazes out at passers-by. Her black braids and embroidered headscarf are distinct markers of traditional female peasant dress. This was Abu Bakr's way of expressing the link between the *fallaḥīn* heritage and the Islamic tradition, which together constitute the main components of Egyptian identity.

Rather than imposing ancient Pharaonic motifs as a whole on the present, these artists hoped to anchor the memory of Egypt's historic martyrs by melding modern and primal Egyptian imagery. Hence, the martyrs in these paintings have wings, which means that they are angels of flesh and blood. Their wings are green, indicating harmony between the Pharaonic and Islamic components of Egyptian identity. The street art depictions of paradise also contain the lotus flower, an image taken from Pharaonic tombs. Such images affirm the linkage between the revolutionary martyrs and the immortality of the Pharaohs. For many Egyptians, simply entering the ancient tombs reinforces their affinity to the past. Since the graffiti artists wanted to draw attention to the present, they used color and contemporary imagery to transform the tomb's ancient funerary images into present-day cemeteries. In one example, a contemporary funeral is juxtaposed with a Pharaonic one. The latter shows women hired by the family of the deceased to accompany the body on its last journey. They mourn, lament, and eulogize while two priestesses, as tradition requires, kneel at the head and feet of the deceased. In the modern scene, the artist paints the martyrs' mothers, dressed in black, mourning their loved ones, who have sacrificed their lives for the sake of the revolution. During the First Intifada (1988), both the *shuhadā'* and their mothers were nationalized by the Palestinian leadership; thus, the Palestinian mothers ululated joyfully in honor of their children, who died for the sake of their country.[51] Unlike them, however, the Egyptian mothers are bereaved (*thakālā*) in every respect. They are depicted next to their dead children, thereby underscoring their personal grief and the privatization of motherhood.[52]

While the composition of images, forms, and colors used in the Pharaonic-themed graffiti made it very relevant to the present, it also revisited the Pharaonic Golden Age and the glory of ancient Egypt, making the latter more accessible to the younger generation who knew less about this era. An Egyptian expatriate and graffiti artist who returned from Germany when the revolution broke out recalls, "We started to revive popular images in order to show the Egyptians that [...] we do have heritage, we do have symbols."[53] The streets of the square may have resembled a Pharaonic temple from afar; in fact, however, they were part of a multilayered memorial site. The walls of the square served as "sites of memory" that blurred and even blotted out the dichotomy between Pharaonic and Islamic identities.[54]

Thanks to the graffiti artists, the martyrs were no longer anonymous. Though the police had attempted to render them faceless, each one now had a face, a name, and an age. The artists took care to stress their youth, even implying that it was eternal. One of the young graffiti artists declared, "When I paint the portrait of a martyr in the public sphere, I bring him back to life again."[55]

Nor were the female martyrs overlooked. Sally Magdī Zahrān was one of those commemorated on the walls of Taḥrīr Square. A 23-year-old student of English language and literature, Zahrān was a member of the "Cairo Complaints Choir," an artistic initiative that encouraged people to get together and sing their complaints in public. She was beaten to death by hired thugs, according to some reports, during a pro-democracy demonstration in the Upper Egypt governorate of Sohāg, her hometown. Another account claims she was attacked on her way to Taḥrīr Square. Upon her death, she was given the honorary titles "the Egyptian Joan of Arc" and "female martyr of the young people's revolution" (*shahīdat thawrat al-shabāb*). Her recognition as a *shahīda* and symbol of the revolution challenged the normative distinction between male and female patriotism in Egyptian society, which maintained that the ultimate male patriot sacrifices his life for his country, while the ultimate female patriot accepts the nationalization of her womb to reduce the shortage of men resulting from war. The Egyptian *shahīda* is not at all like her Palestinian counterpart, who is sometimes forced into suicidal martyrdom (*istishhād*) after breaking codes of virtue and modesty; her suicide purges her sin and she and her family regain their honor. Sally Magdī Zahrān violated no codes and did not choose to become a martyr; it was the ruthless Egyptian internal security forces and their agents who forced martyrdom upon her. During the Taḥrīr revolution, it was enough to die as a young female revolutionary and activist to merit the title of *shahīda*.

In a most impressive feat, the street artists spray-painted surah 59, verse 14 of the Quran (*Surat al-Ḥashr*, The Exile) upon a wall erected on Manṣūr Street to keep demonstrators from accessing the Ministry of the Interior. The verse reads, "They will not fight you all except within fortified cities or from behind walls. Their violence among themselves is severe. You think they are together, but their hearts are diverse. That is because they are a people who do not reason."[56] The deliberate choice of this verse drew attention to the similarities between the leaders of the old regime, including the heads the Supreme Military Council, and the Jewish Banu Naḍīr tribe, who were ordered by the Prophet Muhammad to convert to Islam. When they refused, the Prophet expelled them from al-Madīna to Khaybar.[57] Instead of remaining united against the enemy who threatened their existence as Jews, they chose to fight each other. There were also internal conflicts among Egypt's leaders, who went to the extent of aiming their weapons against their own people. In the eyes of the young revolutionaries, contemporary state leaders were blinded by their lust for political power and their obsessive fear of losing control. They had love and compassion neither for their people nor for their homeland.

The blend of Pharaonic elements and verses from the Quran produced both a hybrid model of the martyr and a hybrid national collective identity. Through an amalgamation of Egypt's Pharaonic and Islamic identities, the concepts of *istishhād* and *shuhadā'* were Egyptianized and the revolution was Islamized; there was no contradiction between the pre-Islamic Pharaonic heritage and the Islamic component of Egypt's collective identity. In his legal ruling (*fatwā*), Sheikh Yūsuf al-Qaraḍāwī—the legal authority of both the Sunni Muslim world and the Muslim Brotherhood movement in Egypt—declared, "These victims are *shuhadā'* since the cause of their death was oppression (*ẓulm*) and aggression (*'udwān*), and because they left their homes with the intention of sacrificing their lives in waging *jihād*... And more importantly, how is it possible that those responsible for protecting the lives of citizens become their murderers? And how is it possible that those responsible for protecting the property of citizens become the ones who rob them and steal their property?" (This is a reference to President Mubarak.)[58] In this pronouncement, the Sheikh sanctioned the claim that the Egyptian revolution was a holy war, a *jihād*, in every respect, and those who died for its sake were *shuhadā'*.

Realizing "the Right to the City," Realizing Sovereignty

Ganzīr the street artist declares, "The city does not belong to them. It belongs to us, the people [...] as a people, I don't think we need permission to use the streets [...] it should be the other way around; they should need permission from us to use it."[59] No longer associated with vandalism, graffiti was now considered a respected artistic genre. The al-Nahḍa Center for Scientific and Cultural Renaissance opened a graffiti workshop in the popular Faggāla district of Cairo, encouraging residents to make their stories public and more accessible through graffiti. These encounters between residents and artists inspired more street art. Graffiti artists who joined this project were veterans who had begun working before the revolution, decorating shop shutters and garage doors after receiving permission from the owners. On one garage wall, they painted the owner's name and the words "sitting in a wooden chair and smiling." Such privatization of public space linked city residents directly to urban spheres and established a clear connection between residents, urban space, and the revolution. It signaled a radical change in consciousness. "I loved the idea of painting beyond the limitations of a gallery, in the streets where everybody could see it," art student and graffiti artist Muhammad Ismā'īl explained.[60]

Even after the first euphoric round ended, the indefatigable revolutionary spirit lived on. Evidence of that is the "Cairo Runners Group," established in 2012, which persuaded residents of Cairo to take responsibility for their health by cycling, running, and jogging in the urban space. The group comprised 3,000 active members of all ages, from primary school pupils to senior citizens. With over 16,000 followers on Twitter,[61] it battled governmental neglect of public space and advocated for civic responsibility in this area. One Cairo Runner linked running to ownership of urban space: "Running is not just about the physical act itself, it's about what you feel, encounter and overcome as you sincerely experience and explore the city."[62] Addressing its 40,000 Facebook followers, the group urged its "dear runners" to abstain from littering and to make the outmost effort to make women feel safe in public, addressing sexual harassment, the rampant social disease in Egypt: "We have a strong duty to keep everyone safe and sound during our runs. Therefore, we would like to highlight our *zero tolerance policy* for any acts of sexual harassment."[63] A bit reluctantly, young Egyptian women nevertheless participated in the group's demonstration of their sport. One of them describes her experience: "I was afraid of being sexually harassed on the street, but to the contrary [...] people stood on the roadside and encouraged us."[64] Cairo Runners conveyed the message that people could now safely communicate, celebrate, and engage in sports within the public space of the city. 'Umar Najātī, an architect and urban planner, commented on this new reality: "Public spaces unite all people, men and women, Muslims and Christians, old and young, liberals and conservatives, rich and poor."[65]

Following the revolution, city squares became places where citizens could meet to demonstrate, express themselves artistically, or hold open discussions. This new ownership of the public arena was a tangible exercise in sovereignty. Though these Egyptian citizens did succeed in preserving the feeling of elation, they chose not to establish political parties or institutions. Nor did they advance any clear social or political agenda or appoint candidates for parliamentary and presidential elections, as they were staunchly opposed to entering politics. However, frustration grew when it became apparent that President Morsi was dominating, "Ikwhanizing," and on the verge of theocratizing Egypt. Only then did they return to Taḥrīr Square demanding his immediate resignation. This time, the leaders of the protest were members of the *Tamarrud* youth movement. Exactly one year and three days after Morsi's election, the revolutionary *coup d'état*[66] of June 30, 2013, led by then Defense Minister 'Abd al-Fattah al-Sisi, put an end to Morsi's regime. With enthusiastic support and high expectations that he would finally fulfill the revolutionary vision, al-Sisi was elected the next president of Egypt.

Ten Years Later: Reassessing the Arab Spring Revolution

Ten years have passed since the Arab Spring revolution broke out, seven years since the second revolution during which President Mohamed Morsi was toppled, and six years since ʻAbd al-Fattah al-Sisi was elected president. Nowadays Taḥrīr Square is empty; no demonstrators or protestors surge into the square, nor is there any graffiti on the city's walls. By the government's decision, the square was recently renovated. Pharaonic monuments were placed at the center of the square; a new lighting system was installed throughout the area, and security forces prevented passers-by from entering the square. The inscription on the ancient obelisk that was recently mounted on the square told those few pedestrians and tourists who succeeded in breaking past the security forces that "Taḥrīr Square symbolizes liberty and steadfastness: after witnessing the anti-colonial revolution of 1919 and the 2011 events, it reached its peak as the symbol of Egyptian freedom in the June 30th, 2013 revolution." There is no doubt that al-Sisi's regime succeeded in reconquering the city and reorganizing it, as well as policing and regulating it.

This inscription, which minimizes the 2011 Arab Spring revolution by referring to it as "events," while maximizing the Egyptian people's experiences during 1919 and 2013 as "revolutions," clearly reflected al-Sisi's policy aimed at preventing demonstrators from flooding the square again. Senior officials, however, declared that the goal of the renovation was to equate the square with similarly famous squares in Europe. This official declaration was in effect no more than an excuse to lock down Taḥrīr Square. "I think the message of this project is that people do not belong to the square and the square does not belong to the people. This is a square that belongs to the state,"[67] proclaimed the Egyptian historian Khaled Fahmy, who participated in the 2011 revolution and ran a short-lived official committee to document it.

Does this necessarily mean that Egyptian youth will never reconquer the square? It is certainly not for us to predict. Nevertheless, in their song *AhYā Midān* (Hey You, the Square), the young Egyptian hip-hop band *Cairokee,* famed for its political lyrics, personifies Taḥrīr Square, where for the first time their voices were loudly raised and heard, where they learned to "say no to the unjust" and to "restore their rights," but above all they learned to not give up their dreams. Their yearning for Taḥrīr Square clearly manifests the change of the Egyptian young generation's mindset from submissive and passive citizens to active citizens who take their fate in their own hands.[68]

Notes

1. As early as the Pharaonic period, the lotus flower was known for its ability to induce euphoria, which was the feeling that Egyptian youths experienced during the revolution. Another reason for the name "Lotus Revolution" was its correspondence to "Jasmine Revolution," the first revolution of the Arab Spring, in Tunis.
2. Tovi Fenster, *Shel Mi Hair Hazot? Tikhnun, Yeda Vehayei Yom Yom* (*Whose City Is This? Planning, Knowledge and Daily Life*) (Tel Aviv: Hakibbutz Hameuchad—Kav Adom, 2012), 11.
3. Henri Lefebvre, *The Production of Space*, trans. Donald Nicholson-Smith (Oxford: Blackwell, 1991).
4. Sherif Gaber, "Beyond Icons: Graffiti, Anonymous Authors, and the Messages on Cairo's Walls," *Cairo Observer* (December 3, 2013).
5. Michel de Certeau, "*Tsaadot ba'Ir*" ("Steps in the City") in Tali Hatuka and Rahel Kalush, eds. *Tarbut Adrichalit-Makom, Yitzug, Guf* (*Architectural Culture: Place, Representation, Body*) (Tel Aviv: Resling, 2005), 59.
6. Michael W. Jennings, Howard Eiland, and Gary Smith, eds., *Walter Benjamin: Selected Writings*, 2, part 1 (Cambridge: Cambridge University Press, 1999), 263.
7. Tovi Fenster, *Shel Mi Hair Hazot?*, 106.
8. Diane Singerman, "The Negotiation of Waithood: The Political Economy of Delayed Marriage in Egypt," in *Arab Youth/Social Mobilization in Times of Risk*, eds. Samir Khalaf and Roseanne Saad Khalaf (London: Saqi, 2011), 67–68.
9. Wael Ghonim, *Revolution 2.0: The Power of the People Is Greater Than the People in Power: A Memoir* (London: Harper Collins, 2012), 28.
10. Public Intelligence, accessed April 26, 2021, http://publicintelligence.net/egyptian-revolution-protest-manual-how-to-protest-intelligently.
11. Ibid.
12. Ibid.
13. http://cairofrombelow.org14/3/2013 (the link is not accessible).
14. Sahar Keraitim and Samia Mehrez, "*Mulid al-Tahrir*: Semiotics of a Revolution," in Samia Mehrez, ed., *Translating Egypt's Revolution* (Cairo: American University of Cairo Press, 2012), 41.
15. Tovi Fenster, *Shel Mi Hair Hazot?*, 105.
16. Gamal Bakhīt, "*Irfa' ra'sak fo' inta Maṣrī*" ("*Raise your head up, you are an Egyptian*"), *Al-Masry Al-Youm* (February 16, 2011).
17. Mira Tzoreff, "The Hybrid Women of the Arab Spring Revolutions: Islamization of Feminism, Feminization of Islam," *Journal of Levantine Studies* 4, no. 2 (2014), 69–70.
18. Noha El-Hennawy, "Sisters Aspire to Equality within Egypt's Muslim Brotherhood," *Al-Masry Al-Yaum* (July 10, 2012).
19. Ibid.
20. "Bravest Girl in Egypt," www.youtube.com/watch?v=jwIY6ivf70A.

21. Sarah A. Topol, "What Happened to My Egyptian Revolution?," *Foreign Policy* (January 24, 2012), http://www.foreignpolicy.com/articles/2012/01/24/what_happened_to_my_revolution?page=0,1.
22. Alaa Al-Aswani, "Five Positions on the Revolution," *Al-Masry Al-Youm* (March 17, 2011). Also: http://www.egyptindependent.com/opinion/five-positions-revolution.
23. Yoram Meital, "Central Cairo: Street Naming and the Struggle over Historical Representation," *Middle Eastern Studies* 43, no. 6 (2007), 857.
24. Andrzej Zieleniec, "The Right to Write the City: Le Febvre and Graffiti," *Environnment Urbain/Urban Environment* 10, 2016.
25. Tal Lanir, *Street Art in Israel* (*Omanut Reḥov beYisrael*) (Tel Aviv: Tel Aviv Museum of Art, 2011), 51.
26. AP, "Egyptians Move to Reclaim Streets through Graffiti," *Al-Ahram Online* (January 30, 2012). Also: http://www.masress.com/en/ahramonline/33223.
27. Chahinaz Gheith, "Graffiti on Cairo Walls: Art or Insult?" *Al-Ahram Online* (February 11, 2013), http://english.ahram.org.eg/NewsContent/5/0/88776/ArtsCulture/0/Graffiti--on-Cairo-walls-Art-or-insult.aspx. The term *artivism* is taken from Yoav Litvin, *Outdoor Gallery: New York City* (New York: Ginko Press, 2014).
28. Adrienne de Ruiter, "Imaging Egypt's Political Transition in (Post-) Revolutionary Street Art: On the Interrelations between Social Media and Graffiti as Media of Communication," *Media, Culture and Society* 37, no. 4 (2015), 584.
29. Hannah El-Ansary, "Revolutionary Street Art: Complicating the Discourse," *Al-Ahram Online* (September 3, 2014).
30. Hagai Marom, *The Graffiti Underground of Tel Aviv* (*Maḥteret hagrafiti shel Tel Aviv*) (Tel Aviv: Halfi, 2011), 16.
31. Jack Shenker, "The Struggle to Document Egypt's Revolution," *The Guardian* (July 15, 2011).
32. Amira el-Noshokaty, "Writing on the Wall," *Al-Ahram Weekly* (September 16, 2011).
33. Israel Gershoni, *Piramida la'uma: Hantsaḥa, zikaron veleumiyut beMitsraim bamea haesrim* (*Pyramid to the Nation: Memorialization, Memory and Nationalism in Egypt in the Twentieth Century*) (Tel Aviv: Am Oved/ Sifriyat Ofakim, 2006), 35.
34. Amira el-Noshokaty, "Writing on the Wall."
35. "Luxor Graffiti: A poem by Abdel Rahman al-Abnoudy," *Al-Masry Al-Youm* (August 31, 2011), http://www.almasryalyoum.com/node/493148.
36. https://www.facebook.com/elshaheeed.co.uk/.
37. Elizabeth Buckner and Lina Khatib, "The Martyrs' Revolutions: The Role of Martyrs in the Arab Spring," *British Journal of Middle Eastern Studies* 14, no. 4 (2014), 369, 379.
38. Lois Farrow Parshley, "For Egypt's Graffiti Artists, Revolution Brings Inspiration and Uncertainty," *The Atlantic*, October 3, 2011.

39. https://suzeeinthecity.wordpress.com.
40. Shadi Rahimi, "Egyptian Graffiti Artists protest Sisi," *Al-Monitor* (May 20, 2014).
41. *Al Jazeera* (June 29, 2012). Also: http://www.ikhwanweb.com/article.php?id=30153.
42. Maoz Azaryahu, *Al Shem: Historiya u'Politika shel Shmot Rehovot beYisrael* (*Named After: The History and Politics of the Street Names in Israel*), (Jerusalem: Carmel, 2012), 15–18, 24, and 29.
43. Henry Lefebvre, *The Production of Space* (Oxford: Blackwell, 1991).
44. Georgiana Nicarea, "Cairo's New Colors: Rethinking Identity in the Graffiti of the Egyptian Revolution," *Romano-Arabica Journal* 14 (2014), 249, and 251.
45. Ibid.
46. According to ancient Egyptian mythology, morning comes when the Sun God Ra opens his eyes; when he closes his eyes, night falls. Every day, Ra wakes up in the East and, with the help of two gods, embarks on his daily journey in his golden ship. During daylight hours the ship sails in the heavenly ocean, and Ra bestows his light and warmth upon the world. When the ship completes its journey, darkness descends and the ship sails to the underworld, where Ra's great enemy, Apophis the snake, lies in wait for him. Every night Ra must battle with his nemesis. His victory enables him to go back to the land of the living and illuminate the world once again.
47. According to certain Islamic traditions, *al-Burāq* is a half-animal, half-human creature with wings. Its body has often been described as a half-mule, half-donkey. In some Islamic traditions, it has the head of a woman, while in some paintings it appears with a male head.... In the Persian and Indian traditions, the *Buraq* is represented as a beautiful-looking half-woman, half-animal, with long black hair and a peacock tail. In some Indian paintings, the body takes the shape of a cow. [Copied from: http:// www. jadaliyya. com/pages/index/5725/ the-buraqs-of-tahrir M.A.]
48. Quran, Sahih International Edition, "The Night Journey" (*Surat al-Isrā'*), ch. 17: "Exalted is He who took His Servant by night from *al-Masjid al-Haram* (the Holy Mosque) to *al-Masjid al-Aqṣā* (the Farthest Mosque), whose surroundings we have blessed, to show him of Our signs. Indeed, He is the Hearing, the Seeing." http:// www.quran.com/171.
49. Mona Abaza, "The Buraqs of Tahrir," http://www.jadaliyya.com/pages/index/5725/the-buraqs-of-tahrir.
50. Latif Bartov, *One Hundred Songs and More of Umm Kulthum* (Jerusalem: Latif Bartov, 2011), 319.
51. Leila Hudson, "Coming of Age in Occupied Palestine: Engendering the Intifada," in *Reconstructing Gender in the Middle East: Tradition, Identity and Power*, Fatma Muge Gocek and Shiva Balaghi, eds. (New York: Columbia University Press, 1994), 127.
52. Mira Tzoreff, "*Me-em hashahid leshahida—ha'imahut basiah haleumi hafalestini*—1987–2005" (*From the Mother of the Shahid to the Shahida:*

Motherhood in the National Palestinian Discourse: 1987–2005), in *Petzatza metakteket* (*A Ticking Bomb*), Haggai Golan and Shaul Shay, eds. (Tel Aviv: Tel Aviv University: Ma'arachot, 2006),119–121. Also Mira Tzoreff, "'Ha'aḥerot' shel 'ha'aḥerim': nashim, migdar uleumiyut baḥevra hafalestinit betzel haintifadot" (The Others' Others: Women, Gender and Nationalism in Palestinian Society in the Shadow of the Intifadas), in *Nashim bamizraḥ-hatikhon bein masoret leshinui* (Women in the Middle East: Between Tradition and Change), Ofra Bengio, ed. (Tel Aviv: Tel Aviv University, The Moshe Dayan Center for Middle Eastern and African Studies, 134, 2004), 114–125.

53. Kate Durham, "Luxor Artists Invoke Pharaonic Heritage in Downtown Cairo's Contemporary Graffiti," *Egypt Today* (April 9, 2012).
54. Adrienne De Ruiter, "Imaging Egypt's Political Transition in (post-) Revolutionary Street Art: On the Interrelations between Social Media and Graffiti as Media of Communication," 590.
55. http://www.youTube.comwatch?V-yZD6. [the link is not accessible]
56. Quran, Sahih International edition: http://quran.com/59.
57. Shelomo Dov Goitein, *The Islam of Mohammed: How a New Religion Developed in the Shadow of Judaism* (*HaIslam shel Muhammad: Keitsad hithavta dat ḥadasha betzel haYahadut*) (Jerusalem: The Hebrew University, 5735 [1975]), 198. When the Prophet expelled the Banū Naḍīr Jewish tribe, he sent their ally from the Banū Aws tribe to tell them that if they left their homes within 20 days, they could return every year to harvest their palm trees. As the Jews prepared to leave, the head of the Khazraj tribe, 'Abdallah Ibn Ubayy, who lived in the south of the Arabian Peninsula, advised them not to give in; instead, he told them to strengthen their fortresses and he would assist them. Aware that Ibn Ubayy was deceitful, the Banū Naḍīr were divided. The head of the tribe tried to reject his offer, but the zealots in the community overpowered him. The Prophet welcomed the Jews' refusal to leave; as he expected, Ibn Ubayy's tribe betrayed the Banū Naḍīr and did not come to their aid. He deserted them "the way the devil abandons a person after seducing him."
58. *25 Yanāyir, thawrat sha'ab—al-shaykh al-Qaraḍāwi wa-l-thawra al-masrīyya, bayānāt wa-khuṭab wa-fatāwa wa-maqālāt wa-ṣuwar* (January 25, Revolution of the People—Sheikh al-Qaraḍāwi and the Egyptian Revolution, Declarations, Sermons, Fatwas, Articles and Images) (Cairo: n.p., 2012), 52.
59. De Ruiter, "Imaging Egypt's Political Transition," 590.
60. Amira el-Noshokaty, "Writing on the Wall."
61. Injy Deif, "Cairo Runners to Celebrate Third Anniversary with a Run and a Dash of Chocolate," *Al-Ahram Online*, January 12, 2016.
62. Amr Kotb, "Running against the Current on Cairo's Hectic Streets," *Ahram Online* (September 18, 2014).
63. facebook.com/notes/cairo-runners/must-read-zero-tolerence-policy/28815932 1305559). [access date: April 27, 2021].
64. "Street Sport Hits Cairo," *Al-Ahram Weekly* (February 27, 2013).
65. http://cairofrombelow.org, May 10, 2013.

66. The term "revolutionary *coup d'état*" reflects the singularity of this event, which was a combination of revolution and *coup d'état*. It started as a classic *coup d'état*: the army ousted a president from power, took over the official broadcasting station, and declared the end of Mohamed Morsi's reign. Within 24 hours a temporary president was appointed, who in turn chose a temporary government of technocrats and announced upcoming elections for the parliament. This latter phase resembled a typical revolution.
67. Aidan Lewis, Nadeen Ebrahim, "Cairo's Tahrir Square Gets a Contested Makeover," *Reuters* (August 10, 2020); (November 16, 2020).
68. https://www.youtube.com/watch?v=ljVTj9yu-ns.

Selected Bibliography

Azaryahu, Maoz, *Al Shem: Historiya u'Politika shel Shmot Rehovot beYisrael* (Named After: *The History and Politics of the Street Names in Israel*) (Jerusalem: Carmel, 2012).

De Certeau, Michel, "Tsaadot ba'Ir" ("Steps in the City") in Tali Hatuka and Rahel Kalush, eds., *Tarbut Adrichalit-Makom, Yitzug, Guf* (Architectural Culture: Place, Representation, Body) (Tel Aviv: Resling, 2005).

Fenster, Tovi, *Shel Mi Hair Hazot? Tikhnun, Yeda Vehayei Yom Yom* (*Whose City Is This? Planning, Knowledge and Daily Life*) (Tel Aviv: Hakibbutz Hameuchad—Kav Adom, 2012).

Ghonim, Wael, *Revolution 2.0: The Power of the People Is Greater Than the People in Power: A Memoir* (London: Harper Collins, 2012).

Jennings, Michael W. Howard Eiland, and Gary Smith, eds., *Walter Benjamin: Selected Writings*, 2, part 1 (Cambridge: Cambridge University Press, 1999).

Lefebvre, Henri, *The Production of Space*, trans. Donald Nicholson-Smith (Oxford: Blackwell, 1991).

Meital, Yoram, "Central Cairo: Street Naming and the Struggle over Historical Representation," *Middle Eastern Studies* 43, no. 6 (2007), 857–878.

Nicarea, Georgiana, "Cairo's New Colors: Rethinking Identity in the Graffiti of the Egyptian Revolution," *Romano-Arabica Journal* 14 (2014), 247–262.

Singerman, Diane, "The Negotiation of Waithood: The Political Economy of Delayed Marriage in Egypt," in Samir Khalaf and Roseanne Saad Khalaf, eds., *Arab Youth/Social Mobilization in Times of Risk* (London: Saqi, 2011), 67–78.

Tzoreff, Mira, "The Hybrid Women of the Arab Spring Revolutions: Islamization of Feminism, Feminization of Islam," *Journal of Levantine Studies* 4, no. 2 (2014), 69–112.

Index

Page numbers in *italics* refer to figures.

'Abd al-'Azīz Fahmī 48
'Abd al-Fattah al-Sisi 45, 116, 126, 150, 165;
  in cartoon 226;
  Civil State under 75–77;
  Egyptian publicists 76;
  regime (1981–2011) 149–152
'Abd al-Ḥalīm Ḥafeẓ 191
'Abd al-Khāleq Tharwat 49
'Abd al-Mun'im, Fāṭima 230
'Abd al-Mu'ṭī Bayyūmī 71–72
'Abd al-Raḥmān al-Abnūdy 252
'Abd al-Raḥmān al-Rafe'ī 165
'Abd al-Wahhāb 166
ad-hoc cooperation 141
administrative revolution 128
aggression (*'udwān*) 259
Ahmad al-Maḥallāwī, Shaykh 74–75
Ah Yā Midān (song) 261
Ajami, Fouad 141
akhwana 208
'Alā' 'Awaḍ 255
al-Ahram 72
al-Azhar 71;
  Azhari students 14–15;
  Shaykh al-Azhar 74
Alexandria, foreign communities in 47
'Alī Gum'a 72
Al Jazeera 28
"alleged middle class" 124
allusions to famous songs 218–219
amalgamation of Islam 254–259
American economic and political hegemony 186
Americanization of Egyptian culture 188
American Presbyterians 96
American University in Cairo 214
Amin, Galal 119–120
'Āmmiyya 204
ancient civilization 94
Anglo-American Protestant concept 96
anti-alcoholism 28
anti-Christian sentiment 56
anti-colonialism 88
anti-establishment slogans 246, 252
anti-Iraqi coalition 122
anti-Mubarak demonstrators 29
anti-Muslim Brotherhood jokes 223
anti-prostitution sentiment 28
anti-revolutionary narrative 56
anti-social behavior 250
Arab:
  boycott 145–146;
  brotherhood 142;
  criticism 144;
  decision making 144;
  historiography 9;
  intelligentsia 142;
  and Islamic heritage 204;
  leadership 137, 144;
  nation-states 11;
  power 183;
  preeminence 148–149;
  regional order 147;
  societies 204;
  -state migrations 100–101
Arab Contractors Company 164
Arabian Gulf oil countries 113, 122
Arabic:
  literature 204;
  mass readership 93;
  -speaking societies 204

Arab–Israeli conflict 98, 114, 122, 147–148
Arab–Israeli hostility 100
Arab League in May 1989 146
Arab Peace Initiative (API) 149
Arab Socialism 164;
  activity 36;
  Arab Socialist Union (ASU) 35–36, 184–185;
  classes 8;
  dialogue 77;
  mobility 183;
  networking 15;
  networks 244;
  parity 102;
  polarization 73;
  sensitivity, July Revolution 183;
  transformation 254
Arab Spring 26–27, 29, 149–150;
  in Egypt 7;
  revolution 251, 261
Arab System declining role (1952–2020):
  Mubarak regime (1981–2011) 145–149;
  Nasser regime (1952–1970) 139–143;
  Sadat regime (1970–1981) 143–145;
  Sisi regime (1981–2011) 149–152
armed violence 150
artistic demonstration 250
artivism 250
Aṣfūr, Gāber' 71
'ashān aḥla' 218
Aswan High Dam project 167, 183
Al-Aswāni, 'Alā' 248–249
Auber de Lapierre, Julien 92
authoritarianism 26, 29
autocratic ruler 242
autonomy 37
Ayalon, Ami 103
Badrāwī 'Āshūr, Muhammad 51
Baghdad Pact (BP) 139
Baghdad summits 144
Bakhīt, Gamāl 246–247
Bakr, Ammār Abu 256
balṭagi 210
balṭagiyya 210
Bandung Conference 179
Bannā, Hasan al- 96
Banque Misr 21
Banu Naḍīr tribe 258
Bastille Day 51
Bayat, Asef 254
Bayt Al-Umma (House of the Nation) 166
Beirut Arab summit 149
Benjamin, Walter 242
Bernstein, Eduard 25
bilingualism 204
Black Saturday riots 14
bloc alliances 57
Bloemaert, Cornelis 92
Bodnar, John 178
"bonanza oil decade" 120–123
British controlled monarchy 190
British occupation 28, 183
British Protectorate 15
British troops, harassment by 14
al-Burāq 255–256
burden of history 25–29
bureaucratic supervision and censorship 250
Bush, George 185

"Cairo Complaints Choir" 258
Cairo Declaration of April 17 141
Cairo Opera House 180–181
Cairo summit 141
Cairo Symphony Orchestra 181
Camp David Agreement 144
Casablanca summit 146
Catholic and Protestant mission schools 96

Catholic missionaries 91–92
centers of power 9
Central Agency for Public Mobilization and Statistics (CAPMAS) *115*
Certeau, Michel de 245–246, 249
charismatic leadership 47, 137, 139
child marriages 117–118
Christian / Christianity:
community 96;
as *dhimmis* 102;
to Egypt 99;
powers 99
Churchill, Winston 47
Church Missionary Society (CMS) 93–94
church–state separation 103
citizenship and religious neutrality 88
civic democratic movement 77
civil administration 58
"Civil, Civil!" (*Madanīyya, Madanīyya!*) youth slogan 74
Civil Democratic Coalition 73
civil equality 70
civilian bureaucracy 45
civilizational integrity 94
civil-ness of Egypt 67–68
civil society, open discourse 69
civil state 71–72, 76;
discourse 70, 75;
nationalization of 71;
in post-revolutionary Egypt 75
civil youth organizations 76–77
collective victimhood 253
colonial influence 47
commemoration:
community 251;
discourse 187–188;
drawings 254–255
Communism 25
conservative nationalist discourse 54–55
consolidated democracy 29
constitutional and legislative amendments 76
constitutional committee 55
constitutional reform 55
constitutional rights and political institutions 59
Coptics / Coptic:
in Arabic language 94;
communal culture 93;
community 27;
Coptic Catholic Church 98–99;
Coptic Orthodox Church 87, 92, 97–100, 103;
in Egypt and abroad 91, 98–101;
eighteenth-century roots 91–93;
energy and debility 87;
fin-de-siècle Coptic intellectuals 91;
Institute of Coptic Studies 99;
interlocutors 89;
and Islamist movements 90;
Lonely Minority, A: The Modern Story of Egypt's Copts 87, 95;
as minority and diaspora 101–103;
missionaries 99;
Museum 165;
Muslim-Coptic fraternity 95;
nineteenth- and early twentieth-century roots of 93–95;
Shanūda al-Manqabbādi, Tādrus 94;
Shenouda III 96–97, 99;
social mobility 96;
"Sunday School Movement" 96
coronavirus pandemic hit 125
corporate mission 37
Corrective Revolution, 1971 33, 36–37, 41, 163
corruption 14, 118
counter-commemoration 178
counter discourse 250

counter-organization 52
counter-revolution 21, 46
coups at the top 11
crude birth rate (CBR) 114, *117*
crude death rate (CDR) 114
Cyril VI, Pope 89

Daftar al-ghaḍab (*Notebook of Anger*) 231
Dā'irat al-Ma'āref (1882) 10
Dam, Aswan 189
al-Damardāsh al-'Aqāli 182
Damascus Declaration 147
Davis, Eric 162
decision-making process 242
decolonization 97
"deep state" 18
democratization 19, 20, 26, 184–187
demographic and military capabilities 142
de-Nasserization project 249–250
De Tocqueville 12
Dhiyāb, Amr 191
digital discourse 244
digital revolution 11
diglossia 204
discrimination 88–89, 97
disenchantment 19
Dishon, Daniel 144
documentation 169
domestication of Egypt's foreign policy 150
domestic stability 137
dominant discourse 68

ecclesiastical statesman 99
economy / economic:
  anxieties 98;
  capability 138;
  failures 118;
  independence 185;
  inequality 124;
  initiatives 40;
  performance 120;
  and political capabilities 139;
  recession 119, 121, 142–143;
  stabilization programs 122
Economic and Structural Adjustment Program 122
education theory 67
Egypt Demographic and Health Survey of 2014 118
Egypt / Egyptian 16, 206;
  antiquity 94;
  Arab System declining role (1952–2020) 137–152;
  British hegemony 27;
  "civil-ness" 75–76;
  civilization 94;
  collective memory and identity construction 254–259;
  constituencies mobilization 53;
  debt-to-GDP ratio 111;
  decision-makers 148;
  economy 118, 121–125, 127;
  fertility rate 114, 117;
  foreign policy 151;
  Gamal 'Abd al-Nasser 34–36;
  governance 33;
  heritage and MSA 220;
  hieroglyphics 255;
  humor 213;
  independence 47–49;
  literature since 2011 230–232;
  military 4, 8;
  modern history 7;
  Nasserist regime 34–36;
  natalist policy 116, 128;
  national identity 161;
  nationalism 16, 102;
  nationalist movement 90;
  nationalist rhetoric 103;
  non-oil industries 123–124;
  petroleum and other liquids production 113;
  political life 35;

polity 189;
pound (LE) 111;
regional aspirations 148;
rental income sources 111;
resources, exploitation 14;
satirical works 214;
security forces 244;
society 52–53, 97, 161, 204;
songs 218;
television channels 180;
territorial nationalism 188;
total non-oil and gas exports 111

Egyptian Arabic 204–205
Egyptian Association for Population Studies 114
Egyptian Christians 97, 101
Egyptian Constitution of 1923 90
Egyptian Museum 244
Egyptian National Archives 52
Egyptian National Museum 165
Egyptian Revolution Research Unit 166
Egyptian Supreme Council of Antiquities 164–165
Egyptian–Syrian alliance:
force in Gulf 147;
military 147;
unification 179

electoral bureaucracy 59
electoral constituencies in 1923 47
electoral districts 48
Elnamoury, Mona 214
emancipation 95
Encyclopedia of the January Revolution 207
Engels, Friedrich 25
enthusiasm 7, 16, 53–54
etymology 9
eudaimonic legitimacy 187
exploitation 14

Fahmy, Khaled 251
Fahmy, Nabil 151
fakka campaign 226–227
Farid, Muhammad 165–166
Farouk, King 187–188
Fatḥi, Muḥammad 230
fill 207
financial policies and reserves 118
firdeh 213
First Five-Year Plan 119
fitna 10
Foda, Farag 69
"food riots" 113–114
foreign capital investment 143
foreign immigration policies 100
foreign policy and economic realms 36
Foucault, Michel 249
freedom of expression 69
Free Egyptian party 75
Free Officers movement 187–188
Free Officers Revolution of July 1952 87, 161
Free Officers' socioeconomic policy 119
French Catholic (Lasallian) institution 96
French monarchy 11
French Revolution 9–12
Fuṣḥā 204
Fuṣḥāmmiyya 205

Gamal ʻAbd al-Nasser 15, 114, 152, 166, 185, 187, 249;
Philosophy of the Revolution, The 140, 152

Gayyed, Naẓir 96–97
Gaza and Jericho agreement 148
gender:
attitudes 248;
segregation 90

geo-strategic location 137
Gershoni, Israel 90
Gezira Island in Cairo 162

Ghali, Boutros 94
Ghonim, Wael 243
Ghūda, Karīm 250
Girgis, Habib 95–98
global/globalization 185–186
Goodwin, Jeff 12
Gouida, Farouq 165, 167
government/governmental:
financial incentives 116–117
Graeco–Roman Museum 165
graffiti 247, 250–251, 257;
foreign graffiti artists 253
Gramsci, Antonio 12
Gran, Peter 87
Grand Egyptian Museum 170
graphic novels 231
Gröndahl, Mia 214
guerrilla raids 11
guided democracy 20
Gulf crisis 150
"*Gumlūkīyya*" ("republican–monarchist") style 14

hadīth 10
Haggāg, Hanān 168–169
Ḥakīm, Tawfīq al- 17
Ḥāmed al-Ghazāli, Abu 10
Ḥammād, Jamāl 188
Hanna, Nelly 93
Hart-Celler Act 100
Harutyunyan, Satenik 214
Hasan, S.S. 97, 101
Hassanein, Ahmad Muhammad 54
Hatimshi 218, *218*
Haykal, Muhammad Hussein 48, 187
hegemony 138–139, 147, 178;
discourse 68;
and leadership 139
Heikal, Muhammad Hassanein 7–8
hereditary monarch 50
hierarchy/hierarchical:
knowledge structures 69;
political system 55;
social relations 52
Ḥilmī ʻĪsā Pasha 54
himāya 14
Hinnebusch, Raymond 46–47, 147
Hishām, Umar 251
historical legacies 26
historic pathways:
2011, remnants, divisions, forces 55–59;
deep state, institutional integrity 46;
ideological divisions 49–52;
middle-class political activists 45;
military power 46;
old regime remnants 47–49;
popular forces 52–55;
private and state-owned businesses 45;
radical revolutionaries 49;
social services and human rights 45
Holsti, Karl 138
Holston, James 246
horizontal discourse 68–69, 75
Hosny, Farouk 177, 190
Human Development Index (HDI) 111
human rights and women's organizations 75
humiliation and anger 14, 16, 20–21, 187, 256
humor, and satire 212–214
Hussein, Ṭaha 166

Ibn Khaldun 46–47, 60
Ibrahim, Saad Eddin 89, 102–103, 116
Ikram, Khalid 120
il-gēsh wish-shaʻb-i īd waḥda 208
il-makhlūʻ 211
il-maʻzūl 211

imagined national community 178
imperialism 27
imshi ba'a ana bardān 218, *218*
individualization of memory 252
industrialization 26, 123
industrial revolution 11
inflation in Egypt 118
ingiz 218, *218*
inqilāb-type seizure of control 20
Institute of Coptic Studies 99
insurgent citizenship 246
intellectual controversy 70
inter-Arab relations 143
internal security:
 forces 244–245;
 system 18
internal stability 139
international Christian forums 98
internationalism 99
International Monetary Fund (IMF) 120, 148, 151
international prestige 99
invisible discourse 76
Inzil 229
Iraq, invasion of Kuwait 147
Iraq–Iran war 146
irḥal 215, *215*;
 irḥal, gabl-i -ṣ-ṣa'āyda ma yaju 216;
 irḥal abl-i ma -ṣ-ṣa'āyda yiwṣalu 216;
 irḥal ba'a īdi waga'itni 215;
 irḥal bil-hiroghlīfi yimkin tifham ya far'ōn 217;
 irḥal bilughit ḥabāybak 217, *217*;
 irḥal īdi waga'itni 215, *215*;
 irḥal mirāti bitiwlid wil-walad mish 'āyiz yishūfak 215;
 irḥal mirāti waḥashitni mutazawwig mundhu 20 yōm 215;
 i-r-ḥ-l yimkin yifham bil-ma'lūb 217
Islam / Islamic:
 disorder 45;
 -dominated parliament 58;
 fundamentalists 28–29;
 groups 53;
 intellectuals (*Wasatīyya*) 69;
 "Islamic, Islamic!" (*Islāmīyya, Islāmīyya!*) 74;
 Islamic Revival 90;
 Islamic Sharī'a 72;
 Islamic Roots of Capitalism: Egypt, 1760–1840 87;
 Islamism 89;
 Islamization of Egypt's law 70;
 state 74
Israel, economic and military capabilities 148
Israeli–Egyptian peace treaty 144
Israeli–Palestinian conflict 148–149;
 negotiations 148;
 relations 149
istibn 210
istishhād concepts 259
Ittiḥād membership 53

Jankowski, James 90
John XXIII, Pope 99
Johnson–Reed Act of 1924 100
jokes, satirical:
 Egyptian revolution, weapons 222–223;
 mocking fundamentalists 223–224;
 Mubarak's indifference 223;
 Mubarak's long rule 221–222;
 revolution's background 220–221
July Revolution 165;
 achievements and failures 182–184;
 commemorating heroes 186–188;
 commemorative discourse 187–188;

democratization process under Mubarak 184–185;
jubilee celebrations 179–182;
revelations and historical accounts 188;
revolution's commemoration, public reception of 191–192;
social sensitivity 183;
socioeconomic legacy 185–186;
vernacular commemorations 188–190

Kaeil, Mustafa 165–166
Kafr al-Dawar 17
Kafr al-Shaykh 54
Kamel, Mustafa 90–91, 220
Kandil, Hazem 118
Karl, Don 253
khala' 211
Khalil, Karima 214
Khartoum summit 141–142
Khashin, Hishām al- 230
Khaṭīb, Linā 251
khirfān 211, 225
knowledge:
as "common sense" 68–69;
forms 69
Kulthum, Umm 166, 191–192, 218, 252
Kuwaiti crisis 122

Labīb, Klūdyūs 94
labour unions 55
language, revolution and humor 206
leadership vacuum 145
Lefebvre, Henri 249, 254
legitimacy 11, 139
libdeh! 213
Liberal-Constitutionals 48;
government 48–49;
monarchy 52;
Party 48;
resignation 51;
rivals 59–60
liberals:
and conservatives 69;
constitutionalists 46;
intellectuals 48, 69, 75;
legitimacy 48;
liberalization 122;
and monarchists 50;
reformers 46
Liberation Rally 35
Library of Alexandria 165
linguistic innovations 203–205
literacy 99, 205;
rate 119;
and semi-literary writing 205
liturgical language 89
Litvin, Yoav 250
living room marriages 243
London-based Minority Rights Group International 103
Lonely Minority, A: The Modern Story of Egypt's Copts 87, 95
Luke, Timothy 162

macroeconomic policy 119–120
al-Madina 72
Mafīsh fayda (There is no hope) 232
Majlis al-Dawla 35–36
Majlis al-Shūrā 37
manuscript writing 93
marginality 117
marginalization 53
market economy 26
marriage crisis 243
martial law 14
Marxism 12
"massacre of the judiciary" 36
mass demonstrations 11, 27
mass mobilization and regime change 12
mawqi'at al-gamal 210–211
McLuhan, Marshall 93

Melbourne community 103
Middle Eastern Catholic churches 98–99
"Middle Easternism" concept 148
Middle Eastern minorities 102–103
Middle East Peace Initiative (MEPI) 185
Midlarsky, Manus 12
military / militarization:
dictatorship 169;
expenditures 119, 120, 146;
process 150–151;
strength 138;
tribunals 57–58
milyonīyya *209*, 209–210
Ministry of Culture 164
Miṣrī, Īrīs Ḥabīb al- 89, 95
Modern Standard Arabic (MSA) 204
modest resurgence 92
Mohyeldin, Ayman 214
monarchists 47, 48;
agents 51;
party 50
Monier, Elizabeth 102
monopolization of political power 101
moral authority 138, 144–145
Morsi, Muhammad 39, 149–150, 165, 260
Mubarak, Hosni 33, 37, 45, 70–71, 96–97, 177, 179, 249–250;
administration 163;
apologizing to 219;
campaign 72–73;
collapse 123;
era 40;
era critics 184;
"eternity" of 222;
long-term presidency 221–222;
presidency 36–38;
regime (1981–2011) 145–149;
sons 220–221;
in Taḥrīr Square 223
Mubārak shūhida yahtifu lil-mutaẓāhirīn 212
Muhammad al-Asad 246
Muhammed Maḥmūd Street 57, 254, 256
Muḥyī al-Dīn, Khāled 181, 187
Muḥyī al-Dīn, Zakārīyya 167
multi-party pluralism 26
museums for 1952 revolution in Egypt 161–171
Muslim Brotherhood 15–16, 20, 28, 35–36, 45, 55–57, 75, 90, 97, 149–150;
anti Muslim Brotherhood jokes 223-224;
appeared triumphant 57;
banned 151;
movement 230, 259;
non-Moslems 88–89;
and Salafi 56;
SCAF and 55;
secret organization of 182;
Muslims / Muslim:
compatriots 97;
cultural values 90–91;
culture and Islamization 102;
leaders and intellectuals 102–103;
religious organizations 101
Mustafa Kamel Museum 165–166
mutinies 11

al-Nahḍa Center for Scientific and Cultural Renaissance 259
Najātī, ʻUmar 260
al-Nāsikh, Ibrahīm 92
Nasser '56 191
Nasser's era 161;
political repression 184;
social and economic reforms 183

Nasserites 20;
Egypt 88;
legacy 179;
Nasserization campaign 20;
regime (1952–1970) 139–143;
state 34
National Center for Translation 71
national commemoration 181–182
National Council for Combating Terrorism and Extremism 150–151
National Democratic Party (NDP) 37, 71, 243
nationalism / nationalist:
credentials 58;
extremism 51;
movement 21;
and patriotism 11, 16, 169–170, 258
nationalization 88
nationalized economy 26
National Library and Archives 180–181
National Museum of Egyptian Civilization 170
National Party 25, 91
National Population Council 116
National Population Strategy 116
National Progressive Unionist Party 181
National Revolution Day 180
National Security Council 150–151
national trait 212
National Youth Conference 116
natural increase rate (NIR) 114
naturalization 101
natural right (*haqquha al-tabī'ī*) 50
Nayrouz Festival 95
Near East Christian Council (NECC) 98
negative connotation 139
neo-authoritarianism 26
neopatriarchal patterns of marriage 243
neo-pharaonism 259–254
New Democratic Party (NDP) 57
New York Times, The 88
nizil 208
non-Arab Muslims 204
non-Arab regional powers 152
non-Christian religions 99
non-discrimination 70
non-Egyptian Arabic speakers 212
non-literary texts 205
non-Muslim foreign rulers 11
non-Muslim polity 10–11
non-Muslim subordination 90
norms of behavior 138
Nostra Aetate 99–100
notably irrigation 51
Nubian Museum 165
al-Nur candidates 57

official memory 178
oil monarchies 146
oppression (*ẓulm*) 259
Orabi, Ahmed 25
Ordinary Egyptians 206
Orthodox:
Islam 10;
leaders 96;
priesthood 96–97
Orwell, George 220
Oslo Accords 148

Palestinians 183, 257
pan-Arabism / pan-Arab 87, 139–140, 142, 179, 188;
commonwealth 27;
hero 141;
identity 249–250;
ideology 137;
leader 142–143;
nationalism 188;
secularism 88
"Pandora's box" 103
parity in Egypt 95

parliamentary life and democracy 185
Peace Conference in Paris 19
personal and gender empowerment 247
personal dominance 35
Pharaohs/Pharaonic 257;
burial structures 255;
golden age 248, 257;
motifs 256–257;
pre-Islamic heritage 259;
themed graffiti 257;
tradition 27
Pharaonicist 94
"Pharaonic Village" entertainment park 168
phased liberalization 29
Philosophy of the Revolution, The 140, 152
Pile, Steve 245–246
pluralism 37
politico-economic system 14
politics/political:
authority 11;
community 10;
contestation 33;
economy 59;
fragmentation 204;
independence 21;
liberalization 34;
mobilization 52;
parties 35;
and religious oppression 184;
social-cultural concept 70;
and social polarization 67;
and socio-economic systems 12;
space 35;
sphere 35;
stability and competence 138;
system, stability 10;
tradition 27;
violence 52
"politics of memory" 162
postcolonial Egypt 101
post-revolution satirical and non-satirical cartoons:
Egyptian Arabic 224;
Egyptian literature since 2011 230–232;
Egyptian revolutions, old and new 227–230;
fakka campaign 226–227;
June 30 Revolution 225;
positive social or political message 226
poverty 14, 118–119
premiership 21
preponderance phenomenon 138–139
presidential domination 37
private sector employment 120, 123
privatization 122, 183, 252;
of motherhood 257;
policies 185–186
pro-Iranian Houthis in Yemen 150
pro-Nasserite protest 190
property rights, redistribution 33
Protectorate 14
protestors as criminals and external agents 56
public awareness 116–117
public commemorative act 177
public discourse 73–75
public performances of piety 90
public sector overstaffing 127–128

Qadhafi, Mu'ammar 179
al-Qā'ed Ibrāhīm mosque 74–75
Al-Qāhira 189
Qosa, William 189
Quran 72, 258

rab'a 207–208
Rabat summit 144
Rabin, Yitzhak 148–149
radicalism 48

Raḍwan, Fatḥī 165
Radwan, Samir 122
Ragab, Eman 151
rampant capitalism 183
recalcitrant state officials 40
recession 119
reformism 16
regimes:
change 58–59;
legitimacy 137–138;
mass mobilization and regime change 12;
Mubarak's regime (1981–2011) 145–149;
Nasser's regime (1952–1970) 139–143;
Sadat's regime (1970–1981) 143–145;
Sisi's regime (1981–2011) 149–152
regional preeminence 139
regular civil 37
Reis ül-Kütab 11
religion/religious:
bias 101;
differences 101;
endowments 51;
heterogeneity 113;
orientation 53;
partisanship 88;
and political power 10;
and polity 11;
scholar 53;
solidarity 248;
state 74
republicanism 51
republican-monarchist style 14
resource endowment 138
restructuring depth, source, pace and sustainability 19–21
Revolutionary Command Council (RCC) 162, 179
Revolutionary Council 20
"Revolution of Workers and Fellahs" 20
revolution/revolutionary 11, 97–98;
colloquial arabic and new vocabulary 206–212;
comprehensive transformation 12;
definition 12;
legacy 161;
nationalists 47;
slogans of 164;
thugs 58;
trials 162–163;
verbal and visual humor 214;
without a revolution 12
"right to the city" 241–243, 249, 259–260
rivalries 14
Rivlin, Paul 113–114
Rizq, Yūnān Labīb 166
Royal Navy fleet 164
Rufīla, Ya'qūb Nakhla 94
ruling power, overthrow and substitution 12
rural notables 52–53
Rushdi, Hussein 49–50
Russian quasiczarist 26

Sabr 'Arab, Muhammad Ṣ 167
al-Sadat, Anwar 33, 96–97, 163;
de-Nasserization efforts 183;
regime (1970–1981) 143–145
Sa'īd, Khāled 252
ṣa'īdīs 216, *216*
Salafi movements 56, 74;
Salafi *al-Nūr* party 77
Samuel, Bishop 99
satire 212–214
Saudi Arabia 152
Sayyid Muhammad al-Biblāwī 54
Scripps-Howard News Service 88
secondary discourse 68

Second Five-Year Plan 119
Second Vatican Council in 1965 99
sectarianism 58, 88, 101
secular governance 101
secular Liberalism 69
secular patriotism 87
security services and the military 40
sedition and internal strife 10
seizing power 14–19;
action 17–18;
external players 19;
ideology 15–16;
intensity 16–17;
organization 15;
participation 14–15;
revolutionary situation 14;
rulers reaction 18
self-communalization 101
self-determination 19
"self-made man" concept 102
self-perceptions 37, 138
Sennett, Richard 242
sequential art 231
sexual revolution 11
al-sha'b yurīd isqāṭ al-niẓām 211
Shafīq, Ahmad 58
Shanūda al-Manqabbādi, Tādrus 94;
Shenouda III 96–97, 99
Sharaf, Sāmī 168
Sharī'a and Islamic punishments 74
Shawqī, Ahmad 166
Al-Shāyib, Galāl 231
Sheḥāta, Asmā' 247
Shehata, Dina 7
sheikhs (religious notables) 53
short-term tactical decisions 36
Shoukri, Sameh 150
shuhadā' concepts 259
al-Shuqayrī, Ahmad 141
Ṣiddīq, Yūsuf 187
Simaika, Marcus 94, 96
Singerman, Diane 243
Sisi's regime (1981–2011) 149–152; *see also* 'Abd al-Fattah al-Sisi
Six-Day War (June 1967) 141, 163
Al-Siyāsa 54
Socialist (*Tagammu'*) Party 55
socioeconomic legacy, July Revolution 185–186
socioeconomic policies:
economic rents 113;
Egypt's current economic challenges 111–113;
Egypt's dire economic future 125–128;
erratic economic development 118–124;
geostrategic rent 113;
indecisive natalist policy 114–118;
Mubarak's regime collapse 124–125;
political structure of Egypt 119;
socio-demographic rents 111–113
socio-economic system 20
socio-economic transformation 20–21
socio-political segments 75
soft revolution 113
Soueif, Ahdaf 56
sovereignty 259–260
Soviet Union in 1989 147
spirit of dignity and pride 17
Stack, Lee 51
state language in modern Egypt 204
state-religion discourse:
after Mubarak's downfall 73–75;
civil camp 74;
Civil State under al-Sisi 75–77;
languages and multiple voices 67–68;

under Mubarak 69–73;
multiple categorizations 68;
nature 67;
oppression and indoctrination, governmental and presidential mechanism for 71;
polarization 74;
radical Islamist organizations 70;
status of Islam 69–70;
vertical *vs.* horizontal discourses 68–69
state-religion relations 67
State Security Law 76
state sovereignty 58
state-sponsored intellectuals 71
steadfastness 244
structural/structuralism 12;
adjustment programs 123;
macroeconomic problems 120–121
subversive art 251
Suez Canal 89, 113, 120, 124–125, 164, 168
suicidal martyrdom (*istishhād*) 258
Sulayman, Omar 223
Sunday School Movement 95–98, 101
Sunni Muslims 111–112
superpower domination 139
supra-Egyptian nationalism 90
supra-state legitimacy 143
Supreme Constitutional Court 39
Supreme Council of the Armed Forces (SCAF) 39, 44, 55–56, 57–58
Sussman, Anna Louie 214
Sustainable Development Strategy 125
symbolic or moral authority 139
Syrian civil war 150
Tagammu‘ 70
Taḥrīr Square 28, 55;
activists 15–16;
administration 242;
anti-government slogans in 247;
daily-life management of 245–246;
demonstrations 16;
demonstrators in 17;
gender norms 247;
Graffiti slogans 247;
history 241–242;
humorous slogans from 215–218;
liberating 243–249;
Pharaonic and Islamic identities 257;
"revolutionaries" 55;
scorched earth policy 248;
"sites of memory" 257;
"the independent republic of Taḥrīr" 246
Tamarrud youth movement 260
Tāmer ‘Abd al-Mun‘im 231
Tanter, Raymond 12
al-Ṭayyib, Ahmad 72
tear gas effect 245
terrorism 150
Thawras:
historical ambiguities of 9–11;
merits of 7–8;
multiple meanings of 8–9;
negative view of 11;
organization types 15;
in political language 10;
rejection 10;
restructuring 19–21;
revolutionary 11–12;
seizing power 14–19
Thawrat al-shabāb 8–9
theatrical reenactments 180
Tignor, Robert 118
total fertility rate (TFR) 116

traditional legitimacy 187
"traditional" rights, hereditary Islamic prince 50
al-Tūnisī, Amānī 230
Tunisian revolutionaries 245
Ṭūsūn, Omar 52
two-stage Revolution 12
tyrannical dictatorship 245

underground art 251
underground subversions 11
unemployed educated youth 126
unemployment 14, 121, 122, 126
Union Party 52
United Arab Republic (UAR) 140
United Nations' Arab Human Development Report 185
unprecedented renaissance 87
unprecedented revival 87
UN Resolution 242 141
urbanization 26
urban notables 52–53
US-led military invasion 27

vaccination campaigns 99
value-added service sectors 123
Vatican II 100
vernacular commemoration 188–190
vernacular memory 178
vertical discourse 68, 76
Victorian orientalism 25
violence 51

Wafd-dominated ministry 50
Wafdist governance 21
Wafd Party 21, 48–49, 52
waḥda waṭaniyya (national unity) 102
Wakin, Edward 87–88
Waltz, Kenneth 138
War of Attrition (1969–1970) 114
Waterbury, John 128
Weber, Max 46–47
Western concept of revolution 10
Western imperialistic powers 27
Western imperialists 27
Western pictorial motifs 92
Western-style nation-states 27
White, James Boyd 76
"White Australia Policy" 100
Williams, Maren 214
Wilsonian political climate 19
World Bank (WB) 148
World Council of Churches (WCC) 98
world economy 122

Yacoubian Building, The 249
Ya misahharni (song) 218
Yemen (1962–1967) 141
Youssef, Hala 117–118
youth cultures 250
Yuḥanna al-Armanī, 92–93
Yūnis, Sharīf 167

Zaghlūl, Sa'd 21, 51, 227–228, *228*, 232
Zahrān, Magdī 257–258
"za'īm al-'umma" 21
Zaki Bey Ibrāshī 48
Zaqzūq, Muhammad Hamdī 72
Zayn al-'ābidīn bin 'Alī 252
zero tolerance policy 260